TO IMPROVE THE ACADEMY

TO IMPROVE THE ACADEMY

Resources for Faculty, Instructional, and Organizational Development

Volume 29

Judith E. Miller, Editor

James E. Groccia, Associate Editor

Professional and Organizational Development
Network in Higher Education

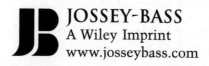

JOSSEY-BASS
A Wiley Imprint
www.josseybass.com

TO IMPROVE THE ACADEMY

To Improve the Academy is published annually by the Professional and Organizational Network in Higher Education (POD) through Jossey-Bass Publishers and is abstracted in ERIC documents and in Higher Education Abstracts.

Ordering Information

The annual volume of *To Improve the Academy* is distributed to members at the POD conference in the autumn of each year. To order or obtain ordering information, please contact:

John Wiley & Sons, Inc.

Customer Care Center

10475 Crosspoint Blvd.

Indianapolis, IN 46256

Phone: 877-762-2974

Fax: 800-597-3299

E-mail: custserv@wiley.com

Web: www.josseybass.com

Permission to Copy

The contents of *To Improve the Academy* are copyrighted to protect the authors. Nevertheless, consistent with the networking and resource-sharing functions of POD, readers are encouraged to reproduce articles and cases from *To Improve the Academy* for educational use, as long as the source is identified.

Instructions to Contributors for the Next Volume

Anyone interested in the issues related to instructional, faculty, and organizational development in higher education may submit manuscripts. Manuscripts are submitted to the current editor early in December of each year and selected through a blind peer-review process. Correspondence, including requests for information about guidelines and submission of manuscripts for Volume 30, should be directed to:

> Judith E. Miller, Ph.D.
> Executive Director of Assessment
> University of North Florida
> 1 UNF Drive, Bldg. 1 Suite 2700
> Jacksonville FL 32224, USA
> Phone: 904-620-2765
> Fax: 904-620-2322
> E-mail: tia@unf.edu

About the POD Network

As revised and accepted by the POD Core Committee, April 2, 2004.

Statement of Purpose

The Professional and Organizational Development Network in Higher Education is an association of higher education professionals dedicated to enhancing teaching and learning by supporting educational developers and leaders in higher education.

Mission Statement

The Professional and Organizational Development Network in Higher Education encourages the advocacy of the ongoing enhancement of teaching and learning through faculty and organizational development. To this end, it supports the work of educational developers and champions their importance to the academic enterprise.

Vision Statement

During the twenty-first century, the Professional and Organizational Development Network in Higher Education will expand guidelines for educational development, build strong alliances with sister organizations, and encourage developer exchanges and research projects to improve teaching and learning.

Values

The Professional and Organizational Development Network in Higher Education is committed to:

- Personal, faculty, instructional, and organizational development
- Humane and collaborative organizations and administrations
- Diverse perspectives and a diverse membership
- Supportive educational development networks on the local, regional, national, and international levels
- Advocacy for improved teaching and learning in the academy through programs for faculty, administrators, and graduate students
- The identification and collection of a strong and accessible body of research on development theories and practices
- The establishment of guidelines for ethical practice
- The increasingly useful and thorough assessment and evaluation of practice and research

Programs, Publications, and Activities

The Professional and Organizational Development Network in Higher Education offers members and interested individuals the following benefits:

- An annual membership conference designed to promote professional and personal growth, nurture innovation and change, stimulate important research projects, and enable participants to exchange ideas and broaden their professional network
- An annual membership directory and networking guide
- Publications in print and in electronic form
- Access to the POD website and listserv

Membership, Conference, and Programs Information

For information, please contact:

Hoag Holmgren, Executive Director
The POD Network
P.O. Box 3318
Nederland, CO 80566
Phone: 303-258-9521
Fax: 303-258-7377
E-mail: podoffice@podnetwork.org
Web: podnetwork.org

CONTENTS

SECTION ONE
Enriching Our Colleagues

SECTION TWO
Enriching Our Campus Contexts

SECTION THREE
Enriching Our Craft

ABOUT THE AUTHORS

Judith E. Miller is executive director of assessment at the University of North Florida in Jacksonville. A former biology faculty member, she currently teaches an online course in college teaching for faculty and graduate students. In 1998 she received the Outstanding Undergraduate Science Teacher award from the Society for College Science Teachers; in 2002 she was named the Massachusetts CASE Professor of the Year by the Carnegie Foundation for the Advancement of Teaching; and in 2004 she won Worcester Polytechnic Institute's Trustees' Award for Outstanding Teaching. Miller is the coeditor (with Jim Groccia and Marilyn Miller) of *Student-Assisted Teaching: A Guide to Faculty-Student Teamwork* (2001), and (with Jim Groccia) of *On Becoming a Productive University: Strategies for Reducing Costs and Increasing Quality in Higher Education* (2005) and *Enhancing Productivity: Administrative, Instructional, and Technological Strategies* (1998). She has published and presented extensively on active and cooperative learning, learning outcomes assessment, team teaching, and educational productivity. She can be contacted at j.miller@unf.edu.

James E. Groccia is the director of the Biggio Center for the Enhancement of Teaching and Learning and associate professor in the Department of Educational Foundations, Leadership, and Technology at Auburn University in Auburn, Alabama. In addition to faculty development work, he teaches graduate courses on teaching and higher education and coordinates the university's graduate certificate in college and university teaching. He is a former POD Network president and Core Committee member. Groccia received his doctorate in educational psychology and guidance from the University of Tennessee. He has presented at dozens of national and international conferences, conducted hundreds of workshops worldwide, has served as an advisor and consultant to institutions nationally and abroad, and has authored numerous articles and book chapters on teaching and learning issues. He is the author of *The College Success Book: A Whole-Student Approach to Academic Excellence* (1992) and coeditor (with Judy Miller) of *On Becoming a Productive University: Strategies for Reducing Costs and Increasing Quality in Higher Education*

(2005); *Student Assisted Teaching: A Guide to Faculty-Student Teamwork* (2001); and *Enhancing Productivity: Administrative, Instructional, and Technological Strategies* (1998). He can be contacted at groccje@ auburn.edu.

The Contributors

Cynthia L. Adams is the manager of distance learning faculty services at Middle Tennessee State University (MTSU) in Murfreesboro. She holds a master of business education degree and teaches in the Regents Online Degree Program. Adams serves as point of contact for MTSU faculty who develop and teach distance courses, including online, hybrid, and correspondence, and Regents Online Degree Program courses. She coordinates the faculty peer assistants program and has presented on the program described in Chapter Thirteen at regional and national conferences. She may be contacted at cladams@mtsu.edu.

Roberta Ambrosino is an educational development specialist at the Academic Center for Excellence in Teaching at the University of Texas Health Science Center in San Antonio. She initiates and supports programs that assist faculty in the advancement of excellence in teaching and learning. Her specialties are media-rich instructional design, faculty learning communities, and mentoring. Her most recent research explores the impact of faculty development activities on instructional practices, student motivation, and learning. She may be contacted at ambrosino@ uthscsa.edu.

Cerri A. Banks is dean of William Smith College and assistant professor of education at Hobart & William Smith Colleges in Geneva, New York. She received her Ph.D. in cultural foundations of education from Syracuse University. Specializing in sociology of education, cultural studies, multicultural education, and qualitative research, Banks draws from critical pedagogy, educational theory, feminist theory, and critical race theory in her scholarship and teaching. She may be contacted at banks@ hws.edu.

Phyllis Blumberg is the director of the Teaching and Learning Center at the University of the Sciences in Philadelphia, where she is also a professor of social sciences. She has focused on how to assist faculty to implement learner-centered teaching approaches for the past eight years. She is the author of *Developing Learner-Centered Teaching: A Practical Guide for Faculty* (2009). She received her Ph.D. in educational and developmental psychology from the University of Pittsburgh. She may be contacted at p.blumbe@usp.edu.

Allison Boye is director of the Teaching Effectiveness And Career enHancement (TEACH) program for the Teaching, Learning, and Technology Center at Texas Tech University in Lubbock. Her work also includes consulting with faculty and leading pedagogical seminars. She holds degrees in English from William and Mary, Bowling Green, and Texas Tech University. Her recent publications focus on patterns of instructor response to feedback and the adaptation of active learning across the disciplines; she also presents on millennial students, classroom management, and teaching writing. She may be contacted at allison. p.boye@ttu.edu.

Thomas M. Brinthaupt is professor of psychology at Middle Tennessee State University (MTSU) in Murfreesboro. He has published several papers related to teaching with instructional technologies. He currently serves as associate editor for the MERLOT Learning Objects Psychology Board. During his time at MTSU, he has received several awards, including the Tennessee Board of Regents Award of Excellence for Online Teaching and Learning, the MTSU Distinguished Educator Award in Distance Learning, and the MTSU Foundation Outstanding Achievement in Instructional Technology Award. He may be contacted at tbrintha@mtsu.edu.

Carl E. Brown Jr. earned a B.S. in human resources development, an M.Ed. in counselor education, and an Ed.S. in family counseling at the University of Florida. At the University of Florida, he worked as a program coordinator in the Office of Academic Support and as the assistant director for technology application in the Career Resource Center. Currently, he is the assistant director in the Center for Excellence in Teaching, Learning, and Assessment at Howard University in Washington, DC. He may be contacted at ce_brown@howard.edu.

Tom Carey is professor of management sciences at the University of Waterloo in Ontario, currently on leave to lead collaborative projects across higher education institutions and systems. In Canada, he is visiting senior scholar at the Higher Education Quality Council of Ontario, leading a research program in knowledge mobilization for exemplary teaching and learning. In the United States, he is visiting senior scholar at San Diego State University, leading the FACCTS program across California community colleges, and the ELIXR program. He may be contacted at tcarey@projects.sdsu.edu.

Andrew N. Carpenter, professor of philosophy and director of the Center for Teaching and Learning at Ellis University, received his Ph.D. from the University of California at Berkeley and also has degrees in philosophy from the University of Oxford and Amherst College. His academic specialty is the history of early modern philosophy; he also has significant expertise in faculty self-governance, assessment of student learning, institutional and program accreditation, continuous quality improvement, and online learning. He may be contacted at acarpenter@ellis.edu.

Nancy Van Note Chism is professor of higher education and student affairs at the Indiana University School of Education in Indianapolis. She has worked in professional and organizational development for twenty-five years at both The Ohio State University and Indiana University–Purdue University Indianapolis. Her interests include professional and organizational development, the faculty profession, and college teaching and learning. She may be contacted at nchism@iupui.edu.

Bob Cole is director of the Teaching and Learning Collaborative at the Monterey Institute of International Studies in Monterey, California. He has taught English as a second language and trained language teachers to integrate technology. His professional work explores the intersections of emerging technologies, constructivist pedagogy, educational and organizational innovation, and reflective practices. He may be contacted at bob.cole@miis.edu.

Alison Cook-Sather is professor of education and coordinator of the Andrew W. Mellon Teaching and Learning Institute at Bryn Mawr College in Bryn Mawr, Pennsylvania. Her research interests include student roles in collaborative approaches to teaching and learning within undergraduate secondary teacher preparation and college faculty development. She has published over fifty articles, chapters, and books, including *Education Is Translation: A Metaphor for Change in Learning and Teaching* (2005) and *Learning from the Student's Perspective: A Sourcebook for Effective Teaching* (2009). She may be contacted at acooksat@brynmawr.edu.

Linda Coughlin, associate provost for academic affairs at St. Mary's College of Maryland (SMCM) in St. Mary's City, is responsible for coordinating faculty development, teaching and learning activities, and cross-disciplinary programs. She oversees new-faculty orientation, teaching workshops offered each fall, and sponsored research activities and is currently chair of both the Academic Planning and Strategic Planning committees. She holds a Ph.D. in neuropharmacology and has taught neuroscience, cell biology, and immunology at SMCM for sixteen years. She may be contacted at lgcoughlin@smcm.edu.

Donna Ellis is interim director of the Centre for Teaching Excellence at the University of Waterloo in Ontario. She cochaired the 2004 POD conference and served on POD's Core Committee as chair of the Finance and Audit Committee from 2005 to 2008. She has also received two

POD Menges awards for her research. Her research interests include the professional development of graduate students and educational developers, organizational development strategies, and students' responses to innovative instructional methods. She may be contacted at donnae@uwaterloo.ca.

Sarah M. Ginsberg is an associate professor and program coordinator of the speech-language pathology program at Eastern Michigan University in Ypsilanti, where she is also a faculty consultant supporting adjunct lecturers. Her research focuses on university teaching and faculty classroom communication. She has published in the *Journal of Scholarship of Teaching and Learning*, the *Journal of Cognitive Affective Learning*, and the *Journal on Centers for Teaching and Learning*. She is codirector of the annual SOTL Academy conference. She can be contacted at sarah.ginsberg@emich.edu.

Joe Grimes was director of faculty development and founder of the Center for Teaching and Learning at California Polytechnic State University in San Luis Obispo. At Cal Poly, he has been a consultant to government agencies and industry, director of campus computing services, and director of computer engineering. He has publications and presentations in the areas of computer science and scholarship of teaching and has hosted three faculty participant conferences with more than 150 participants at each. He may be contacted at jgrimes@calpoly.edu.

Mikaela Huntzinger holds a Ph.D. in ecology. She is an academic developer in the teaching resources center at the University of California, Davis, where she served as a graduate fellow and coordinator in the teaching assistant consultant program. Her areas of interest include inclusive teaching, the unique needs of international instructors, teaching science effectively, and communities of practice. She teaches undergraduate courses on ecological conservation, the land art movement, and student preparedness. She may be contacted at pmhuntzinger@ucdavis.edu.

Jonathan Iuzzini is assistant professor of psychology and an affiliate of the interdisciplinary program in public policy studies at Hobart & William Smith Colleges in Geneva, New York. He teaches courses in social psychology, political psychology, and the psychology of prejudice, discrimination, and intergroup relations. His current research focuses on the social psychology of group privilege and disadvantage. He may be contacted at iuzzini@hws.edu.

Sally Kuhlenschmidt has been the director of the Faculty Center for Excellence in Teaching at Western Kentucky University in Bowling Green since 1994. She received her Ph.D. in clinical psychology from Purdue University. Kuhlenschmidt's current research interests include assessment of faculty development and using technology to enhance development. She may be contacted at sally.kuhlenschmidt@wku.edu.

Virginia S. Lee is principal and senior consultant of Virginia S. Lee & Associates, a consulting firm specializing in teaching, learning, and assessment in higher education. She is a former president of the Professional and Organizational Development Network in Higher Education. She edited *Teaching and Learning Through Inquiry: A Guidebook for Institutions and Instructors* (2004), based on the inquiry-guided learning initiative at North Carolina State University, which she led from 2000 to 2004. She may be contacted at vslee@virginiaslee.com.

Deandra Little is associate professor and assistant director of the Teaching Resource Center at the University of Virginia in Charlottesville. Her research interests include teaching consultation techniques, graduate student professional development, student and faculty writing, and teaching with images across the curriculum. She received a Ph.D. in English from Vanderbilt University and teaches courses on science and gender in U.S. literature. Her publications include articles focused on using critical theory to examine educational development and on visual learning. She may be contacted at dlittle@virginia.edu.

Whitney Ransom McGowan is a social growth analyst at FamilyLink and the editor of more than 140 industry publications. In her academic career, she has authored several journal articles and has presented at a variety of conferences. McGowan received her Ph.D. in instructional psychology and technology at Brigham Young University, where she developed a system to identify contributing factors for improved teaching and learning and established a model for midcourse evaluations. She may be contacted at whitney.ransom@gmail.com.

Flora McMartin is the founder of Broad-based Knowledge, LLC (BbK), a consulting firm focused on assisting educators in higher education to evaluate the use and deployment of technology-assisted teaching and learning. BbK specializes in building organizational and project-level evaluation capacities and integrating evaluation into management activities. Current research projects focus on relationships among technology, student learning, and faculty roles; development of collaborative faculty work groups; and the institutionalization of educational innovations. She may be contacted at flora.mcmartin@gmail.com.

Paul McPherron is an assistant professor of linguistics at Southern Illinois University Carbondale (SIUC). He is a former fellow and coordinator in the teaching assistant consultant program at the University of California, Davis. His research interests include reforms of English teaching in China and cross-cultural communication in the language classroom. At

SIUC, he teaches courses in language teaching methods and materials, intercultural communication, and language assessment and supervises a student teaching practicum course. He may be contacted at mcpherron@ siu.edu.

Micah Meixner is a lecturer of voice at the Texas Tech University School of Music at Lubbock. While at Texas Tech, she has worked closely with the Teaching Effectiveness And Career enHancement (TEACH) program at the Teaching, Learning, and Technology Center, where she helped facilitate events, present seminars, and provide consultations to faculty and graduate students. Her research interests include graduate student development, student-teacher immediacy, peer observation, and reflective teaching. She may be contacted at micah.meixner@ttu.edu.

Sal Meyers is director of faculty development and a professor of psychology at Simpson College in Indianola, Iowa, and chair of the POD's Small College Committee. As Simpson's first director of faculty development, she has developed an ongoing new faculty orientation program, twenty-minute faculty development sessions, and formats for longer workshops during the summer and immediately before the start of fall classes. She may be contacted at sal.meyers@simpson.edu.

Susanne Morgan retired as associate professor of sociology at Ithaca College in Ithaca, New York, where for many years she also served as the designer and coordinator of faculty development activities. She holds a Ph.D. from Case Western Reserve University and taught medical sociology and research methods. Now an independent faculty development professional, she writes and consults in areas including mentoring and the tenure process, generational transitions, and building community through integrating Web 2.0 environments. She can be contacted at morgan@ ithaca.edu.

Russell T. Osguthorpe, a professor of instructional psychology and technology, serves as director of the Center for Teaching and Learning at Brigham Young University in Provo, Utah. He has served as chair of his department and associate dean of the David O. McKay School of Education. He has authored five books; has collaborated on educational projects in China, Europe, and Polynesia; and has been a visiting scholar at the University of Toronto and the University of Paris. He may be contacted at russell_osguthorpe@byu.edu.

Megan M. Palmer is assistant dean for faculty affairs and professional development at Indiana University School of Medicine, director of faculty development in the Health Professions at Indiana University–Purdue University Indianapolis, and visiting assistant professor at Indiana University School of Education. She holds a master's degree in higher education from Colorado State University and a Ph.D. from Indiana University. Her research focuses on college teaching, faculty development, and the experience of faculty. She may be contacted at mmpalmer@iupui.edu.

Michael S. Palmer is associate professor and assistant director of the Teaching Resource Center at the University of Virginia in Charlottesville. He holds a Ph.D. in chemistry from the University of Wyoming. His educational development research centers on teaching consultation techniques and graduate student professional development. His pedagogy interests include course design, active learning, student motivation, and creativity. He served on the core faculty of the 2009 New Faculty Developers Institute and is the 2010 POD conference program cochair. He may be contacted at mpalmer@virginia.edu.

Susan M. Pliner is associate dean for teaching, learning, and assessment and assistant professor of education at Hobart & William Smith Colleges in Geneva, New York. She has a certificate of advanced graduate studies in social justice education and an Ed.D. in human development. Her areas of specialty include universal instructional design for teaching and learning, multicultural and social justice education, college student learning and development, and social identity development theory and practice in higher education. She may be contacted at pliner@hws.edu.

Mark Potter is director of the Center for Faculty Development at Metropolitan State College of Denver, Colorado. He received his Ph.D. in history in 1997 and moved in 2008 from a faculty position at a different institution to establish the newly founded center. He continues to teach European history while developing programs in support of course design and pedagogy, peer observation of instruction for improvement, and early career faculty development. He may be contacted at mpotte10@mscd.edu.

Christopher Price is the director of the Center for Excellence in Learning and Teaching and instructor for the department of political science and international studies at the College at Brockport, State University of New York. He received his Ph.D. in political science from the State University of New York at Albany in 2004. His current research looks at how the power-balanced classroom can serve as a means of citizen education. He may be contacted at cprice@brockport.edu.

Madhumitha Rajagopal is a postdoctoral fellow in the division of nephrology at the Stanford University School of Medicine in Palo Alto, California. She served as a fellow in the teaching assistant consultant program at the University of California, Davis while earning her doctorate. Her areas of teaching interest include international teacher training, communities of practice, teaching diverse student populations, and teaching laboratory courses. She serves as a teacher training coordinator for the Stanford Education Services Program. She may be contacted at rmadhu@stanford.edu.

Teresa M. Redd is a professor of English and director of the Center for Excellence in Teaching, Learning, and Assessment at Howard University in Washington, D.C. A recipient of the Vice President's Teaching Excellence Award, she holds a Ph.D. in education from the University of Maryland, College Park. Redd has published articles, chapters, and books about teaching with technology, writing across the curriculum, service-learning, and teaching African American students. She may be contacted at tredd@howard.edu.

Tamara Rosier is the academic dean at Kuyper College in Grand Rapids, Michigan. Prior to her current position, she was assistant director of the Pew Faculty Teaching and Learning Center at Grand Valley State University and founding director of the Center for Excellence in Learning and Teaching at Cornerstone University, where she taught for eight years in the teacher education department. She earned her Ph.D. in leadership in higher education from Western Michigan University. She may be contacted at trosier@kuyper.edu.

Dianna Z. Rust is the associate dean of the College of Continuing Education and Distance Learning at Middle Tennessee State University (MTSU) in Murfreesville. She directs distance learning courses and online degree programs, off-campus courses and degree programs, and the evening school at MTSU. She has instructed online courses at the undergraduate and graduate level. Rust has received the Middle Tennessee State University Administrative Employee of the Year award and the TBR Lana Doncaster Innovations Award. She may be contacted at drust@mtsu.edu.

Dieter J. Schönwetter is an associate professor and director of educational resources and faculty development with the Faculty of Dentistry at the University of Manitoba in Winnipeg, Manitoba, Canada. He has cross-appointments with the department of psychology, the Faculty of Education, and the department of medicine education. As a social psychologist, he enjoys exploring the cognitive dynamics between effective teaching and student learning in higher education. These dynamics include different teaching behaviors and styles as well as different student learning predispositions. He may be contacted at schönwet@cc .umanitoba.ca.

Genevieve G. Shaker recently completed her Ph.D. at Indiana University. Her dissertation research, the basis for Chapter Four in this volume, was recognized by the Association for the Study of Higher Education as the Bobby Wright Dissertation of the Year and by the POD Network with the Robert J. Menges Award. Her academic interests center on university employees who are ineligible for tenure, particularly contingent faculty. She is an administrator in the School of Liberal Arts at Indiana University–Purdue University Indianapolis. She may be contacted at gshaker@iupui.edu.

Peter Shaw has taught French, English, and Spanish and trained language teachers in Nigeria, Mexico, and Egypt. He is currently professor of educational linguistics in the Graduate School of Translation, Interpretation, and Language Education at the Monterey Institute of International Studies in Monterey, California. His interest in learning-centered pedagogy and faculty development complements his academic and professional work in learning, instruction, and curriculum in language education. He may be contacted at pshaw@miis.edu.

Brian C. Smith is an associate professor of psychology and chair of the Division of Social Science at Graceland University in Lamoni, Iowa. He has served on Graceland's Faculty Development Committee, and in 2008 he received Graceland's Excellence in Teaching Award. He earned a J.D. from the University of Texas at Austin and a Ph.D. in social psychology from the University of Minnesota. He may be contacted at bcsmith@graceland.edu.

Tasha J. Souza is professor of instructional communication, the faculty development coordinator for the Center for Excellence in Learning and Teaching at Humboldt State University in Arcata, California, and the faculty development lead for the ELIXR project. Her specialties include gender, intercultural, and organizational communication; mediation, training, and facilitation skills; active learning pedagogies; and universal design for learning. Souza's current interests lie in instructional communication, including research on gender and communication and cold-calling in the classroom. She may be contacted at tasha@humboldt.edu.

James B. Young was the founding chief information officer at Harrisburg University of Science and Technology in Harrisburg, Pennsylvania. His research interest is interdisciplinary faculty learning collaboration. Previously, he was employed for nine years at George Mason University, where he led initiatives in curriculum development and integration, libraries, learning communities, and assessment. He regularly publishes and presents at professional conferences in the areas of knowledge management, learning communities, alternative assessment, information literacy, technology-across-the-curriculum, and e-portfolios. He may be contacted at jamesbyersyoung@gmail.com.

PREFACE

This volume presents twenty-two contributions from authors across an array of institutions on a variety of topics. Some focus on providing insights on the preparation and support of those engaged in doing the work of teaching and learning: faculty and staff colleagues, graduate students, and even undergraduates. Others share research on improving teaching and learning within different campus contexts. Some contributors offer center- or unit-focused insights that suggest pathways for continued growth and development of our practice and profession. Still others encourage us to expand our horizons by providing a view of our work from an international perspective. We have organized the chapters in this volume to reflect the various levels at which our work as developers has impact on our colleagues, our campuses, and our craft.

The contributions to this book reflect both the challenges higher education face and the maturation of our practice as faculty, staff, and organizational developers. They also reflect the fact that as a profession, we address challenges with optimism and energy.

Section One: Enriching Our Colleagues

Dieter Schönwetter and Donna Ellis report in Chapter One on the results of a two-stage study identifying key competencies in graduate student development programs at Canadian and U.S. institutions and developer perceptions of the importance and coverage of each competency in their programming. They find that numerous potential gaps exist in the training of those who deliver graduate student development programs that organizations such as the Professional and Organizational Development (POD) Network can help address.

In Chapter Two, Allison Boye and Micah Meixner describe a model of group peer observation that turns the usual classroom observation practice on its head. Their Teaching Effectiveness And Career enHancement (TEACH) program encourages thoughtful self-reflection on the part of the observer rather than the observed. By removing the evaluative component, TEACH supports introspection and community among beginning teachers.

Sarah Ginsberg reports in Chapter Three a study investigating the support needs of adjunct lecturers. The results indicate they want additional information about students and effective teaching methods beyond lecturing. As this group of faculty now comprises more than half of our instructional population, teaching and learning programs must integrate new approaches and be more responsive to their needs in providing faculty development support.

In Chapter Four, Genevieve Shaker, Megan Palmer, and Nancy Chism describe the results of a phenomenological qualitative study of full-time, non-tenure-track English faculty that provides a point of departure for recommendations on expanding organizational and faculty development strategies for supporting, integrating, and encouraging these faculty members.

In Chapter Five, Tasha Souza, Tom Carey, Flora McMartin, Roberta Ambrosino, and Joe Grimes describe the use of multimedia case stories to help faculty share in the experience of using an innovative teaching strategy and the process of implementing it. Such stories can help faculty to realize that they can overcome pedagogical challenges and institutional constraints in order to better meet the learning needs of students.

In Chapter Six, Tamara Rosier describes the process of developing social intelligence skills in one faculty member in a series of ten coaching sessions. The findings of her exploratory study suggest that social intelligence can be developed and that such a coaching strategy has the potential to have a positive effect on teaching practices and faculty success.

In Chapter Seven, James Young addresses how faculty from disparate backgrounds collaborate in interdisciplinary learning communities and how this cross-domain collaboration leads to a tangible change in identity. The experience is both rewarding and transformative for faculty, who become better equipped to communicate across the disciplinary landscape and gain a rhetorical awareness that is invaluable to learning community participation.

In Chapter Eight, Deandra Little and Michael Palmer describe a process-oriented consultation model based on effective practices from literature on individual consultations, coaching, learning, and motivation. Using a three-step model, educational developers can systematically create a collaborative environment that is nonjudgmental and nonprescriptive and draws on the client's capabilities, experiences, aspirations, and resourcefulness.

In Chapter Nine, Peter Shaw and Bob Cole describe a consultation model they label the professional conversation. In this structured interaction, a speaker explores a topic of professional and personal significance through the facilitation of an understander. Assessment data indicate that the struggle to master the model is worthwhile in terms of community building, professional development, and, unexpectedly, pedagogical practice.

In Chapter Ten, Cerri Banks, Jonathan Iuzzini, and Susan Pliner propose that faculty developers' work around issues of diversity, social justice, and inclusive excellence can be enhanced by developing a foundation in the theory of intersectionality, which engages the complexity of identity and the resulting power structures that inform institutions. They discuss this theoretical perspective and provide examples of faculty development initiatives that can be strengthened through the use of an intersectional lens.

Section Two: Enriching Our Campus Contexts

In Chapter Eleven, Sal Meyers and Brian Smith discuss the results of three studies that rated first-day-of-class satisfaction. Student interest on or before the first day, or, for faculty, excitement and confidence in students' abilities, strongly predicted satisfaction. Both student and instructor satisfaction were positively associated with time spent on the first day on course hows and whys, course content, and introductions. These findings contradict previous empirical studies of student satisfaction but are consistent with faculty development recommendations.

In Chapter Twelve, Whitney Ransom McGowan and Russell Osguthorpe report on faculty and student perceptions of the effects of midcourse evaluations on teaching improvement and student learning. Faculty who read their midcourse feedback, discussed it with their students, and made pedagogical changes saw the most improvement in their ratings.

In Chapter Thirteen, Cynthia Adams, Dianna Rust, and Thomas Brinthaupt combined a mentoring and peer review process for development and subsequent revision of online courses. The Faculty Peer Assistants (FPA) Program incorporates a peer review and evaluation form that outlines course standards and guides the faculty course developer, the peer reviewer, and the department chair.

In Chapter Fourteen, Phyllis Blumberg reports on assessment of the impact of her faculty development programming by looking for evidence of learner-centered practices in seventy-two recently approved courses.

The documents revealed a disappointing lack of evidence of learner-centered course design features. The results prompted discussions with administrators and faculty and yielded calls to action for greater implementation of learner-centered practices.

In Chapter Fifteen, Andrew Carpenter, Linda Coughlin, Susanne Morgan, and Christopher Price investigated the social capital of four very different colleges and universities on five dimensions: civic engagement, norms and trust, collective action, bonding capital, and bridging capital. They argue that confronting the complexities of social capital can help faculty developers understand diverse campus communities with greater nuance and in ways that improve their ability to design and implement development initiatives.

Section Three: Enriching Our Craft

In Chapter Sixteen, Alison Cook-Sather describes a model of professional development that invites undergraduate students to serve as pedagogical consultants to faculty members. Feedback suggests that this approach affords faculty and students an unusual opportunity to coconstruct a more informed model of faculty development, deepens the learning experiences of both, and recasts the responsibility for those learning experiences as one shared by faculty and students.

In Chapter Seventeen, Teresa Redd and Carl Brown Jr. discuss how Howard University's Center for Excellence in Teaching, Learning, and Assessment (CETLA) includes students in everything, from the design of CETLA's infrastructure to the implementation of instructional technologies and assessment of student learning. Survey results confirm that working with students at CETLA is a win-win opportunity for the university, faculty, students, and CETLA.

In Chapter Eighteen, Mikaela Huntzinger, Paul McPherron, and Madhumitha Rajagopal describe a teaching assistant consultant program designed to improve professional development opportunities for campus teaching assistants. Recommendations are offered for creating similar programs and for greater emphasis on the development of communities of practice for graduate students to improve their teaching, cross-disciplinary collaboration, and service skills.

In Chapter Nineteen, Nancy Chism reports the results of an international survey of educational developers, describing their entry-level background knowledge and skills, how they obtained them, and the preparation of new entrants to the profession. Results are used as a basis for recommending increased professionalization of educational development through more systematic preparation of future developers.

In Chapter Twenty, Sally Kuhlenschmidt reports on a systematic study of 1,267 U.S. teaching-learning development units (TLDUs) that provides strategic planning and research tools previously unavailable. Results indicate that TLDUs occur in at least 21.2 percent of U.S. higher education institutions. The study provides normative data on the nature of higher education in the United States and on TLDUs by Carnegie classification, location, and type and special focus of institution.

In Chapter Twenty-One, Mark Potter critically examines the scholarship of faculty development and reflects on the primary currents identifiable in the literature. He observes that much of what is published in the field of faculty development consists of descriptions of particular programs. What is largely missing, he notes, are metastudies that preserve the findings of scholar-practitioners.

In Chapter Twenty-Two, Virginia Lee offers examples of international engagement and a framework for thinking about them. She argues that international engagement in the form of an evolving global scholarship and practice of educational development represents the ultimate extension of our thought and practice as educational developers.

To Improve the Academy allows professionals engaged in faculty development to share expertise, research, and best practice supporting the enhancement of higher education teaching and learning. *TIA* represents the true spirit of the POD Network in the unselfish sharing of our wisdom and expertise to enrich our profession and those with whom we work, be they colleagues or students, teachers or learners. This volume joins those that have preceded it in recording our evolving knowledge of what works and bringing our collective wisdom to bear on promoting improvement in faculty, instructional, and organizational development.

ACKNOWLEDGMENTS

A volume of this type would not be possible without the dedication and enthusiasm of myriad members of the community whose work it reflects and documents. We received forty-four manuscripts, all of them with significant merit, and fortunately we were able to trust our reviewers to help us make some very hard choices. We distributed 176 reviews across sixty-nine reviewers. Many experienced reviewers from volume 28 of *To Improve the Academy* signed on again for this volume, and dozens of new colleagues volunteered to join us. The reviews we received were, for the most part, timely, thorough, thoughtful, and constructive. Taken together, the four reviews of each manuscript reflected the diversity of perspectives that is one of the many strengths of the Professional and Organizational Development Network in Higher Education (POD). Many authors whose manuscripts were ultimately rejected expressed their thanks for helpful comments that would inform continuation of their work.

Those reviewers who worked so diligently to bring the best possible edition of *To Improve the Academy* are Roberta Ambrosino, Gabriele Bauer, Danilo Baylen, Laurie Bellows, Donna Bird, Phyllis Blumberg, Jim Borgford-Parnell, Jeanette Clausen, Eli Collins-Brown, Bonnie Daniel, Michele DiPietro, Sally Ebest, Bonnie Farley-Lucas, Kip Finnegan, Christopher Garrett, Judy Grace, Stacy Grooters, Jace Hargis, Nira Hativa, Jennifer Herman, Sue Hines, Eric Hobson, Katherine Hoffman, Mikaela Huntzinger, Carol Hurney, Sallie Ives, Wayne Jacobson, Douglas James, Kathleen Kane, Bruce Kelley, Mick La Lopa, Bruce Larson, Marion Larson, Jean Layne, Virginia Lee, Rachel Levin, Deandra Little, Alice Macpherson, Jean Mandernach, Jean Martin-Williams, Leslie McBride, Lillian McEnery, Gerald Meredith, Sal Meyers, Cheryl Miller, Theresa Moore, Joy Morrison, Bonnie Mullinix, Ed Neal, Linda Noble, Edward Nuhfer, Leslie Ortquist-Ahrens, Patrick O'Sullivan, Pratul Pathak, Donna Petherbridge, Susan Polich, Nancy Polk, Michael Potter, Gerald Ratliff, Stewart Ross, Brian Rybarczyk, Derina Samuel, Beez Schell, Peter Shaw, Ike Shibley, Jennifer Shinaberger, Julie Sievers, Suzanne Tapp, Karen Ward, and Mary Wright.

Thanks are due to Hoag Holmgren, executive director of the POD Network, for supporting our efforts, and to David Brightman, Aneesa Davenport, and Carolyn Dumore of Jossey-Bass for their prompt responses and gentle reminders. My sincere appreciation goes to the University of North Florida for providing logistical support for this endeavor. Special thanks are due to Summer Sullivan for her quick mastery of APA formatting and her sharp editorial eye.

Based on my past collaborations with associate editor James Groccia, my expectation, in which I have not been disappointed, was that he would bring to our partnership broad knowledge and incisive insights into higher education generally and faculty development particularly. His skills include a wonderful sense of when to give authors direction and when to give them space, and his ability to conceptualize a broad vision is the perfect counter to my tendency to get mired in detail and process. This volume is truly a team effort, and its quality and comprehensiveness are attributable in no small measure to his work.

Judith E. Miller
University of North Florida
Jacksonville, Florida
March 16, 2010

ETHICAL GUIDELINES FOR EDUCATIONAL DEVELOPERS

Adopted by the Professional and Organizational Development Network in Higher Education

Preamble

As professionals, educational developers (faculty, teaching assistant, organizational, instructional, and staff developers) have a unique opportunity and a special responsibility to contribute to the improvement of the quality of teaching and learning in higher education. As members of the academic community, they are subject to all the codes of conduct and ethical guidelines that already exist for those who work or study on campuses and those who belong to disciplinary associations. Educational developers have special ethical responsibilities because of the unique and privileged access they have to people and often to sensitive information. This document provides general guidelines to inform the practice of professionals working in educational development roles in higher education.

Educational developers in higher education come from various disciplinary areas and follow different career tracks. Some work as educational developers on a part-time basis or for simply a short time, but for others educational development is a full-time career. The nature of their responsibilities and prerogatives as developers varies with their position in the organization, their experience, interests, and talents, and with the special characteristics of their institutions. This document attempts to provide general ethical guidelines that should apply to most developers across a variety of settings.

Ethical guidelines indicate a consensus among practitioners about the ideals that should inform their practice as professionals, as well as those behaviors that would constitute misconduct. Between the ideal of exemplary practice and misconduct lies a gray area where dilemmas arise: choices may seem equally right or wrong; different roles and/or responsibilities may place competing, if not incompatible, demands on developers; or certain behaviors may seem questionable but no consensus can determine that those behaviors are examples of misconduct.

It is our hope that these guidelines complement typical programmatic statements of philosophy and mission and that educational developers can use the guidelines effectively to promote ethical practice. This document describes the ideals of practice, identifies specific behaviors that typify professional misconduct, and provides a model to think through situations which present conflicting choices or questionable behavior.

Guidelines for Practice

Ideals of Practice

Ideals that should inform the practice of educational developers include the following areas of professional behavior: providing responsible service to clients, demonstrating competence and integrity, assuring that the rights of others are respected, maintaining the confidentiality of any information regarding contact with clients, and fulfilling responsibilities to the profession of educational development as a whole. It is expected that educational developers will understand and integrate these ideals into their daily practice. Even though the following categories are viewed as ideals of practice, many of the individual statements are quite concrete and practical, while others encourage educational developers to attain a high standard of excellence.

Educational developers evince a high level of responsibility to their clients and are expected to:

1. Provide services to everyone within their mandate, provided that they are able to serve all clients responsibly;

2. Treat clients fairly, respecting their uniqueness, their fundamental rights, dignity and worth, and their right to set objectives and make decisions;

3. Maintain appropriate boundaries in the relationship, avoid exploiting the relationship in any way, and be clear with themselves and their clients about their specific role;

4. Protect all privileged information, obtaining informed consent from clients before using or referring publicly to client cases in such a way that the client could be identified;

5. Continue service only as long as the client is benefiting, discontinue service by mutual consent, and suggest other resources to meet needs they cannot or should not address.

Competence and Integrity

Aspects of competence and integrity discussed in these guidelines include the behavior of educational developers, the skills and the boundaries they should respect and enforce, and the need for them to assure the rights of their clients. Educational developers should also interact competently and with integrity in relationships with their co-workers, supervisees, and the community.

BEHAVIOR

In order to assure evidence of competence and integrity, educational developers should:

a. clarify professional roles and obligations;

b. accept appropriate responsibility for their behavior;

c. make no false or intentionally misleading statements;

d. avoid the distortion and misuse of their work;

e. clarify their roles and responsibilities with each party from the outset when providing services at the behest of a third party;

f. accept appropriate responsibility for the behavior of those they supervise;

g. model ethical behavior with co-workers and those they supervise and in the larger academic community.

SKILLS AND BOUNDARIES

To practice effectively, educational developers need an awareness of their belief systems, personal skills, and personal knowledge base and cognizance of their own and their clients' boundaries. Ethical practice requires that educational developers:

a. Be reflective and self-critical in their practice;

b. Seek out knowledge, skills, and resources continually to under-gird and expand their practice;

c. Consult with other professionals when they lack the experience or training for a particular case or endeavor or if they seek to prevent or avoid unethical conduct;

d. Know and work within the boundaries of their competence and time limitations;

e. Know and act in consonance with their purpose, mandate, and philosophy, integrating the latter insofar as possible;

   f. Strive to be aware of their own belief systems, values, biases, needs, and the effect of these on their work;

   g. Incorporate diverse points of view;

   h. Allow no personal or private interests to conflict or appear to conflict with professional duties or clients' needs;

   i. Take care of their personal welfare so they can facilitate clients' development; and

   j. Ensure that they have the institutional freedom to do their job ethically.

CLIENTS' RIGHTS

Because educational developers work in a variety of settings with a variety of clients and interact within different teaching and learning contexts, they must be sensitive to and respectful of intellectual, individual, and power differences. Educational developers should thus:

   a. Be receptive to different styles and approaches to teaching and learning, and to others' professional roles and functions;

   b. Respect the rights of others to hold values, attitudes, and opinions different from their own;

   c. Respect the right of clients to refuse services or to request the services of another professional;

   d. Work against harassment and discrimination of any kind, including race, ethnicity, gender, class, religion, sexual orientation, disability, age, nationality, etc.; and

   e. Be aware of various power relationships with clients (e.g., power based on position or on information) and not abuse their power.

Confidentiality

Educational developers maintain confidentiality regarding client identity, information, and records within appropriate limits and according to legal regulations. Educational developers should:

   a. Keep confidential the identity of clients, as well as their professional observations, interactions, or conclusions related to specific clients or cases;

   b. Know the legal requirements regarding appropriate and inappropriate professional confidentiality (e.g., for cases of murder, suicide, or gross misconduct);

c. Store and dispose of records in a safe way; and comply with institutional, state, and federal regulations about storing and ownership of records; and

d. Conduct discreet conversations among professional colleagues in supervisory relationships and never discuss clients in public places.

Responsibilities to the Profession

Educational developers work with colleagues in the local, national, and international arena. In order to assure the integrity of the profession, they:

a. Attribute materials and ideas to their creators or authors;

b. Contribute ideas, experience, and knowledge to colleagues;

c. Respond promptly to requests from colleagues;

d. Respect colleagues and acknowledge collegial differences;

e. Work positively for the development of individuals and the profession;

f. Cooperate with other units and professionals involved in development efforts; and

g. Are advocates for their institutional and professional missions.

Professional Misconduct

The professional misconduct of educational developers would reflect gross negligence and disdain for the guidelines for practice stated above. Unethical, unprofessional, and incompetent behaviors carried out by educational developers should be brought to the attention of the association. Individual educational developers should take responsibility if or when they become aware of gross unethical conduct by any colleague in the profession.

Ethical Conflicts in Educational Development

CONFLICTS ARISING FROM MULTIPLE RESPONSIBILITIES, CONSTITUENTS, RELATIONSHIPS, AND LOYALTIES

Educational developers may encounter conflicts that arise from multiple responsibilities, constituents, relationships, and loyalties. Because educational developers are responsible to their institutions, faculty, graduate students, undergraduate students, and themselves, it is inevitable that conflict will arise. For example, multiple responsibilities and relationships to various constituencies, together with competing loyalties, may lead to conflicting ethical responsibilities. The following examples point out situations in which conflicts may arise and identify the specific conflict.

Example 1: An instructor is teaching extremely poorly and students in the class are suffering seriously as a result. *Conflict*: In this situation the educational developer is faced with a conflict between the responsibility of confidentiality to the client-teacher and responsibility to the students and the institution.

Example 2: A faculty member wants to know how a teaching assistant with whom the educational developer is working is progressing in his/her consultation or in the classroom. *Conflict*: In this situation the educational developer is faced with a conflict between responding to the faculty member's legitimate concern and with maintaining confidentiality vis-à-vis the teaching assistant.

Example 3: The educational developer knows first hand that a professor-client is making racist or sexist remarks or is sexually harassing a student. *Conflict*: In this situation the educational developer is faced with a conflict between confidentiality vis-à-vis the professor-client and not only institutional/personal ethical responsibilities but responsibility to the students as well.

Example 4: A fine teacher who has worked with the educational developer for two years is coming up for tenure and asks that a letter be written to the tenure committee. *Conflict*: In this situation the educational developer is faced with a conflict between rules regarding client confidentiality and the educational developer's commitment to advocate for good teaching on campus and in tenure decisions.

In such instances of conflict educational developers need to practice sensitive and sensible confidentiality. It is best that they:

1. Consult in confidence with other professionals when they are faced with conflicting or confusing ethical choices.
2. Inform the other person or persons when they have to break confidentiality, unless doing so would jeopardize their personal safety or the safety of someone else.
3. Break confidentiality according to legal precedent in cases of potential suicide, murder, or gross misconduct. In such cases, to do nothing is to do something.

4. Decide cases of questionable practice individually, after first informing themselves to the best of their ability of all the ramifications of their actions.

5. Work to determine when they will act or not act, while being mindful of the rules and regulations of the institution and the relevant legal requirements.

CONFLICTS ARISING FROM MULTIPLE ROLES

Educational developers often assume or are assigned roles that might be characterized as teaching police, doctor, coach, teacher, or advocate, among others. They are expected to be institutional models or even the conscience for good teaching on their campuses. Yet, in their work with professors and graduate students, they endeavor to provide a "safe place" for their clients to work on their teaching. Another potential area for conflict arises from the fact that educational developers may serve both as faculty developers and as faculty members. As developers, they support clients in their efforts to improve their teaching; in their role as faculty they often serve on review committees that evaluate other faculty. Either role may give them access to information that cannot appropriately be shared or communicated beyond the committee or the consultation relationship (even if it would be useful for the other role).

An important area of potential conflict exists in the case of the summative evaluation of teaching. Departmental faculty and campus administrators (chairs, deans, etc.) are responsible for the assessment of teaching for personnel decisions. Educational developers should not generally be placed in this situation because of the confidentiality requirements noted in the section on guidelines for practice. In general, educational developers do not make summative judgments about an individual's teaching. In particular, they should never perform the role of developer and summative evaluator concurrently for the same individual unless they have that person's explicit consent and with proper declaration to any panel or committee involved. However, educational developers may:

1. Provide assessment tools

2. Collect student evaluations

3. Help individuals prepare dossiers

4. Educate those who make summative decisions

5. Critique evaluation systems

Conclusion

This document is an attempt to define ethical behaviors for the current practice of educational development in higher education. In creating this document the association has referred to and borrowed from the Ethical Guidelines of the American Psychological Association, the American Association for Marriage and Family Therapy, Guidance Counselors, the Society for Teaching and Learning in Higher Education in Canada, and the Staff and Educational Development Association in the United Kingdom. The association will continue to refine these guidelines in light of the changes and issues that confront the profession. The guidelines will be updated on a periodic basis by the Core Committee of the Professional and Organizational Development Network in Higher Education.

SECTION ONE

ENRICHING
OUR COLLEAGUES

TAKING STOCK

CONTEMPLATING NORTH AMERICAN GRADUATE
STUDENT PROFESSIONAL DEVELOPMENT
PROGRAMS AND DEVELOPERS

Dieter J. Schönwetter, University of Manitoba
Donna Ellis, University of Waterloo

A two-stage study was conducted to identify key competencies in graduate student development programs at Canadian and U.S. institutions. Once thirty-nine key competencies were identified, developers of graduate students were asked to rate the importance of each competency in their programming, the extent to which each competency was explicitly taught, and their own confidence in the training received to help teach these competencies. One key finding suggests that numerous potential gaps exist in the training of those who deliver graduate student development programs, which organizations such as the Professional and Organizational Development Network in Higher Education can help to address.

Central to educational development organizations is the development of our future professoriate through services and programs. In North America, there is a recent sense of urgency about the perception that graduate students are lacking an array of nontechnical skills that are critical for new academics, including communication and interpersonal skills, critical

This project was supported by a POD research grant (2007) and an Educational Developers Caucus Grant from Society for Training and Learning in Higher Education (2007). It received the 2009 POD Robert J. Menges Outstanding Research Award in Educational Development.

and creative thinking, integrity and ethical conduct, teaching competence, leadership, research management, knowledge mobilization and knowledge translation, and social and civic responsibility (Bilodeau, 2007). Although the literature on graduate student development (GSD) is prolific (Marinco-vich, 1998; Nyquist, 2002; Schönwetter & Taylor, 2001), little is known about the core competencies to which U.S. and Canadian GSD programs ascribe. There is also a gap in the knowledge about educational developers' confidence in and preparation for developing these competencies in their graduate students. The former need will guide GSD, whereas the latter will enable identification of key areas for career development of educational developers, especially neophyte developers responsible for GSD.

Literature Review

Researchers with a historical focus have discussed the importance and the types of programs offered to develop graduate students (Boyer, 1990; Chism, 1998). Numerous articles identify themes viewed as significant in training graduate students (Chism, 1998). Postsecondary teaching courses are included as just one of many facets of this training (Ronkowski, 1995). The literature also provides ample information on how to set up and run such programs (Marincovich, Prostko, & Stout, 1998). However, core program elements, including core competencies, are not clearly artic-ulated in this literature.

   Based on an extensive literature review and a panel interview using the Delphi method with thirty-three American leaders in GSD, Smith and Simpson (1995) validated twenty-seven competencies as critical for grad-uate students. However, the leaders' years of expertise in graduate student development, their level of confidence in facilitating each competency, and the extent to which they were trained in these competencies were not addressed. Canadian educational developers have built on this founda-tional work. One study included a comprehensive review of university teaching courses offered to graduate students and identified a set of com-mon course competencies (Schönwetter, Ellis, Taylor, & Koop, 2008). Although core competencies were proposed, they represented only one component of GSD: competencies addressed in courses on university teaching rather than in more comprehensive programs.

   In other research, Schönwetter and Taylor (2003) asked graduate stu-dents enrolled in one certification in higher education program to rank the importance of specific program competencies with respect to teaching development. Schönwetter and Ellis (2007) created a list of potential competencies that reflect core elements in many GSD programs. A related longitudinal study focused on GSD programs in two Canadian universities demonstrated that similar competencies were critical in both programs but that students' perceptions of the key competencies before the program had changed by the end of the program (Taylor, Schönwetter, Ellis, & Roberts, 2008). These studies' findings were specific to graduate student participants, not to those who teach them. The experiences and perceptions of GSD developers are critical as well and are the focus of the study reported in this chapter.

The findings of this study add an international perspective to existing research (Chism, 1998; Lewis, 1992; Marincovich, 1998; Marincovich et al., 1998; Nyquist, 2002; Nyquist et al., 1999; Smith, 2001). We hope our findings will guide the training of educational developers who are responsible for GSD and may be new to the profession and assist developers in creating and refining their own GSD programs. In addition, we hope our findings will provide direction to groups such as the Professional and Organizational Development Network in Higher Education (POD)'s Graduate Student Professional Development (GSPD) subcommittee in identifying and meeting membership needs.

Research Questions

This project tapped into the experiences of educational developers responsible for GSD programs in the United States and Canada and sought to discover (1) a list of common and unique GSD program competencies, (2) which of these competencies are explicitly taught as part of GSD programs, (3) the importance of these competencies, and (4) the confidence levels and training that GSD developers have and need in order to help their graduate student participants develop these competencies. To capture these data, two studies were conducted. The second study is the primary focus of this chapter.

Study 1: Identifying Critical GSD Program Competencies

Seventy GSD developers belonging to POD's GSPD subcommittee were invited in January 2007 to provide a list of the top competencies currently included in their institution's GSD programs on teaching development. Seventeen GSD developers (representing 24.4 percent of developers belonging to the GSPD subcommittee) provided 152 responses.

We conducted a theme analysis, guided by Smith's (2001) ten pivotal events in graduate teacher preparation for a faculty career. Numerous competencies were identified within the ten resulting categories.

Table 1.1 Categories of GSD Program Competencies Identified
by GSD Developers

Category Label	Percentage Responses Within Category
Lesson and course design	17.8%
Teaching skills	17.1
Evaluation and feedback	13.2
Self-reflection	11.8
Interpersonal skills	10.5
Scholarship of teaching and learning	7.9
Presentation and communication skills	7.2
Management of time and people	7.2
Accessing and providing resources	4.6
Being mentored and mutual learning	2.6

Table 1.1 provides a synopsis of the competency categories and the percentage of responses that fell within each category.

The overall results replicate studies that captured content of GSD courses on teaching in higher education (Schönwetter et al., 2008) and what graduate students found as being most important in their teaching training (Taylor et al., 2008). Although study 1's findings reveal what GSD developers perceive are important program competencies, they do not indicate which are most important, which are taught, or how competent the GSD developers feel in teaching these competencies. Study 2 addressed these limitations.

Study 2: Exploring GSD Program Competencies

Exhibit 1.1 lists the thirty-nine competencies identified by GSD developers in study 1. A Web-based survey was created to address the research questions. The first section focused on participant demographics such as age, gender, and number of years in graduate student development. The second set of questions focused on evaluating each of the thirty-nine competencies on a five-point Likert scale (1 = not at all to 5 = very much so) in terms of four criteria: how important this competency is for preparing graduate students to teach as future faculty, the extent to which it is explicitly taught in their graduate student development programs, how confident they feel in preparing graduate students in this area, and the extent to which their training prepared them to teach graduate students these competencies. The survey was distributed to two groups of GSD developers: members of the POD GSPD subcommittee and members of the Canadian Teaching Assistant Developers listserv. Both groups have Canadian and American members, but respondents were asked to identify their country as part of the demographic information. The survey was housed on the QuestionPro.com website and was made available for three months. Reminders were sent in weeks 5 and 9.

Exhibit 1.1 Competencies Assessed in a Survey of GSD Developers

- Exhibit respect and understanding for all students.
- Construct valid and reliable assessments of their students' learning.
- Able to use effective discussion techniques.
- Able to use effective questioning techniques.
- Able to use effective assessment methods.
- Communicate and manage appropriate expectations for achievement in the course.
- Design courses that challenge students to pursue higher-level learning, such as critical thinking and problem solving.
- Develop a reflective approach to teaching through collecting feedback and continually modifying instructional approaches.
- Match varying teaching methods with specific learning objectives.
- Match varying assessment methods with specific learning objectives.
- Able to write specific and assessable learning objectives.
- Engage in professional development related to teaching.
- Document their teaching effectiveness.
- Communicate effectively in oral format in English.
- Provide a welcoming and safe environment for their students.
- Able to articulate the values of their teaching approach (i.e., teaching philosophy).
- Adhere to institutional policies (i.e., discipline, academic honesty, and legal information).
- Communicate effectively in written format in English.
- Able to use effective lecturing techniques.
- Seek out mentoring on teaching.
- Able to teach small and large classes.

- Perceive teaching as a scholarly endeavor.
- Use student-centered teaching methods.
- Recognize that teaching requires lifelong reflective learning.
- Select course material suited to the background, ability level, and interest of their students.
- Apply their knowledge of learning principles and learning theories.
- Present material that is sequenced and paced appropriately for their students.
- Enhance motivation of their students through conveying personal enthusiasm for the subject.
- Accommodate different learning styles of their students.
- Able to adapt teaching material to students' needs.
- Demonstrate mastery of their subject.
- Encourage cooperation and collaboration among their students.
- Build confidence in students by helping them to successfully meet learning objectives.
- Use research in teaching as it applies to instruction in one's field.
- Communicate important values inherent to the discipline or profession.
- Be self-aware of their teaching biases.
- Know how to uncover departmental norms regarding teaching.
- Use technology to enhance learning.
- Advise students of career opportunities in the discipline or profession.
- Demonstrate relationships between the course and the broader liberal education curriculum.

Study 2 Results and Discussion

From December 2008 to February 2009, 149 GSD developers viewed the online survey, 106 started the survey, and 34 completed it (32.1 percent completion rate). The average time required to complete the survey, thirty-one minutes, may explain the relatively low response rate.

GSD DEVELOPER DEMOGRAPHICS

The ratio of the respondents reflects the number of GSD programs in the United States and Canada: eighteen (52.9 percent) Americans, thirteen (38.2 percent) Canadians, and three unspecified (8.8 percent) (Schönwetter et al., 2008). Years of experience in GSD ranged from one to twenty-five (M = 8.97; SD = 5.98), and the age of the respondents ranged from thirty-two to sixty-four (M = 44.03; SD = 9.69). The lowest age seemed somewhat high, given the number of younger GSD developers in both the POD and Society for Teaching and Learning in Higher Education (STLHE) associations. Twenty-five (73.5 percent) females and nine (26.5 percent) males responded, indicative of many GSD programs being directed by females.

GSD DEVELOPER TRAINING AND PROFESSIONAL DEVELOPMENT

The highest degrees earned by respondents were twenty-five doctorates (73.5 percent), eight master's (23.5 percent), and one other (2.9 percent). In response to the question, "As a faculty developer, is it (or would it be) helpful in your current position to have a doctorate degree?" the majority (N = 32; 94.1 percent) indicated yes. This result suggests that further graduate education may be desirable and provides support for doctoral programs in faculty development, as well as support for the ongoing movement toward professionalization of faculty development (Gosling, McDonald, & Stockley, 2007; McDonald & Germain-Rutherford, 2009). The most common forms of professional development for GSD developers are POD and STLHE conferences, workshops, and research projects. GSD developers are involved in important professional development activities that not only keep them current in the areas of graduate student development, but are likely to promote networking among them. The number of conference presentations on GSD ranged from none (N = 4) to thirty (N = 30; M = 9.27; SD = 9.07). The number of publications on GSD ranged from none (N = 12) to fifteen (N = 22; M = 4.36; SD = 4.249), and the number of research grants received for GSD projects ranged from none (N = 20) to nine (N = 14; M = 2.64; SD = 2.307). As a group, GSD developers are well trained, have a fairly established record of conference presentations and publications, and have received research grants, reinforcing the legitimacy of the GSD field.

INSTITUTIONS, CENTERS, AND PROGRAMS REPRESENTED

Institutions represented were twenty-three doctoral (67.6 percent), nine comprehensive (26.5 percent), one undergraduate (2.9 percent), and two other (3.9 percent). These results seem reasonable given that most institutions with GSD programs have graduate programs. The types of centers represented were twenty-nine teaching centers (85.3 percent), two graduate student centers (5.9 percent), and three other (8.8 percent), a distribution that is reflected in other studies (Schönwetter et al., 2008). The GSD programs offered at these institutions include workshop series (91.2 percent of all programs), graduate student teaching certificate or certification programs

(85.3 percent), teaching in higher education courses (70.6 percent), peer consultations (70.6 percent), and mentor programs (47.1 percent). These results mirror literature that highlights the importance of such programming for graduate student development (Marincovich et al., 1998; Nyquist, 2002; Richlin, 1995; Schönwetter & Taylor, 2001, 2003; Smith, 2001; Svinicki, 1989). The number of graduate students in the institutions ranged from 300 to 15,000 ($N = 31$; $M = 5,316$; $SD = 4,220$), and the number of graduate students enrolled in GSD programs ranged from 23 to 3,091 ($N = 31$; $M = 515$; $SD = 647$).

PERCEPTIONS ABOUT THE COMPETENCIES

The data were organized according to mean scores and then compared across the four question areas of importance, explicitly taught, confidence to train, and developer preparation. Synopses of the highest- and lowest-scored items for each question area are in Tables 1.2 and 1.3.

All thirty-nine GSD competencies were perceived as important by GSD developers, scoring well above the midpoint of the scale (the lowest was 3.60). Table 1.2 shows a pattern in that the six most important competencies (those scoring above 4.60) match basic requirements for effective teaching, particularly active learning strategies. These competencies also fit with the themes often represented in POD and STLHE conference sessions. Interestingly, the items most often explicitly taught (in column 2 of Table 1.2) do not completely match those listed as most important. The areas taught in GSD programming tend to fall more into the area of reflective practice, replicating the reflective emphasis found in a synopsis of graduate courses on teaching in higher education (Schönwetter et al., 2008).

As anticipated, the top items about which graduate student developers feel most confident teaching overlap substantially with those explicitly taught, reflecting that confidence tends to build with practice. However, with the exception of "being able to use effective discussion techniques," the areas of most confidence do not overlap with those rated as most important. The mismatch between areas of confidence and importance suggests a gap that professional associations such as POD and STLHE could fill through professional development activities. The high ratings for discussion techniques in all four columns also raise questions (not addressed in the survey) about the disciplinary backgrounds of those who responded to the survey, since discussions occur much more frequently in humanities and social science courses.

Also not surprising, the areas of most confidence overlap considerably with the competencies that developers feel best prepared to teach, yet these competencies focus primarily on attitudes, such as reflecting on

Table 1.2 **Highest-Rated Competencies for Each Question Category**

Importance of Competency ($M \geq 4.62$)	Explicitly Taught ($M \geq 4.30$)	Confidence to Train ($M \geq 4.62$)	Developer Preparation ($M \geq 4.00$)
Exhibit respect and understanding for all students	Able to use effective discussion techniques	Able to articulate the values of their teaching approach (teaching philosophy)	Able to use effective discussion techniques
Construct valid and reliable assessments of their students' learning	Engage in professional development related to teaching	Document their teaching effectiveness	Document their teaching effectiveness
Able to use effective discussion techniques	Develop a reflective approach to teaching through collecting feedback and continually modifying instructional approaches	Develop a reflective approach to teaching through collecting feedback and continually modifying instructional approaches	Able to articulate the values of their teaching approach (teaching philosophy)
Able to use effective questioning techniques	Document their teaching effectiveness	Engage in professional development related to teaching	Engage in professional development related to teaching
Able to use effective assessment methods		Able to use effective discussion techniques	
Communicate and manage appropriate expectations for achievement in the course		Provide a welcoming and safe environment for their students	

teaching and engaging in further development, rather than on concrete skills needed to succeed in teaching, such as setting assessments or conveying course expectations. Again, with the exception of "being able to use effective discussion techniques," GSD developers were not most confident with those competencies deemed most important, so they could

Table 1.3 Lowest-Rated Competencies for Each Question Category

Importance of Competency ($M \leq 3.93$)	Explicitly Taught ($M \leq 2.83$)	Confidence to Train ($M \leq 2.96$)	Developer Preparation ($M \leq 2.79$)
Be self-aware of teaching biases	Communicate effectively in written format in English	Know how to uncover departmental norms regarding teaching	Select course material suited to the background, ability level, and interest of their students
Know how to uncover departmental norms regarding teaching	Communicate important values inherent to the discipline or profession	Advise students of career opportunities in the discipline or profession	Demonstrate relationships between the course and the broader liberal education curriculum
Use technology to enhance learning	Select course material suited to the background, ability level, and interest of their students	Demonstrate mastery of their subject	Use technology to enhance learning
Advise students of career opportunities in the discipline or profession	Demonstrate relationships between the course and the broader liberal education curriculum		Demonstrate mastery of their subject
Demonstrate relationships between the course and the broader liberal education curriculum	Know how to uncover departmental norms regarding teaching		Know how to uncover departmental norms regarding teaching
	Demonstrate mastery of their subject		Communicate important values inherent to the discipline or profession
	Advise students of career opportunities in the discipline or profession		Advise students of career opportunities in the discipline or profession

benefit from receiving training in these areas (see Table 1.2). Such training is unlikely to be an explicit part of most discipline-specific graduate programs, thus reinforcing the value of graduate programs in faculty development.

The competencies rated least important by GSD developers (Table 1.3) tended to link directly to discipline-specific information (departmental norms, career opportunities, and course connection to liberal education curriculum) or strategies that fall outside traditional classroom teaching (using technology to enhance learning). Discipline-specific competencies appear in almost every column as those with the lowest scores, many falling below the midpoint of the scale (3.0). A primary reason could be that developers typically have received their own postsecondary education in one or two disciplines. Since developers are unable to be experts in every discipline, perhaps they need professional development to help connect their work to the disciplines in the form of conference sessions that describe models for involving graduate students or faculty members as GSD developers. Training in the field of organizational development, an increasing area of focus for POD, may help attain the competency of uncovering departmental norms.

Surprisingly, being self-aware of teaching biases was rated among the lowest in importance, and yet some of the competencies that scored the highest in all areas except importance (see Table 1.2) were documenting teaching effectiveness and articulating teaching values. How can one provide a critically reflective teaching philosophy without being aware of biases? Perhaps graduate student developers could benefit from learning about tools such as teaching perspective inventories (Angelo & Cross, 1993; Pratt, 2001) so both they and their students can learn more about the benefits and limitations of different approaches to teaching.

Another troubling result is the low importance ascribed to teaching with technology. This result raises questions about whether developers feel that technology is so ubiquitous that graduate students no longer require training in how to use it in pedagogically effective ways or if developers themselves do not have the training to provide this type of assistance. The results from the developers' training column in Table 1.3 suggest the latter is the more likely explanation. Perhaps graduate student developers could benefit from training in this area since it is unlikely that technologies will disappear from higher education. Again, professional associations could assist with this knowledge gap, particularly with face-to-face or virtual training.

Finally, it is surprising to see that the students' ability to communicate effectively in written English was one of the least often taught competencies.

Presumably students in GSD programs are assessed in some way and written assignments may be a common format, particularly with the prevalence of teaching portfolios in GSD teaching courses and certificates. If students need to communicate what they have learned in writing, is it not important to also assist them with this skill as part of the program? Reflective writing, which is common for documents such as teaching portfolios, is quite different from the writing used in technical reports or research essays. However, faculty members in many disciplines struggle to teach written communication skills to their students; perhaps graduate student developers face a similar challenge. Organizations like POD and STLHE could provide conference sessions or online resources on effective strategies for teaching and assessing written work.

A number of one-way ANOVAs were conducted to determine if any differences existed based on gender or experience cohorts. With gender, statistically significant differences were found in relation to two competencies on the extent to which these are taught in GSD programs: "presenting material that is sequenced and paced appropriately for their students" and "ability to adapt teaching material to students' needs." In both cases, female graduate student developers reported higher frequencies of teaching these competencies than males did. These findings call into question whether differences are related solely to gender or whether men and women have different training or disciplinary backgrounds. Unfortunately, the study does not provide information needed to clarify this difference.

One-way ANOVAs were also performed using experience cohorts (one to five, six to ten, and ten or more years of experience) on each of the competencies. In terms of GSD developers' confidence, the "be self-aware of their teaching biases" competency demonstrated differences ($p < .01$). Least squares difference post hoc t-tests ($p < .05$) showed that the more experienced cohort (ten or more years of experience) reported statistically significant higher perceptions of confidence than either the younger cohort (one to five years) or the middle experience cohort (six to ten years). This result may suggest that it takes time to learn effective tools or questions to feel confident when helping graduate students uncover their teaching biases.

In terms of explicitly teaching competencies in their programs, the "seeking out mentoring on teaching" competency demonstrated statistically significant differences based on experience ($p < .01$). Least square differences post hoc t-tests ($p < .01$) showed that the more experienced cohort (ten or more years of experience) taught this competency more than the younger cohort (one to five years) did. Again, increased experience may make it more likely that these developers have either had their own mentor or served as a mentor, an experience that could help them recognize the importance of mentoring and know how to teach their graduate students to engage effective mentors as part of their professional development.

Limitations and Implications for Future Research

Although the findings presented here extend the research of previous studies by providing a larger sample of participants from both the United States and Canada, the study has its limitations. Only one-third of current graduate student developers who were solicited responded to the online survey. Future research needs to find ways to engage more of this population. Possibilities are reducing the number of survey items, providing incentives to encourage participation, or running the survey as part of a conference registration.

The study sought primarily quantitative data and in many cases could benefit from additional open-ended questions or follow-up interviews to provide in-depth explanations of the findings. Also important would be a comparison of graduate student developers from other countries, including those from the European Union nations, Australia, and New Zealand, to provide a more global perspective. Finally, a comparison of GSD programs and developers to new faculty programs may be of interest, given that there may be substantial overlap between the two types of programs.

Conclusion

Graduate student development is a critical component of many teaching centers' programming. The international and multi-institutional study discussed in this chapter provides guidance and questions for the development of our future professoriate and those directly responsible for their development. The findings suggest the existence of numerous gaps that professional associations and higher education institutions can fill through conference sessions, other professional development activities or resources, and graduate programs targeted to GSD developers and the programs they offer. Graduate students represent the future professoriate, and their teaching preparation is vitally important to the future of higher education. But to help this key cohort, we cannot overlook those who support their development. This study suggests a need to promote and provide solid preparation for graduate student developers. Let us hope that the members of our professional associations rise to meet this need.

REFERENCES

Angelo, T., & Cross, K. P. (1993). *Teaching goals inventory*. Retrieved from www.uiowa.edu/~centeach/tgi/

Bilodeau, P. (2007). *Tri-agency statement of principles on key professional skills for researchers*. Retrieved from www.tss.uoguelph.ca/pdfs/ProfSkills4Re searchers.pdf

Boyer, E. L. (1990). *Scholarship reconsidered: Priorities of the professoriate*. Princeton, NJ: Carnegie Foundation for the Advancement of Teaching.

Chism, N.V.N. (1998). Evaluating TA programs. In M. Marincovich, J. Prostko, & F. Stout (Eds.), *The professional development of graduate teaching assistants* (pp. 249–262). San Francisco: Jossey-Bass/Anker.

Gosling, D., McDonald, J., & Stockley, D. (2007). We did it our way! Narratives of pathways to the profession of educational development. *Educational Developments, 8*(4), 1–5.

Lewis, K. G. (1992). *Teaching pedagogy to teaching assistants: A handbook for 398T instructors*. Austin: University of Texas, Center for Teaching Effectiveness.

Marincovich, M. (1998). Teaching teaching: The importance of courses on teaching in TA training programs. In M. Marincovich, J. Prostko, & F. Stout (Eds.), *The professional development of graduate teaching assistants* (pp. 145–162). San Francisco: Jossey-Bass/Anker.

Marincovich, M., Prostko, J., & Stout, F. (Eds.). (1998). *The professional development of graduate teaching assistants*. San Francisco: Jossey-Bass/Anker.

McDonald, J., & Germain-Rutherford, A. (2009). *Conceptualizing our teaching: A reflective process*. Paper presented at the Society for Teaching and Learning in Higher Education, Fredericton, New Brunswick.

Nyquist, J. D. (2002). The PhD: A tapestry of change for the 21st century. *Change, 34*(6), 12–20.

Nyquist, J. D., Manning, L., Wulff, D. H., Austin, A. E., Sprague, J., Fraser, P. K., et al. (1999). On the road to becoming a professor: The graduate student experience. *Change, 31*(3), 18–27.

Pratt, D. D. (2001). *Teaching perspectives inventory*. Retrieved from www.teachingperspectives.com

Richlin, L. (1995). Preparing the faculty of the future to teach. In W. A. Wright (Ed.), *Teaching improvement practices: Successful strategies for higher education* (pp. 255–282). San Francisco: Jossey-Bass/Anker.

Ronkowski, S. A. (1995). Trends in TA training: An analysis of national conferences on TA-ing from 1986 to 1993. In T. A. Heenan & K. F. Jerich (Eds.), *Teaching graduate students to teach: Engaging the disciplines.* Chicago: University of Illinois Press.

Schönwetter, D. J., & Ellis, D. (2007). *Sharing competency commonalities and uniqueness across Canadian TA programs.* Paper presented at the Educational Developers Caucus Winter Conference, University of Guelph, Ontario, Canada.

Schönwetter, D. J., Ellis, D. E., Taylor, K. L., & Koop, V. (2008). An exploration of the landscape of graduate courses on college and university teaching in Canada and the USA. *Journal of Graduate and Professional Student Development, 11*(1), 7–29.

Schönwetter, D. J., & Taylor, K. L. (2001). Academic morphing: From graduate student to faculty member. *University Teaching Services Newsletter, 9*(3), 1–2.

Schönwetter, D. J., & Taylor, K. L. (2003). Preparing future professors for their teaching roles: Success strategies from a Canadian program. *Journal of Graduate Teaching Assistant Development, 9*(3), 101–110.

Smith, K. S. (2001). Pivotal events in graduate teacher preparation for a faculty career. *Journal of Graduate Teaching Assistant Development, 8*(3), 97–105.

Smith, K. S., & Simpson, R. D. (1995). Validating teaching competencies for faculty members in higher education: A national study using the Delphi method. *Innovative Higher Education, 19*(3), 223–233.

Svinicki, M. D. (1989). The development of TAs: Preparing for the future while enhancing the present. In A. F. Lucas (Ed.), *New directions for teaching and learning: No. 37. The department chairperson's role in enhancing college teaching* (pp. 71–80). San Francisco: Jossey-Bass.

Taylor, K. L., Schönwetter, D. J., Ellis, D. E., & Roberts, M. (2008). Profiling an approach to evaluating the impact of two certification in university teaching programs for graduate students. *Journal of Graduate and Professional Student Development, 11*(1), 78–108.

2

GROWING A NEW GENERATION

PROMOTING SELF-REFLECTION THROUGH PEER OBSERVATION

Allison Boye, Micah Meixner, Texas Tech University

Many faculty developers understand the value of self-reflection in effective teaching and aim to cultivate the practice in their programming. However, many instructors regard peer observation as punitive or evaluative in nature and overlook how the practice can promote thoughtful self-reflection by the observer. This chapter outlines a model of group peer observation that supports introspection and community, thereby transforming that negative perception. We discuss how the process promotes cross-disciplinary open-door teaching and reflective practice in teaching improvement and how faculty developers from institutions and programs of all sizes can help nurture that growth.

In our work as graduate student developers facilitating an intensive fellowship program at Texas Tech University, the Teaching Effectiveness And Career enHancement (TEACH) program, we are constantly searching for ways to help new instructors improve their teaching and encourage them to engage in teaching as reflective practice. Reflection is a core value of our program, and we try to incorporate it into virtually everything our TEACH fellows do in the hope that it will become a habit that they take with them into their careers, not just something they engage in for the two semesters while they are working with us. Teaching so often takes place behind closed doors, so we strive to foster a culture of collegiality and open-door teaching.

We expect a significant amount of work from our fellows, including extensive teaching portfolios and scholarship of teaching and learning

(SoTL) projects, twenty hours of workshop attendance, and having consultants videotape their classes; each element asks for self-reflection in some way. Nevertheless, we felt that there was room for improvement and so introduced a peer observation element. Now in its third year, we have found peer observation to be effective in building community as well as fostering self-reflection, and it has become one of the most popular elements of the program. Moreover, it has helped instructors open the closed doors not only of their classrooms, but also of their disciplines, and discover that they can learn a great deal by talking about teaching with colleagues from across the university.

A Brief Overview of the Literature

A study of the literature provided resounding support for the addition of peer observation to the program. Many institutions employ evaluative teaching observations in the tenure review process, and many of these same institutions support peer observation to inform teaching development (DeZure, 1993; Millis, 1992, 1999; Richardson, 2000; Weimar, 1990; Wilkerson & Lewis, 2002). Nonevaluative peer observation is also cited as an important element in increased teaching effectiveness (Beaty, 1999; Chism, 1999; DeZure, 1993; Millis, 1992).

In the discussion of teaching observations for developmental purposes, the impact of reflection is continually emphasized as key to the success of the exercise. Findings on reflection suggest that instructors who reflect on their teaching and engage in dialogue about their teaching with colleagues, administrators, and faculty developers show continued or increased teaching effectiveness (Bell, 2001; Brookfield, 1995; Bullough & Gitlin, 1991; Cosh, 1999; Hammersley-Fletcher & Orsmond, 2005; Loughran, 2002; Wilkerson & Lewis, 2002). In addition, the collegial dialogue that frequently results from peer observation often prompts the observer to reflect on his or her own teaching (Brookfield, 1995; Cosh, 1999; Hammersley-Fletcher & Orsmond, 2005; Wilkerson & Lewis, 2002).

Seasoned developers (Barnett, 1983; Millis, 1999; Weimar, 1990; Wilkerson & Lewis, 2002) call attention to the tendency for classroom observations to be viewed as a punitive or negative experience, and they suggest peer observation and collegial conversation as ways in which this perception might be changed. To achieve an open culture, scholars such as Brookfield (1995), DeZure (1993), Millis (1992), and Shulman (2000) recommend encouraging classroom observations within the department as well as across the campus. These authors suggest that opening classrooms to observation by colleagues and other instructors is likely to establish a culture of reflective and improved teaching.

Our Peer Observation Model

Recognizing the power of reflection in conjunction with observation (Richardson, 2000), we use a reciprocal peer observation model that aims to emphasize the self-reflection of the observer rather than the feedback presented to the observed. Through the model, we endeavor to change the negative perception of observation as simply evaluative and instead support introspection and the collegiality of the peer relationship. In pursuit of those goals, we encourage observers to use the observation experience as an opportunity to think about their own teaching rather than an opportunity to critique their colleagues. Our experience has been that many fellows struggle with self-reflection in other TEACH program components, as they find it difficult to look at themselves from the outside in and contemplate the reasoning behind their classroom decisions. We therefore believe that putting them in an external position of observer, watching a peer in action, offers them another aperture through which they might gaze back at themselves and consider "Why don't I do that?" Or, "Do I do that too?"

TEACH fellows are assigned to groups of three to four that encompass similar and dissimilar disciplines as well as varying levels of experience. Although the groups change each semester, it is not unusual for at least two group members to be paired again in subsequent semesters. One fellow made the following comment about the benefit of continued partnership: "What was most encouraging was seeing the growth of one teacher the second semester that I observed her. I realized that I had grown significantly as well." (All participants quoted in this chapter gave permission to quote them.)

To dispel the idea that observations are conducted solely for evaluative purposes, we believe it is important for each instructor to experience all aspects of observation. After groups are assigned, each fellow must observe at least one other group member and be observed by at least one group member each semester. Brookfield (1995) asserts, "Peer observation must be reciprocal. If you are going to invite colleagues into your classrooms, it should be on the understanding that you'll return the favor by visiting theirs. All too often, peer observation reproduces the power dynamics on campus" (p. 85). Reciprocity helps diminish the stigma of evaluative observation and shifts the focus to a strengthened sense of collegial dialogue and association. Although only one observation is required, we encourage fellows to conduct multiple observations each semester, and at least three or four typically do so.

The act of simply going into a colleague's classroom to think about your own teaching helps show fellows that teaching does not have to be an isolated experience and furthers the program goal of cultivating an open-door teaching culture. The group follow-up discussion fosters collegiality and the idea that teaching does not have to be private *or* perfect. Many fellows appreciate the opportunity to observe others who are at the same level, in contrast to other models that highlight the observation of only excellent teaching (DeZure, 1993). In observing their peers, they are not intimidated and are therefore in a better position to observe and reflect on their own practices. As one fellow remarked in our survey, "It has been a very enlightening experience. I realized that we all have similar situations, problems, and students."

The interdisciplinary cohort also enables cross-disciplinary observation, and for many fellows, observing a class that is completely different from their own has been an eye-opening experience. In observing across disciplines, these new instructors are exposed to different modes of teaching, and they are forced to focus on the teaching without getting bogged down in the content because the content itself is unfamiliar (Beaty, 1999). Cross-disciplinary observation demonstrates that an open-door teaching culture does not have to be limited to one's own department; rather, there are universal issues surrounding teaching and learning that can extend well beyond the confines of a single discipline. One fellow noted in our 2008 survey, "It was fascinating to watch a class in a discipline so different from mine, one that was strongly lecture-based and yet still involved the class. I was impressed that such a large lecture could still require student input and involvement."

Because reflective teaching is something that we constantly promote with faculty and graduate students alike, we ask that each of the fellows submit a piece of postobservation reflective writing in response to a series of questions provided to them in their TEACH Program Handbook. Writing often serves as an instrument for guided reflection (Maas, 1991), and we therefore ask the fellows to respond to a handful of questions that encourage them to reflect on their experience as observers and their thinking about their teaching. In recognition of the fact that many inexperienced instructors might need a familiar location to begin their observations and reflection, and in spite of the fact that many instructors struggle with the seemingly visceral impulse to critique, we include questions such as, "What suggestions might you share with the instructor?" This question helps the instructors establish a basis of what they like or dislike in a classroom, and then more easily enter into reflection about their own teaching.

The fellows submit their written reflections to their consultant prior to any follow-up discussion. When they turn in a bulleted list or time line of the observation, we request that they more fully explain and reflect on their observations before sharing their write-up with the remainder of the group. We have seen considerable growth in rewritten statements. It has been our observation that the writing component is critical to the success of the peer observation process, as it is often through writing that these instructors begin to reflect and consider their own teaching, producing thoughtful insights like this one: "Witnessing B's class also made me consider the difference between process and end result. In other words, can it be effective to teach students in a manner that emphasizes the process rather than the end result? Perhaps the learning process may be more effective when the final result isn't always so obvious."

After everyone in the group has observed and been observed and has submitted reflective writing to one of the consultants, the group meets for a discussion with both the group members and consultants to share their reflective writings and engage in conversation about their ideas and observation experiences. Many fellows view this discussion as a significant part of the process that provides a forum to discuss their most intimate teaching concerns and challenges. As Bell (2001) states, "Truly collegial and developmental activities involving observation encourage shared critical reflection on real-life teaching experiences—and can lead to transformation of both perspective and practice" (p. 29). Most important, the group setting offers the fellows a safe haven and a support system for introspection. In this venue, young instructors can come to the liberating realization that teaching "is a learning process and I am not alone."

While many models of peer observation (Bell, 2001; Hammersley-Fletcher & Orsmond, 2005; Millis, 1992, 1999) outline a process of observation based on a system of consultation before the observation, followed by the observation, and then a follow-up, we have elected not to include a preobservation consultation in our model. Though the value of preobservation consultations is indisputable, we decided that it might emphasize the evaluative rather than the reflective aspects of observation by focusing too much on what the observed person hopes to gain. In addition, the logistical implications of preobservation meetings in which the observation process is not always reciprocal could potentially create a scheduling ordeal as well as overwhelm fellows with even more commitments on top of the other highly rigorous program requirements.

Allen (1991) asserts that the notion of reflective teaching "has the advantage of being relatively uncomplicated" (p. 314), drawing on Posner's (1989) model, which indicates that experience plus reflection equals growth. Our model of reflective teaching, if encapsulated into a similar formula, would be similarly uncomplicated: experience plus observation plus dialogue can foster reflection, which can lead to growth. We offer a purposefully simple paradigm because we maintain that growth does not necessitate complexity, particularly for novice teachers. Furthermore, we do not expect that all reflection will be critical reflection for these young instructors, for, as Brookfield (1995) agrees, "just because reflection is not critical does not mean it is unimportant or unnecessary" (p. 8). For instance, during an observation, some instructors might realize that it is valuable to repeat questions for students, or ask students to put away their cell phones, or as one fellow realized, simply "slow down and make sure all the details are known." For these instructors, or even seasoned instructors, those are valuable realizations; it is reflection, and it has led to growth.

The Role of the Faculty Developer

Our role as faculty developers within this model is primarily supportive. We assist with essential logistics: collecting schedules, making introductions, or stepping in on the rare occasion when groups experience difficulties scheduling their observations of one another. In creating groups, we must make sure that class times do not conflict and that every member of a group will have the opportunity to observe at least one other peer. However, we also work to create groups that we think will be a good fit with one another based on what we know about experience, discipline, and personality. Sometimes that means matching more experienced instructors with newer instructors, or teachers who favor traditional methods with those who like to experiment. Of course, we cannot ultimately predict group dynamics, but our goal is to make the process as free as possible from conflict while exposing the instructors to new experiences. So far this approach has proven successful. For instance, a shy music instructor whose students were talking throughout her classes experienced an epiphany by observing a gregarious theater instructor speak out and tell her students to quiet down; at that moment, she finally realized that she too could "manage a tranquil environment for a class and stop unnecessary talking among students while the instructor speaks without hurting students' feelings." That moment was made possible by her cross-disciplinary peer observation experience with an instructor she might otherwise have never met.

During the observation process itself, we provide guidance to instructors in the form of the questions that we ask them to ponder as they reflect on the experience as well as classroom elements, such as content, classroom management, student engagement, and delivery and communication, they might consider during their classroom visit (Exhibit 2.1). Because our clients are primarily novice instructors working outside their discipline, we recognize the importance of providing them with structure and focus for the experience so that they have a foundation for their observation and reflection.

Exhibit 2.1 Peer Observation Reflective Questions and Guidelines

- What did this observation help you recognize about your own teaching? Did you identify with anything that happened in the class? Did this experience make you want to change or implement something new in your own classroom?

- In conducting this observation, what thoughts did you have about the practice of teaching and learning in general? For instance, did your observation inform your thinking about big picture issues like classroom management or student engagement? Did you change your mind about anything, or confirm beliefs you already had?

- What did the instructor do particularly well?

- What suggestions or ideas might you share with the instructor?

- If you observed someone in a discipline different from your own, what was that experience like?

Here are some general matters you might consider as you observe your peers in the classroom (yes, there is a lot that goes into teaching!). You don't need to address ALL or any of these; these are just to help you focus during your observation and to assist you in your reflections on teaching. And you can certainly think about issues that are not included here!

Content: Content knowledge; answering questions; variety; challenging and stimulating; use of examples and analogies; clarity; application; synthesis of information and connections; organization

Classroom management: Student attention; student participation; student preparation; student civility

Student engagement: Instructor enthusiasm; rapport with students; active involvement; asking questions; discussion; class activities; student participation

Delivery and communication: Eye contact; clarity; volume; movement; pace; visuals; technology

Following the observations, the consultants are present to help facilitate follow-up discussion. We help initiate the discussion and, more important, are there to promote deeper reflection during the discussion and shift the focus away from evaluation when necessary. The impulse to evaluate when observing is a natural one, so during the group discussion, we strive to steer the instructors gently back toward self-evaluation and reflection, often by asking questions as simple as, "So what does that make you think about your own teaching? Is that something you would be interested in trying?" or "How does this influence your thoughts on . . .?" In addition, participating in the discussions benefits us as consultants by allowing us to get to know the fellows on a deeper level.

The group discussion and dynamic are vital to promoting self-reflection, for much of the reflection begins to happen in the dialogue among peers and consultants (Maas, 1991). Although the instructors have engaged in reflection during the writing process, that reflection truly blossoms as they bounce ideas off one another and begin to think of things that occurred to them during dialogue. As one fellow stated, "I think the most valuable part of the process was when the peer group sat down together and talked about the things that they learned from each other."

Assessment

Several strategies have been used to determine the success of our peer observation model as a component of the TEACH program, and in general we have received a very positive response from our fellows. One method of assessment is a year-end anonymous online survey with qualitative and quantitative questions designed to elicit feedback on the peer observation process. Data were gathered from two cohorts over the course of two academic years (Table 2.1). In 2009, the cohort contained an unusually high number of graduating fellows who were understandably busy at the end of the year, which could explain the lower response rate for that year.

Significantly more (82 percent) of the 2009 respondents indicated that they felt engaged in community with other fellows, compared to only 44 percent of the 2008 respondents. Similarly, 82 percent of the 2009 respondents compared to 56 percent of the 2008 respondents claimed to have enjoyed the opportunity to compare another discipline to their own and to focus solely on teaching rather than content. We attribute these dramatic increases to the expansion of the group dynamic. We expanded the observation model from pairs to groups in 2008 and 2009, realizing that the more complicated logistics were worth the significant benefits.

Table 2.1 Peer Observation Participant Quantitative Survey Responses

	2008	2009
Regarding the Peer Observation Process	(*N* = 16)	(*N* = 11)
Felt more engaged in community with other TEACH fellows	44%	82%
Gained insight into my teaching	38	82
Took away some good ideas to try in my own teaching	69	82
Engaged in critical reflection about teaching in general	38	91
Felt more confident in my teaching	38	73
Felt discouraged about my teaching	0	9
Enjoyed the opportunity to watch someone else teach	81	73
Enjoyed the opportunity to compare another discipline to my own and just focus on teaching rather than content	56	82
Found it difficult to observe another discipline	NA	0
Felt inspired to do more in my teaching	NA	64
Felt reaffirmed that other instructors were dealing with similar issues	NA	45
Regarding the Group Follow-Up Discussion		
The discussion helped me think about my own teaching.	NA	91
I felt uncomfortable talking about my own teaching with the group.	NA	0
I enjoyed the group dynamic.	NA	91
I learned from others' observations and reflections.	NA	82
The consultants encouraged my personal reflection.	NA	73
I made a personal connection with my peers.	NA	27

Note: The response rate for 2008 was 80 percent, and for 2009, it was 58 percent.

The fellows achieved a greater sense of community, instructors who wanted to engage in multiple observations had more options, and the opportunity to interact with more than one colleague and discipline ultimately created a significantly richer discussion and reflective experience.

In a similar jump in ratings, 91 percent of the 2009 respondents compared to 38 percent of the 2008 respondents felt that the observation process caused them to engage in critical reflection about teaching in general. We credit the new structure of the guidelines (Exhibit 2.1) and the addition of the formal written element for the improvement in our fellows' self-reflection. When we piloted the model in 2007, we simply asked the instructors to observe each other and talk with us about what they had observed. We soon discovered that the instructors needed structure and guidance to reap the most benefits from the experience. As a result of the additional structure, their self-reflections were much more thoughtful, and the discussions were deeper and more fruitful.

Feedback was also gathered from current and former fellows by e-mail in which we asked them to answer questions such as, "How did the peer observation process affect your teaching approach or teaching philosophy?" In those exchanges, many fellows listed peer observation among their favorite elements of the program. They similarly found the observation process to be beneficial to their development as effective teachers. One example of these sentiments is expressed in the following statement: "It made me think about what it meant to be a good teacher. It made me think about my role as an instructor and what kind of teacher I wanted to be. It made me think critically about things that I hadn't noticed about myself. I am still trying to work on some of those things."

In regard to interdisciplinary observation, we met with varied reactions from the fellows. Nevertheless, most welcomed the interdisciplinary experience and found it to be highly beneficial, as these examples show:

> This disconnect between the observer and the classroom has greater potential to drive both fellows to a deeper sense of reflection because of the lack of familiarity.

> The commonalities of teaching in all subjects really spurred me on to make sure I was doing the best job possible for my students.

Overall, as shown in Table 2.1, the fellows found the peer observation process to be a useful way to engage in community and critical reflection, and they enjoyed the disciplinary intersection and the group dynamic. Since adding the peer observation component, we have seen a significant increase in the sense of collegiality and camaraderie within the cohort.

Discussion

In dismal economic times, faculty developers cannot underestimate the value of inexpensive programming for offering great impact for young instructors and faculty alike. This model requires no cost beyond the salaries (the "consultants" here are not consultants in the sense that they get paid by the hour; they are employees who refer to themselves as consultants to the process) of the consultants who facilitate its implementation and requires no large facility. Although our groups met in conference rooms in our own teaching and learning center, they could meet anywhere on campus—classrooms, lounges, offices, even the bookstore coffee shop. All that is truly required is willing participation from instructors, time from consultants, a basic spreadsheet to aid in coordinating schedules, and patience during the scheduling process.

The process of observing one another and discussing their beliefs was particularly powerful for young graduate student instructors who are relatively new to the college classroom and still discovering their personal teaching philosophies. However, much literature reveals the importance of collegiality and relationships to the success and satisfaction of both new and experienced faculty (Baldwin, DeZure, Shaw, & Moretto, 2008; Boice, 1991, 1993; Karpiak, 1997; Sorcinelli, 1992). The self-reflective peer observation process could also be valuable for new faculty members in search of guidance and community, or seasoned midcareer faculty looking to reenergize their teaching. We have seen that instructors are interested in seeing how others "negotiate the classroom terrain and how they resolve challenges similar to those they face daily" (DeZure, 1993, p. 28), finding support and building connections with one another, and discovering that they are not alone in their experiences. As DeZure also notes, the involvement of a teaching and learning center can help structure the peer observation experience and alleviate concerns about intrusiveness for instructors who are interested in observing others but are perhaps reticent to initiate the relationship on their own. Assistance from a faculty developer in the scheduling of observations and meetings can also help avert potential procrastination from busy faculty who might be excited about the idea of peer observations but slow to follow through.

Regarding the reflective process, we have found that ultimately, as Cranton (2006) remarks, "an educator can do nothing to ensure that transformative learning takes place. Learners must decide to undergo the process themselves" (p. 135). Nevertheless, "We do not leave the possibility of students engaging in critical self-reflection, increasing self-knowledge, and potentially transforming perspectives to chance. It is our responsibility to help people articulate and examine beliefs and assumptions that have been previously assimilated without questioning" (p. 135). So while we cannot coerce instructors to reflect, we do continue to believe in the value of reflection and that we can help them reexamine their teaching in new ways with a little bit of guidance. We will continue to modify our model toward the goal of promoting deeper thoughtfulness in our instructors and their subsequent growth.

What began for us as a simple invitation to watch others teach has been confirmed as a truly rewarding experience for graduate instructors and an undeniable opportunity for their growth as reflective teachers. By embracing peer observation as a vehicle for self-reflection and community rather than critique and evaluation, fellows become a cohort of thoughtful faculty members who are comfortable engaging in open dialogue about teaching and learning.

REFERENCES

Allen, R. R. (1991). Encouraging reflection in teaching assistants. In J. D. Nyquist, R. D. Abbott, D. H. Wulff, & J. Sprague (Eds.), *Preparing the professoriate of tomorrow to teach: Selected readings in TA training* (pp. 313–317). Dubuque, IA: Kendall/Hunt.

Baldwin, R., DeZure, D., Shaw, A., & Moretto, K. (2008, September/October). Mapping the terrain of mid-career faculty at a research university: Implications for faculty and academic leaders. *Change, 40*(5), 46–55.

Barnett, M. A. (1983). Peer observation and analysis: Improving teaching and training TAs. *ADFL Bulletin, 15*(1), 30–33.

Beaty, L. (1999). The professional development of teachers in higher education: Structures, methods and responsibilities. *Innovations in Education and Teaching International, 35*(2), 99–107.

Bell, M. (2001). Supported reflective practice: A programme of peer observation and feedback for academic teaching development. *International Journal for Academic Development, 6*(1), 29–39.

Boice, R. (1991). Quick starters: New faculty who succeed. In M. Theall & J. Franklin (Eds.), *New directions for teaching and learning: No. 48. Effective practices for improving teaching* (pp. 111–121). San Francisco: Jossey-Bass.

Boice, R. (1993). Primal origins and later correctives for midcareer disillusionment. In M. J. Finklestein & M. W. LaCelle-Peterson (Eds.), *New directions for teaching and learning: No. 55. Developing senior faculty as teachers* (pp. 33–41). San Francisco: Jossey-Bass.

Brookfield, S. D. (1995). *Becoming a critically reflective teacher*. San Francisco: Jossey-Bass.

Bullough, R. V., & Gitlin, A. D. (1991). Educative communities and the development of the reflective practitioner. In B. R. Tabachnick & K. M. Zeichner (Eds.), *Issues and practices in inquiry-oriented teacher education* (pp. 35–55). Bristol, PA: Falmer Press.

Chism, N.V.N. (1999). *Peer review of teaching: A sourcebook*. San Francisco: Jossey-Bass/Anker.

Cosh, J. (1999). Peer observation: A reflective model. *ELT Journal, 53*(1), 22–27.

Cranton, P. (2006). *Understanding and promoting transformative learning*. San Francisco: Jossey-Bass.

DeZure, D. (1993). Opening the classroom door. *Academe, 79*(5), 27–28.

Hammersley-Fletcher, L., & Orsmond, P. (2005). Reflecting on reflective practices within peer observation. *Studies in Higher Education, 30*(2), 213–224.

Karpiak, I. E. (1997). University professors at mid-life: Being a part of . . . but feeling apart. In D. DeZure (Ed.), *To improve the academy: Vol. 16. Resources for faculty, instructional, and organizational development* (pp. 21–40). Stillwater, OK: New Forums Press.

Loughran, J. J. (2002). Effective reflective practice: In search of meaning in learning about teaching. *Journal of Teacher Education, 53*(1), 33–43.

Maas, J. (1991). Writing and reflection in teacher education. In B. R. Tabachnick & K. M. Zeichner (Eds.), *Issues and practices in inquiry-oriented teacher education* (pp. 211– 225). Bristol, PA: Falmer Press.

Millis, B. J. (1992). Conducting effective peer classroom observations. In D. H. Wulff & J. D. Nyquist (Eds.), *To improve the academy: Vol. 11. Resources for faculty, instructional, and organizational development* (pp. 189–201). Stillwater, OK: New Forums Press.

Millis, B. J. (1999). Three practical strategies for peer consultation. In C. K. Knapper & S. Piccinin (Eds.), *New directions for teaching and learning: No. 79. Using consultants to improve teaching* (pp. 19–28). San Francisco: Jossey-Bass.

Posner, G. J. (1989). *Field experience: Methods of reflective teaching*. New York: Longman.

Richardson, M. O. (2000). Peer observation: Learning from one another. *Thought and Action, 16*(1), 9–20.

Shulman, L. S. (2000). Teaching as community property: Putting an end to pedagogical solitude. In D. DeZure (Ed.), *Learning to change: Landmarks in teaching and learning in higher education from* Change *magazine, 1969– 1999* (pp. 24–26). Sterling, VA: Stylus.

Sorcinelli, M. D. (1992). New and junior faculty stress: Research and responses. In M. D. Sorcinelli & A. E. Austin (Eds.), *New directions for teaching and learning: No. 50. Developing new and junior faculty* (pp. 27–37). San Francisco: Jossey-Bass.

Weimar, M. (1990). *Improving college teaching*. San Francisco: Jossey-Bass.

Wilkerson, L., & Lewis, K. G. (2002). Classroom observation: The observer as collaborator. In K. H. Gillespie, L. R. Hilsen, & E. C. Wadsworth (Eds.), *A guide to faculty development: Practical advice, examples, and resources* (pp. 74–81). San Francisco: Jossey-Bass/Anker.

3

SUPPORT NEEDS OF UNIVERSITY ADJUNCT LECTURERS

Sarah M. Ginsberg, Eastern Michigan University

Little is known about the support needs of the part-time instructors on university campuses, despite the fact that they represent more than 50 percent of the instructors teaching in higher education. This study of adjunct lecturers investigated their support needs and their preferences for receiving support. Results indicated that adjuncts wanted information about their students and effective teaching methods beyond lecturing. They expressed frustration over the fact that there was no systematic approach to information sharing, particularly with the tenure-track faculty in their programs. They evenly favored resources provided either electronically or face-to-face.

Thirty-five years ago, 58 percent of faculty members were in tenure-track positions (Gappa, 2008). Fewer than half of the faculty teaching today are eligible for tenure (Gappa, 2000, 2008; Schuster, 2003; Umbach, 2006). Numerous studies, particularly at community colleges, have shed light on who these part-time instructors are, why they teach, and how they teach. However, little research has been conducted to learn what types of assistance they need and how best to deliver it. Successfully supporting the teaching of part-time faculty would seem to be critical to institutional mission and student learning outcomes.

Part-time teachers provide colleges and universities with flexibility to manage fluctuations in enrollments and decreases in government funding. The financial value of part-time instructors, typically paid less than their

This research was generously funded by the Faculty Development Center at Eastern Michigan University.

tenure-track counterparts, cannot be overlooked. Part-time instructors typically do not get paid benefits, are paid only for the courses they teach, and do not require a commitment on the part of the institution from one semester to the next (Ellison, 2002; Gappa, 2000; Umbach, 2006).

Gappa and Leslie (1993) noted that instructors taught part time for one of four basic reasons. More than half described themselves as experts employed full time in their field, motivated to teach more by satisfaction derived from the educational process than by economic and career interests (Leslie & Gappa, 2002). "Career enders" (p. 49) were either transitioning into retirement or had already retired. A third group chose to teach part time because of a preference for greater professional flexibility than tenure-track positions might offer. The final category was termed "aspiring academics" (p. 60): those teaching in part-time or term-limited positions, often at more than one institution at a time, in the hopes of obtaining a tenure-track position.

Teaching Effectiveness and Satisfaction

Given the financial trends in higher education, we are not likely to see a significant departure from the extensive use of adjunct lecturers in the near future. Part-time faculty not only offer the university flexibility, they bring a potentially unique quality to their classrooms. Adjunct lecturers bring real-world experience to the class that helps to ground the lessons that they teach for their students (Gappa, 2000; Nutting, 2003). They share a level of expertise, particularly in the application of concepts, that is valuable to students in many programs. Despite the low pay, lack of benefits, and limited reliability of work from one semester to the next, part-time instructors have demonstrated a remarkable dedication to their teaching positions, staying in them for an average of 6.3 years, in contrast to 11.2 years for full-time faculty (Gappa, 2000). Part-timers report having the same degree of interest in professional development activities as their full-time counterparts (Leslie & Gappa, 2002; Schuetz, 2002).

Studies of the instructional effectiveness of part-time instructors have yielded mixed results. Numerous studies have suggested that there is little to no difference in the instructional practices of part-time and full-time faculty (Leslie & Gappa, 2002; Schuetz, 2002; Schuster, 2003). Findings suggest that class time use by full-time and part-time instructors is very similar; however, closer examination indicates that part-time instructors are less likely to use techniques that increase active, engaged learning such as collaboration and group activities, technology, and guest lecturers (Schuetz, 2002; Umbach, 2006). This may be partially due to their lack of exposure to a variety of teaching practices because they are not in an academic department full time.

Another significant distinction between full-time and part-time instructors is the amount of knowledge they hold regarding available campus services. Part-time teachers receive less orientation to their jobs than tenure-track teachers do, which results in limited knowledge regarding resources for students, such as library services, tutoring, counseling, and extracurricular activities that support and reinforce classroom learning (Gappa, 2000; Nutting, 2003; Schuetz, 2002; Schuster, 2003). If part-time instructors are unaware of mechanisms on campus that may increase students' success, there is little likelihood that they will refer students to support resources for additional learning opportunities. This situation places the students of part-time faculty at a distinct disadvantage in comparison to students of full-time faculty.

Despite the many challenges that part-time faculty face, overall they are relatively satisfied with their teaching jobs. In comparison to their full-time faculty peers, part-time, term-limited faculty report no difference in satisfaction levels with their academic careers (Gappa, 2000, 2008; Howell & Hoyt, 2007). It may be that part-time teachers are able to achieve their goals, which are different from those of tenure-track faculty members, through their part-time status and thus are satisfied. However, there are numerous aspects unique to the part-time teaching positions with which there is dissatisfaction, including limited notification of teaching assignments prior to the beginning of the term; poor pay compared to that of full-time teachers; few, if any, benefits; inadequate opportunities for advancement; and low status in the academic community (Gappa, 2000, 2008; Leslie & Gappa, 2002).

Our Study

Despite our increased understanding of their numbers, their teaching effectiveness, and their job satisfaction, we know relatively little about how to help part-time faculty be more effective in their primary role as teachers. Leslie and Gappa (2002) note that "there remains a serious gap in our understanding of part-timers' teaching in community colleges" (p. 60), and even less focus has been placed on understanding adjunct lecturers teaching in universities.

Methods

This study used qualitative data collected in an individual interview format and using electronic communication with adjunct lecturers. The primary question asked of all participants was, "What areas would you like to receive support in to maximize your teaching effectiveness at this university?" The secondary question, asked of all participants, was their preferred format for receiving the support that they identified.

Participants

This study was conducted at a large, public university with an enrollment of twenty-three thousand students. The university employs 690 full-time, tenure-track faculty and an average of 450 adjunct lecturers for each of the two main terms of the year. Adjunct volunteers were solicited from the university's e-mail list of 457 adjunct lecturers who were teaching that term. Approximately 80 adjunct lecturers responded to the e-mail, volunteering to participate in an individual interview. It was not feasible to interview all volunteers, in large part due to the demands of the instructors' schedules. Seven adjunct lecturers were purposefully selected to represent a range of teaching experience and disciplines. The participants taught in sociology, marketing, engineering, education, theater arts, foreign languages, and chemistry programs and had been teaching at the institution for between one and eight terms. Although the sample of those interviewed is small, it reflects each major organizational division of the university. Such a naturalistic generalization (Eisner, 1998) using a smaller sample size is a common approach to guiding learning about one educational setting in order to inform our knowledge of comparable settings.

After reaching saturation by interviewing the seven adjunct lecturers, a second e-mail solicitation was sent to the remaining seventy-three individuals who had originally volunteered, offering them the opportunity to respond by e-mail to a series of questions based on the questions asked during the individual interviews. Thirty-four responded to the e-mail questions. The average number of terms that these adjunct lecturers had been teaching at this institution was ten, and again respondents represented each of the colleges within the university.

Data Collection

The face-to-face individual interviews were semistructured and focused on the primary and secondary questions. The use of interviews offered insights into each individual's perceptions and attitudes (Creswell, 2003). Because data from the electronic communication did not provide the same degree of rich detail and "thick descriptions" (Denzin & Lincoln, 2003, p. 98), they were used for corroborating evidence with the interview results.

Data Analysis

Each interview was audiorecorded and then transcribed in full following Creswell's reduction and interpretation guidelines (1998). The same process was used with the written responses of the thirty-four e-mail respondents. All data were sorted sentence by sentence into categories related to concerns, comments, and needs of adjunct lecturers. These categories were then compared and consolidated into broader categories. Each unit of data, from both interviews and electronic communication, was compared with these broader categories.

Results

From our analysis of interview and e-mail data, several consistent themes emerged.

"No Systematic Plan" for Information Sharing

Despite the fact that the primary question focused on what support adjunct lecturers needed to be effective instructors, most responded by first explaining what type of support they had been given when they began teaching. All interviewed participants indicated that they were provided with "no systematic plan" for getting information about teaching. Many stated that though they knew their topic well, they knew so little about teaching that they did not know where to begin asking for help. Peter (names and identifying information have been altered to protect participant identity), who has taught an engineering course twice, stated, "I am not enough of an educator to know . . . I don't know what I don't know," and he was at a loss as to what questions he should be asking. No information regarding teaching was offered by their department to any of the adjunct lecturers interviewed other than to share a copy of the syllabus from a previous semester. Dan, teaching a sociology course for the first time, was told, "We will give you full support," but he never received more than the syllabus for the course. This experience made him "feel like I'm sort of out there" on his own.

Several adjunct lecturers indicated that they took it upon themselves to gather information about teaching because they realized their department would not give them any. Bob, a retired high school drama teacher now teaching theater arts for his eighth semester, indicated that when he began, he asked for information every semester. He had to "ferret out" the information from people in the department by asking many specific questions over his first several terms of teaching. Had he not been an experienced teacher, he said, he would have "not known things to ask. I can imagine feeling extremely confused, disconnected, and anxious" had he not pursued this information diligently. Lidia, teaching marketing for her second term, realized that "there wasn't really any structure set up" for her to be given information about teaching. She took the initiative to seek out a tenured member of the faculty in her department and ask if she could visit his classroom several times. "We went to lunch one day, and so he's kind of been my mentor."

Lidia also had a friend who was a full-time faculty member at another institution whom she used as a resource for teaching questions. She was one of three adjunct lecturers who indicated that faculty at other universities served as a resource for teaching support. Knowledge that adjunct lecturers gained regarding teaching was due to their taking the initiative to seek out answers or initiate relationships that would provide them with mentoring. Their persistence was rewarded with information that they were seeking, but it typically gave them answers only to the questions that they knew to ask. As Dan noted, without some structured, planned orientation, he was left feeling "out there" on his own, with large gaps in his knowledge base. It was striking that the adjunct lecturers' experiences with early support made such a strong impression that they needed to share it before talking about what their current desires were.

Teaching-Related Concerns

Many adjunct lecturers were looking for skills that would improve students' in-class experience but were unable to specify what was needed. Lidia said, "I feel like I do a decent job of keeping the material interesting." But she would like to move past her reliance on lectures and "jump to the next level. . . . Those are the skills I need to develop." Eddy noted that although he knows that there are "interactive types of things" that could be done in his chemistry class, he is not familiar with alternative methods for "how you can present [information] so that they will actually understand." Lois, who has been teaching in preschools and kindergartens for over thirty years, is an instructor in the early elementary program. She feels confident about her content knowledge but would like help "gearing my teaching to people who are entering the profession" and "knowing some new things to try" to adapt her teaching skills to college students. Consistent with the literature (Schuetz, 2002), the adjunct lecturers tended to rely primarily on lectures. Nevertheless, they recognized that there are alternatives for teaching and expressed interest in gaining knowledge about new delivery methods.

Support with grading issues was one of the most commonly identified needs. Some adjunct lecturers noted that they were uncomfortable grading anything other than multiple-choice exams and therefore avoided other forms of assessment. Dan was unsure how much latitude a teacher has in determining grades in his sociology class. He had a student who was "negotiating for grades" because despite her apparent best efforts, she was barely passing the course. He was uncertain and "could have used some guidance" in handling the challenge of a student who was trying to haggle over her grade. Adjuncts indicated that they were uncertain about how to handle common grading challenges, such as poor grammar, work turned in late, grading curves, and whether to grade for participation.

For full-time faculty, many of these issues may seem routine and obvious. However, instructors not immersed in the culture of the institution and with no regular contact with colleagues are at a disadvantage in handling common grading concerns (Schuster, 2003; Umbach, 2006). In addition, if there is a prevailing culture in a program regarding grading issues, such as whether other faculty grade participation, then the students of adjunct lecturers may be hindered by being graded by a teacher who does not grade in a manner consistent with the full-time instructors.

Understanding Students

Many participants were confused, dismayed, and caught off guard by the behaviors or characteristics of their students. Admission to this university's undergraduate program is minimally competitive: it accepts most applicants with high school diplomas. Prior to beginning his class, Eddy did not "understand the level of the student that I was going to face." Dan noted that there are "a good percentage that are really good" and impressive, but he was "shocked" by the lack of "overall academic curiosity" he saw in his students. In a discussion with a student who was struggling with a concept in his class, Dan asked if she had read the chapter. She told him, "I really don't like to read." Like most other adjunct lecturers, Dan did not understand the nature of some of the university's students, who are often working one or two jobs to put themselves through school and have family obligations in addition to their student roles.

Contributing to Dan's confusion may have been a lack of understanding of his students' majors: "I assumed that most of these [students] were going to be sociology majors. I was wrong." He soon learned that many students were in the class because his course was a core requirement for a number of programs. He was unprepared for the disparity in student backgrounds. Eddy was also surprised that students in his chemistry class were not chemistry majors and felt that more than half of them were not "functionally prepared for the course": "The second semester I asked [students] about their educational foundation in chemistry, and that is when it became clear to me that the majority of them were really not suitably prepared."

Because Eddy now recognizes the disparity among his students, he encourages them to succeed by talking to them about expectations for progress and learning so that they understand that they are not all starting from the same point and do not have the same goals. Peter has his engineering students write a brief biography so that he can find out how much application experience they have. Lois realized that in her early elementary teaching course, "Some people have a rich background in teaching. They've already had jobs that prepared them for teaching young people. Other people are coming right out of high school." She now begins the semester by asking the students to introduce themselves and talk about their experiences so that she understands what level of knowledge they have when they come to her class. Lois notes that it "would have been nice [to] participate in professional conversations" with members of the program's faculty to learn how to manage classes.

Given a formal orientation to the university or to the programs in which they teach, adjuncts might have been able to prepare for the heterogeneity of students' academic majors and preparation more appropriately and without the element of surprise. Despite being caught off guard in their first semester of teaching, the adjunct lecturers demonstrated a commitment to understanding more about their students so that they are able to meet their learning needs.

Desired Supports

The secondary question regarding the ideal format for the provision of support was open-ended to allow adjunct lecturers to offer suggestions of formats or modes for support delivery. Several were aware of the existence of the campus's faculty support center for teaching and suggested that the programs offered through the teaching center include them on a regular basis. They expressed interest in having a consultant watch them teach so that they could sit down and discuss their teaching. Several suggested seminars on specific topics, such as test design or active learning techniques. The possibility of "quarterly meetings" and "open forum discussions" that would allow adjunct lecturers to come together and discuss challenges and solutions for teaching was also raised. Those requesting face-to-face support noted that it would need to be provided either at the end of the workday, after 5:00 P.M., or on weekends. Peter suggested a weekend seminar, modeled on executive M.B.A. programs. Resources in the form of readings, either hard copy or electronic, were commonly requested.

Some adjunct lecturers indicated that although they were interested in learning more about teaching, they did not see any extra time in their schedule to attend meetings on campus. They preferred materials to be provided to them electronically so they could be accessed at their convenience. Eddy requested a "virtual toolbox . . . there could be a more global tool set . . . with educational type of tools." He noted that this type of tool box would be valuable to all faculty, including adjuncts. Online courses, listservs, and videotapes were also suggested as helpful electronic forms of support. Responses were nearly equally divided between those wanting support to be provided in face-to-face formats and those wanting support to be in an electronic format. Many indicated that they would be amenable to either option.

Frustrations of Being a "Necessary Evil"

An unexpected response to the question regarding how adjunct lecturers would like to receive support was frustration about how they were treated by full-time faculty in their department. Bob noted that while there is regularly a large contingent of adjuncts teaching, "[we] feel to be somewhat of a necessary evil to the university. I think we don't feel enormously valued. . . . I don't think they have enormous faith and trust in us." He observed that full-time faculty "make decisions without the input from the people that are teaching [the class] and they make decisions that are not well communicated to the people in the trenches. This to me is exceptionally shortsighted because number one you are losing a tremendous talent pool that may be very willing to assist . . . and secondly, you are handing over the future of that department every semester to adjuncts who may or may not be terribly committed." Many of the adjunct lecturers who participated in the study echoed these sentiments. For some, the lack of interaction and opportunity for conversation with full-time faculty was a source of anger and frustration. Peter said, "I thought I might get invited to a faculty mix or something like that where I'm rubbing elbows with the department head, just to learn more about who the people are and all that. They haven't done any of that, so that's a minor disappointment." The lack of formal and informal communication between full-time and part-time faculty contributes to a sense of marginalization and low status in the professional community (Gappa, 2000, 2008; Leslie & Gappa, 2002). Given that some of the communication missing is directly associated with teaching and curricular issues, this limited interaction may have a negative effect on student learning.

Discussion

Consistent with previous findings, the adjunct lecturers in this study felt the impact of being "unappreciated" and "undervalued," "a necessary evil" whom the university tolerates because finances and student fluctuations force it to (Gappa, 2000, 2008; Leslie & Gappa, 2002). Remarkably, few of the comments addressed the low pay scale or the limited notice that adjuncts were given prior to teaching. The observations addressed concerns regarding limited communication between full-time and part-time faculty. Although it is clear that better communication between the two groups would ameliorate feelings of marginalization, more important to the adjunct lecturers was that the lines of communication should be open for the benefit of students in their classes. They were looking for opportunities to collaborate regarding curriculum decisions that appear logical in light of their role in the classroom.

Also compatible with the literature, the adjuncts interviewed relied primarily on lectures for teaching (Schuetz, 2002; Umbach, 2006). While Leslie and Gappa (2002) found an interest in professional development in their discipline, previous literature has not identified a desire on the part of adjunct lecturers to learn more techniques for increasing active, engaged learning. Although they were not able to identify specific methods that would improve teaching and learning in their courses, they knew that there must be alternatives to lecture available that would help them teach, "so that [students] will actually understand." These data shed new light on the awareness that part-time faculty have that there are probably pedagogical methods available and that they are looking for ways to obtain that information. Several were aware of the campus's faculty teaching center but were unaware that services offered were available to them as part-time instructors, and few mentioned resources available to assist struggling students. Our finding of their lack of awareness is congruent with other studies, which have documented the limited knowledge of campus resources for students (Gappa, 2000; Nutting, 2003; Schuetz, 2002; Schuster, 2003). Unfamiliarity with student characteristics proved to be a source of frustration for part-time instructors. What has not been documented in previous studies are the strategies that these adjunct lecturers reported for coping with this lack of information, such as asking for the information in introductions and written biographies.

Implications and Limitations

Despite the low pay, the unpredictability of teaching assignments, and the limited information sharing, adjunct lecturers demonstrate persistence in their willingness to teach at an institution that gives them little in return. The fact that the average respondent had been teaching for over ten semesters confirms that part-time faculty are a dedicated group (Gappa, 2000). The investment that they appear willing to make to learn about students and teaching and to work collegially with full-time faculty suggests that they are a resource worthy of cultivation.

Given the financial limitations that lead most colleges and universities to make extensive use of part-time faculty in the first place, the question remains, "How do we support adjunct lecturers?" Significant increases to pay are likely not feasible on many campuses. The literature from community colleges is replete with recommendations to increase professional development opportunities for part timers (Ellison, 2002; Thompson, 2003; Wallin, 2007). Campuses that already have a faculty teaching center can readily adapt their focus to include part-time faculty. With limited investments, programs can be redesigned specifically to meet some of the more basic needs that adjuncts have, such as dealing with grading, syllabus creation, and active teaching techniques.

Another solution to improving the teaching of adjunct lecturers that would cost little money is to increase the opportunities for communication between the full-time and part-time faculty in a program or department. Creating opportunities for formal or informal collegial interactions once or twice each semester would be of benefit to both parties and would provide adjunct lecturers with a sense of appreciation as well as an opportunity to share information with individuals who make the majority of curricular decisions. Basic orientation to the college and its students is commonly provided to the majority of permanent new faculty hires but because of the adjunct lecturers' time-limited status, this orientation is commonly overlooked (Ellison, 2002; Thompson, 2003; Wallin, 2007). Brief orientations provided at the beginning of each term could easily increase the amount of information adjuncts receive about the campus and its students that would have a direct impact on the quality of their teaching.

New models of professional development for part-time instructors need to be explored (Wallin, 2007). The results of this study demonstrate that administrators, from those overseeing the university's human resource department to individual department heads, need to work together to provide as much information as possible to newly hired part-time faculty. Connections need to be made between part-time teachers and the campus as a whole, between part-time teachers and the department in which they teach, and, most important, between part-time teachers and their students. Staff at university teaching centers need to be inclusive of adjunct lecturers and work to make resources available to them in a variety of formats on an ongoing basis. Programs and consultations need to be offered after hours, on weekends, and electronically. Web-based formats, such as online course platforms, need to be used to provide 24/7 access to those who cannot find the time to make it to campus for an extra meeting but want to learn more about teaching. Campuses that do not have their own centers for teaching and learning will face more challenges to supporting part-time teachers; however, a number of resources are available online, such as AdjunctNation (www.adjunctnation.com).

The results of this study reflect the experiences and perceptions of one group of part-time faculty at one institution. It is possible that adjuncts who responded to the opportunity to participate in this study represented a highly dedicated group of teachers. However, many of these adjuncts were in their first few terms of teaching, leaving their long-term dedication in question. It is also possible that those who did not respond had no time to learn more about teaching. The large number of individuals who responded to the offer of study participation may have been motivated to do so in hopes of having their voices heard on a topic that is important to them. The sample interviewed in this study was representative of the university's individual colleges and a wide range of disciplines; however, it was a small sample. Even when combining the written responses from the thirty-four e-mail participants with those of the seven interviewees, the sample remains but a small percentage (just under 10 percent) of adjunct lecturers on this particular campus at the time. Future practices would be aided by larger-scale studies at a variety of universities. Although the views and experiences of this group may not generalize to all institutions, they do provide a place to begin the conversation about how to improve the teaching of part-time instructors and thus improve the learning of their many perhaps hundreds of thousands, or more, students.

REFERENCES

Creswell, J. N. (1998). *Qualitative inquiry and research design: Choosing among five traditions*. Thousand Oaks, CA: Sage.

Creswell, J. N. (2003). *Research design: Qualitative, quantitative, and mixed methods approaches* (2nd ed.). Thousand Oaks, CA: Sage.

Denzin, N. K., & Lincoln, Y. S. (2003). *Collecting and interpreting qualitative materials*. Thousand Oaks, CA: Sage.

Eisner, E. W. (1998). *The enlightened eye: Qualitative inquiry and the enhancement of educational practice*. Upper Saddle River, NJ: Prentice Hall.

Ellison, A. (2002). *The accidental faculty: Adjunct instructors in community colleges*. Tampa: University of South Florida. (ERIC Document Reproduction Service No. ED466874)

Gappa, J. M. (2000). The new faculty majority: Somewhat satisfied but not eligible for tenure. In L. S. Hagedorn (Ed.), *New directions for institutional research: No. 105. What contributes to job satisfaction among faculty and staff* (pp. 77–86). San Francisco: Jossey Bass.

Gappa, J. M. (2008). Today's majority: Faculty outside the tenure system. *Change, 40*(4), 50–54.

Gappa, J. M., & Leslie, D. W. (1993). *The invisible faculty*. San Francisco: Jossey-Bass.

Howell, S. L., & Hoyt, J. (2007). *Part-time faculty job satisfaction in higher education: A literature review*. Provo, UT: Brigham Young University. (ERIC Document Reproduction Service No. ED499387)

Leslie, D. W., & Gappa, J. M. (2002). Part-time faculty: Competent and committed. In C. L. Outcalt (Ed.), *New directions for community colleges: No. 118. Community college faculty: Characteristics, practices, and challenges* (pp. 59–67). San Francisco: Jossey-Bass.

Nutting, M. M. (2003). Part-time faculty: Why should we care? In E. Benjamin (Ed.), *New directions for higher education: No. 123. Exploring the role of contingent instructional staff in undergraduate learning* (pp. 33–39). San Francisco: Jossey-Bass.

Schuetz, P. (2002). Instructional practices of part-time and full-time faculty. In C. L. Outcalt (Ed.), *New directions for community colleges: No. 118. Community college faculty: Characteristics, practices, and challenges* (pp. 39–46). San Francisco: Jossey-Bass.

Schuster, J. H. (2003). The faculty makeover: What does it mean for students? In E. Benjamin (Ed.), *New directions for higher education: No. 123. Exploring the role of contingent instructional staff in undergraduate learning* (pp. 15–22). San Francisco: Jossey-Bass.

Thompson, K. (2003). Contingent faculty and student learning: Welcome to the strativersity. In E. Benjamin (Ed.), *New directions for higher education: No. 123. Exploring the role of contingent instructional staff in undergraduate learning* (pp. 41–47). San Francisco: Jossey-Bass.

Umbach, P. D. (2006). How effective are they? Exploring the impact of contingent faculty on undergraduate education. *Review of Higher Education, 30*(2), 91–123.

Wallin, D. L. (2007). Part-time faculty and professional development: Notes from the field. In R. L. Wagoner (Ed.), *New directions for community colleges: No 140. The current landscape and changing perspectives of part-time faculty* (pp. 67–73). San Francisco: Jossey-Bass.

4

UNDERSTANDING AND SUPPORTING FULL-TIME NON-TENURE-TRACK FACULTY

A NEEDED CHANGE

Genevieve G. Shaker, Megan M. Palmer,
Nancy Van Note Chism,
Indiana University–Purdue University Indianapolis

As the face of the American faculty profession changes, targeted academic development becomes more important. A phenomenological qualitative study of full-time, non-tenure-track faculty in English portrays an experience characterized by a love of teaching but fraught with professional challenges stemming from low status and poor reward and recognition structures. These data provide the point of departure for recommendations on expanding organizational and faculty development strategies for supporting, integrating, and encouraging full-time, non-tenure-track faculty.

The literature on faculty development is built around the traditional notion of the faculty member progressing along a stable career line, enjoying equal status with other faculty colleagues, and having relative autonomy and variety in teaching assignments. Faculty development centers often do workshops on documenting tenure dossiers, advice to developers stresses engaging "respected faculty leaders" in programming or on advisory boards, and workshops often assume that participants are free to alter their course syllabi, change course assessment methods, and develop new offerings. Enter the contingent faculty member, now among the majority of newly hired faculty members in the United States (Schuster & Finklestein, 2006).

In qualitative and mixed-method studies of full-time, non-tenure-track (FTNT) faculty, the emphasis has usually been quite broad (Baldwin & Chronister, 2001) and has not attended to FTNT faculty in depth at the discipline, institution, department, or individual level. Schuster and Finkelstein (2006) argued the FTNT trend may be "the most consequential but most under-investigated faculty-related phenomenon of the past several decades" (p. 355). In spite of the growing body of scholarship about the FTNT, the phenomenon remains well stocked with opportunities for further research. This qualitative study was guided by the question: What are the essential features of the experience of being FTNT faculty? Our goal is to understand more fully the conditions in which FTNT faculty work for the purpose of customizing development programs to their needs.

Context of the Study

The American public's unease with the necessity for and practicality of tenure, declining government financing for higher education, an abundance of Ph.D. recipients, changing patterns of student enrollment, concern about overreliance on part-time faculty, and new curricular demands all have contributed to an environment conducive to the hiring and continued employment of FTNT faculty (Baldwin & Chronister, 2001). In 1987, 8 percent of all full-time faculty at higher education institutions worked off the tenure track; by 2003, FTNT faculty accounted for 21 percent of faculty nationwide. And in 2003, FTNT faculty represented 59 percent of newly hired instructors, up from 51 percent a decade earlier (Schuster & Finklestein, 2006). Today, as institutions face diminished budgets, they report they are just as likely to consider cuts in individual tenure-line appointments as in nontenure positions (Association of Public and Land-Grant Universities, 2009), suggesting that FTNT faculty are now deeply embedded in their institutions.

All disciplines are affected by this shift (National Center for Education Statistics, 2005), but few are more concerned about and fundamentally affected by reliance on contingent faculty than English departments (Association of Departments of English, 1999; Bousquet, Scott, & Parascondola, 2004; Cayton, 1991; Laurence, 2001; Modern Language Association & Association of Departments of English, 2008). What happens in English, with its near universally required undergraduate writing courses and the foundational skills transmitted in those courses, has ripple effects across campus. It appears that English, in its reliance on FTNT faculty, is not the exception but the rule throughout academe

(AFT Higher Education, 2009; Schuster & Finkelstein, 2006), and for this reason, it is the setting for this chapter.

Literature Review

Schuster and Finkelstein (2006) found that FTNT faculty were more likely to focus on teaching than research and were both younger and more proportionately female than tenure-eligible faculty. Baldwin and Chronister (2001) and others (Evans, 1996; Harper, Baldwin, Gansneder, & Chronister, 2001; Smith & Hixson, 1987) studied select aspects of the FTNT experience, finding these faculty to be diverse in background, experience, and professional responsibilities. Dual labor market theory has been used to seek theoretical grounding for the circumstances of FTNT employment, arguing that a two-tiered system explains, to some extent, the nontenure experience (Roemer & Schnitz, 1982; Rosenblum & Rosenblum, 1996; Smith & Hixson, 1987). FTNT employment looks very much like a secondary market when it is unstable, exists in poor conditions, is based on tasks that tenured faculty do not want to complete, lacks opportunities for professional or scholarly development, offers fewer professional perks than those afforded tenure-line faculty, and provides limited paths for advancement (Roemer & Schnitz, 1982).

Using data from the National Study of Postsecondary Faculty, one study criticized institutions for failing to attend appropriately to the effects of the FTNT appointment on diminished individual productivity and commitment (Bland, Center, Finstad, Risbey, & Staples, 2006). Administrators surveyed in a national study recognized FTNT faculty for their important contributions in the classroom and beyond, despite their poor salaries and low status (Center for the Education of Women, 2007). As a group, FTNT faculty have been perceived as a threat to faculty power, norms, and job markets based on assumptions that they have poor institutional ties, are disempowered by their lack of tenure, and fill positions that might otherwise be tenure-track (Finkin, 1996; McPherson & Schapiro, 1999). Scholars have begun to use data to examine the effects of FTNT faculty on students (Ehrenberg & Zhang, 2005), finding a correlation between these faculty and lower graduation rates. Critics, however, often do little to accommodate for the professional identity issues of nontenure-track faculty resulting from their employment conditions (Levin, Shaker, & Wagoner, 2010) or to recognize the central role FTNT faculty play when it comes to accomplishing the core missions of colleges and universities. Agreeing that FTNT faculty are in academe to stay, a range of best practices for employment policies, including longer contracts and promotion structures, has been proposed and endorsed (Baldwin & Chronister, 2001; Center for the Education of Women, 2007; Gappa, Austin, & Trice, 2007; Rhoades & Maitland, 2008; Tolbert, 1998).

Methods

The best way to deeply consider being FTNT faculty was nearness to that experience. Thus phenomenology, as a philosophy and a method, was selected for its "focus on exploring how human beings make sense of experience and transform the experience into consciousness" (Patton, 2002, p. 104) and attention "to mak[ing] the invisible visible" (Kvale, 1996, p. 53). In this research, the essential features of FTNT "facultyness" were deeply explored through compilation, analysis, and interpretation of the lived reality of English FTNT faculty members.

The three public universities in this study spanned two states, ranged from twenty thousand to thirty-five thousand students, and were doctoral or research institutions. One was unionized; two were in urban settings. With department support and through the administration of questionnaires, faculty participants were purposefully selected to create a sample stratified in gender, academic experience, educational degree, and professional responsibility. All study faculty were engaged with rhetoric and composition programs to some degree, but many also had administrative responsibilities or taught classes in subjects other than first-year writing.

Eighteen FTNT English faculty from the three institutions were interviewed during the second half of 2007. Of interest in a phenomenological study is the confluence of participant and phenomenon—"how they perceive it, describe it, feel about it, judge it, remember it, make sense of it, and talk about it with others" (Patton, 2002, p. 104). Thus, participants, interviewed once for between one and three hours, were asked to reflect deeply and speak openly about being FTNT faculty members.

The analysis was based on a series of steps adapted from Carspecken (1996), Creswell (1998, 2003), and Moustakas (1994). Interviews were transcribed and then reviewed by the researcher and participants. Raw codes were developed and reduced to eliminate unsubstantiated or underdeveloped ideas. Clustering of remaining codes formed themes and connections between the essential features of being FTNT in English and systems governing and relating to that experience were sought. Just as they reviewed interview transcriptions, participants read the study findings and shared comments.

This study had its limitations, including its small size and scope. The research lacked a comparative perspective and did not incorporate perspectives of part-time, tenure-track, and tenured faculty, or those in other disciplines. Because qualitative studies seek depth rather than breadth and do not require a large sample or comparative element for the findings to have value (Patton, 2002), we decided to attend deeply to the lived experiences of the selected group of faculty rather than expand the study to address its limitations. Because we focused on one discipline, the study findings were affected by English-specific conditions that may or may not be relevant to the other disciplinary contexts of FTNT work. However, our conclusions align with what is thought and reported to be true about the broader FTNT faculty experience (Shaker, 2008).

Results

The FTNT faculty followed nontraditional academic career paths, often situating personal priorities before professional advancement, and they planned to continue working in higher education. Their hopes and visions for the future, however, varied based on possession or lack of a terminal degree. One respondent stated,

> I think I always wanted to teach. I come from a family of teachers. I'm one of those people who probably doesn't thrive in the marketplace because I love the role of ideas and I'm not eminently practical about things. I've never been real job oriented or career oriented. I've more wanted to do things where I've felt like I've made a difference, and it's taken me a long time to realize that that may not be the best thing for me professionally, or that my professional future may not be the same as what makes me happy or satisfied. But I just . . . I love talking to students. I love interacting with students. I love classroom discussions. I've just always thrived on that culture and that environment.

FTNT faculty struggled with heavy workloads, salary structures perceived to be out of balance with their contributions and often underdeveloped reappointment and promotion policies. Nevertheless, they evidenced high levels of confidence in job security due to the quality of their contributions and their field's importance in the curriculum. Another respondent replied, "It's too much. It is too much to be entirely fair to the students you have. It is too much work for one person to handle at given points of the semester, particularly at the end when . . . other faculty can run their tests through Scantron machines, and we are literally grading hundreds of papers during finals week. Even if they're papers that we've seen drafts of before, that's a lot of work, and it's a lot of responsibility. It is too much work."

Within composition programs, FTNT faculty felt valued, understood, and influential. In their departments, they reported a measure of respect and protection. At the institution level, participants described some marginalization and underappreciation, but responses were institution specific. According to one faculty member, "Tenure-track people, mostly in other departments . . . have no idea. The tenure-track people in the English department know about the hard work that we do, and they're relieved because they don't want to teach those freshman classes, and they know they get us on the cheap. Somebody in art or history or psychology or criminal justice or whatever, they don't know. They've got their idea of what the ivory tower is, and we don't fit into it."

The FTNT experience in English was negatively affected by the position of composition in the discipline. Moreover, the positioning of the FTNT faculty in composition appeared to exacerbate and perpetuate disciplinary divisions, as indicated by the following statement: "What they really need to do is open more tenure lines and recognize that teaching composition is as valid as teaching a class on Milton and is more important really, because who walks away with more skills? The student who's had a research writing class, and knows how to use the research library and all the databases, and put together a number of different types of writings, from PowerPoint presentations to pamphlets to term papers? Or the person who can quote Milton? And, not that I don't think that the Milton class is important too. It is."

Although most participants professed stronger disciplinary than institutional loyalties, their close connections to students, workplaces, and communities were repeatedly demonstrated. Rationales for disciplinary prioritization, moreover, hinged on what the discipline enabled them to do, not who it enabled them to be.

FTNT second-class status was amplified by lingering and outdated stereotypes about "the faculty" and professorial work. These stereotypes had a harmful effect on FTNT faculty work experiences and self-perceptions, particularly participants' sense of worth and confidence. As one faculty member stated: "I think there was one point where they were saying 'faculty and [FTNT people].' Whereas, we have the same obligations as faculty do. We're faculty for all practical purposes, because in this particular meeting [the chair] had been delineating 'faculty' and '[FTNT people].' But the [FTNT people] didn't know they were supposed to participate in graduation, because the language of the meeting seemed to imply that [FTNT people] were not faculty."

Despite undesirable aspects of FTNT work-life, faculty chose to continue in these appointments because they loved teaching, were committed to students, and believed in serving society; they opted to cope and manage the difficult components of the work rather than surrender their positions. One respondent expressed, "I'm sure you've gathered, people who teach at the contract level, they're not trying to climb the ladder, madly trying to get over the top of everybody else. They're looking for an environment in which they can feel useful and content with what they do and feel like they're making a difference."

Discussion

Collectively, the experience described by FTNT faculty portrays a career characterized by maintenance of a tenuous balance between the positive and negative—positioning each individual on a shifting scale with potential to move in one direction or another. FTNT faculty were fulfilled by their work. Yet their experiences were nuanced and at times emotionally draining. Although they expressed broadly positive sentiments about being FTNT faculty, nagging doubts threatened their equilibrium on a daily basis. Their concerns often originated from externally governed aspects of their work and workplace, including professorial stereotypes, compensation levels, and heavy workload. Fluctuating emotions and personal circumstances as well as contextual factors mandated constant need for readjustment and revalidation. Essentially FTNT faculty were engaged in an ongoing balancing act in which much could influence their emotional stability and mental well-being.

Recommendations

Factors in the FTNT experience that are institutionally affected may be moderated, modified, or supported by academic developers.

For Organizational Development

Those working in organizational development are ideally positioned to play an active role in several issues that influence the effectiveness, satisfaction, and growth of FTNT faculty members. By providing support, practical suggestions for change, and information from the scholarly literature, developers can work to bring about improvement in the environment of FTNT faculty on multiple fronts, including tenure, appointments, stereotypes and status distinctions, communication, and participation.

The findings of this study support a substantial reconsideration of the continued viability of tenure in American higher education. It is clear from the participants' struggles to endure their secondary status that parity among today's faculty population is impossible in the current, tenure-emphasizing context. So long as disregard for academe's egalitarian principles continues and outdated conceptions of faculty life are perpetuated, the bifurcation will continue. Faculty divides will become progressively more intractable as time passes. Both nationally and at their own institutions, developers can help to raise awareness of the work of scholars who have analyzed the question of tenure and made helpful recommendations (Chait, 2002; Finkin, 1996; Plater, 2008; Rice, 2006). They can serve as local advocates in calling on their institutions to take a hard look at what tenure is, what it should be, and whether it should be at all.

Should the system continue as it is with the placement of faculty in non-tenure-eligible roles, a series of improvements is necessary. Institutions, perhaps with help from scholars, professional organizations, and unions, need to fully develop and refine the policies and systems governing these appointments. Developers can take their lead from this study and those of other scholars (Baldwin & Chronister, 2001; Center for the Education of Women, 2007; Gappa et al., 2007; Rhoades & Maitland, 2008) to support implementation of the following: renewable multiyear contracts with clear evaluation standards following an established probationary period, professorial titles with a sequential rank promotion system featuring well-documented guidelines and criteria, and equitable salaries with some compensation for the lack of security afforded by tenure.

As part of their advocacy role, developers working at the organizational level can help to identify ways in which the culture of the institution is perpetuating inequality at the expense of educational effectiveness. The questioning of stereotypes about faculty life is critical for creating an equitable academic workforce and respecting all those doing the work of teaching, research, and service in America's universities. Going forward, a fair representation of what it is to be faculty will encourage FTNT and other nontraditional faculty to focus on their work and not the dated conceptions surrounding their appointments. Developers can help to dispel the false and damaging notion that only those in the tenure ranks are the "regular" or "normal" faculty—distinctions that should be disregarded. They also might champion those who work in the core course areas that are often undervalued by their own departmental faculty (for example, writing composition, speech communication, and developmental mathematics). A sea change in representation cannot come fast enough and can be accomplished only through continued attention to the whole professoriate and educating the academic community and the public at every turn. Developers can examine their own literature, priorities, and programmatic assumptions to make sure that they are not making harmful delineations based on status in their own work.

Faculty studied were burdened by what they believed their tenure-line colleagues thought about them and their work. In some cases, their fears were validated through interactions; in others, the participants received recognition and appreciation from the tenure ranks. They were also concerned that these colleagues and others throughout the institution did not understand the course loads, salary structures, and appointment policies that FTNT faculty endured. Developers can help to create improved communication among the faculty to address these informational issues. They may organize mentoring arrangements or workshops at the campus or departmental levels to explore these topics, coordinate recognition for the contributions of FTNT faculty, and disseminate thoughtful articles about the differentiated but complementary work of all within the faculty community. Faculty need to know the roles and challenges of one another's positions, and developers can help to ensure that FTNT faculty receive opportunities to be judged on their own merits rather than on hierarchical notions of faculty appointments.

Findings indicate that many FTNT faculty members want a larger role in their institutions. Gappa et al. (2007) proposed that FTNT faculty need "opportunities to participate in governance, and recognition and rewards for contributions to the academic department or institution" (p. 209). FTNT faculty also need to take on a manageable amount of responsibility beyond the classroom as those who invest in this way will make certain that future campus decisions are not made without their input. Developers working at the organizational level can participate in policy discussions to help others see that disparities of eligibility should be addressed and that FTNT faculty should be encouraged to take available opportunities for participation.

For Faculty Development

Faculty developers need to recognize that the number of FTNT faculty has expanded to 30 percent nationwide and that they have become the majority of new full-time hires in academia (National Center for Education Statistics, 2005; Schuster & Finklestein, 2006). They need to be aware of the composition of the FTNT faculty group, as well as those in other contingent categories. Developers must learn about the demographic variety within these populations and about the motivations and goals of their members. Through this empirical knowledge, academic developers will be prepared to act efficiently and appropriately to meet the educational and organizational needs of FTNT faculty and will be able to respond to new challenges and work with institutional leaders to provide constructive solutions (Sorcinelli, Austin, Eddy, & Beach, 2005). Understanding that many FTNT faculty place more value on their personal than professional lives might help developers to filter their expectations for faculty commitment and participation through a different lens. Developers might collaborate with human resource colleagues to develop work-life balance programs specifically geared to faculty. Recognizing that FTNT faculty struggle with lower salaries than their tenure-line peers, developers might consider compensating FTNT faculty for time they contribute to projects undertaken by their centers.

If they do not already, developers must see themselves as advocates for all faculty, especially those who are marginalized. As advocates, developers must take the lead in ensuring that the recommendations made regarding organizational development are acted on while at the same time making programming changes to serve FTNT faculty better. Furthermore, faculty developers can be at the center of creating campus climates that foster inclusiveness by creating opportunities for tenure-line and FTNT faculty to work together.

Academic developers should develop a comprehensive plan for FTNT faculty development to include non-tenure-track programs as well as additions to existing development activities. For example, an FTNT faculty learning community could help participants discuss many of the individual challenges they face while also creating cross-campus connections and overcoming isolation (Cox, 2004). Programming that addresses work-life balance, teaching and grading efficiency, scholarship of teaching and learning, and navigating the political climate of the academy will help to support FTNT faculty. In an effort to accommodate the many demands placed on FTNT faculty, offerings should be held at varying times and in several formats (for example, face-to-face, online seminar, and online self-paced modules).

Encouraging better understanding of and recognition for FTNT faculty, meanwhile, could become among the objectives for new faculty orientation, awards programs, and department-specific activities. Teaching centers might consider offering small grants to support FTNT faculty who want to attend conferences related to teaching and learning. Listservs or other online communities to help build connections between FTNT and tenure-line faculty also could be useful.

While programs that integrate faculty across appointment types are very important, developers might also consider offering workshops or facilitated conversations specifically designed for FTNT faculty. These could include panels of established FTNT faculty or discussions facilitated by new and longer-serving FTNT faculty members. Open-ended questions, structured reflection, and self-assessment activities could help participants understand challenges and triumphs that cut across the group and those that they may find are theirs alone. Such workshops might explore the trade-offs that FTNT faculty make in order to create deeper conviction and satisfaction among those who feel that the choice is right for them, and brainstorm alternatives for those who are dissatisfied.

A multipronged approach would target both FTNT faculty and tenure-track perceptions and would benefit institutions, FTNT faculty, the students they teach, and the tenure-line faculty who are their colleagues within the professoriate.

Conclusion

The findings of this study inevitably lead to concern about the sincerity of the lofty values professed by our academic system. One of the study participants expressed it well:

> How do I put this? Are [tenure-line and FTNT faculty] equals? No. Is there a power difference? Yes. [Laugh] Because this is the truth about university life. We preach diversity here, right? And egalitarian quali-ties. But the truth is, universities, in many ways, are the very worst institutions for institutionalizing a hierarchy where some people are considered more valuable than others. Even though that's not what we preach to our students. It's very funny to me.

FTNT faculty in this study sacrificed personal time to grade paper after paper, published numerous books, and pushed the limits of what FTNT faculty could and could not do on their campuses. These individu-als were deeply committed to higher education, put their students before themselves, and loved their work. Developers, with their commitment to improving the academy, should be among the first to appreciate those who choose FTNT careers and the many contributions these faculty make. Developers should also recognize and address the realities of the FTNT faculty, which can include shocking workloads, staggeringly low salaries, institutions' refusal to initiate promotion structures, the burden of the not-tenure-eligible branding, and unkind words of colleagues and leaders.

Developers are positioned to use knowledge about FTNT faculty to lead discussions that go to the heart of how faculty are thought of in America. Discussions, which can be initiated by academic developers, must be broad and include contemplation of whether tenure still makes sense. Furthermore, academic developers can work to ensure that all parties are at the table, not just those in the tenure ranks. Policies about faculty appointments cannot be one size fits all, as was made abundantly clear by the specific challenges faced by FTNT faculty in English. Proposals can consider institutional needs and tenured faculty, but they must also value individuals serving their institutions so well in their nontenured capacities.

Knowledge of the experiences of FTNT faculty, the work of concerned national organizations, and the research of many scholars interested in this issue provide the tools necessary for reconsidering and reconfiguring FTNT faculty work life. FTNT faculty, meanwhile, are using their voices, words, and actions to speak out about the realities of their work through publications, conferences, and faculty unions. Only by working together can optimal solutions be found and appropriate policies be developed for the new landscape of professorial life.

REFERENCES

AFT Higher Education. (2009). *American academic: The state of the higher education workforce 1997–2007*. Washington, DC: American Federation of Teachers.

Association of Departments of English. (1999). Report of the ADE Ad Hoc Committee on Staffing. *ADE Bulletin, 122*, 3–26.

Association of Public and Land-Grant Universities. (2009). *Coping strategies of public universities during the recession of 2009: Results of a survey on the impact of the financial crisis on university campuses*. Washington, DC: Author.

Baldwin, R. G., & Chronister, J. L. (2001). *Teaching without tenure: Policies and practices for a new era*. Baltimore: Johns Hopkins University Press.

Bland, C. J., Center, B. A., Finstad, D. A., Risbey, K. R., & Staples, J. (2006). The impact of appointment type on the productivity and commitment of full-time faculty in research and doctoral institutions. *Journal of Higher Education, 77*(1), 90–123.

Bousquet, M., Scott, T., & Parascondola, L. (Eds.). (2004). *Tenured bosses and disposable teachers: Writing instruction in the managed university*. Carbondale: Southern Illinois University Press.

Carspecken, P. F. (1996). *Critical ethnography in educational research: A theoretical and practical guide*. New York: Routledge.

Cayton, M. K. (1991). Writing as outsiders: Academic discourse and marginalized faculty. *College English, 53*(6), 647–660.

Center for the Education of Women. (2007). *Making the best of both worlds: Findings from a national institution-level survey on non-tenure track faculty.* Ann Arbor, MI: Author.

Chait, R. P. (Ed.). (2002). *The questions of tenure.* Cambridge, MA: Harvard University Press.

Cox, M. D. (2004). Introduction to faculty learning communities. In M. D. Cox & L. Richlin (Eds.), *New directions for teaching and learning: Vol. 97. Building faculty learning communities* (pp. 5–23). San Francisco: Jossey-Bass.

Creswell, J. W. (1998). *Qualitative inquiry and research design: Choosing among five approaches.* Thousand Oaks, CA: Sage.

Creswell, J. W. (2003). *Research design: Qualitative, quantitative, and mixed method approaches* (2nd ed.). Thousand Oaks, CA: Sage.

Ehrenberg, R. G., & Zhang, L. (2005). Do tenured and tenure-track faculty matter? *Journal of Human Resources, 40*(3), 647–659.

Evans, L. C. (1996). *An examination of the expectations between core and peripheral workers.* Unpublished doctoral dissertation, Iowa State University, Ames.

Finkin, M. W. (1996). *The case for tenure.* Ithaca, NY: Cornell University Press.

Gappa, J. M., Austin, A. E., & Trice, A. G. (2007). *Rethinking faculty work: Higher education's strategic imperative.* San Francisco: Jossey-Bass.

Harper, E. P., Baldwin, R. G., Gansneder, B. G., & Chronister, J. L. (2001). Full-time women faculty off the tenure-track: Profile and practice. *Review of Higher Education, 24*(3), 237–257.

Kvale, S. (1996). *InterViews: An introduction to qualitative interviewing.* Thousand Oaks, CA: Sage.

Laurence, D. (2001). *The 1999 MLA survey of staffing in English and foreign languages.* New York: Modern Language Association.

Levin, J. S., Shaker, G. G., & Wagoner, R. (2010, January). *Post-neoliberalism: The professional identity of faculty off the tenure-track.* Paper presented at the Global Collaboration Conference Series, Centre for Social Innovation and Education, Monash University, Melbourne, Australia.

McPherson, M. S., & Schapiro, M. O. (1999). Tenure issues in higher education. *Journal of Economic Perspectives, 13*(1), 85–98.

Modern Language Association & Association of Departments of English. (2008). *Education in the balance: A report on the academic workforce in English.* New York: Author.

Moustakas, C. (1994). *Phenomenological research methods.* Thousand Oaks, CA: Sage.

National Center for Education Statistics. (2005). *2004 national study of postsecondary faculty (NSOPF: 05): Data file.* Washington, DC: U.S. Department of Education.

Patton, M. Q. (2002). *Qualitative research and evaluation methods* (3rd ed.). Thousand Oaks, CA: Sage.

Plater, W. M. (2008). The twenty-first-century professoriate. *Academe, 94*(4), 34–40.

Rhoades, G., & Maitland, C. (2008). Bargaining for full-time, non-tenure track faculty: Best practices. In *The NEA 2008 Almanac of Higher Education.* Retrieved from www2.nea.org/he/healma2k8/images/a08p67.pdf

Rice, R. E. (2006). From Athens to Berlin to L.A.: Faculty work and the new academy. *Liberal Education, 92*(4), 6–13.

Roemer, R. E., & Schnitz, J. E. (1982). Academic employment as day labor: The dual labor market in higher education. *Journal of Higher Education, 53*(5), 514–531.

Rosenblum, G., & Rosenblum, B. R. (1996). The flow of instructors through the segmented labor markets of academe. *Higher Education, 31*(5), 429–445.

Schuster, J. H., & Finkelstein, M. J. (2006). *The restructuring of academic work and careers.* Baltimore: Johns Hopkins University Press.

Shaker, G. G. (2008). *Off the track: The experience of being full-time non-tenure-track in English* (Unpublished doctoral dissertation). Indiana University, Bloomington.

Smith, C. B., & Hixson, V. S. (1987). The work of the university professor: Evidence of segmented labor markets inside the academy. In H. Z. Lopata (Ed.), *Current research on occupations and professions* (Vol. 4, pp. 159–180). Greenwich, CT: JAI Press.

Sorcinelli, M. D., Austin, A. E., Eddy, P. L., & Beach, A. L. (2005). *Creating the future of faculty development: Learning from the past, understanding the present.* San Francisco: Jossey-Bass/Anker.

Tolbert, P. S. (1998). Two-tiered faculty systems and organizational outcomes. In D. W. Leslie (Ed.), *New directions for higher education: Vol. 10. The growing use of part-time faculty: Understanding causes and effects* (pp. 71–80). San Francisco: Jossey-Bass.

5

USING MULTIMEDIA CASE STORIES OF EXEMPLARY TEACHING FOR FACULTY DEVELOPMENT

Tasha J. Souza, Humboldt State University

Tom Carey, Higher Education Quality Council of Ontario

Flora McMartin, Broad-based Knowledge, LLC

Roberta Ambrosino, UT Health Science Center at San Antonio

Joe Grimes, California Polytechnic State University

Faculty are more likely to embrace the possibility of change when they see change modeled by their colleagues. Through a multimedia case story, faculty can share in the experience of using an innovative teaching strategy and the process of implementing it. Integrating multimedia case stories into our work with faculty can help us meet diverse faculty needs and encourage more faculty to embrace pedagogical change. Such stories

We thank the conscientious attention of the reviewers and editors of this volume. We are pleased to acknowledge the stellar contributions of the MERLOT ELIXR program staff—Season Eckardt, Lou Zweier, Joel Bennett, and Cynthia Desrochers—and the ongoing support of MERLOT's executive director, Gerry Hanley, to our success with using multimedia case stories in faculty development. We also thank the ELIXR faculty development fellows, Kathy Ross, Kiren Dosanjh Zucker, Roberta Ambrosino, and Joe Grimes, for their active engagement with the case stories. We appreciate the thirty faculty development centers that created ELIXR case stories, providing us with engaging and valuable resources to enhance teaching and learning. The MERLOT ELIXR program was supported in part by a grant from the Department of Education, Fund for the Improvement of Post-Secondary Education.

can help faculty to realize that they too can overcome pedagogical challenges and institutional constraints in order to better meet the learning needs of students.

Centers for teaching and learning need to provide professional development opportunities focused on innovative pedagogies that meet twenty-first-century faculty members' "unique professional development and support needs, especially in the area of teaching and learning" (Diaz et al., 2009, p. 54). Universities today must consider changes in faculty development programs in the same way that they consider new teaching and learning approaches for their students. Vrasidas and Glass (2004) contend that "the demands of world and family life for teachers [coupled with the rise in part-time faculty] . . . underline the need for professional development activities that can be delivered anytime, anywhere" (p. 4). Diaz and others (2009) suggest that successful faculty development programs "incorporate flexible scheduling and various delivery options" (p. 54), "provide access to online resources" (p. 54), and include delivery in diverse formats (face-to-face, blended, online, and self-paced).

Freidus and Hlubinka (2002) note in a study of early users that sharing faculty experiences with innovative teaching and learning approaches through digital storytelling using case stories and supporting documents enhances and accelerates the adoption of exemplary teaching practices. Multimedia case stories, as developed for the MERLOT ELIXR (2009) project, combine faculty storytelling with course artifacts and interactive resources to illustrate exemplary teaching practices. ELIXR offers an online repository of multimedia case stories and resources on innovative pedagogy. These stories highlight different disciplinary approaches to pedagogical innovation, relevant teaching contexts, unique design or assessment methods, and student-centered teaching approaches. Viewing a changed classroom strategy through a multimedia case story lens provides an example of how faculty implement new pedagogical strategies and redesign courses to promote significant learning (Fink, 2003). To see such examples, readers are encouraged to scan one or more case stories on the ELIXR website (MERLOT ELIXR, 2009) or from the list in the WikiPODia article on Digital Case Stories for Faculty Development (POD Network, 2009).

Multimedia Case Stories Defined

The use of cases has a long history in various educational contexts (Ellet, 2007; Grossman, 1992; Kim et al., 2006). Cases reveal interpersonal complexity in context with all its connections to other aspects of classroom life (Anson, Jolliffe, & Shapiro, 1995). Cases are useful in preparing preservice teachers for the classroom (Anson et al., 1995). A case-based approach to teacher development encourages thoughtfulness among teachers (Boyer, 1990; Abell, Bryan, & Anderson, 1998) by capturing the wisdom of practice (Bransford, Brown, & Cocking, 1999). "Because cases are rich retellings of real classroom events, they encourage teachers to move beyond the 'idea' of a teaching issue by seeing it played out in a particular context" (Anson et al., 1995, p. 26). Hutchings (1992) contends that cases are a powerful tool for faculty development and offer a productive way for faculty to improve teaching and learning. Research suggests that cases can improve faculty learning by addressing context and relevance (Lowenthal, 2008).

Building on the success of cases, multimedia case stories combine elements of both case studies and digital storytelling. Multimedia case stories are a relatively new genre with two distinct attributes. First, they are real or realistic stories about teaching—not lessons, presentations, or even reflections (although a good story may contain all or some of these elements) presented through a digital medium. The power of stories to improve learning is well documented (Abrahamson, 1998; Connelly & Clandinin, 1994; McDury & Alterio, 2003). The key characteristic of a good story is that it draws in the audience members to imaginatively relate to the story. A good story about teaching helps other teachers experience what the storyteller has done and feel what the storyteller has felt. Second, these stories are also cases organized for learning. In the ELIXR multimedia case stories described here, the learners are teachers in higher education, and so storytellers reflect on questions their faculty colleagues might ask as they consider a new pedagogical approach.

Each ELIXR multimedia case story is unique, reflecting both a particular teaching method and the unique qualities that all teachers bring to their classes. However, most contain the following elements, either as individual components or integrated in sections customized to the story and the faculty storyteller's perspective:

- *Overview*. Before diving into a story, most viewers start with the overview, a short video thumbnail of the case story that previews the content and affective dimensions of the case in order to help viewers decide whether they want to explore the case further.

- *Story narrative*. The story narrative outlines, in video and text, why the practice was adopted, the resulting changes, how students responded to these changes in teaching, and evidence that these changes made a difference in student learning. Although the case is created by a team that includes experts in faculty development and digital media, the authorship of the story is personalized to reinforce the notion that the faculty member is the author-storyteller. Critical to the story are the successes and difficulties the author-storyteller encountered.

- *Personal reflection.* The author's personal reflection, in video and text, provides the viewer with a more personal account of the changes the innovator experienced in teaching and learning.

- *More detail.* The detail on this story provides resources that will help others understand the course more fully in order to use the methods demonstrated in the story. Example resources include course syllabi, assignments, links to outside resources, and assessment data such as actual examples of student work. A potential video element would be students at work demonstrating the implementation.

- *Faculty development resources.* The faculty development resources section, if there is one, contains resources and tools for faculty developers to use with the case stories.

Benefits of Multimedia Case Stories in Faculty Development

The following benefits are ones that we specifically targeted in our design and use of multimedia case stories for faculty development.

See New Strategies in Action

Multimedia case stories present new ways of demonstrating particular teaching and learning innovations (Mitchem et al., 2009). Instead of simply talking about goals for the first day of class, for example, faculty can see a first-day-of-class goal described by the faculty member and the process of achieving that goal (Desrochers & Grimes, 2007).

Provide Discipline-Specific Examples

A recent study in the United Kingdom noted that most faculty, when considering approaches to teaching and learning, primarily seek and respect advice and guidance given by colleagues in their own discipline. Faculty are, at best, broadly tolerant of a generic approach; they would rather be provided with stepping-stones to link pedagogical strategies with their disciplinary context (Supporting New Academic Staff Project Team, 2006). For example, faculty in the sciences may prefer examples from the sciences about integrating active learning strategies, and faculty in the humanities may prefer to learn about the same topic from their own disciplinary colleagues. "Without contextualizing and making things relevant, attracting faculty and hence helping support the transfer of what faculty learn to their own classroom to improve their teaching is futile" (Lowenthal, 2008, p. 351).

Demonstrate Both the Product and Process of Innovations in Teaching

Reciprocal classroom visits are a way for faculty developers to promote dialogue among faculty while ensuring the learners' perspective is a focal point (Helling & Kuhlmann, 1988; Hutchings, 1996), but what is most visible in these visits is the product of change. Multimedia case stories provide a similar experience, with the added benefit of showing both the product and process of innovations in teaching. Recent research documents the effectiveness of process-oriented case studies in fostering a learning-centered perspective in faculty workshops. "Process-oriented information refers to the principled (why) and strategic (how) information that experts use when solving problems . . . adding process-oriented information to worked examples can enhance transfer performance" (Hoogveld, Paas, & Jochems, 2005, p. 287).

Target Evolving Faculty Concerns with Just-in-Time Learning

Multimedia case stories provide a rich resource for faculty to use to follow up on workshop programs as their questions about a particular method evolve. The concerns-based adoption model (CBAM) provides a framework for typical questions teachers ask over time in considering a change in teaching methods (Hord, Rutherford, Huling-Austin, & Hall, 1987). Initial ELIXR case story work used CBAM to target evolving faculty concerns with just-in-time learning, weaving stories around a CBAM question sequence that might arise for another instructor considering use of a new teaching approach. Questions covered reasons for the approach, approaches to using it, impact on students and the course, challenges and rewards, and assessment.

Extend Access to Faculty Development Opportunities

Typical faculty development programs offer one-time workshops or institutes as ways to attract participants to faculty development efforts. While such programs are convenient for some, research suggests that lack of time and competing priorities are two major obstacles to faculty participation in such programs (Stevens et al., 2005). Using multimedia case stories in combination with more traditional methods can extend access to faculty development opportunities and more efficiently reach a broader range of faculty (DiPietro et al., 2009). Because multimedia case stories and their related resources are available online, faculty can explore the stories when the time is convenient, and repeatedly if necessary. Faculty who might be reluctant to ask for help can use such online resources anonymously (DiPietro et al., 2009). While the multimedia case stories from the ELIXR project were developed with the intention of faculty development events as the primary access method, the stories are also used by individual faculty by means of websites to support teaching. For example, the Pedagogy in Action website (SERC, 2009) uses multimedia case stories as illustrations within a rich set of online resources on particular teaching methods like concept tests and just-in-time teaching. Online multimedia case stories are especially useful for underserved faculty such as adjuncts who cannot easily take advantage of traditional faculty development programs and consultations.

Using Multimedia Case Stories in Faculty Development

Faculty development professionals have used multimedia case stories in face-to-face workshops, online learning opportunities, faculty learning communities (FLCs), and consultations. The stories are stand-alone tools or supplements to any faculty development activity. The multimedia case stories offer the flexibility needed for different faculty development needs. The faculty developer must, of course, review the potential case story before use to be sure that it will provide the desired outcomes and ensure the appropriate pedagogical placement of the story in the larger program design. Faculty developers have incorporated multimedia case stories into face-to-face workshops in the following ways:

- Asking participants to preview cases as preparation for a workshop
- Showcasing story elements to demonstrate a point or lead into an exercise
- Forming groups to review and reflect on the case story
- Providing links to cases in workshop materials as suggested follow-up resources

- Sending new faculty links to case stories relevant to new faculty orientation

- Sending cases to faculty as orientation to new instructional initiatives

Similar approaches can be used with FLCs and consultations with faculty. Faculty can preview cases prior to a meeting, view cases during a meeting or consultation, or review cases after a meeting or consultation as a follow-up resource.

Face-to-face workshops and programs are often expensive and fail to attract a large number of faculty members (Lowenthal, 2008). Case stories used for online faculty development offer a less expensive alternative. Such self-paced online learning opportunities "can help address attracting faculty to attend workshops by eliminating issues of time and place" (Lowenthal, 2008, p. 351). Given the increasing popularity of online learning and teaching (Shea, Sherer, & Kristensen, 2001; Vrasidas & Glass, 2004), the need for online faculty development may increase, especially in times of declining resources.

Evaluating the Use and Usability of Case Stories in Faculty Development

The ELIXR program team is evaluating the outcomes of the project as a whole while examining three areas in particular: use in face-to-face faculty development, use in online faculty development, and the usability of the cases for faculty developers. Evaluators collect data along three dimensions: participation, faculty learning, and impact on teaching and learning. The ELIXR project, begun in 2006, has focused primarily on developing the case stories. Since 2008, case stories have been available for use online, so given the early stage of the project, the focus to date is on faculty satisfaction and learning, not student learning.

Through the ELIXR website, faculty developers have access to survey instruments to evaluate the effectiveness of face-to-face or online workshops. Additional survey instruments measure knowledge prior to the workshop or allow participants to report what they have learned and how they have applied it to their teaching. Collection of these data is ongoing, and the information provided in this chapter illustrates the types of responses received to date. Preliminary analysis indicates that faculty and faculty developers find the case stories meaningful, appreciate the variety of disciplines and topics represented, and believe the stories would be most useful for less experienced instructors.

Face-to-Face Faculty Development Evaluation Data

Evaluation conducted by the faculty developers who used case story resources in face-to-face workshops and FLCs reported faculty reactions as well as data regarding actual and anticipated changes to teaching practice. The small numbers of participants in the workshops make it inappropriate to report anything beyond descriptive statistics. The following information from several of these faculty developers provides an overview of their evaluation efforts.

California State University, San Luis Obispo used the Universal Design for Learning in Information Systems (UDL) case story (Beckman, 2009) as part of a UDL meeting of FLCs five times for two hours each time. Over the course of these sessions, each faculty member reviewed and discussed material on the fundamentals of UDL and planned the transformation of his or her courses by receiving suggestions from others in the learning community. After completing the activities and prior to the final meeting, members reviewed the ELIXR case story on how to improve learning using UDL principles. Members reviewed the case at this stage so that their initial designs would not be unduly influenced by the case story. The case story provided confirmation of the value of UDL, illustrated a variety of UDL techniques (for example, small group discussions, guided notes, use of online multimedia), and included sample assessment techniques that reinforced the importance of assessment and evaluation.

FLC participants confirmed two main benefits of case story use: seeing UDL happen is better than just talking about or reading about how it should happen, and interdisciplinary discussions of the case stories allow different insights to emerge. All FLC participants felt the case story was valuable for them, and all followed through by implementing UDL in revised courses.

University of Texas Health Science Center took a different approach and used the First Day of Class case story (Desrochers & Grimes, 2007) in two face-to-face workshops with participants from various disciplines, different teaching environments, and varying years of experience. Seasoned faculty led the workshops and related case stories to their own experiences with discussions of their own questions, tips, and reflections, resulting in rich interactions around first-day instructional strategies, especially about framing course content and motivating students. Both the workshop facilitators and the participants rated the workshops favorably. The facilitators felt that the story format of the ELIXR resources promoted a story-sharing atmosphere, which led to the faculty openly identifying and comparing their differences in disciplines and teaching environments. The workshop evaluations indicated that 60 percent of the thirty participants found that the case stories contributed to their learning, which compared favorably with the other aspects of the workshop (for example, 80 percent for discussions with peers and 47 percent for handouts).

California State University, Fullerton used the First Day of Class (Desrochers and Grimes, 2007) case story as well but in a ninety-minute session as part of a two-day orientation for new faculty. Approximately fifty faculty attended, viewing the First Day of Class case story at the end of the two days. The case story revived the fatigued group, who seemed to appreciate the ability to work on their own classes. The session used many methods and resources, including a handout of the most common goals for the first day of class, a case story video showing two instructors dealing with first-day classes, a large group discussion about individual goals, a writing activity for participants to select upcoming first-day goals, a pair-share of those goals, and completion of a first-day planning template with references to the relevant disciplinary case stories. Participants chose methods to achieve goals and shared first-day plans in small groups. The overall average rating of the value of the workshop was 4.2 on a scale of 1 to 6, with the case story rated at 4.0 and discussion with colleagues at 4.7. Such scores suggest that discussion of the case stories can be more valuable than simply viewing the case stories. Many favorable comments were written about the use of the case stories, and 75 percent of the respondents reported that they would likely use what they had learned in the workshop in their own first day of class.

Looking more closely at the kind of behavioral change that Fullerton's data suggest, Humboldt State University conducted a focus group with new faculty a week after they attended a similar first-day-of-class workshop, where the value of the workshop case stories was rated as a 3.7 on a 1 to 5 scale. The inquiry focused on the kinds of changes participants made to their first day of class that they attributed to the workshop and in particular to the case stories. Twelve participants attended the meeting, and all reported that they made changes to their classes as a result of attending the workshop and viewing the case stories.

Each evaluation effort shows that the methods used were specific to the context of the campus. The results were useful to the faculty developers in refining their workshops, a primary goal for the program's evaluation efforts.

Online Professional Development Data

A secondary use of the ELIXR case stories is through individual faculty accessing online resources such as a discipline-specific teaching portal. The Science Education Resource Center (SERC) at Carleton College studied the ELIXR case stories to assess the value and utility of integrating the First Day of Class and Just in Time Teaching stories into their existing website, Teach the Earth, which makes pedagogical modules available for use by for geosciences faculty. Faculty reported that the case stories contributed to their knowledge about the topic or affirmed their existing knowledge. One participant wrote, "I have spent 20-something years walking into the first day of class, right, every semester, all different kinds of settings. And, what I have learned on the fly through shear [sic] years of experience is captured here in this website. So, in a way, it's completely reinforcing of knowledge I have acquired the hard way" (SERC, 2009, p. 7). Two study participants noted, when reflecting on the use of the videos, "By actually demonstrating the ideas, the videos provided concrete examples," and, "It would be difficult to conceptualize the techniques without the videos" (SERC, 2009, pp. 8–9).

The faculty who participated in the SERC study found that multimedia case stories demonstrating techniques, using real faculty in real classroom settings, are effective complements to the textual descriptions in the existing modules. Findings from this initial study indicate that faculty exploring the case studies in an online environment learn from the ELIXR stories because they relate to the genuineness of the stories and see how to apply the techniques in their own classroom settings.

Usability Data of Case Stories for Faculty Development

At the ELIXR program level, two evaluation questions regarding usability and potential for dissemination are of prime importance. To better understand faculty developers' views of the cases and determine methods for disseminating them, the ELIXR evaluators conducted an observational user study of the case stories with faculty developers who attended the 2009 MERLOT International Conference. In this study, we asked participants to view a case story for fifteen to twenty minutes, after which they responded to a survey or participated in a one-on-one structured interview. Participants tended to be experienced instructors in addition to being faculty developers. Study participants reported that the case stories were engaging, content well organized, and video segments compelling.

We observed that most participants viewed the entire case story, even though the study did not require them to do so.

In their role as instructors, around 60 percent of the participants reported that the case story piqued their interest in trying out a new teaching strategy or in integrating it into a future course or class. About 35 percent reported that the cases added to what they already knew about the story topic, which suggests that experts chose to view the stories to test their accuracy and validity, while people new to the topic viewed them to learn more about the topic. In their role as faculty developers, 70 percent of respondents reported that they would share the case stories with other instructors or administrators on their campus. In a follow-up survey conducted in November 2009, respondents reported that they had not changed their teaching practices because of viewing the case story. This finding must be viewed with caution, however, because many of the participants were experienced teachers already expert in the topic area of the case story they reviewed. In their faculty developer roles, over half of the respondents reported they had recommended the case stories to faculty, faculty development colleagues, or administrators on their campus. However, none of the respondents reported using them in formal faculty development programs. This could be the result of the timing of the survey (given that their fall programming may have already been in place at the time they first viewed the case stories) or might suggest that exposure to a resource one time may not be enough to encourage immediate use.

These findings are generally encouraging but also reveal the challenges of adopting innovative faculty development resources. Successful adoption requires more than simply making people aware of a resource. In particular, faculty developers must have the time and support to examine the case story resources in some depth and redesign programs to integrate them. The consensus from the faculty developers using the ELIXR case stories is that faculty participating in their programs benefited from use of the cases.

Conclusion

Our experiences and observations, along with the emerging evaluation data, convince us of the value of multimedia case stories as a new genre for faculty to share knowledge about exemplary teaching. The reports in this chapter represent initial efforts to understand, apply, and evaluate multimedia case stories in our programs for faculty. We encourage readers to make use of ELIXR resources, available for use at no charge, and to contribute to the knowledge exchange about their use and value.

REFERENCES

Abell, S. K., Bryan, L. A., & Anderson, M. (1998). Investigating pre-service elementary science teacher reflective thinking using integrated media case-based instruction in elementary science teacher preparation. *Science Education, 82*(4), 491–509.

Abrahamson, C. E. (1998). Storytelling as a pedagogical tool in higher education. *Education, 118*(3), 440–451.

Anson, C. M., Jolliffe, D. A., & Shapiro, N. (1995). Stories to teach by: Using narrative cases in TA and faculty development. *Writing Program Administration, 19*(1), 24–37.

Beckman, P. (2009). *Universal design for learning in information systems case story.* Retrieved from http://pachyderm.cdl.edu/elixr-stories/udl-information-systems/

Boyer, E. L. (1990). *Scholarship reconsidered: Priorities of the professoriate.* Princeton, NJ: Carnegie Foundation for the Advancement of Teaching.

Bransford, J. D., Brown, A. L., & Cocking, R. R. (1999). *How people learn: Brain, mind, experience, and school.* Washington, DC: National Academy Press.

Connelly, F. M., & Clandinin, D. J. (1994). Telling teaching stories. *Teacher Education Quarterly, 21*(1), 145–158.

Desrochers, C., & Grimes, J. (2007). *Making your 1st class session really first class.* Retrieved from http://pachyderm.cdl.edu/elixr-stories/1stday-slo/

Diaz, V., Garrett, P. B., Kinley, E. R., Moore, J. F., Schwartz, C. M., & Kohrman, P. (2009). Faculty development for the 21st century. *EDUCAUSE Review, 44*(3), 46–55.

DiPietro, M., Ambrose, S. A., Bridges, M., Fay, A., Lovett, M. C., & Norman, M. K. (2009). Defeating the developer's dilemma: An online tool for individual consultations. In L. B. Nilson & J. E. Miller (Eds.), *To improve the academy: Vol. 27. Resources for faculty, instructional, and organizational development* (pp. 183–198). San Francisco: Jossey-Bass.

Ellet, W. (2007). *Case study handbook: How to read, discuss, and write persuasively about cases.* Boston: Harvard Business School Press.

Fink, L. D. (2003). *Creating significant learning experiences: An integrated approach to designing college courses.* San Francisco: Jossey-Bass.

Freidus, N., & Hlubinka, M. (2002). Digital storytelling for reflective practice in communities of learners. *ACM SIGGROUP Bulletin, 23*(2), 24–26.

Grossman, P. L. (1992). Teaching and learning with cases: Unanswered questions. In J. Shuman (Ed.), *Case methods in teacher education* (pp. 227–239). New York: Teachers College Press.

Helling, B., & Kuhlmann, D. (1988). The faculty visitor program: Helping teachers see themselves. In K. G. Lewis & J.T.P. Lunde (Eds.),

Face to face: A sourcebook of individual consultation techniques for faculty instructional developers (pp. 135–148). Stillwater, OK: New Forums Press.

Hoogveld, A.W.M., Paas, F., & Jochems, W.M.G. (2005). Training higher education teachers for instructional design of competency-based education: Product-oriented versus process-oriented worked examples. *Teaching and Teacher Education, 21*(3), 287–297.

Hord, S. M., Rutherford, W. L., Huling-Austin, L., & Hall, G. (1987). *Taking charge of change*. Alexandria, VA: Association for Supervision and Curriculum Development.

Hutchings, P. (1992). Using cases to talk about teaching. *AAHE Bulletin, 44*(8), 6–8.

Hutchings, P. (1996). *Making teaching community property*. Washington, DC: American Association for Higher Education.

Kim, S., Phillips, W. R., Pinsky, L., Brock, D., Phillips, K., & Keary, J. (2006). A conceptual framework for developing teaching cases: A review and synthesis of the literature across disciplines. *Medical Education, 40*(9), 867–876.

Lowenthal, P. R. (2008). Online faculty development and storytelling: An unlikely solution to improving teacher quality. *MERLOT Journal of Online Teaching and Learning, 4*(3), 349–356.

McDrury, J., & Alterio, M. (2003). *Learning through storytelling in higher education: Using reflection and experience to improve learning*. London: Kogan Page.

MERLOT ELIXR. (2009). *Welcome to MERLOT ELIXR*. Retrieved from http://elixr.merlot.org

Mitchem, K., Koury, K., Fitzgerald, G., Hollingsead, C., Miller, K., Tsai, H. H., et al. (2009). The effects of instructional implementation on learning with interactive multimedia case-based instruction. *Teacher Education and Special Education: The Journal of the Teacher Education Division of the Council for Exceptional Children, 32*, 297–318.

POD Network. (2009). *WikiPODia*. Retrieved from http://sites.google.com/site/podnetwork/

SERC. (2009). *The Science Education Research Center*. Retrieved from http://serc.carleton.edu/sp/library/conceptests/index.html and http://serc.carleton.edu/sp/library/justintime/index.html

Shea, T. P., Sherer, P. D., & Kristensen, E. W. (2001). Harnessing the potential of online faculty development: Challenges and opportunities. In D. Lieberman & C. M. Wehlburg (Eds.), *To improve the academy: Vol. 20. Resources for faculty, instructional, and organizational development* (pp. 162–179). San Francisco: Jossey-Bass/Anker.

Stevens, E., Dunlap, J., Bates, B., Lowenthal, P., Wray, M., & Switzer, T. (2005). *Faculty development attitudes and motivators*. Paper presented at the annual meeting of the Northern Rocky Mountain Educational Research Association, Jackson, WY.

Supporting New Academic Staff Project Team. (2006). *The generic meets the discipline*. Retrieved from www.medev.ac.uk/docs/generic_meets_the _discipline_update.pdf

Vrasidas, C., & Glass, G. V. (2004). *Online professional development for teachers*. Greenwich, CT: Information Age.

6

THERE WAS SOMETHING MISSING

A CASE STUDY OF A FACULTY MEMBER'S SOCIAL INTELLIGENCE DEVELOPMENT

Tamara Rosier, Grand Valley State University

Some faculty members seem to lack the social intelligence or relational skills needed to successfully "read" and respond to their students. This chapter describes the process of developing social intelligence skills in one faculty member. During a series of ten coaching sessions, there was demonstrable change in the faculty member's behavior and a self-reported increase in his social intelligence skills. The findings of this exploratory study suggest that social intelligence can be developed, and it has the potential to have a positive effect on teaching practices and faculty success.

John, a faculty member in a science department, is intelligent and articulate. He spends a great deal of time crafting tests and lectures for his students and wants his students to fully grasp the details of his field. John was referred to me by an administrator because of the high withdrawal rate from his courses, numerous student complaints, below-average student evaluations, and a very low student grade point average.

For years I met with faculty members who were not successful in the classroom, coaching them to use more appropriate pedagogical strategies. Yet in spite of using good theory-driven practices, a few professors still experienced a significant disconnect in their classroom. I was missing something. Teaching is a multifaceted, complex process and involves far more than merely conveying information. Research has demonstrated that successful teachers "read" their students' nonverbal signals, discern how their students might be feeling, manage the affective elements in a class, understand how to influence the behaviors of their students, and show appropriate concern (Hall, Rosenthal, Archer, DiMatteo, & Rogers, 1977; Wilmington, 1992). Some faculty members, however, seem to lack the relational skills needed to read and respond to their students. In these cases, better teaching strategies alone are not enough.

Social Intelligence Theory

The notion of social intelligence was originally put forth by Thorndike (1920) as "the ability to understand and manage men and women, boys and girls, to act wisely in human relations" (p. 228). A person who is socially intelligent understands what another person is feeling and is able to act effectively and appropriately based on that understanding. While some researchers (Eisner, 1986) have restricted the definition to deal only with knowledge of social situations, others agree that social and emotional intelligence overlap (Kang, Day, & Meara, 2005; Mayer, Salovey, & Caruso, 2000; Salovey & Mayer, 1990). However, social intelligence is differentiated from other intelligences by its focus on others (Weis & Süb, 2007).

The key elements of many social intelligence models include social understanding and the ability to respond appropriately. Weis and Süb (2007) have created a social performance model that includes understanding, memory, perception, creativity, and knowledge. Cantor and Kihlstrom (1986) have outlined the kinds of concepts people use to make sense of their social relations, the rules they use to draw inferences, and their rules for planning actions. Albrecht (2005) has proposed a five-part model of social intelligence: situational awareness, presence, authenticity, clarity, and empathy.

The conceptual framework for this case study is the social intelligence paradigm put forth by Goleman (2006). Drawing on concepts from neuroscience and psychology, Goleman presents a model of social intelligence that includes the synergistic interplay of brain and biology. He explains that our brain physiology is shaped by our social interactions. He describes the difference between two brain processes: "high road" and "low road." The high road uses a comparatively slow neurological pathway when we analyze and consciously think. High-road thinking runs through neural systems that work methodically with deliberate effort. Low-road thinking is instinctive and provides us with intuitive feelings (LeDoux, 1998; Gallese, 2007). Low-road operations in the amygdala are emotionally based; they allow us to walk into a room and sense a silent disagreement. According to Goleman, social intelligence is the ability to effectively use both low-road and high-road processes. Goleman's model of social intelligence is descriptive, not definitive. In his model, social intelligence is organized into two broad categories: social awareness and social faculty.

Social Awareness

Goleman's (2006) first category of social intelligence, social awareness, encompasses primal empathy, attunement, empathetic accuracy, and social cognition. All of these skills are important to effective teaching and can be developed to improve faculty-student relationships:

- *Primal empathy* is the ability to sense and make meaning of another's nonverbal emotional signals, communicated unconsciously through facial muscles (Ekman, 2007). Faculty members who do this well can spontaneously read nonverbal clues and are viewed as more effective by their students (Hall et al., 1977).

- *Attunement* refers to the ability to listen with full receptivity. When faculty members focus attention on the individual speaking, they are making an effort to connect on a personal level by listening intentionally.

- *Empathetic accuracy* has to do with understanding another person's thoughts, feelings, and intentions. Research performed in the area of empathetic accuracy suggests that our readings of the thoughts and feelings of others can be accurate (Ickes, 2001). Faculty members who do this well remember what it was like to be a student, can accurately project how their students may be feeling, and can relate to their students' goals.

- *Social cognition* is an understanding of the norms and mores of a changing environment. Faculty members who do this well can read the politics of a classroom. They can accurately interpret the social currents to see which students will influence other students, how some behaviors affect the entire class, and how their presence affects class interactions.

Social Faculty

Goleman's (2006) second category of social intelligence, social faculty, encompasses synchrony, self-presentation, influence, and concern. Development of these skills is important to faculty interactions with students:

- *Synchrony* refers to individuals' interacting smoothly at the nonverbal level. Since much of our communication is nonverbal (Mehrabian, 1981), we perform a mostly unconscious social dance that causes individuals to react to social cues without thinking about it. Faculty who do this well interact smoothly and effectively with their classes.

- *Self-presentation* is the ability to present oneself effectively. Professors who do this well convey a confident, calm, knowledgeable, and caring persona to the class. They effectively convey behavioral expectations to their class without words because they have convinced their students that they are leading the class.

- *Influence* is the understanding of and ability to shape the outcome of social interactions. A colleague once stated that he was able to convince his students that completing the final class assignment would help them in their future teaching careers. He understood his influence and its effect on his students. Therefore, he was able to motivate them to invest considerable time and effort in the assignment.

- *Concern* extends the idea of empathy by adding action and caring about others' needs and then behaving accordingly. Busy schedules threaten this aspect of social intelligence, as seen in the classic Darley and Batson (1973) experiment with seminary students who believed they were late to give a talk about the parable of the Good Samaritan. Subjects in a hurry were far less likely to stop and provide assistance to an actor playing the role of a groaning man who was apparently in distress. Effective teaching faculty manage their numerous professional tasks while focusing on their students' needs, acting in ways that address students' needs.

Method

An exploratory case study approach was chosen to observe what happened when a professor who did not seem to have a relational connection to his students was coached in the use of social intelligence. In this case study, Goleman's (2006) social intelligence framework guided the work with the participant. Three research questions were investigated:

1. What areas of social intelligence can be developed in ten coaching sessions?

2. How does the faculty member describe his own perceptions of social intelligence?

3. How does the faculty member understand the impact of social intelligence on his classroom?

Participant

The case study focused on a single participant—a male science professor with several years of teaching experience, identified here as John. He was an ideal candidate for three reasons: he needed to develop social intelligence, he had a desire to learn a new approach, and he seemed to genuinely care for his students.

I am a full-time faculty development professional and was the researcher. I recognized from the beginning that a case study with one participant would generate empirical findings specific only to that case. However, it could contribute to faculty developers' understanding of how to coach colleagues who lack interpersonal connection with their students.

Data Collection

John and I had ten meetings, lasting from 60 to 150 minutes each. During each meeting, a problem was defined and planned interventions discussed. After John implemented these plans, subsequent meetings evaluated the interventions and defined another problem. I analyzed my notes from each session and e-mail messages between John and me for signs of progress.

I also collected data from reports, other e-mail messages, and student evaluations of teaching, which helped set the baseline of behavior and goals for improvement. Due to confidentiality assurances, it was not possible to validate my observations by triangulating with other observers. However, John's midterm teaching evaluation provided some cross-checking. I also relied on his self-reflective comments to provide substantiation.

The Initial Meeting

The goals of the initial meeting were to establish a relationship and assess if John needed improvement in the area of social intelligence. I developed rapport with him by accessing my own social intelligence skills, carefully listening to his story, responding empathetically, and showing concern.

In this first conversation, John explained that he was very irritated with the student behavior that he saw in his classes. He described his students as "lacking of character"; they worked only for a grade and appeared lazy. He had developed a distanced relationship with his students by categorizing them as very different from himself. Although John was frustrated, he wanted to do something about the student behavior.

When I asked him if he liked his students, he responded emphatically that he did care for his students as both individuals and learners. At that point, I had two observations that began to shape my understanding about this case. Although John appeared to genuinely care for his students, he seemed disconnected from them. He also perceived this gap and stated that this was not how he wanted to be viewed by them.

As a result of our first meeting, we agreed to work on how he understood his students (primal empathy, empathetic accuracy, and concern), how he could communicate empathetically with his students (influence, concern, and self-presentation), and how he could act in a way that would alter his students' perceptions (concern and self-presentation).

Coaching Sessions

The topics of the ten coaching sessions followed this general progression:

- Acknowledgment of who John's students were
- Analysis of how his behavior affected students
- Identification of teaching behaviors that were likely to have a positive effect on student learning
- Exploration of John's personal vision of who he wanted to be as a professor
- Introduction of social intelligence
- Discussion of nonverbal behaviors that communicated social intelligence
- Discussion of verbal communication behaviors that communicated social intelligence
- Reflection on John's learning

Primal Empathy, Empathetic Accuracy, and Concern

In discussing the results of this case study, I am grouping the subcategories primal empathy, empathetic accuracy, and concern together because simultaneous growth occurred in these areas. Each of these subcategories built on one another as John examined his approach to teaching and our first goal of understanding his students. We worked first on empathetic accuracy (the ability to accurately understand how another is feeling) and then on primal empathy (the ability to read another's thoughts or feelings). Concern (acting with the understanding gained from primal empathy and empathetic accuracy) developed as John responded to his students.

At the beginning of the coaching process he asked, "I know what empathy is, but what does it look like in a class?" By the end of our work together, he was responding to class situations with increased empathy. He had discovered what empathy in the classroom looked like; practiced understanding another person's thoughts, feelings, and intentions; and demonstrated caring for his students' needs and acting accordingly. He had developed primal empathy by beginning to see student distress, empathetic accuracy when considering how his students felt, and concern when acting on his observations.

STEPS TOWARD EMPATHY

In the third meeting, John acknowledged that his frustration with students was counterproductive and that it was not helping him solve his problem. In an effort to build a better understanding of his students, develop his empathetic accuracy, and deconstruct some labels that kept him at a distance from his students, we discussed his recent readings on the millennial generation. John analyzed his own beliefs from a generational perspective and contrasted his sense of responsibility to work and learn with that of his students. We discussed the needs of students in his classes. After a few meetings, John could explain that his students were concerned about their ability to pass his difficult required course.

Showing empathy became the topic of discussion at many of our meetings. I insisted that empathy was not merely a "touchy-feely concept to use to make students feel good about themselves," as John once had said, but instead was a significant part of learning. From there we discussed how to show empathy in front of the class and to individuals during office hours.

PRACTICING EMPATHY

During one meeting, John brought a contentious e-mail message from a student and his response to it. To give him the feedback he wanted, we went over the message like coaches analyzing a football game. He had responded to the student's complaints in a factual tone, carefully addressing each of the student's points. His message was precise, logical, and correct, but there was something missing. I suggested that he could have responded more empathetically and let the student know that he had been heard. I suggested specific phrases that eventually became useful to him, such as, "In your e-mail, you seemed very upset" and "From your e-mail, I can tell that you are frustrated with . . ." John took notes and expressed the wish that he had these types of sound bites for other situations.

In a later meeting, John brought a second student e-mail message to discuss. The student felt that the questions on an exam were unfair and that the answers to the questions contradicted class discussion. The e-mail ended with the student expressing his frustration that all of his studying was not "paying off." This time, John explained to me, he had begun writing an empathetic answer in response but felt as if he were "pandering, insincere, and condescending." We looked at the student's message and analyzed it for emotion first. John identified the emotions of fear and frustration expressed in the message. Then he went back to his office and sent the following e-mail message to the student:

> Your message seems to indicate that you are feeling frustrated and perhaps anxious about successfully completing the course. If this is correct I am sorry to hear this. I would very much like to talk with you about developing strategies to improve the effectiveness of the time you spend studying. If you would like to meet to do this send me an email so we can find a time that will work for both of us. Please be assured that it is never my intent to write questions that are either tricky or misleading, although I do compose questions that I hope will access students' depth of understanding.

The first e-mail message John had sent expertly explained why the student's perceptions were incorrect and invalid. This second message illustrated two changes: he addressed the emotions expressed (empathetic accuracy) and invited the student to join a process to improve (concern).

JOHN'S PARADIGM SHIFTS

By our fifth meeting, John was questioning his assumptions about students and teaching. At one point he explained that they were "all wrong." Although he remained confident in the effectiveness of his teaching methods and wished that students would be responsible and hard working, he recognized that as a professor, he was responsible for motivating students and meeting their needs. He wasn't sure how to do that. When I explained the concept of social intelligence as it relates to empathy and concern— and that it could help him understand how to engage students in a new way—he became emotional and said, "I've felt this." At the end of that discussion he said, "I'm missing something." This was an important moment for John: he acknowledged that he lacked social intelligence, specifically in the areas of primal empathy, empathetic accuracy, and concern.

Self-Presentation

Self-presentation is the ability to portray ourselves effectively. John had received feedback from his students that they felt "disrespected," that he was arrogant, and that he did not care about their success. John was not presenting himself accurately; that is, he did not want to be viewed that way. We worked on ways to help him present himself as confident and caring.

In the sixth meeting, we discussed the use of midterm teaching evaluations. He noted my suggested language for introducing the idea of a midterm evaluation to students. He wrote in his notebook the specific phrases, "I'm interested in . . .," "Help me understand . . .," and "Let's . . ." He wanted to be seen as inviting students to join him in a learning process.

MIDTERM EVALUATIONS

In an effort to improve his self-presentation skills and receive specific student feedback, John decided to conduct midterm evaluations. Because he had never done this before, we discussed the kind of feedback he desired and how to ask questions. The evaluations ultimately provided valuable feedback to him and suggested that he was making progress.

Students were asked to rate their responses to seven prompts on a scale of A to E (A = totally agree, C = generally agree, E = totally disagree), with an area for comments beneath each prompt. One question, "I believe I am free to talk with my professor about my progress in the course if I desire," provided surprising feedback. The answers to this question revealed that he had made progress in portraying himself as someone who could be approached. His upper-level course responded with 90 percent indicating "generally agree" to "totally agree." The majority of the introductory classes (73 percent), his most challenging and critical group, responded with "generally agree" to "totally agree." Some comments from the introductory-level classes showed that he still had some work to do with some students. For example, one student wrote that she agreed she was able to talk with him about her progress, but that it was sometimes "nerve wrecking [sic]" to approach him.

What John did with this feedback was impressive, and it showed his commitment to the process as well as his growing awareness of self-presentation. After carefully reading and reflecting on the midterm evaluations and preparing and rehearsing a response, he talked with his students. He described the theme of fear and anxiety about successfully completing the course and provided some strategies to help them become more successful. He also explained that the majority of the class reported that they found him accessible; he invited those who did not to e-mail him or come to his office. Finally, intentionally ending with this point, he addressed a perception that the class moved too quickly through the material. He explained that there was a great deal of content and that he tried to support their learning by preparatory or subsequent assignments. Speaking to his classes this way not only illustrated empathetic accuracy and concern, but also helped him to present himself effectively and authentically. He was building a relationship with his classes.

CHANGING SELF-PRESENTATION

In our tenth meeting, John explained how he was more effectively addressing some of the myths perpetuated in his field. In the past, he had explained in detail why textbook authors were incorrect or misguided; this was likely one of the behaviors that led students to think he was arrogant. John changed his self-presentation by making a joke when drawing attention to a common myth.

Social Cognition and Influence

As John practiced his empathetic and self-presentation skills, he noticed situations in his classroom that needed his attention. He began by analyzing how the social elements in his class worked and how he could shape the outcomes of many social interactions. For example, a pair of students would sigh loudly or exchange eye-rolling looks with one another during his class, especially when he was talking about a test or assignment. Because the behavior was noticeable to the entire class, it affected the tone of the room. When John noticed these subtle behaviors, he realized how distracting it was for others and began to strategize ways to intervene.

In another situation, he described a student who would ask questions that seemed to be "nonthinking" inquiries. Instead of becoming irritated (his previous response) and saying, "I'm not going to answer that question," John decided to open the discussion to the class and say, "So, how do we answer that question?" Students responded by chiming in with appropriate answers. In addition to improving his self-presentation, John demonstrated his social cognition and influence skills when he encouraged the class to respond to their classmate's question. He influenced student behavior by asking the class to cooperate and began to understand that students learn better when they are included in the discussion.

John's Progress

In one of my last meetings with John, I encouraged him to continue the progress he was making. He looked at me and said, "I was doing many things right, but there was something missing." John explained his progress in this way. First, he became aware of the affective environment surrounding him. Then he practiced specific skills to match his acquired sensitivity. Next, he reflected on his social interactions. Finally, he accumulated "sound bites" to help in specific situations. After ten coaching sessions, he was feeling more aware and sensitized to his class environment. Although he is still learning what it means to act in socially intelligent ways, John has become aware of the possibilities inherent in this model.

Overall Results of Coaching

The first research question was, "What areas of social intelligence can be developed in ten coaching sessions?" I found that John demonstrated great progress in six areas of social intelligence: primal empathy, empathetic accuracy, concern, self-presentation, social cognition, and influence.

The second research question was, "How does the faculty member describe his own perceptions of social intelligence?" After ten coaching sessions, John was able to articulate a shift in his perception of students and his approach to building relationships in his classes.

The third research question was, "How does the faculty member understand the impact of social intelligence on his classroom?" John reported that he had become more aware of his students' affective states and understood more clearly how to respond to what he observed. He also appeared to be more satisfied with what happened in his classes.

Discussion

This case study affirms the importance of acknowledging and caring for the interpersonal communication skills of faculty members who have been identified as not being successful in the classroom due to an apparent lack of interpersonal skills. It is not a clear, simple process, but it is worth the investment of a faculty developer's time and energy.

What should be done when faculty developers suspect that a professor is unsuccessful in the classroom due to low social intelligence? Goleman's (2006) framework has the potential to help faculty developers identify and understand what may be missing in a faculty member's teaching.

As faculty developers, trusting our own instincts and monitoring our own social intelligence can be informative. For example, does the conversation with a faculty member seem uneasy? To test our assumptions, faculty developers can ask open-ended questions about teaching and learning. Signs of problems with social intelligence in a faculty member could include egocentrism, blaming students for not succeeding, talking extensively about oneself, awkward discussion patterns, the inability to read another's facial cues, misunderstanding of social patterns, and appearing to lack empathy.

When faculty developers are preparing to help faculty members improve their social intelligence, they need to consider how to build rapport with the individual faculty member, develop a commitment to a process, and coach social intelligence skills.

Building Rapport

Individuals help other individuals grow through relationship with one another. I understood that I had a tremendous opportunity to influence and shape John's classroom behavior by developing an effective coaching relationship. To develop rapport, I modeled social intelligence by attuning with him, focusing on empathetic accuracy, and showing genuine concern. I employed my interpersonal skills by asking questions, listening well, mirroring John's demeanor, showing understanding, and expressing optimism about his success. Taking the time to establish rapport helped make the coaching process more successful.

Developing a Commitment

Although John's superiors strongly recommended that he work with me, I needed his commitment to the process (Boyatzis, 2009) without which he would not have invested in improving his social intelligence. I asked him about his goals and convinced him that I wanted to help him achieve them. We became partners in the process of improving his teaching experience.

Coaching Social Intelligence

I found it useful to begin with social awareness so John could begin to be sensitized to his environment. Empathy skills, attuning skills, and social cognition were the topics of our first several discussions. We discussed the basics of empathy and what it looks like in a classroom: using body language, reflecting on the other person's statement or feeling, and validating the other's emotions. We discussed how to attune to students: listening with full receptivity; monitoring his own feelings and responses; and focusing on the whole message, spoken and unspoken. We practiced the skills by talking through scenarios, rehearsing dialogues, and reviewing class events. Doing these activities reinforced the high-road aspect of these skills and encouraged the low-road neural pathways to pay attention to new cues.

I learned that providing individuals with "sound bites" can be useful when developing or reinforcing new behaviors. Basic phrases like, "I would like to understand . . ." or, "You feel confused when . . ." are useful when learning the basics of showing empathy. Other phrases that helped John were inclusive in their language or engaged students in a partnership: "Let us work this out together" or, "After we talk a little more, perhaps we can come up with some solutions that may help."

Limitations of the Study

The limitations of this case study point to the need for further research. First, baseline data such as classroom observations and analyses of student evaluations of teaching could have been collected before the coaching sessions began. Without early access to such data, my understanding of John's specific deficiencies in social intelligence was limited.

Second, because this case study was exploratory in nature, only my observations and coaching experience have been discussed. As a result, observations in the case study are limited to one participant in a specific time frame and are restricted to what could be observed during the coaching sessions. Additional research, particularly classroom observation and other student data, is needed to determine if improving a professor's social intelligence affects student learning.

Conclusion

John is not the only faculty member who is "missing something." Many faculty are missing one or more of the key social intelligence skills that allow other faculty to communicate effectively and smoothly with their classes. Goleman's social intelligence paradigm offers faculty developers a model that can be used as a basis for coaching social and communication skills. John made a great deal of progress toward becoming the professor he would like to be in just ten coaching sessions. By improving his social intelligence, he has overcome a substantial teaching barrier and has improved his chances for professional success.

REFERENCES

Albrecht, K. (2005). *Social intelligence: The new science of success*. San Francisco: Jossey-Bass.

Boyatzis, R. E. (2009). Developing emotional, social, and cognitive intelligence competencies in managers and leaders in educational settings. In M. Hughes, H. L. Thompson, & J. B. Terrell (Eds.), *Handbook for developing emotional and social intelligence* (pp. 219–241). San Francisco: Pfeiffer.

Cantor, N., & Kihlstrom, J. (1986). *Personality and social intelligence*. Upper Saddle River, NJ: Prentice Hall.

Darley, J. M., & Batson, C. D. (1973). From Jerusalem to Jericho: A study of situational and dispositional variables in helping behavior. *Journal of Personality and Social Psychology, 27*, 100–108.

Eisner, E. (1986). Aesthetic modes of knowing: An expansive perspective on intelligence. In *Proceedings from the 10th Annual Research Symposium: The World of the Mind*. Evanston, IL: Northwestern University.

Ekman, P. (2007). *Emotions revealed: Recognizing faces and feelings to improve communication and emotional life*. New York: Times Books.

Gallese, V. (2007). Before and below "theory of mind": Embodied simulation and the neural correlates of social cognition. In N. Emery, N. Clayton, & C. Frith (Eds.), *Social intelligence: From brain to culture* (pp. 276–279). New York: Oxford University Press.

Goleman, D. (2006). *Social intelligence*. New York: Bantam Dell.

Hall, J. A., Rosenthal, R., Archer, D., DiMatteo, M. R., & Rogers, P. L. (1977). Nonverbal skills in the classroom. *Theory into Practice, 16*(3), 162–166.

Ickes, W. (2001). Measuring empathetic accuracy. In J. A. Hall & F. J. Bernieri (Eds.), *Interpersonal sensitivity: Theory and measurement* (pp. 219–241). Mahwah, NJ: Erlbaum.

Kang, S., Day, J. D., & Meara, N. M. (2005). Social intelligence and emotional intelligence: Starting a conversation about their similarities and differences. In R. Schulze & R. D. Roberts (Eds.), *Emotional intelligence: An international handbook* (pp. 91–105). Cambridge, MA: Hogrefe & Huber.

LeDoux, J. (1998). *The emotional brain: The mysterious underpinnings of emotional life*. New York: Simon & Schuster.

Mayer, J. D., Salovey, P., & Caruso, D. R. (2000). Models of emotional intelligence. In R. J. Sternberg (Ed.), *Handbook of intelligence* (pp. 396–420). New York: Cambridge University Press.

Mehrabian, A. (1981). *Silent messages: Implicit communication of emotions and attitudes* (2nd ed.). Belmont, CA: Wadsworth.

Salovey, P., & Mayer, J. D. (1990). Emotional intelligence. *Imagination, Cognition and Personality, 9,* 185–211.

Thorndike, E. L. (1920). Intelligence and its use. *Harper's Magazine, 140,* 227–235.

Weis, S., & Süb, H. M. (2007). Reviving the search for social intelligence. *Personality and Individual Differences, 42,* 3–14.

Wilmington, S. C. (1992). Oral communication skills necessary for successful teaching. *Educational Research Quarterly, 16,* 5–17.

7

CROSS-DOMAIN COLLABORATIVE LEARNING AND THE TRANSFORMATION OF FACULTY IDENTITY

James B. Young

This chapter addresses how faculty from disparate backgrounds collaborate in interdisciplinary learning communities and how this cross-domain collaboration leads to a tangible change in identity. Faculty enter learning communities playing the more common roles of expert and teacher, but they leave taking on the additional roles of novice, learner, and knowledge integrator. The experience of cross-domain interaction is both rewarding and transformative for faculty as they are well equipped to communicate across the disciplinary landscape and gain a rhetorical awareness that is an invaluable ingredient for learning community participation.

Faculty play multiple, simultaneous roles in interdisciplinary learning communities in the Anonymous College (AC) integrative studies program at Large State University. They assume the expected roles of expert and teacher in collaboration with other faculty from across the disciplinary landscape on diverse cross-domain projects such as course design, instruction, and assessment in both the general education and upper-division curriculum in integrative studies. Within collaborative circles of two to eight instructors, faculty take on the additional, and often new, roles of novice, learner, and knowledge integrator. The creative tension that results from cross-domain interaction is both a rewarding and transformative experience for individuals, faculty teams, and the students who have ready access to faculty who do much more than teach; they model collaborative learning as context-sensitive experts.

How Faculty Typically Interact

Faculty are knowledge workers with deep expertise in a particular field. As part of their day-to-day work, they interact regularly with colleagues both within and outside their departments and, as part of their academic responsibilities, with peers from other institutions who share their intellectual pursuits or associational interest. Faculty collaboration is common, but the interactions within these collaborations are almost always framed in a sociocultural domain of like-minded experts protective of discipline-specific boundaries. Discipline-driven curricula, increased specialization, traditional rewards and motivations, and university organizational structures that resist change all help form and reinforce this prevailing culture of faculty interaction.

Most faculty collaboration, and therefore most faculty learning, occurs in the field in which they have been trained to be experts. As most universities and colleges organize their programs into departments by discipline or field, faculty typically interact with faculty of similar discipline, intellectual training, and professional background. For the most part, faculty members are not socialized, encouraged, or rewarded for cross-domain collaboration. Faculty ways of knowing, fostered in graduate study and individual scholarly pursuit, are increasingly governed by pressure to specialize. They have little choice but to become more conversant in areas they already know a great deal about. The dearth of opportunities or motivations for bridging chasms promoted by this pervasive culture of expertise hinders faculty opportunities to collaborate on cross-domain teaching and learning and therefore blunts chances to learn from each other across boundaries. One way to chip away at this prevailing university culture is for faculty to collaborate in learning communities.

Literature Review

It is relatively rare, in the literature and in practice, for faculty from diverse areas of expertise to work in intense, interdisciplinary work teams or cross-functional groups (Cox, 2004; Creamer, 2005). There are, however, multiple, broader frameworks in the higher education literature in which to place learning communities (Becher & Trowler, 2001; Smith, Macgregor, Matthews, & Gabelnick, 2004; Tagg, 2003; Tierney, 2008). The literature on communities of practice comes from the fields of knowledge management and organizational learning (Berthoin Antal, Lenhardt, & Rosenbrock, 2001; Davenport & Prusak, 1998; Dixon, 2000; Nonaka, 2008; Wenger, 1998; Wenger, McDermott, & Snyder, 2002). The common thread in the learning community and community of practice literature is that learning is social, dynamic, and rooted in the exchange of knowledge across organizational or disciplinary boundaries.

One way to understand cross-domain faculty learning is to frame it as a dynamic community of practice. According to Wenger (1998), communities of practice are formed by people who engage in a process of collective learning in a shared domain. As such, "ways of doing things, ways of talking, beliefs, values, power relations—in short, practices—emerge in the course of this mutual endeavor. As a social construct, a community of practice is different from the traditional community, primarily because it is defined simultaneously by its membership and by the practice in which that membership engages" (Eckert & McConnell-Ginet, 1992, p. 462). At AC, layers of communities of practice emerge around individual courses, which serve as vehicles to allow a wide diversity of participants to engage in ongoing social practice, reflecting the value placed on ongoing negotiation among multiple perspectives. In collaboratively taught communities of practice, faculty need expertise in a particular content area ("know what"), experience putting their expertise into practice ("know how"), and a willingness to learn.

Lave and Wenger (1991) use an apprenticeship model to illustrate how individuals gain knowledge in communities of practice. They do not, however, sufficiently explain how experts from disparate fields play the simultaneous roles of expert, teacher, novice, learner, and, ultimately, knowledge integrator. Their apprenticeship model assumes a one-way, almost top-down approach to social learning. In a co-apprenticeship model, novices or newcomers are exposed over time to a social culture in which they gain skills, learn subtle ways of functioning, and sharpen their judgment through interactions and experiences guided by a mentor or group of co-mentors. Learning is therefore situated in the team's social interaction in a common situation in which all members have a stake. In the AC learning context, knowledge is practical, linked to action, and integral to the creation of meaning, and increased participation in communally experienced situations leads faculty to the interdependent outcomes of richer understanding and the construction of identity.

Participants and Data Collection

Data for this chapter were collected in part from a larger study that investigated how faculty learn outside the domain of their expertise in interdisciplinary learning communities (Young, 2003). As part of this study, ten experienced instructors of various backgrounds, disciplines, and faculty status self-selected to participate in two or three individual semistructured interviews using the same series of questions. Their responses shed light on how the participants reflect on learning or gain knowledge in a learning community.

Participants ranged in age from thirty-four to sixty-one and came from a variety of disciplines—one each from biology, cultural studies, philosophy, history, political science, psychology, and public policy, and three from English. They were diverse in faculty status (two doctoral students, three adjunct, two tenure-track, and three tenured faculty) and years of general teaching experience. Each participant had taught at least three years in learning communities, and some as many as ten years. The participants' individual ways of knowing, rooted in professional and personal experiences, were colored by disciplinary training but also shaped by collaborative experiences from across the university landscape.

Cross-Domain Learning in the AC Community of Practice

A requirement of learning community work is faculty collaboration. This collaboration is interdisciplinary and cross-domain, with participants who vary in age, experience, discipline, status level, theoretical outlook, and personal background. The common goal is the desire to collaborate intensely in order to improve undergraduate learning. AC faculty collaborate in teams of four to eight for the cohort-driven general education program, they pair up for interdisciplinary upper-level courses, and they work together outside class in intense planning meetings, shared governance activities, and active participation in student-centered issues and concerns. An inclusive faculty model underscores AC's commitment to broad-based expertise as librarians, student service professionals, instructional designers, graduate students, practitioners, and university administrators are invited to the table and into the fold.

Given the intense nature and the complex structure of interdisciplinary team-taught courses, it is impossible for individual AC faculty members to be conversant in all parts of an individual course, let alone contextualize the course within the larger integrated curriculum. Faculty also need to "create practice" in the soft areas of cross-domain faculty collaborative work, including how to contextualize and properly teach a particular concept from both one's own disciplinary perspective and the perspectives of their varied colleagues; divide and share complex tasks; work toward common goals; publicly address intellectual and interpersonal conflict; and collectively strive to improve the teaching process, approach to content, or interactions with students. In some of these areas, faculty have a deep level of experience in the "know how" of teaching in a cross-domain context; however, some faculty are beginners.

Three examples illustrate how situating diverse faculty in complex courses sets the stage for cross-domain collaborative learning:

- A tenured biologist and a doctoral student in cultural studies collaborate to teach When Cultures Collide, an upper-level literature, film, and Web-based course that investigates cultural representations of change through music, art, food, folklore, tradition, and social habits.

- The former AC associate dean, an expert in political communication, and a librarian team-teach Presidential Primary 2004, an experiential learning course that challenges students to analyze the intersection of presidential candidacies, media coverage, and how technology has forged changes in the political process.

- A team of five teaches Community of Learners, the first in a suite of four eight-credit cohort-based general education courses for freshmen that conveys credits for composition, communication, and computer science. It is taught jointly by a tenured English professor, an experienced contract instructor with a background in Appalachian studies, a tenured community psychologist, and two graduate students with backgrounds in philosophy.

These courses reflect the diversity of faculty backgrounds, experience, and expertise in AC as "a full member of a community of practice requires access to a wide range of ongoing activity, old-timers, and other members of the community; and to information, resources, and opportunities for participation" (Lave & Wenger, 1991, p. 100). Despite an impression of implied hierarchy within these courses, faculty collaborate on even footing because despite their external status, disciplinary background, or years of training, none can be expert in the entire course. For a course to work, collaboration is mandatory; for collaboration to work effectively, learning is required. In such a rich collaborative context, knowledge is socially constructed by communities of individuals, and meaning making is grounded in the context of relationships with others. Faculty are therefore motivated to think about thinking and reflect on their learning. They also become aware of, and attuned to, their colleagues' various ways of knowing. Acceptance of difference, coupled with a common appreciation for learning theory, helps faculty realize that new knowledge is ultimately a rich, continual process of give-and-take as reflected here by one instructor who conceptualizes her learning by stressing the importance of the team:

> I'm not sure of precisely the kinds of ways [AC helps me think differently about my teaching] because I think of it more in terms of the

team. I've learned more ways of how to talk about framing an issue in the class. I tap into the expertise of the team. I think the most dramatic learning lesson of working in the teams has to do with thinking about how different our epistemologies and cognitions are and those are obviously very intertwined.

Sustained collaboration across domains allows faculty to model concepts important to undergraduate learning: viewing problems from multiple perspectives, approaching and addressing difference, and engaging expert colleagues from diverse fields who offer themselves as learners, mentor each other, and, in the process, create new knowledge. In offering such an intellectually charged, integrative, and social learning environment, AC communicates high expectations of both faculty and students. The AC curricular model encourages faculty to learn to think like students again. As the college deemphasizes top-down communication of received knowledge from instructor to pupil, students are encouraged to be active participants in their learning by communicating and working with peers and faculty. Like faculty, students are given latitude and strong encouragement to make connections across boundaries, apply their learning in various contexts, and, by the very nature of nonclassroom learning, gain the perspective that comes from the primacy of real world experience.

On Not Knowing: Faculty as Novice and Learner

A cultural by-product of working in intense, collaborative work teams is that faculty learn the multiple, simultaneous roles of expert, teacher, learner, and novice. They do not simply take on these roles; they are constructed through interactions with peers as they learn to share expertise, pose new questions, and use storied examples to explain their perspective. They challenge colleagues' perceptions, negotiate conflict, and debate vigorously. In playing perhaps the trickiest role of all, that of novice, faculty trip, stumble, and shrug in frustration. Although it takes great courage to expose ignorance or admit confusion, novice thinking is quite useful in AC. The novices often question their partner (or the group) into rethinking fundamental assumptions about teaching and learning, as an AC instructor explains:

> Novices are naive. I don't think it's a deliberate thing. You can't possibly be moving towards expertise on everything so it's just somebody who is naive who hasn't been exposed to something yet. A novice is good to a teaching team because they ask a lot of questions that require you to rethink your assumptions and be explicit about

assumptions you're making. They also ask questions from a student perspective. Things they don't understand are things that students aren't going to understand, so they help you think about ways that you need to present material so that somebody hearing it for the first time can deal with it. They also get you to think. Sometimes there is new information that doesn't shake your world and then there are new ways of thinking about things that completely call into question values that you hold dear. They clue you in.

Playing multiple roles allows faculty to tap into other ways of knowing outside their field. These different ways of knowing serve as lenses that broaden each instructor's original area of expertise. Tapping into other ways of knowing can help one feel more confident as a newcomer. The curriculum, serving as a vehicle for learning, motivates faculty to share ideas and work together to solve the inevitable problems that arise in course design, teaching, or the facilitation of day-to-day activity. As faculty need to share "know how" in the successful creation and teaching of a AC course, they also need to learn how to appropriately share their "know what" in a way that is meaningful to lesser-knowing peers from other disciplines and widely divergent backgrounds. This intellectual stretching is not, however, an exercise in attempting to know all. Instead, it is an exercise in gaining perspective. Over time in AC, content experts move toward becoming context experts. Context experts are aware of their experiences enough to put those aside in order to be adaptable to the culture of the community:

> Even if you're a four-year-old novice, you still have experiences to bring to the table. When I'm a novice at something and I'm trying to be a good novice, or when I'm trying to be good at approaching material for the first time, I try to be aware of my similar experiences. Somebody who's aware of his or her experiences and is willing to put those aside in an open fashion in a group dynamic is slightly different because you have other responsibilities, not just to yourself but to others. So a good novice to a learning community will perform the actions of a learning community, which is to be an active participant but then be adaptable to the culture of the community.

This does not mean that faculty specialization ceases to be important; rather, in lieu of each instructor teaching his or her own course or topic within the context of the team, faculty collaborate, depend on each other, and teach together. "Shared participation is the stage on which the old and new, the known and the unknown, the established and the hopeful, act out their differences and discover their commonalities, manifest their fear of one another, and come to terms for their need for one another" (Lave & Wenger, 1991, p. 116). For a faculty member learning as nonexpert, it is important to have a flexibility to transfer and apply knowledge in multiple contexts. In short, they need to become conversant at integrating knowledge so as relate to students better. As one AC instructor reflects:

> Well, the efficacy of the generalist is that person can relate to students better. You're not so buried in your discipline that you can't pay attention to the students. Don't get me wrong. I know tons of people who have incredible depth in their discipline and who are very attentive to students. But I think when we become obsessed by the discipline, we miss so many other opportunities, and part of that is learning around the periphery, around the edges, learning to contextualize things. And I don't know of a field that hasn't become more interdisciplinary. In a lot of ways we live in a time that demands academics to know more. We may not acknowledge it but I think about the broad learning.

In a cross-domain collaborative community of practice, faculty are both encouraged and enabled to know more than their specific area. They need to know the ways in which it is understood and how others might experience their subject. Despite the general willingness to learn that most faculty have, the experience they gain in their colleagues' areas of expertise tends to vary from course to course. Newcomers to AC tend to rely on stored knowledge that is comfortable for them to express; veteran AC faculty take more chances and are open to new mentorship opportunities. One faculty member feels that long-term exposure in an intense group culture results in knowledge rubbing off over time:

> We [always] have newcomers but we never had anybody who's a complete novice. Newcomers tend to feel panicked, and feel like they actually are novices. A term that Anne Moore and Melinda Smith [pseudonyms] coined in talking about shared authority and collaboration is *co-mentorship*. It is so powerful. You may be the newcomer on the team and you may be a graduate student and you may be a novice in the course and what it means to integrate knowledge. You may be a novice as a teacher! But all of a sudden in topic X, you are *the* expert on that topic. And it may be a conflict resolution graduate student and so there's something about group collaboration that's very obvious to that person [who will] have insight and knowledge that nobody else has.

The term *co-mentorship* underscores a breakdown in status and helps to bring equality to each of the roles that faculty members play. Faculty become helpers, freely willing to assist their peers. They also become accustomed to out-of-field learning, reinforcing the notion that they can become comfortable learning across boundaries. Sustained communication, interaction, and negotiation become increasingly important to faculty expertise:

> There are all kinds of ways in which co-mentorship emerges in an integrative environment. I've yet to be on a team in which there wasn't real expertise demonstrated by somebody who would have been labeled a novice because of their relative inexperience in team work or in teaching in one of these courses. It's easier for me to think in terms of newcomers. We all remain novices to some extent, even veteran novices in certain areas, while we may gain expert status in some other areas. The co-mentorship thing is absolutely crucial to understanding what happens with these teams. And how that role reverses and reverses and reverses.

As AC faculty play myriad interdependent, overlapping, and shifting roles, they take on the key role of veteran novice. Faculty challenge each other, learn to ask basic questions, and demonstrate role flexibility. However, they do not become complacent in their role as novice; as the curriculum adapts and as student expectations and needs evolve, faculty become more practiced in the functioning of a collaborative learning culture that they as a group helped form.

Deep Experts and the Evolving Learning Conversation

One original goal of AC was to become a teaching incubator where disciplinary-based faculty would leave their department and join AC "on loan" for a semester or two. Communities of practice do not work for everyone, however. Some faculty returned to their department cynical about group work. Innovation did not diffuse, and the multiplier effect was blunted at the learning community doors. AC has also had talented faculty who resist the community of practice as passive observers, polarizers, or dominators. They are unable to adapt to the intellectual subtleties of knowledge integration. When certain faculty do not fit in, their resistance can sometimes add punch to a team in need of a spark of dissension—or the outlier faculty member can be a nuisance:

> Well, I don't do social contact. I have for years drawn a very strong boundary and it has to be *solely* with personal preferences. I *like* all the people. I enjoy collaborating with them professionally. But I find the AC system is too rigid. That things had to be negotiated and it had to be consensus of all seven people. Frankly I thought that was

bullshit. I understand the arguments about equity and I think they're nonsense. I find it extremely difficult to talk to people who just want to sit around all day and fondle something. You come up with a proposed reading and you spend three hours discussing it and you think you have a consensus and you get back and somebody sent an e-mail saying, "I found another reading." It just drove me nuts.

Deep experts are indispensable to learning communities; however, deep experts who are overly rooted in a particular domain struggle as they tend to be unpracticed at framing what they know in the context of other experts from other fields. They are unable to relate what they know in a manner that is knowable or learnable to a broadly educated audience of faculty peers. The following is an example from a faculty member with a background in cultural studies who collaborated with a biologist to teach When Cultures Collide:

> When I first taught When Cultures Collide, both of us were in the classroom together. We were friends before that, so we really had a sense for each other as people. We really had a high regard for each other, and that made it a lot easier. But it was still hard on some levels. You model conflict. You learn that your way isn't always necessarily right. You're forced into working out differences of opinion. My colleague would say something and I'd think, "God that's such a scientific point of view." So you have to figure out how to introduce your perspective without undercutting the other instructor whose point of view is just as valid.

Unless faculty are able to share what they know or express interest in learning from experts in other fields, their role in cross-domain collaboration will be diminished. Similarly, faculty who lack either expertise or a social context by which to communicate with peers from diverse knowledge areas, share existing knowledge, or gain new knowledge are ultimately less effective in helping students integrate their knowledge. Unless faculty have learned to embrace integration, it will be difficult for them to teach in a highly integrated fashion. Faculty need a community of peers in order to learn how to integrate knowledge from many fields. To be an integrator of diverse knowledge fields requires being an adept builder of bridges, and these bridges must be sturdy enough to cross diverse intellectual, interpersonal, and practical terrain yet flexible enough to support questioning, negotiation, and openness required of integrative learning:

> In terms of disciplinary background or fields of inquiry, I think lots of different people could teach well in Anonymous College as long as

they weren't completely wedded to one disciplinary perspective.
I think you need to have people who understand that knowledge is
constructed, the multiple perspectives, that multiple ways of knowing
are valid and certain people are unable to do that.

Knowledge integration, often elusive and difficult to achieve, is "making connections across disciplines" by "placing them in a larger context" (Boyer, 1990, pp. 18–19). It requires faculty to take great professional and personal risk as they regularly place themselves in uncomfortable positions of learning outside their original area of expertise. Knowledge integration is an outcome of faculty playing multiple simultaneous roles in the context of a rich cross-domain community of practice. Ironically it is optimally achieved when confidence, certainty, and intellectual heft are combined with the uncertainty, ambiguity, or confusion that comes with being a novice or learner.

Implications for Faculty Identity

Faculty who teach individual courses have responsibilities to students, their department, and the broader curriculum; cross-domain collaborative faculty also have responsibilities to one another. This mutual responsibility helps both reinforce and embolden the AC community of practice in which faculty embrace more robust conceptions of expertise with important implications for faculty identity. This new expertise is rooted in community that pushes faculty beyond the limitations of decontextualized deep knowledge. As faculty are better able to frame problems in their own area, they are also better equipped to communicate across disciplinary languages, and they become better and more knowledgeable instructors both inside and outside the AC community. As they gain knowledge and learn about others, they also learn about themselves, while gaining an improved tolerance for ambiguity and a better understanding of local and broader surroundings. The cross-domain collaborative learner has a rhetorical awareness that allows him or her to communicate complex ideas to a wide array of audiences in a wide variety of contexts. It is, in part, rhetorical awareness that helps faculty form rich communities of practice, freely share what they know, learn outside the domain of their expertise, and co-create knowledge.

For integrated undergraduate learning community programs like AC to flourish, faculty need the organizational latitude to collaborate across boundaries. To do so, they need to be rewarded for demonstrating how being exposed to other areas of inquiry can improve their own practice. In the fifteen years since the college's inception, one of the more pleasant surprises at AC has been how senior faculty have learned from graduate students or faculty at the beginning of their careers. This is due in large part to the generosity of more experienced faculty who are willing mentors and are open to being mentored by a junior faculty member or graduate student. In the end, faculty acculturated in this rich community-of-practice process and philosophy pass on the cultural baton to learning community students as well as the next generation of learning community faculty.

REFERENCES

Becher, T., & Trowler, P. (2001). *Academic tribes and territories: Intellectual enquiry and the culture of disciplines* (2nd ed.). London: Open University Press.

Berthoin Antal, A., Lenhardt, U., & Rosenbrock, R. (2001). Barriers to organizational learning. In M. Dierkes, A. Berthoin Antal, J. Child, & I. Nonaka (Eds.), *Handbook of organizational learning and knowledge* (pp. 865–885). New York: Oxford University Press.

Boyer, E. L. (1990). *Scholarship reconsidered: Priorities of the professoriate.* Princeton, NJ: Carnegie Foundation for the Advancement of Teaching.

Cox, M. D. (2004). Introduction to faculty learning communities. In M. D. Cox & L. Richlin (Eds.), *New directions for teaching and learning: No. 97. Building faculty learning communities* (pp. 5–23). San Francisco: Jossey-Bass.

Creamer, E. G. (2005). Insight from multiple disciplinary angles: A case study of an interdisciplinary research team. In E. G. Creamer & L. R. Lattuca (Eds.), *New directions for teaching and learning: No. 102. Advancing faculty learning through interdisciplinary collaboration* (pp. 37–44). San Francisco: Jossey-Bass.

Davenport, T. H., & Prusak, L. (1998). *Working knowledge: How organizations manage what they know.* Boston: Harvard Business School Press.

Dixon, N. M. (2000). *Common knowledge: How companies thrive by sharing what they know.* Boston: Harvard Business School Press.

Eckert, P., & McConnell-Ginet, S. (1992). Think practically and look locally: Language and gender as community-based practice. *Annual Review of Anthropology, 21,* 461–490.

Lave, J., & Wenger, E. C. (1991). *Situated learning: Legitimate peripheral participation.* Cambridge: Cambridge University Press.

Nonaka, I. (2008). *The knowledge creating company.* Boston: Harvard Business School Press.

Smith, B. L., Macgregor, J., Matthews, R., & Gabelnick, F. (2004). *Learning communities: Reforming undergraduate education.* San Francisco: Jossey Bass.

Tagg, J. (2003). *The learning paradigm college.* San Francisco: Jossey-Bass/Anker.

Tierney, W. G. (2008). *The impact of culture on organizational decision making: Theory and practice in higher education.* Sterling, VA: Stylus.

Wenger, E. C. (1998). *Communities of practice: Learning, meaning, and identity.* New York: Cambridge University Press.

Wenger, E. C., McDermott, R., & Snyder, W. M. (2002). *Cultivating communities of practice.* Boston: Harvard Business School Press.

Young, J. B. (2003). *How experts learn outside the domain of their expertise: An exploration of a faculty community of practice.* Fairfax, VA: George Mason University.

8

A COACHING-BASED FRAMEWORK FOR INDIVIDUAL CONSULTATIONS

Deandra Little, Michael S. Palmer, University of Virginia

Educational developers committed to promoting effective teaching and learning practices often make the same mistake we advise instructors to avoid: privileging content over process in individual consultations. We describe a process-oriented consultation model based on effective practices from the literature on individual consultations, coaching, learning, and motivation. Using this three-step model, educational developers can systematically create a collaborative environment that is nonjudgmental and nonprescriptive and draws on the client's capabilities, experiences, aspirations, and resourcefulness.

When Michael was on leave, Deandra consulted with a faculty member he had worked with extensively over the previous three years. During that time, Karen (not her real name) had gradually begun to incorporate student-centered teaching methods into her courses. That day's discussion of various ways to make her lectures more interactive seemed fairly straightforward; however, Karen's concluding remark suggested she valued it for more than just the ideas she left with: "I enjoy working with folks from your center. You ask good questions that help me see what is already there." It was clear that she was responding to the coaching-based framework we both use in individual consultations. Her remarks underscored what we have experienced with other faculty and graduate instructors: the process, as much as the content, matters in consultations. Often it can be difficult to find the right balance between the two. We frequently hear this concern echoed by other educational developers. Ironically those of us committed to promoting effective teaching and learning practices often find ourselves inadvertently making the same mistake we advise the instructors we work with to avoid: focusing on content delivery rather than on engagement and learning.

In an attempt to keep consultations process oriented and collaborative, in 2005 we adopted a three-step coaching framework that includes best practices from literature on instructional consultations, coaching, learning and motivation theory, question asking, and active listening. It organizes effective consultation strategies into a heuristic with three interrelated components: deep listening, asking powerful questions, and prompting action. We find that using this consultation framework reminds us of the importance of inclusion, relevance, and autonomy for motivation and learning (Svinicki, 2004; Theall, 2001). Moreover, it provides a language and systematic structure for consultations that is aligned with the literature on effective consultation (Brinko, 1993; Brinko & Menges, 1997; Gillespie, Hilsen, & Wadsworth, 2002; Knapper & Piccinin, 1999; Lewis & Lunde, 2001).

We became interested in professional coaching techniques because they emphasize interactions that are nonprescriptive, instructor centered, goal based, and action oriented. Coaching models focus on promoting professional or personal development through facilitated discussion (Costa & Garmston, 1994; Stober & Grant, 2006) and incorporate principles of knowledge construction and adult learning theory (Brookfield, 1986; Cranton, 2006). We also found basic metaphors for coaching that aptly described the educational developer's role in consultations. In consultations, developers help move or convey (Costa & Garmston, 1994) instructors from one point to another. Or, to use another metaphor, developers, like coaches, work as catalysts for change.

We use the coaching framework in our own consultations, our training of faculty and graduate student consultants, and a number of workshops for new and experienced educational developers. In these settings, coaching strategies have helped both consultant and instructor "see what is there" by reminding us to keep the focus trained on the individual, including his or her understanding of the issues, and readiness for and motivation to change.

Individual Consultations: Opportunities and Challenges

In spite of a good deal of variation in the conditions of educational development work—whether working alone or as part of a center or system, whether full or part time—individual consultations make up a large part of the workload. Depending on how the position is defined, educational developers may consult with faculty, graduate and professional students, administrators, and support staff, among others. The literature on instructional consultations suggests they are "the most promising way of fundamentally changing postsecondary teaching" (Brinko, 1997, p. vii) and "the best way to instill lasting commitment to and change in a faculty member's teaching" (Lewis & Lunde, 2001, p. iii). In short, individual consultations are at their core about learning and transformation—changing perspectives and practices to improve student learning, create opportunities for instructors to explore and further their own goals for teaching or professional development, and even, at times, help administrators anticipate and respond to changes in ways that promote the core institutional mission.

One way to think about the variety and complexity of educational development is to consider the specific tasks or roles involved in working with individual instructors. Lewis (2002) organizes the tasks into distinct categories: collecting and managing data, providing information and support, and serving as facilitators and sometimes even counselors. Clearly these tasks require a range of skills, including providing empathy and positive reinforcement, recognizing institutional support structures and cultures, identifying and summarizing the literature, and analyzing data and motivating change. For new developers and experienced faculty members alike, trying to manage these can seem overwhelming, particularly given that as a whole, developers "receive little systematic training for their role—an irony, because the lack of training in teaching for faculty is the very reason such consultation is needed in the first place" (Knapper & Piccinin, 1999, pp. 4–5).

Tiberius, Tipping, and Smith (1997) posit that developers can be effective outside their range of expertise by focusing on problem solving. Such a process-oriented framework can help beginning developers address teaching problems or scenarios new to them. One former graduate student consultant at our center explained that being trained to use the process-oriented framework changed the way she viewed the consultant's role: "My job is not to tell the instructor my ten ideas for how to improve his or her teaching. Rather, my job is to be a listener, to offer suggestions when asked for, but primarily, to help the instructor think, reflect, and decide for him- or herself how to improve teaching. This was hard to do at first, but ultimately, it was freeing."

More experienced developers face a related but different challenge: how to manage multiple roles while navigating the tension between knowledge of teaching and learning practices and the urge to provide solutions. For such developers, a coaching framework can be a useful cue to remain mindful of how our practices enact our intentions, to listen first, and to be aware of when and how we intervene during a consultation.

Deep Listening

Listening, specifically listening attentively and with empathy, is key to a successful consultation. This observation may seem self-evident, but the difficulty and value of deep listening can easily be underestimated. As Brinko (1997) notes, our reported behavior may differ greatly from our observed behavior in the consultation setting; we may think we are listening more and talking less than we actually do. Focused, empathetic listening can be difficult to sustain, yet it is often key to effective consultations. Garmston and Wellman (1999) describe several types of listening that can hinder collaboration and learning. Building on their work, we have found that categorizing different types of listening according to their focal point—the listener-developer, the problem, or the speaker-instructor—helps us consider whether our listening habits facilitate learning.

In the first category, listener- or self-focused listening, the consultant listens to the words but focuses only on what they mean to him or her. This may take any of the following forms: distracted listening, or pretending to listen while focused on other thoughts; autobiographical listening, or shifting the focus from speaker to listener; interruptive listening, or stopping the speaker impatiently to focus on the listener's ideas; and inquisitive listening, or listening with self-serving curiosity. We might, for example, find ourselves listening in a self-focused way when we ask questions about the content of a course because it overlaps with our own interests or when we interrupt to relate similar situations.

In the next category, what we term problem-focused listening, the listener pays close attention to the words being spoken but lacks an awareness of the context and is inattentive to the speaker's nonverbal cues. Examples include editorial listening and solution listening. Editorial listening is just that—playing editor to the speaker's words by interrupting to correct, revise, or finish the speaker's sentences. Often when we listen in this way, we mentally make judgments about the speaker or situation rather than paying attention to nonverbal cues or how the listener expresses his or her feelings or values. Another form of problem-focused listening, solution listening, can be a trap into which many of us fall in spite of our best intentions. As educational developers who want to help instructors solve their problems, we often begin to provide answers or offer advice without hearing the full scope of the problem or allowing the speaker to begin addressing answers on his or her own.

In daily interactions, we often move between types of listening depending on our mood, energy level, attachment to the topic or person, or the situation. There are times, for example, when solution listening is called for. For instance, if institutional policies are clearly involved, there may be only one possible answer. Similarly there are times when inquisitive or autobiographical listening allows us to connect with the speaker or begin to build rapport. In general, however, self- and problem-focused listening result in less effective consultations because they introduce digressions, shift the focus away from the speaker, and can create a didactic rather than a dialogic relationship.

In the coaching framework, the developer strives for the third category: speaker-focused or deep listening. We describe deep listening as a form of empathetic communication similar to that central to social work (Rhoedick, 2006) and other helping professions. Empathetic communication is more than just mirroring the speaker's words; it engages both affective and cognitive processes in an effort to see the world from the other person's perspective (Stober, 2006). Identifying the speaker's feelings and communicating an understanding of them helps reduce perceived threats and defensiveness, while creating an atmosphere conducive to behavior change (Rhoedick, 2006). Our experience using deep listening mirrors the findings of psychotherapists and coaches (Rogers, 1951; Stober, 2006) that empathetic listening builds trust, establishes rapport, and encourages reflective thought.

When we practice deep listening, we work to reside in the moment, focus intently on the instructor's verbal and nonverbal cues, and listen without jumping to conclusions. To maintain a focus on the instructor, we advise developers to try not to spend time contemplating whether the instructor is "right" or "wrong," focusing on the next question to ask, or thinking about how they would solve the instructor's problems. Instead, pay attention to what the speaker is communicating verbally and nonverbally, and consider which topics the instructor shows most enthusiasm about, which points he or she avoids, or how gestures or facial expressions reveal unspoken values or beliefs about teaching and learning. By occasionally summarizing and paraphrasing the instructor's emotions and ideas, developers can check comprehension and reflect back the instructor's feelings and values in their responses. One instructor described the value of being deeply listened to this way: "The consultation was immeasurably helpful. I especially appreciated how you listened to and paraphrased back my comments and let me figure things out by talking them through. . . . I gain so much when I am given the space to do that."

Deep listening requires becoming comfortable with the silences and pauses necessary for the speaker to talk it through. Purposefully extending the wait time in consultations, as in the classroom, models thoughtfulness and restraint while encouraging a higher level of critical response. Based on the research on productive wait time in classroom discussion (Rowe, 1972), we recommend pausing at least three to five seconds after asking a question and before responding to the instructor's comments. To avoid immediate responses, developers can examine their motives for speaking by briefly answering the following questions: Why am I offering a suggestion? To whom is this comment really directed? Who will benefit from it? In short, deep listening means listening attentively to the speaker with the intention to understand rather than to judge, react, or instantly solve the problem. Being mindful of our level of listening, stray thoughts, and motivations to speak can help keep the focus of the consultation on the instructor.

Asking Powerful Questions

Deep listening promotes feelings of trust and a safe, supportive atmosphere. However, empathetic listening and descriptive feedback alone do not add new ideas or provoke change (Border, 1997). Combining deep listening with a series of powerful, thought-provoking questions can help interrupt the rush to premature judgment or action and slow the pace to provide a space for reflection.

Questions lie at the heart of everything we do. They are "fundamental for gathering information, building and maintaining relationships, learning, thinking clearly, creatively, and critically, making requests, and initiating action" (Goldberg Adams, 2004, p. 2). Our actions and our understanding of self and others spring from our questions. Postman (1995) explains, "Everything we know has its origins in questions. Questions, we might say, are the principal intellectual instruments available to human beings" (p. 172). Powerful questions can alter subsequent thinking and behavior; however, some intellectual instruments are better suited for promoting critical thought and reflection than others.

In workshops about consultation techniques that we facilitate, we end a listening exercise by discussing the types of questions that arose during it. This conversation helps participants become more aware of the kinds of questions they ask. Did they ask for greater clarification or elaboration out of general curiosity, or because they were relating it to personal experiences? As developers ask questions during individual consultations, it is helpful to consider motives by mentally answering the following: What will the question accomplish? What is its purpose? Whose needs does it serve?

The first category, consultant-focused questions, springs from the same tendencies as self-focused listening: these questions are motivated by the consultant's autobiography or interests, and they interrupt or distract the speaker from his or her concerns. Solution-focused questions can have negative effects: leading the speaker toward a particular answer, provoking the speaker through a veiled challenge or implied judgment, or closing down thought by having only one or two possible answers. In consultation with an instructor struggling with student attendance, for instance, asking, "Do you take attendance?" implies a solution connected to this act. Because they focus primarily on information gathering or either-or thinking, consultant- and solution-focused questions are not often transformative.

We refer to the third category of instructor-focused questions, which includes questions focused on the speaker, as powerful questions. Powerful questions, such as those in Exhibits 8.1 and 8.2, ask the instructor to think about something to which she or he does not know the answer beforehand. In consultations, we find these types of questions often elicit such responses as "I don't know" or "I've never thought about that." Powerful, open-ended questions produce more significant learning (Brookfield & Preskill, 2009) and can lead to higher levels of engagement, thought, resourcefulness, and follow-through. They can benefit both developer and instructor by fostering curiosity, provoking thought, or invoking new possibilities or perspectives. Asking thoughtful questions can promote trust by demonstrating the developer's interest in the instructor's ideas and learning by allowing the instructor to think out loud.

Powerful questions allow the instructor to gather information, organize thoughts, clarify problems, discover novel possibilities, and unlock creativity. In short, they can "shake people out of their conventional thinking, deepen understanding, and help lead the way toward envisioning new possibilities" (Brookfield & Preskill, 2009, p. 127). Because questions by their very nature call for answers, they also initiate movement, propelling the instructor toward decisions and actions to meet short- and long-term goals. Powerful questions can clarify the situation, including the perceived and underlying issues, create possibilities, shift perspectives (Exhibit 8.1), and prompt future action (Exhibit 8.2).

Exhibit 8.1 Examples of Powerful Questions That Clarify and Create Possibility

QUESTIONS THAT CLARIFY

- What happened? What are the facts of the situation?
- What do you think is really going on? What's really at stake here?
- What would you like to see happen?

- What is working well? What is not?
- Which of your values are you honoring in this situation? Which are you not honoring?
- What is really important to you about this?
- Why does it matter to you?

QUESTIONS THAT CREATE POSSIBILITY

- What is another perspective you could have about this?
- What do you want to happen? What is really important to you about this?
- In what ways are you stuck? What would it take to get unstuck?
- What are potential risks? Benefits?
- What other options can you think of? Would you like to brainstorm ideas?

A consultation with John (not his real name) highlights the collaborative nature of this process. After several meetings revealed that John's attempts to redesign a course failed to move beyond the coverage model, Michael decided to take a new approach. Rather than telling John that his approach was less likely to produce significant learning experiences, he asked a question to elicit new possibilities: "What are the big questions underlying all this content that first excited you about the subject?" Reflecting on his own passion for the subject from a different perspective transformed John's understanding of course design. As a result, he reorganized his course around a series of big questions and let his goals, rather than his concerns about coverage, guide his decisions about content and assignments.

Prompting Action

The third component in the coaching-based framework focuses on one particular category of powerful questions: those that elicit commitments to future action. As a question-centered practice, coaching is grounded in forward-moving change: "Questions (including requests) initiate behavior or action, be it mental or physical. Questions focus and direct attention and energy" (Goldberg, 1998, p. 7). By being aware of the ways questions can initiate behavior or action, a developer can prompt instructors to take meaningful and significant action and discuss ways to follow through on them. Exhibit 8.2 offers suggested questions to prompt instructors to set realistic goals, identify what actions they will take when, and think about how they will assess whether they are meeting their goals.

Exhibit 8.2. Examples of Powerful Questions That Prompt Action

QUESTIONS THAT PROMPT GOAL SETTING

- What would you like to get out of this consultation? What questions about teaching are you trying to answer?
- What specifically are you going to do? When are you going to do it?
- What obstacles might you meet along the way? .
- What will be the hardest part for you in taking this action?
- What support do you need? How and when will you get this support?
- What first steps will you take?

QUESTIONS THAT PROMPT ASSESSMENT

- How will you know that you are making progress toward these goals?
- How will you measure success?
- How will you know this made a difference?
- How can I be of help to you? What other resources can I provide?

By encouraging goal setting and concrete actions, the final component of the coaching framework allows the instructor to define and initiate change and to determine how she or he will measure the effects of change. At this point in the consultation, offering additional resources, ideas, and a range of possible best practices applicable to the situation can help the instructor devise a plan of action. During a collaborative discussion, the instructor can select options based on his or her values, short- and long-term goals, energy, and time.

Keeping the end in mind can help developers guide the first part of the consultation as we help the instructor clarify short- and long-term goals with an eye toward translating these into specific actions. Consulting with Karen about improving the lecture, Deandra began with a clarifying question: "What do the teacher-student and student-student interactions currently look like in your lectures?" Next she asked Karen a question to elicit new possibilities: "What would these interactions look like in your ideal class?" Then together, they explored ways Karen might realize these goals ("What kinds of learning activities would lead to the types of change you are interested in?") and respond to challenges to those goals ("What if students resist being asked to take a more active role in class?"). Shifting focus, Deandra asked Karen which of these strategies best matched her goals and the course content; then they identified small, concrete steps in response to the question: "What is the first thing you plan to do to engage the students?" As a result, Karen left with specific ideas in mind. After the lecture, Karen assessed student engagement, reporting that "things went well. They [students] applauded at the end and there was a lot of good class discussion. I don't usually get applause until the last day [of the semester—an institutional tradition]."

The Role of Data Collection

Data management and analysis play an important role in the coaching-based framework. (For more on specific data collection methods, see Brinko & Menges, 1997; Gillespie et al., 2002; Lewis & Lunde, 2001.) When combined with data collected by the instructor or developer, powerful questions can engage the instructor in reflective practice, a marker of professional self-development (Brookfield, 1995; Schön, 1983) and transformative learning (Cranton, 2006). Because questions serve as engines of knowledge creation and the language of our questions helps structure reality, how we frame a question determines the kind of answers we receive. Powerful questions ask the instructor to examine the assumptions underlying his or her teaching, compare these assumptions with data the instructor or developer has collected, and commit to future actions that better align those beliefs and practices.

Using the framework also means providing and analyzing data in a value-neutral manner, avoiding praise or criticism. Discussing an in-class observation, for example, a developer might comment: "You asked five questions in the first ten minutes of class. Four of these questions asked students to recall information. One asked them to apply it to a novel situation." Developers can then nonjudgmentally ask the instructor to consider what the data reveal and what kinds of responses they warrant. In all cases, the wording matters: carefully formulated questions require the instructor to process information cognitively in different ways (Costa & Garmston, 1994). Questions that ask "Who? What? Where?" help clarify the situation by asking the instructor to gather and recall information, activities among the lower levels of Bloom's taxonomy (Krathwohl, 2002). Questions starting with, "What?" typically require more inference and analysis. And questions such as, "How do you think this would be different if . . .?" or, "What are you going to do?" ask the instructor to hypothesize, synthesize, or apply ideas in new ways. Because they imply the need to justify one's actions, questions beginning "Why did you . . . ?" are better avoided. Reframing "why" questions to ask, "What was your motivation to do X?" or "How did X accomplish your goals?" makes them more powerful. (For more examples of ways that question syntax can affect the cognitive processes of the instructor, see Cranton, 2006; Costa & Garmston, 1994; or Auerbach, 2006.)

Important Considerations

Occasionally instructional consultations touch on areas of personal and professional identity that threaten to cross the line between consulting and therapy. This is particularly true for the coaching framework because it relies on empathetic communication and a question-centered orientation, both hallmarks of counseling practice (Goldberg, 1998). As with any other consultation, developers should remain aware of and maintain professional boundaries, particularly if they do not have counseling training. If the consultation begins to take on a therapeutic quality, encourage the instructor to seek other resources.

Paying attention to the instructor's nonverbal or verbal cues can also reveal whether the instructor is comfortable with the method. Cultural, developmental, or personal differences may require different modes of interaction. In some cultures, for example, asking direct questions might be perceived as rude, or deep listening may be misinterpreted. The developmental stage of the instructor can also affect the consultation (Wergin, Mason, & Munson, 1976); novice instructors who have fewer strategies to call on may prefer that developers assume the role of expert rather than facilitator and may expect answers or quick tips and a less collaborative consultation.

In all cases, we recommend being explicit about the framework. We typically start a consultation by explaining that our consultations rely on open-ended questions and deep listening and that we see our roles as facilitators (Border, 1997). If the instructor expresses or demonstrates discomfort with the process after this explanation or at any point during the consultation, we shift to a different consultative style or allow the instructor to choose whether to continue (Brinko, 1997).

Conclusion

Taken together, deep listening, asking powerful questions, and prompting action enable us to act as agents of positive change during consultations, in alignment with the values and guidelines of our profession (Professional and Organizational Development Network in Higher Education, 2009). The empathetic quality of deep listening allows the developer to be receptive to different styles and approaches to teaching while respecting others' rights to hold values, attitudes, and opinions different from his or her own. The question-centered method and self-awareness it requires encourages instructor and developer reflective practice and can empower client action, based on the client's needs and motivations. Coaching allows developers to provide formative feedback to instructors in a nonjudgmental environment. In short, developers using coaching methods find themselves asking good questions that help the instructor unlock and act on what is already there.

REFERENCES

Auerbach, J. (2006). Cognitive coaching. In D. Stober & A. M. Grant (Eds.), *Evidence based coaching handbook* (pp. 103–128). Hoboken, NJ: Wiley.

Border, L. (1997). Identifying and assessing your consultation style. In K. T. Brinko & R. J. Menges (Eds.), *Practically speaking: A sourcebook for instructional consultants in higher education* (pp. 211–216). Stillwater, OK: New Forums Press.

Brinko, K. T. (1993). The practice of giving feedback to improve teaching: What is effective? *Journal of Higher Education, 64*(5), 574–593.

Brinko, K. T. (1997). The interactions of teaching improvement. In K. T. Brinko & R. J. Menges (Eds.), *Practically speaking: A sourcebook for instructional consultants in higher education* (pp. 3–8). Stillwater, OK: New Forums Press.

Brinko, K. T., & Menges, R. J. (Eds.). (1997). *Practically speaking: A sourcebook for instructional consultants in higher education.* Stillwater, OK: New Forums Press.

Brookfield, S. (1986). *Understanding and facilitating adult learning: A comprehensive analysis of principles and effective practices.* San Francisco: Jossey-Bass.

Brookfield, S. (1995). *Becoming a critically reflective teacher.* San Francisco: Jossey-Bass.

Brookfield, S., & Preskill, S. (2009). *Learning as a way of leading: Lessons from the struggle for social justice.* San Francisco: Jossey-Bass.

Costa, A. L., & Garmston, R. L. (1994). *Cognitive coaching: A foundation for Renaissance schools.* Norwood, MA: Christopher-Gordon.

Cranton, P. (2006). *Understanding and promoting transformative learning: A guide for educators of adults.* San Francisco: Jossey-Bass.

Garmston, R., & Wellman, B. (1999). *The adaptive school: A sourcebook for developing collaborative groups.* Norwood, MA: Christopher-Gordon.

Gillespie, K. H., Hilsen, L. R., & Wadsworth, E. C. (Eds.). (2002). *A guide to faculty development: Practical advice, examples, and resources.* San Francisco: Jossey-Bass/Anker.

Goldberg, M. C. (1998). *The art of questions: A guide to short-term question-centered therapy.* Hoboken, NJ: Wiley.

Goldberg Adams, M. C. (2004). Expert question asking: The engine of successful coaching. *Institute for Inquiring Leadership.* Retrieved from www .inquiryinc.com/knowledge/pdf/ExpertQuesAsking.pdf

Knapper, C., & Piccinin, S. (1999). Consulting about teaching: An overview. In C. Knapper & S. Piccinin (Eds.), *New directions for teaching and learning: No. 79. Using consultants to improve teaching* (pp. 3–8). San Francisco: Jossey-Bass.

Krathwohl, D. (2002). A revision of Bloom's taxonomy: An overview. *Theory into Practice, 41*(4), 212–218.

Lewis, K. G. (2002). The process of individual consultations. In K. H. Gillespie, L. R. Hilsen, & E. C. Wadsworth (Eds.), *A guide to faculty development: Practical advice, examples, and resources* (pp. 59–73). San Francisco: Jossey-Bass/Anker.

Lewis, K. G., & Lunde, J.T.P. (Eds.). (2001). *Face to face: A sourcebook of instructional consultation techniques for faculty/instructional developers.* Stillwater, OK: New Forums Press.

Postman, N. (1995). *The end of education.* New York: Vintage.

Professional and Organizational Development Network in Higher Education. (2009). *Ethical guidelines for educational developers.* Retrieved from www.podnetwork.org/ faculty_development/ethicalguidelines.htm

Rhoedick, S. (2006). *Using the helping process to strengthen our consultation skills.* Paper presented at the 31st annual meeting of the Professional and Organizational Development Network in Higher Education, Portland, OR.

Rogers, C. (1951). *Client-centered therapy: Its current practice, implications, and theory.* Boston: Houghton Mifflin.

Rowe, M. B. (1972). *Wait time and rewards as instructional variables: Their influence in language, logic, and fate control.* Paper presented at the National Association for Research in Science Teaching, Chicago. (ERIC Document Reproduction Service No. ED061103)

Schön, D. A. (1983). *The reflective practitioner: How professionals think in action.* New York: Basic Books.

Stober, D. R. (2006). Coaching from the humanistic perspective. In D. R. Stober & A. M. Grant (Eds.), *Evidence based coaching handbook* (pp. 17–50). Hoboken, NJ: Wiley.

Stober, D. R., & Grant, A. M. (Eds.). (2006). *Evidence based coaching handbook.* Hoboken, NJ: Wiley.

Svinicki, M. D. (2004). *Learning and motivation in the postsecondary classroom*. San Francisco: Jossey-Bass/Anker.

Theall, M. (2001). Thinking about motivation: Some issues for instructional consultants. In K. G. Lewis & J.T.P. Lunde (Eds.), *Face to face: A sourcebook of instructional consultation techniques for faculty/instructional developers* (pp. 77–91). Stillwater, OK: New Forums Press.

Tiberius, R., Tipping, J., & Smith, R. (1997). Developmental stages of an educational consultant: Theoretical perspective. In K. T. Brinko & R. J. Menges (Eds.), *Practically speaking: A sourcebook for instructional consultants in higher education* (pp. 217–221). Stillwater, OK: New Forums Press.

Wergin, J. F., Mason, J., & Munson, P. J. (1976). The practice of faculty development: An experience-derived model. *Journal of Higher Education, 47*(3), 289–308.

9

PROFESSIONAL
CONVERSATIONS

A REFLECTIVE FRAMEWORK FOR
COLLABORATIVE DEVELOPMENT

Peter Shaw, Bob Cole, Monterey Institute of
International Studies

A small team of faculty and faculty developers at the Monterey Institute of International Studies launched a professional development initiative by adapting Edge's (1992, 2002) framework of cooperative development into a model they labeled the professional conversation. This structured interaction involves a speaker exploring a topic of professional and personal significance through the facilitation of an understander. The details of the model are presented, along with heuristics for practicing the two roles. Assessment data indicate that the struggle to master the model is judged worthwhile for community building, professional development, and, unexpectedly, pedagogical practice.

Edge's (1992, 2002) cooperative development process was adapted, renamed the professional conversation, and implemented by a small team of faculty and faculty developers at the Monterey Institute of International Studies. We came quite rapidly to appreciate the powerful impact of the process and to see its value in resolving issues, including selecting the best of a number of possible research projects, solving assessment difficulties, and dealing with difficult students. From our reading of Edge and other sources, we expected positive outcomes. We were not prepared, however, for the direct and transformative transfer of the respect, empathy, sincerity, and humility generated in the professional conversation process to our teaching behaviors and interactions with colleagues.

Background

In order to situate our work, we first carefully distinguish professional conversation from other types of collegial interaction in the academy. Because professional conversation involves peers, it is not a form of mentoring, though we found value in comprehensive accounts of mentoring (Lottero-Perdue & Fifield, 2010; Neal & Peed-Neal, 2009), insightful case studies (Dailey-Hebert, Donnelli, & Mandernach, 2010), online tools (DiPietro et al., 2009), and team models (Gray & Birch, 2008). Similarly, we separate professional conversation from consulting (Jacobson, Wulff, Grooters, Edwards, & Freisem, 2009) and coaching (Blumberg, 2009; Glickman, 2002; Thomas, 1995; West & Staub, 2003). We view it as more like the small group-based professional development program that complemented the campus expedition approach of Carlson-Dakes and Pawley (2006), and the Spiritual Book Club, Breakfast for the Soul, and other initiatives (Qualters, Dolinsky, & Woodnick, 2009). Professional conversation shares the spirit of the seminar for exploring the inner landscape of teaching described by Jones (2005), where the sessions, with twelve to sixteen participants, were characterized by a "calm, slow" pace and an "open, honest and supportive" tone (p. 132).

In broader terms, ideas informing our general thinking around professional conversation come from a variety of sources; the notion of professional collaboration in education is, after all, nothing new. Particularly fundamental is the work of Rogers (1973) in establishing empathy as a necessary condition for facilitating personal development and its subsequent application (Rogers & Freiberg, 1994) to education. Freire (1970) describes liberation from the old models of education not as a gift or a self-achievement but as a mutual process. Education is a mutual, world-mediated process in which the participants become conscious of their incompletion. The transformation to a state of being more fully human is achieved by dialogics, which Freire presents as the essence of education and thereby the practice of freedom. Ferguson (1980) describes the process of personal transformation as developing the open and collaborative teacher who is fully attuned to all aspects of the educational context, having "a healthy level of self-esteem, little defensiveness, few ego needs" and being "willing to let go, to be wrong" (p. 293). Chomsky (2000) urges educators away from a "pedagogy of lies" toward (echoing Freire's phrase) a "pedagogy of hope." Gabriel (2005) calls for educational leaders to foster collaboration among teachers and describes how collaborators morph into partners in learning who are equally motivated to facilitate each other's development.

A second important background element in professional conversation is the significance of open dialogue and storytelling among educators. Postman (1995) discusses William James and his notion that there is nothing more human than telling the stories of our errors and how we have overcome them to reach new truths. Knowledge is not passed directly down, but is modified, refined, and enriched by conversation. Johannesen (1994) starts from Martin Buber's I-thou relationship, where participants in a dialogical interaction display a range of qualities from openheartedness and directness to a sense of responsibility for the other and a complete lack of interest in boosting their own ego. In discussing critique as signature pedagogy in the arts, Klebesadel and Kornetsky (2009) conclude that creating an effective learning community crucially involves developing a space featuring the free and open exchange of ideas. In each case—telling stories, exchanging ideas, offering critiques—the emphasis is on open sharing in order to understand and be understood.

Four Guiding Themes

In pursuit of our own understanding of such intentional collaboration within a learning community, four key themes emerged: empowerment, respect and empathy, humility, and mutuality.

Empowerment

The first theme is the liberating and empowering potential of professional conversations that we saw particularly in the work of bell hooks, who includes transcripts of conversations with educator and philosopher Ron Scapp in *Teaching Community* (2003). Scapp expresses the basic position in this way: "The practice of critical thinking requires that we all engage in some degree of critical evaluation of self and other. . . . It helps if we can engage individuals in ways that promote self-motivated interrogation rather than reactive response to outer challenge" (p. 107). hooks responds: "Our dialogues together stimulate us. They lead us back to the drawing board and help us strengthen ideas. We have continued to support each other as friends, as colleagues, crossing the boundaries of race, gender, and status. . . . You and I together strengthened the bonds of personal closeness and professional solidarity by always maintaining a space where we listen to one another when the other is raising critical questions" (pp. 111–112). It was essential for us to remember that such "self-motivated interrogation" can take place only in an appropriately safe and meaningful space.

Respect and Empathy

Given the conditions hooks described, the second theme to emerge in our work was the role of respect and empathy in professional interactions. Makau and Marty (2001) describe the need for empathetic and respectful exchanges in the academy as the basis for effective decision making and the quality of human life. Respectful listening and compassionate responses underlie constructive deliberation, leading to a definition of *dialogue* as "a process of communicating with (rather than at, to, or for) others and the sharing of a mutual commitment to hear and be heard" (p. 46). Philosopher Martha Nussbaum coined the phrase "narrative imagination" to characterize complex imaginative abilities required for moral interaction with others. Among these abilities is the capacity to imagine the experience of others so deeply that we are able to empathize with them and experience true compassion for them. She speaks of the capacity to "imagine what it is like" to be in someone else's place and the "ability to stand back and ask whether the person's own judgment has taken the full measure of what has happened" in any given set of circumstances (1997, p. 91). Our understanding of empathy was further informed by Pink's (2005) urging for a more right-brain approach to solving problems. He defines *empathy* as an instinctive, spontaneous act of putting oneself in another's position—"a stunning act of imaginative derring-do, the ultimate virtual reality—climbing into another's mind to experience the world from that person's perspective" (p. 159). We thus recognize that an effective participant in the professional conversation must combine empathy and respect with a strong dose of imagination.

Humility

Palmer (1993) discusses humility as both a classic spiritual virtue and an epistemological virtue. He defines *humility* as "the virtue that allows us to pay attention to 'the other'—be it student or subject—whose integrity and voice are so central to knowing and teaching in truth" (p. 108). Palmer acknowledges the clarity of Karl Deutsch's (1966) writing on humility as "an attitude towards facts and messages outside oneself . . . openness to experience as well as criticism . . . a sensitivity and responsiveness to the needs and desires of others" (p. 230). Palmer links humility with teaching in the following way: "It takes humility for a teacher to create and sustain silence, a silence in which we withhold the instant answer so the question can be really heard. The teacher who lacks humility will be unable to create a space for any voice except his or her own. . . . In humility we allow ourselves to know and be known in relationship, and in that allowing we draw our students into the community of truth" (Palmer, p. 109). We found this notion of humility important as a reminder to the understander (who is inspired by the call for empathetic imagination) of the constant need for restraint, self-monitoring, and the mindful suppression of advice and critical commentary.

Mutuality

Mutuality is at the heart of professional conversations. One of Fullan's (2008) six secrets of change is "connecting peers with purpose," which is described in educational terms as "social and intellectual glue" (p. 47) at a variety of levels: teachers learn from each other in professional learning communities; schools learn from each other; school districts learn from each other in "lateral capacity building." Although the informing and modifying of pedagogical practice was not the primary concern of our group, we describe how the flow of insight and energy into teaching practice was fairly immediate and had a high impact.

Edge's Cooperative Development

Edge's model is a proven framework of professional self-development through cooperation with colleagues. Edge (1992) makes the case that self-development cannot be done in isolation; rather, through cooperation with colleagues, we can understand more deeply our own experiences and ways of thinking. It is important, however, that our collaborators are not invested in changing or persuading us so that our thinking and practice more closely approximate theirs. The collaborator does not offer advice or recommendations. The aim is to help the colleague through the process, keeping the development in the speaker's own hands. Cooperative development is thus "a mixture of awareness-raising and disciplined cooperation" (Edge, 1992, p. 4). In refining the model, Edge (2002) characterizes the locus of the work as "the space between our common humanity and our individual, contextualized differences that constitutes the territory of our potential development as teachers. It is exactly this space that I want to explore. It's a big country" (p. 6).

The model involves two participants: the speaker and the understander. The former learns by speaking: that is, she selects an issue, problem, or challenge and sets out to learn more about it by putting together thoughts sufficiently coherent for someone else to understand them. The understander has a very constrained role within the discourse framework. Since the core of cooperative development is an agreement for the two to work together according to mutually agreed rules, the understander must follow the contract closely, deliberately making as much space as possible for the speaker by withholding his suggestions, advice, and commentary. The understander role, however, is not passive: it involves actively working to help the speaker to use this space creatively. Edge (2002) notes: "The collaborating colleague's entire purpose is to understand in a deep and rich sense . . . because of the growth that can arise from the experience from being understood" (p. 25).

To clarify the nature of cooperative development discourse, Edge outlines three macrophases—exploration, discovery, and action—each with three possible components (Table 9.1). The result is what Randall and Thornton (2001) call "nine ways of interacting which are important for encouraging and nurturing collaborative development" (p. 62), developing interpersonal skills and promoting empathetic and respectful attitudes and behaviors

Table 9.1 Cooperative Development Discourse Phases

Macrophase	Components	Characterization of Roles
Exploration	Attending	Making the speaker (S) feel well listened to; understander (U) pays close attention with nonjudgmental acceptance
	Reflecting	U is a "warm, human mirror," reflecting back meanings at all levels to check comprehension
	Focusing	U helps S review aspects of topic and identify the central issue
Discovery	Thematizing	U brings together two or more of S's ideas to see if they are related; S may or may not accept the connection
	Challenging	U asks S to reconcile two or more statements that seem to conflict
	Disclosing	Within S's frame of reference, U discloses his or her own experience as a point of comparison

(Continued)

Table 9.1 (*Continued*)

Action	Goal setting	U nudges S toward action by asking what goals might be set
	Trialing	U helps S describe a plan to reach the goal with clear and organized steps
	Planning	The most practical step, including arrangements for the next conversation

Our Process

The group whose work we describe here emerged from a chance conversation between two faculty members from different academic programs about talking less in class. After making contact with the campus faculty development group, the Teaching and Learning Collaborative, an informal group formed around discussions of Finkel's (2000) book, *Teaching with Your Mouth Shut*. There was great interest from other faculty once news spread that a group had formed to discuss learning- and student-centric teaching strategies. The original group of six expanded to a mixed group of students and faculty numbering more than twenty. This quickly proved to be unmanageable; we learned that scalability presents dynamic challenges to teaching and learning communities. With a smaller group, norms and expectations can be discussed and shared reasonably, while with the larger group, it became much more difficult to attend to everyone. The following semester we fell back to a purposefully small teaching and learning community to explore the Edge model, an approach that we had identified as fundamentally transformative given that it is based on a role-based discourse framework that requires participants to reframe professional development as purposeful reflection. This community consisted of three full-time faculty members and three faculty developers who also maintained regular teaching assignments.

Our amended version of the process (Table 9.2) has emerged directly from our own experiences. From recording, transcribing, and analyzing speaker-understander sessions, we found evidence for four phases rather than three. In particular, we found the need to identify the purpose of the first phase as acknowledging the speaker-understander space and launching the topic, with focusing moved into phase 2. In order to facilitate the role of the understander within our group, we modified Edge's original stages of cooperative development into four main phases, each representing a couple of possible moves. Our modifications reflect our shared

Table 9.2 The Professional Conversation Framework

Macrophase	Components	Characterization of Roles	Outcomes
1. Establishing mutual attention	Attending	Understander (U) and speaker (S) acknowledge roles and purpose in the conversation; S sees that U is listening with close attention and respect	S feels comfortable, respected, and listened to, and is willing to disclose issue
	Reflecting	S presents issue; U helps S to define limits of the topic under consideration	S and U are clear about the topic or nature of the issue
2. Mapping the topic	Focusing	U guides S to narrow and refine topic scope, identifying key elements	Topic boundaries are defined and key elements articulated for mutual reference
	Connecting and relating	Meaningful connections emerge for S	Relationships between key elements form
3. Exploring the topic	Reconciling	U presents points of perceived disconnect or vagueness; S resolves to achieve maximum clarity	Inconsistencies presented by S are addressed and resolved
	Speculating	U points to possible solutions or actions already mentioned; S contemplates	Solutions become visible and their potential is explored
4. Making a plan	Goal setting	S identifies desired outcomes; U seeks clarity and priority	S is satisfied with relevance of the goal and ready to consider next steps
	Planning action	S identifies actionable steps; U is encouraging	S gains confidence to undertake plan for action
	Appreciating	S and U reflect appreciatively	Both participants recognize the value of their roles in the cooperative development process

appreciation for the reinforcing and mutual nature of the speaker-understander relationship in jointly working through unexplored issues, dilemmas, and questions.

While Table 9.2 captures our group's experiences with Edge's original framework and our subsequent revisions, it is important to emphasize that the speaker-understander interaction is far from linear. At first the process may feel somewhat formulaic, but the fluid, intuitive nature of the process emerges through repeated practice and reflection. As we continued to discuss our own practice during our weekly meetings, other metaphors and visualizations (fluid layers, a spiral staircase, a garden walk, a tango) were suggested as a means of illustrating the dynamic, reflective pathways available within the revised framework. Figure 9.1 offers one such visualization, highlighting mutual attention as a constant while the understander intentionally helps the speaker to map, explore, and eventually plan action. To further enhance our ability to practice

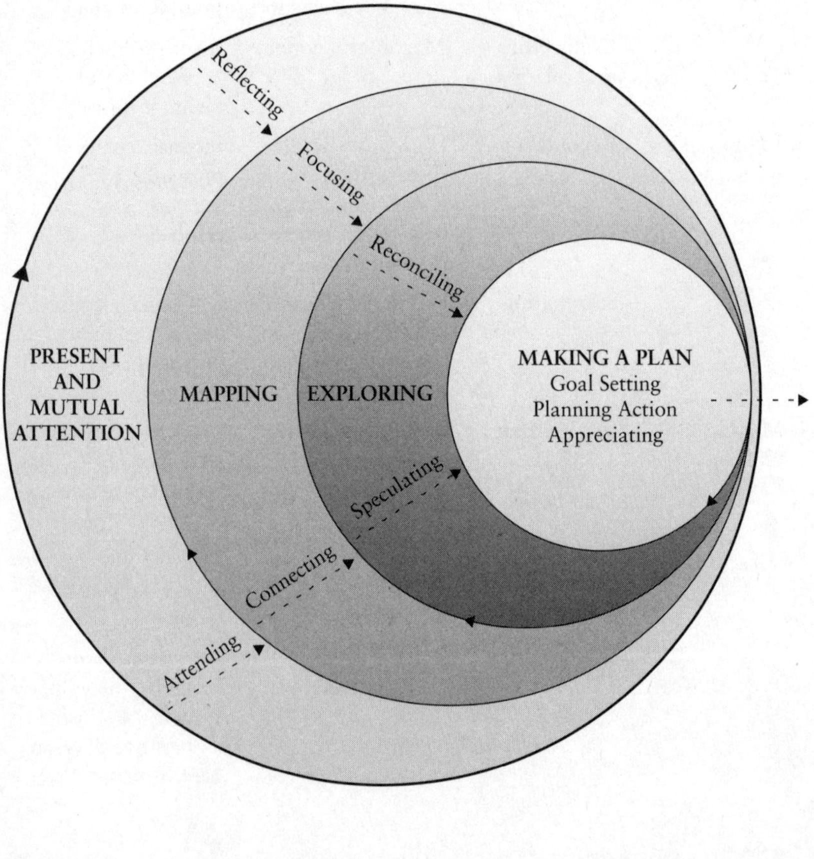

Figure 9.1   Visualization of the Emended Professional Conversation

the understander's role as a guide we created a heuristic (Table 9.3) for the understander to have available as a prompt.

To contextualize further the revised framework, we present an extract from a twenty-minute speaker-understander conversation between two faculty colleagues. In the first phase (attending, reflecting), the speaker, Maria (not her real name), talks about her "troubled writing class." She describes the challenge of her mixed-level class, articulating her frustrations with a group of higher-level students who, she feels, are taking advantage of her and not completing course assignments. In the second phase (focusing, relating), Maria's understander, Jake, prompts her to summarize how she has responded to the confusing behavior of this group of students. She explains that the issue is not simply a conflict of personalities or her lack of clarity in her course design or communication:

Table 9.3 The Understander's Quick Reference Guide

Macrophase	Component	Understander Cues
1. Presence and mutual attention	Attending	I am actively and supportively listening to you.
	Reflecting	If I understand you correctly, you think . . .
2. Mapping the topic	Focusing	What is the most important aspect? What do you want to concentrate on? What is your underlying assumption about this?
	Connecting and relating	Do you think there is a connection between A and B?
3. Exploring the topic	Reconciling	How does that fit with what you said about X?
	Speculating	I am wondering . . .
4. Making a plan	Goal setting	So what might be the takeaway here? What would it take to move forward?
	Planning action	So how might you go about this?
	Appreciating	I really appreciate your . . .

"This feels different in a way that I feel that I've been so clear in explaining what we're doing and in trying to be extraordinarily supportive to them, that I guess that's where I see the frustration, I'm confused as to why, why the expectations are so out of balance." As Maria and Jake continue, she considers how accommodating she should be given the conflicting attitudes, diverse learning needs, and preestablished course requirements. We join their interaction in phase 3 (exploring) as Jake helps Maria try to reconcile her frustration with the direct stance she has taken with these students:

Jake: So it's possible that some of this intense discomfort results from your being moved away from where you would normally be in your roles as a teacher, in the ways that you would behave, to another place that is not where you want to be?

Maria: Yeah—

Jake: That's not Maria the—

Maria: And it's not necessarily the type of, I mean I like the clarity. Sometimes I hear myself saying sentences to them and I'm like "hmm?" (laughter) Interesting because it's so clear and so direct and so just, there's no ambiguity in it.

Jake: Mm-hmm. (nodding)

Maria: That, yeah, I think that is what it is, but I don't necessarily think that that's the best teacher. I mean I don't think that's necessarily the best approach. I mean I—I don't know, that's up for debate but, um, yeah, I don't think it's necessarily how I see myself as a teacher.

Jake: But clearly there's something there in the complex Maria makeup (laughter) that is also the professional who is not going to be pushed around by rude people.

Maria: Yeah, I mean I, yeah. (nodding)

Jake: And you're obviously prepared to go there when it's necessary.

Maria: Mm-hmm, yeah, I think so, it's just hard to go there. (nervous laughter)

Jake: And would it, do you think it would ever get any easier? I mean if you were forced to go there again in the future?

As the conversation enters phase 4 (planning action), Maria expresses a sense of resolve in her flexible yet uncompromising approach to working with the difficult group of students. While she expresses discomfort in having to take on the role of rule enforcer, a renewed voice of confidence emerges: "You know, like, I'm here to work with you [the students] on these things but, one, you have to do my assignments as much as you would do another assignment and, two, you have to, you can't just also, at two in the morning just e-mail me." In this way, Maria takes away from the session a thoughtfully considered plan to resolve the classroom issue and, beyond that, has gained valuable insights for her practice.

Practicing the Roles

As we came to grips with the speaker-understander model and our emerging version of the professional conversation, we created a repertoire of procedures for rehearsing and becoming more comfortable with the roles:

- Pairs of participants rehearsing in private
- Pairs of participants rehearsing in public, with feedback from the other four
- The group watching and critiquing a recorded professional conversation
- The dummy understander: one participant is the speaker and one the understander, but the latter participates only when prompted by the four observers, who are thus making joint decisions about when and how to intervene
- Using a videorecorded conversation and pausing each time the understander was about to speak in order to predict what would be most appropriate to say
- Creating laminated cards with the sequence shown in Table 9.3, with the cards used by understanders as a heuristic reference

Conclusion

In a focus group format, participants discussed positive aspects of their experiences with the professional conversation framework and their reservations to date. They identified these aspects as the most prominent:

- The small scale was greatly valued in terms of both the size of the community (six) and the self-contained nature of the conversations.
- The small scale has proved a manageable way of meeting multiple goals and needs.

- The process itself has become a valuable outcome as we have learned to really listen to each other; this is always useful, even when there is no immediate outcome. Simply framing an issue fully leads to significant reflection, which leads to better understanding the world around us, to putting things into context through personal exploration.

- Because the model creates a space for exploration, there is both a mental transformation as we gain clarity in our thinking process and a personal transformation that combines heart and mind. Truly attending (including to oneself) is a difficult process, but one we have found helpful. "Being clear to myself" is a crucial outcome.

- As teachers, the model has led us away from focusing on ourselves to pedagogical developments and a much better connection with students. As one participant put it, "The ego goes away, leaving real communication with the students and with the material." This new humility leads to a more student-centered approach: "We can allow greater energy to flow through us rather than trying to capture it." This pedagogical infusion has been extended to our graduate teacher training programs, where students learn PC procedures as they develop their own reflective practice through a teaching practicum.

- The lack of hierarchy and the resulting depth of collegiality permit risk taking. Using Edge's phrase, which captures the excitement and the fear implicit in the first few experiences with the model, we found we could put ourselves on "the crumbling edge of our understanding."

- The group appreciated the symmetry between the understander role and our institutional approach to cross-cultural issues in development. That is, the value for the speaker (or client) is greater because no advice is given; rather, a fruitful process of reflection and planning is facilitated.

The group's reservations about the model centered initially on the discomfort of the somewhat therapeutic feel of the interaction. The process seemed overly personal (the phrase *touchy-feely* was used more than once), and we had to confront the challenge of locating the zone between the personal and the professional where the real work gets done. The second issue of concern was finding the appropriate means of dissemination, that is, broadening the project to become more inclusive. Because of the recognized value of the small scale, the next stages have been approached with caution. The original group continues to hone its practice and also work individually with interested colleagues. In short, the process of overcoming the initial awkwardness of the model and mastering the two roles was not easy, but it nevertheless has been judged worthwhile in terms of professional development, community building, and, somewhat unexpectedly, pedagogical practice.

REFERENCES

Blumberg, P. (2009). Practical tools to help faculty use learner-centered approaches. In L. B. Nilson & J. E. Miller (Eds.), *To improve the academy: Vol. 27. Resources for faculty, instructional, and organizational development* (pp. 111–134). San Francisco: Jossey-Bass.

Carlson-Dakes, C., & Pawley, A. (2006). Expeditionary learning: A low-risk, low-cost, high-impact professional development model. In S. Chadwick-Blossey & D. R. Robertson (Eds.), *To improve the academy: Vol. 24. Resources for faculty, instructional, and organizational development* (pp. 259–275). San Francisco: Jossey-Bass/Anker.

Chomsky, N. (2000). *Chomsky on miseducation.* Lanham, MD: Rowman & Littlefield.

Dailey-Hebert, A., Donnelli, E., & Mandernach, B. J. (2010). Access to success: A new mentoring model for women in academia. In L. B. Nilson & J. E. Miller (Eds.), *To improve the academy: Vol. 28. Resources for faculty, instructional, and organizational development* (pp. 327–340). San Francisco: Jossey-Bass.

Deutsch, K. (1966). *The nerves of government: Models of political communication and control.* New York: Free Press.

DiPietro, M., Ambrose, A., Bridges, M., Fay, A., Lovett, M., & Norman, M. (2009). Defeating the developer's dilemma: An online tool for individual consultations. In L. B. Nilson & J. E. Miller (Eds.), *To improve the academy: Vol. 27. Resources for faculty, instructional, and organizational development* (pp. 183–198). San Francisco: Jossey-Bass.

Edge, J. (1992). *Cooperative development.* Harlow, UK: Longman.

Edge, J. (2002). *Continuing cooperative development.* Ann Arbor: University of Michigan Press.

Ferguson, M. (1980). *The Aquarian conspiracy.* Los Angeles: Tarcher.

Finkel, D. (2000). *Teaching with your mouth shut.* Burlington, MA: Heinemann.

Freire, P. (1970). *Pedagogy of the oppressed.* New York: Continuum.

Fullan, M. (2008). *The six secrets of change.* San Francisco: Jossey-Bass.

Gabriel, J. G. (2005). *How to thrive as a teacher leader.* Alexandria, VA: Association for Supervision and Curriculum Development.

Glickman, C. (2002). *Leadership for learning: How to help teachers succeed.* Alexandria, VA: Association for Supervision and Curriculum Development.

Gray, T., & Birch, A. J. (2008). Team mentoring: An alternative way to mentor new faculty. In D. R. Robertson & L. B. Nilson (Eds.), *To improve the academy: Vol. 26. Resources for faculty, instructional, and organizational development* (pp. 230–241). San Francisco: Jossey-Bass.

hooks, b. (2003). *Teaching community: A pedagogy of hope.* New York: Routledge.

Jacobson, W., Wulff, D., Grooters, S., Edwards, O., & Freisem, K. (2009). Reported long-term value and effects of teaching center consultations. In L. B. Nilson & J. E. Miller (Eds.), *To improve the academy: Vol. 27. Resources for faculty, instructional, and organizational development* (pp. 223–246). San Francisco: Jossey-Bass.

Johannesen, R. (1994). *Ethics in human communication.* Prospect Heights, IL: Waveland Press.

Jones, L. F. (2005). Exploring the inner landscape of teaching: A program for faculty renewal. In S. Chadwick-Blossey & D. R. Robertson (Eds.), *To improve the academy: Vol. 23. Resources for faculty, instructional, and organizational development* (pp. 130–143). San Francisco: Jossey-Bass/ Anker.

Klebesadel, H., & Kornetsky, L. (2009). Critique as signature pedagogy in the arts. In R.A.R. Gurung, N. L. Chick, & A. Haynie (Eds.), *Exploring signature pedagogies: Approaches to teaching disciplinary habits of mind* (pp. 99–117). Sterling, VA: Stylus.

Lottero-Perdue, P. S., & Fifield, S. (2010). A conceptual framework for higher education faculty mentoring. In L. B. Nilson & J. E. Miller (Eds.), *To improve the academy: Vol. 28. Resources for faculty, instructional, and organizational development* (pp. 37–62). San Francisco: Jossey-Bass.

Makau, J., & Marty, D. (2001). *Cooperative argumentation.* Prospect Heights, IL: Waveland Press.

Neal, E., & Peed-Neal, I. (2009). Experiential lessons in the practice of faculty development. In L. B. Nilson & J. E. Miller (Eds.), *To improve the academy: Vol. 27. Resources for faculty, instructional, and organizational development* (pp. 14–31). San Francisco: Jossey-Bass.

Nussbaum, M. (1997). *Cultivating humanity: A classical defense of reform in higher education.* Cambridge, MA: Harvard University Press.

Palmer, P. (1993). *To know as we are known.* San Francisco: HarperSanFrancisco.

Pink, D. (2005). *A whole new mind*. New York: Penguin Books.

Postman, N. (1995). *The end of education*. New York: Vintage Books.

Qualters, D., Dolinsky, B., & Woodnick, M. (2009). Searching for meaning on college campuses: Creating programs to nurture the spirit. In L. B. Nilson & J. E. Miller (Eds.), *To improve the academy: Vol. 27. Resources for faculty, instructional, and organizational development* (pp. 166–179). San Francisco: Jossey-Bass.

Randall, M., & Thornton, B. (2001). *Advising and supporting teachers*. New York: Cambridge University Press.

Rogers, C. (1973). *Encounter groups*. New York: Penguin Books.

Rogers, C., & Freiberg, H. (1994). *Freedom to learn* (3rd ed.). New York: Macmillan.

Thomas, A. (1995). *Coaching for staff development*. Leicester, UK: British Psychological Society.

West, L., & Staub, F. (2003). *Content-focused coaching*. Burlington, MA: Heinemann.

10

INTERSECTING IDENTITIES AND THE WORK OF FACULTY DEVELOPMENT

Cerri A. Banks, Jonathan Iuzzini, Susan M. Pliner,
Hobart and William Smith Colleges

On increasingly diverse college campuses, faculty members look to faculty developers for support in facilitating difficult classroom dialogues and in handling challenging interactions around their students' identities and their own. We propose that faculty developers' work around issues of diversity, social justice, and inclusive excellence can be enhanced by developing a foundation in the theory of intersectionality, which engages the complexity of identity and the resulting power structures that inform institutions. We discuss this theoretical perspective and provide examples of faculty development initiatives that can be strengthened through the use of an intersectional lens.

What does it feel like to be a faculty member preparing to teach on a Monday or Tuesday, just as a racist incident that occurred on campus over the weekend has begun to gain attention? Suppose a noose was found hanging from a tree on campus, as was the case at the University of Maryland, California State University at Fullerton, Purdue University, and Columbia University in recent years (Jones, 2007). Perhaps a predominantly white fraternity hosted a party at which students dressed in blackface, or as slaves, or entered the party by crawling under a barbed-wire fence as part of a "crossing the border" theme (Jones, 2007).

Students are likely to arrive at class with a range of emotions about what they have heard or experienced. For students of any background who are passionate about the struggle for social justice, such incidents are deeply troubling and may evoke feelings of disappointment, fear, or anger. For students who have had less interaction with people different from themselves or whose attitudes lead them to minimize the power of such incidents, the reaction of their peers may seem to be blowing the event out of proportion, an overreaction. One explanation for the divergence in how such events are processed is that the acts themselves are not always intended to be offensive. Because the actors in these incidents may be focused on the ways in which their acts are humorous and ironic to themselves as a group, they may fail to think through the ways in which others could perceive their acts as hurtful, insensitive, offensive, and threatening. Students from across this spectrum will be looking for guidance from faculty about how to process these events, but many faculty members feel unprepared to discuss them.

In faculty development workshops, new faculty orientations, campus forums, and classroom observations, we have heard educators articulate their concerns about dealing with difficult conversations in their classrooms in a number of ways. These include feeling unprepared to answer unexpected questions, feeling disconnected from issues related to identity, feeling culturally different from students, and feeling worried that attention to these matters will result in less content being covered. In addition, at institutions that lack support for matters related to diversity, inclusive excellence, and social justice, faculty can feel isolated in their classrooms and apprehensive about reaching out to departmental colleagues for support. A successful faculty developer must be prepared to support professors in the work of acknowledging, facilitating, and at times confronting controversial topics in the classroom.

Historically, academic literature and faculty development practice has focused on classrooms, where the course content lends itself easily to discussions about difficult topics and faculty have chosen to engage with students in this way (Duncan-Andrade, 2008; Fox, 2001; Newman, 2007). For example, in a course on race, class, and gender, both students and faculty expect controversial conversations, heated debate, challenging questions, and collaborative inquiry related to identity and power. This is not always the case in a chemistry class. Yet controversy may arise not only from verbal interactions or course themes. Classroom practices—for example, group work, who gets called on in class and is therefore seen as knowledgeable, and decisions about class content—are always connected to who is in the classroom at any given time. Student and faculty relationships are always in flux based on the interactions that occur, making it inevitable that classroom challenges connected to identity will arise.

The Theory of Intersectionality

Dill and Zambrana (2009) described intersectionality as "an innovative and emerging field of study that provides a critical analytic lens to interrogate racial, ethnic, ability, age, sexuality, and gender disparities and to contest existing ways of looking at these structures of inequality, transforming knowledges as well as the social institutions in which they have found themselves" (p. 1). In other words, intersectionality examines identity and its relationship to power. It moves beyond individual examinations of difference and highlights institutional structures and the ways in which unequal power relationships are recreated and reinforced in everyday language, media, legal systems, and higher education (Banks, 2009; Howard, 1999). Intersectionality incorporates systemic reasons for inequality with a goal of institutional change.

Feminist scholars have outlined specific features that explain the usefulness of intersectionality (Brewer, 1999; Collins, 1998, 2000; Crenshaw, 1993; Dill & Zambrana, 2009). The following specific components of the theory relate directly to the work of faculty developers:

• Race, class, gender, sexuality, and other markers of identity are "simultaneous and overlapping spheres of oppression" that are important to daily life on both individual and systemic levels (Collins, 2000, p. 22). Thus, all of the features of identity that an individual holds are at play in every experience. For example, intersectionality recognizes that biological features (skin color) have social consequences (race). Individuals may share identities, but there are differences both among and between groups. In their work, faculty developers must recognize that societal norms like stereotypes are connected to identity and played out in college classrooms. They must acknowledge the social consequences of both privilege and oppression that faculty and students may face concurrently as a result of their multiple, intersecting identities (Kendall, 2006; Rothenberg, 2008). Understanding these points requires making opportunities for dialogue and reflection.

• Intersectionality employs "*both/and* rather than *either/or* categorizations" of identity and experience (Brewer, 1999, p. 33). Either-or categorizations force individuals to rank the significance of features of identity in any given experience. Both-and categorization is inclusive and recognizes that all aspects are significant. For example, a black woman and a white woman will both experience sexism. Yet the black woman cannot separate her struggle against racism from her struggle against sexism, while the white woman can make choices unburdened by her racial identity. Along these lines, it is important for faculty developers to recognize the multiple complexities to consider when consulting with faculty members on issues related to identity in the classroom. Faculty developers should understand that both-and categorization makes space for all features of identity to be included in conversations. This can help faculty understand the complexities of student lives and lead inclusive and expansive classroom discussions.

• Intersectionality "challenges traditional modes of knowledge production in the United States and provides an alternative model that combines advocacy, analysis, theorizing, and pedagogy" (Dill & Zambrana, 2009, p. 1). Such a multifaceted approach to pedagogy incorporates the idea that educational practices should move beyond traditional ways of teaching and learning. It posits that valuable knowledge originates from individuals and groups whose voices are often marginalized. Including these voices can create new dialogues and new outcomes. For example, faculty developers can help faculty understand that all students bring important knowledge into a classroom setting. This knowledge comes from many places and is not always connected to traditional understandings. Faculty must find ways to show that they value all student voices in order to facilitate equity in the classroom. Faculty developers must also understand, and be prepared to address in training and consultations, that because of both visible and presumed identity markers, faculty may be challenged by students regarding the validity of their authority and knowledge on a given topic or discipline.

• Intersectionality "reconstructs lived experiences, historical positioning, cultural perceptions, and social constructions" (Brewer, 1999, p. 33). It thus challenges assumed knowledge about the lives of others. For example, much of the knowledge about marginalized groups is steeped in stereotypes. Intersectionality challenges stereotypes by examining history, culture, and society, thereby providing a more expansive analysis that looks at social, political, and economic structures. Since institutional change requires sharing knowledge and power, such analysis fosters a broader way of seeing and understanding others and solving problems. Faculty developers can help faculty members recognize that an intersectional approach supplies them with a wider knowledge base and group of strategies to draw on when they face challenging issues in the classroom.

Faculty developers using an intersectional analysis will help alter the ways educators think about content, policy, and practice. Intersectionality teaches us that no students or faculty, in spite of shared identities, have the same lives or experiences; that systemic inequities and the resulting social, political, and economic power relationships inform our classrooms in complex and dynamic ways; and that the choices we make about managing controversial topics are as important to students' success as course content. In the next section, we show the connection among these four features of the theory of intersectionality and the practical work of faculty developers.

Intersectionality and Faculty Development: Connecting Theory to Practice

When considering specific practices that faculty developers can employ to help educators prepare to handle difficult discussions or interactions in the classroom, we build on the ideas put forth by Salazar, Norton, and Tuitt (2010), who stated, "Faculty developers are vital to interrupting the cycle of inequity. They can be catalysts for faculty to weave inclusive excellence into their practices" (p. 220). Many faculty are anxious or fearful about confronting hot topics and difficult interactions in their classrooms because they feel ill equipped to do so. They may also believe that the potential impact they could have as an individual would be limited.

Faculty developers can lead faculty members to a greater sense of competence and efficacy. One of the lessons we learn from an intersectional analysis is that the embodiment of a particular identity and the understanding of the systemic impact of that embodiment on oneself and others are two different conversations that stem from two different knowledge bases. The first relies on lived experience, and the second draws from learned theoretical understandings. Faculty developers cannot make assumptions about the values that a professor or student may hold and the reasons they do so. They must be prepared to help all faculty members across the range of identities gain the necessary academic knowledge, skills, and strategies to handle hot topics in the classroom. Faculty developers and faculty members must engage in an ongoing process of teaching and learning, with theory informing practice.

Scenarios

Here we present four scenarios generated by faculty and faculty developers. These examples come from workshops we have facilitated on difficult dialogues and classroom challenges and from classroom observations. For each example, we discuss how a faculty developer's approach to addressing the issue is broadened through an intersectional perspective.

SCENARIO 1

A faculty member in history reported that during a discussion of a radical film about race, the one black student in the class appeared to be the most reluctant of the students to discuss the issues in the film. One of the white students challenged him, essentially calling him racist, and the whole class became deeply uneasy and unsure how to proceed.

Intersectional analysis recognizes that structural inequality has individual consequences. Using this concept can help faculty developers support individual faculty members who are working to make structural changes that will have an impact on student learning. An intersectional analysis would help the professor in this situation recognize that the one black student who was uncomfortable speaking in class should not be expected to carry a special responsibility to do so simply because the discussion focuses on race. For this student, who carries the biological marker of race, a social consequence is the expectation that he should have an advanced understanding of race and that it is his responsibility to teach others who do not have that marker. An additional consequence is that if he does speak about race often, he runs the risk of being pigeonholed by the professor and students as the authority on race rather than as a student who is also there to learn about race. Other students in the classroom may believe that explaining race can be his only worthwhile contribution.

An intersectional analysis allows a faculty developer to help the faculty member challenge the typical inequitable dynamic in which white students sit silently through discussions about race. For example, the faculty developer could provide the faculty member with strategies like the use of a free-write, which would require all students to write a response to the question or incident that arose and then share that response in pairs, a small group, or the class as a whole. In addition, since many white students are reluctant to participate in conversations about race because they believe their lives are not connected to this issue, a professor can be encouraged to include a short assignment (for example, an interview with family members about their history, an autobiography in which they discuss their first experience with difference) to help students recognize that they all have knowledge to share about this topic. Thus, the faculty developer helps the faculty member hold all students accountable to participate fully in classroom discussions as they examine the power relationships at play.

SCENARIO 2

During a conversation about reproductive rights, a white student said, by way of arguing for the legal right to abortion, "Imagine how many Puerto Ricans there would be in Rochester if abortion was illegal." This student is relying on stereotypes about people of Puerto Rican descent to advocate for maintaining the legality of abortion. Interestingly, the student is making use of a racist ideology to support a "liberal" attitude toward this particular public policy that is most often represented as a matter of gender.

In this instance, we suggest an approach informed by the second and third tenets of intersectionality. A faculty developer could point out how stereotypical assumptions about multiple social identities (that is, social class, ethnicity, and women's reproductive rights) are at play and intertwined in this student's statement. He or she can remind the faculty member about the ways in which identities and inequalities are socially constructed and about how to interrupt the stereotypical assumptions at play. Employing both-and categorization allows a professor to combine advocacy and pedagogy by asking, "What does this discussion mean for a woman who is Puerto Rican?" and then facilitating a conversation that can create new knowledge. Brookfield and Preskill (2005) and Fox (2001) provide excellent ideas for facilitating civil conversations and classroom confrontations, including setting guidelines, making certain there are opportunities for all voices to be heard, using a range of different models for discussion, and helping faculty members make connections to their specific disciplines.

SCENARIO 3
In a midsemester evaluation of an introductory economics course, it became clear to the faculty developer that a group of male students who challenged the credibility, preparation, and credentials of the professor, a young white woman, did so based on sexist expectations.

This situation illustrates the third tenet of intersectionality. In traditionally male-dominated disciplines, it is not uncommon for female professors to face skepticism from young males who are used to knowledge in that discipline coming from men. Thus, the professor feels obligated to work harder to prove herself competent since the students' sexist expectations are likely to serve as a filter through which they evaluate her performance. In some cases, it may not occur to the professor that the source of the hostility is gender bias, and the faculty developer may have to point this out. The faculty developer could encourage her to expand her pedagogy, model for students how to challenge traditional ideas about how knowledge is made in that discipline, and provide a broader context for knowledge construction. For example, the faculty developer could suggest that the faculty member assign a reading that deals with sexism in the discipline, construct classroom activities where men and women discuss their experience with the discipline, and invite professionals who engage identity and economics to speak in class.

CHALLENGING ASSUMED KNOWLEDGE
In each of the scenarios, the fourth described feature of intersectionality is evident. Using intersectionality to reconstruct lived experiences and cultural perceptions will help a professor understand that students

arrive in the college classroom from a variety of backgrounds and with deeply ingrained cultural values and beliefs. An intersectional under- standing motivates the professor to be open to discussing a range of ideas, recognizing both the privilege and oppression from which a stu- dent may be speaking and their consequences. The reconstruction of historical positioning and social constructions also gives faculty devel- opers and faculty a wider range of strategies on which to draw in the classroom.

Programming for Intersectionality

Cook and Sorcinelli (2005) suggest that faculty developers can convey this information at an institutional level through a range of programming methods. We present here examples of specific programmatic initiatives that faculty developers can use to integrate this theory into their practice, taking into consideration the culture of their individual institutions.

TEACHING CONSULTATIONS

Much has been written about specific methods of individual instructional consultation in developing classroom practice (Brinko & Menges, 1997; Lewis & Lunde, 2001; Stanley & Ford, 2001). Given that consultations can be significant in helping faculty members enrich their pedagogy, we urge faculty developers to view them as an opportune time and safe envi- ronment in which to introduce an intersectional perspective. Developing ongoing relationships with faculty, observing classroom interaction, and discussing teaching philosophies are key elements of teaching consulta- tions. With feedback loops, faculty developers can identify problem areas and then work through them with faculty.

In our experience, faculty can make significant gains in inclusive teaching when faculty developers are prepared to conduct individual consultations, observations, and feedback using an intersectional approach. For exam- ple, faculty developers can observe and record gender dynamics in the classroom; pay attention to who speaks and who gets called on, and with what frequency, during class discussion; note how faculty members use language and the extent to which that language is inclusive; and look for ways that students use their identity-based privilege to manipulate class- room interactions.

FACULTY READING GROUPS

In one common practice of faculty developers, the faculty reading group, faculty typically read a common text and engage in discussion and analysis of that text with one another and the faculty developer in several meetings over a semester. Reading groups can serve as a catalyst for engaging faculty developers and faculty in construction of foundational knowledge about the principles of intersectionality, diversity, and the complexity of identity. Faculty developers can also guide faculty members immersed in an analysis of selective texts, such as bell hooks's teaching trilogy—*Teaching to Transgress* (1994), *Teaching Community* (2003), and *Teaching Critical Thinking* (2010)—or Paulo Freire's *Pedagogy of the Oppressed* (2007), to move beyond critical analysis to practical applications for teaching. In addition, the reading group format can illuminate for faculty developers and faculty their own intersecting identities and the subsequent impact those identities have on pedagogy, classroom dynamics, and in the work of faculty development.

Without the foundation of the intersectional approach, these reading groups would likely involve the faculty developer's leading faculty members in a discussion that relies almost exclusively on their personal experiences and disciplinary backgrounds. Certainly there is value in a discussion that stems from these sources of information, but we suggest that discussion of the same text can be deepened by asking critical questions that go beyond individual experiences to an analysis of systemic influences on beliefs and behavior. For example, in the third book in her teaching trilogy, hooks (2010) discusses the often isolating experience of being an African American woman in the predominantly white academy. In a related vein, she presents her framework for engaged pedagogy: "Because engaged pedagogy highlights the importance of independent thinking and each student finding his or her unique voice, this recognition is usually empowering for students. This is especially important for students who otherwise may not have felt that they were 'worthy,' that they had anything of value to contribute" (p. 21).

In a recent discussion of this book, a white woman faculty member commented that it was impossible for her to relate to hooks's experience as an African American and that this disconnect prevented her from understanding the utility of hooks's framework for engaged pedagogy. This faculty member's focus on the racial difference between her and hooks created an obstacle to being able to consider the identities they shared: both are women, and both are academics.

Using an intersectional approach, the faculty developer (also a white woman) facilitated the faculty member's understanding of embodying multiple identities and the impact of these on classroom dynamics. The developer began by modeling how she thought about hooks's framework: that being a woman and an academic enables her to understand certain important aspects of the text. Hearing hooks address race reminds her of the need to think about the ways identities intersect and make certain that this insight informs her practice. Including all aspects of identity (both-and categorization) helps her to find points of connection. After sharing her perspective with the group, the faculty developer then posed these questions: Have you had an experience, perhaps in a classroom or at a conference, where you felt disenfranchised in some way, where your voice was not being heard? How might we (perhaps unconsciously) be replicating this dynamic in our classrooms?

We maintain that a faculty developer whose work is informed by intersectionality is better equipped to pose these kinds of critical questions and facilitate faculty members' exploration of material that can enrich their teaching. We have found that the most successful conversations emerge from cross-disciplinary groups where ideas are shared, critiqued, and tested in a supportive, low-stakes environment.

Workshops

Faculty developers have long used workshops as opportunities to support the professional development of faculty members and socialize them to the campus culture and academic expectations. Workshops can also be used to create a visible institutional expectation for developing one's own understanding of diversity, as well as creating inclusive classrooms. These workshops should include discussions and resources that enable faculty to explore their own intersecting identities and what they mean for classroom practice (Ouellett, 2005).

Developing a workshop on dealing with difficult conversations is a useful tool. Asking faculty members to reflect on their own experiences as students or teachers and to describe scenarios they may have heard from colleagues provides a fertile source of material to establish foundational expectations and a springboard for further faculty development initiatives. Faculty developers can help faculty members brainstorm, critique, and examine a range of responses to these scenarios. For example, having faculty members participate in role plays can help them develop language and model behaviors that facilitate conversation about difficult topics. By working in groups led by the faculty developer, faculty members access the many ways in which complicated issues arise across disciplines and a multitude of perspectives about how to respond. Faculty can learn from the struggles of their colleagues and be encouraged by their success as they discuss what worked well, what did not, and why.

Developing relationships through these activities provides a support network that lasts well beyond the workshop and can be useful when these issues arise in the classroom or on campus. These workshops should take place on a regular basis at a time when faculty of all career stages can participate, so they can keep current on evolving pedagogical theory and practice related to identity and difference.

Conclusion

Intersectional analysis transforms knowledge in ways that challenge structures of inequality in institutions like higher education. The classroom is a space where interactions and relationships are as significant to student learning as course content is, although they are not always recognized as such. Intersectional analysis fosters different ways of knowing, pushes the boundaries of traditional pedagogical approaches to include radical critical thinking and analysis skills, and can lead to teaching that supports academic excellence and prepares students for life after college (Banks, 2009; Franklin, 2002).

The concept of intersectionality creates space for all features of identity to be included for critique, application, and analysis in practices associated with teaching and learning. It points to the systemic nature of identity markers and their connection to privilege, power, and dominance. Intersectionality examines how systemic relationships connected to identity reinforce inequitable power relationships that influence both institutions, like higher education, and individual lived experiences. These relationships are often the foundation for challenging classroom dynamics.

Handling hot topics and challenging interactions connected to identity, like the ones described at the start of this chapter, require knowledge and preparation. Faculty developers must learn the relevant theoretical concepts and then make the practical application of that theory visible. To that end, faculty developers must understand their own identities as intersectional and use this understanding to inform their work. They must teach faculty to engage in the same analysis. Faculty developers must be open to learning about and understanding the complexity of the lived experiences of others and how these inform teaching and learning. They cannot assume that identity markers alone make one qualified or not to engage intellectually with issues of difference. By using the concept of intersectionality, faculty developers can help educators across identity backgrounds and academic disciplines create and maintain classrooms that challenge inequitable power relations and are committed to inclusive excellence and student learning.

REFERENCES

Banks, C. A. (2009). *Black women undergraduates, cultural capital, and college success*. New York: Peter Lang.

Brewer, R. M. (1999). Theorizing race, class, and gender: The new scholarship of black feminist intellectuals and black women's labor. *Race, Class, and Gender, 6*(2), 29–47.

Brinko, K. T., & Menges, R. J. (Eds.). (1997). *Practically speaking: A sourcebook for instructional consultants in higher education*. Stillwater, OK: New Forums Press.

Brookfield, S. D., & Preskill, S. (2005). *Discussion as a way of teaching: Tools and techniques for democratic classrooms* (2nd ed.). San Francisco: Jossey-Bass.

Collins, P. H. (1998). *Fighting words: Black women and the search for justice*. Minneapolis: University of Minnesota Press.

Collins, P. H. (2000). *Black feminist thought: Knowledge, consciousness, and the politics of empowerment*. New York: Routledge.

Cook, C. E., & Sorcinelli, M. D. (2005). Building multiculturalism into teaching development programs. In M. Ouellett (Ed.), *Teaching inclusively: Resources for course, department, and institutional change in higher education* (pp. 74–83). Stillwater, OK: New Forums Press.

Crenshaw, K. (1993). Mapping the margins: Intersectionality, identity politics, and violence against women. *Stanford Law Review, 43*, 1241–1299.

Dill, B. T., & Zambrana, R. E. (2009). Critical thinking about inequality: An emerging lens. In B. T. Dill & R. E. Zambrana (Eds.), *Emerging intersections: Race, class, and gender in theory, policy, and practice* (pp. 1–21). New Brunswick, NJ: Rutgers University Press.

Duncan-Andrade, J. (2008). Teaching critical analysis of racial oppression. In M. Pollock (Ed.), *Everyday antiracism: Getting real about race in school* (pp. 156–160). New York: New Press.

Fox, H. (2001). *When race breaks out: Conversations about racism in college classrooms*. New York: Peter Lang.

Franklin, V. P. (2002). Introduction: Cultural capital and African American education. *Journal of African American History, 87*(2), 175–180.

Freire, P. (2007). *Pedagogy of the oppressed*. New York: Continuum.

hooks, b. (1994). *Teaching to transgress: Education as the practice of freedom*. New York: Routledge.

hooks, b. (2003). *Teaching community: A pedagogy of hope*. New York: Routledge.

hooks, b. (2010). *Teaching critical thinking: Practical wisdom*. New York: Routledge.

Howard, G. R. (1999). *We can't teach what we don't know: White teachers, multiracial schools*. New York: Teachers College Press.

Jones, V. E. (2007, December 5). "They're sitting right next to us": On college campuses, students continue to struggle with ethnic tensions and racist attitudes. *Boston Globe*. Retrieved from www.boston.com/lifestyle/articles/2007/12/05/theyre_sitting_right_next_to_us/

Kendall, F. E. (2006). *Understanding white privilege: Creating pathways to authentic relationships across race*. New York: Routledge.

Lewis, K. G., & Lunde, J.T.P. (Eds.). (2001). *Face to face: A sourcebook of individual consultation techniques for faculty/instructional developers*. Stillwater, OK: New Forums Press.

Newman, D. M. (2007). *Identities and inequalities: Exploring the intersections of race, class, gender, and sexuality*. New York: McGraw-Hill.

Ouellett, M. (Ed.). (2005). *Teaching inclusively: Resources for course, department and institutional change in higher education*. Stillwater, OK: New Forums Press.

Rothenberg, P. S. (Ed.). (2008). *White privilege: Essential readings on the other side of racism* (3rd ed.). New York: Worth.

Salazar, M. D., Norton, A. S., & Tuitt, F. A. (2010). Weaving promising practices for inclusive excellence into the higher education classroom. In L. B. Nilson & J. E. Miller (Eds.), *To improve the academy, Vol. 28. Resources for faculty, instructional, and organizational development* (pp. 208–226). San Francisco: Jossey-Bass.

Stanley, C. A., & Ford, T. F. (2001). Using climate assessment data to consult about multicultural teaching. In K. G. Lewis & J.T.P. Lunde (Eds.), *Face to face: A sourcebook of individual consultation techniques for faculty/instructional developers* (pp. 275–296). Stillwater, OK: New Forums Press.

ENRICHING OUR CAMPUS CONTEXTS

THE FIRST DAY OF CLASS

HOW SHOULD INSTRUCTORS USE CLASS TIME?

Sal Meyers, Simpson College

Brian C. Smith, Graceland University

Students and instructors rated first-day class satisfaction and completed scales assessing the time that instructors spent on introductions, course policies, procedures, and course content. For students, interest on or before the first day, and for faculty, excitement and confidence in students' abilities, strongly predicted satisfaction on the first day. Student and instructor satisfaction also were positively associated with time devoted to hows and whys, content, and introductions. Findings contradict previous empirical studies of student satisfaction but are consistent with faculty development recommendations.

Instructors are often advised to make sure the first day of class goes well (Clement, 2007; Lang, 2008) because the impressions students form on that day can have a lasting impact on satisfaction with the instructor, their motivation, and their performance throughout the semester (Wilson & Wilson, 2007). Given the assumption that what instructors do on the first day of class is important, what should instructors do?

One way to answer that question is to ask students what they consider to be most effective on the first day of class. Perlman and McCann (1999) asked students open-ended questions regarding the "most useful things a faculty member can do during a first class meeting" and the students' "pet peeves about what faculty do during a first class meeting" (p. 277). Students were most likely to list as useful activities reviewing the syllabus and course expectations; receiving information regarding assignments, exams, and grading; and having the instructor introduce himself or herself. Despite the tendency for published advice to recommend the use of icebreakers (McGlynn, 2001, offers an entire chapter on this topic), students more often listed icebreakers as a pet peeve than as something that works well. They also listed as pet peeves poor use of class time (for example, including noncrucial information and reading the syllabus aloud) and the instructor's beginning to teach course content.

Based on what students said they liked and disliked in Perlman and McCann's (1999) study and a replication by Henslee, Burgess, and Buskist (2006), Wilson and Wilson (2007) randomly assigned students to a positive or a negative first day of class. Students in the positive first-day-of-class condition left early after viewing a fifteen-minute video of the professor reviewing the syllabus in a friendly manner. Students assigned to the negative first-day-of-class condition viewed a video of the professor reviewing the same syllabus but without any emotional tone, then learned course content by watching a film and received a homework assignment about the film. Wilson and Wilson found not only that the students with the positive first-day experience rated the course and professor more positively than students with the negative first-day experience, but also that those students reported greater motivation and received better course grades at the end of the semester.

Based on the findings of these three studies (Henslee et al., 2006; Perlman & McCann, 1999; Wilson & Wilson, 2007), an instructor deciding what to do on the first day of class would likely opt to review the syllabus in a friendly manner, avoid icebreakers and introductions, avoid teaching course content, and let class out early. In contrast, advice from faculty developers suggests using icebreakers and introductions and teaching some course content, or at least having a meaningful discussion of the course objectives (Davis, 2009; Lang, 2008; McGlynn, 2001; McKeachie & Svinicki, 2006; Nilson, 2003).

The Student and Faculty Studies

The studies we present here seek to determine whether the advice of faculty developers or the advice based on student preferences is associated with greater satisfaction with the first day of class. The first two studies focus on student perceptions and the third one on instructor perceptions. Because people are often not able to accurately describe the true causes of their behavior (Nisbett & Bellows, 1977), rather than asking people to identify the things that increase their satisfaction with the first day of class, we asked participants to report how much time the instructor spent on specific activities and then to report how satisfied they were with the first day of class overall.

Study 1

To examine which instructor behaviors are associated with a good first day of class, we asked students to indicate what happened on the first day of class and report their satisfaction with that first day.

METHOD

On the second day of the semester, students at a small midwestern liberal arts college were invited by e-mail to complete an anonymous online questionnaire about the first day of class in one of their courses. In order to increase the variability of students' responses, students were randomly assigned to complete the survey about a course that was the best, the worst, or the most recent of the various first days of class they had attended that spring.

The 164 respondents consisted of 37 men, 126 women, and 1 person who did not indicate gender. Respondents were fairly equally distributed across year in college: 23.8 percent were first-year students, 23.8 percent were sophomores, 30.5 percent were juniors, and 22.0 percent were seniors. The mean age of the respondents was 20.14 years (SD = 2.51).

Students indicated how much time the instructor spent on introductions, explaining how and why the course would be taught the way it would, course policies, and course content. Respondents were asked, "How much time did the instructor spend on" each item on a scale from 1 (no time) to 9 (a great deal of time). Time spent on introductions was assessed with a five-item measure that had adequate internal reliability (Cronbach's alpha = .79). The five items were introducing himself or herself, having students meet each other, starting to learn students' names, having students provide information about themselves in writing, and having students provide information about themselves in an activity or discussion. Time spent explaining the hows and whys of the course was assessed with a five-item measure that had adequate internal reliability (Cronbach's alpha = .85). These five items were discussing course objectives, discussing how the course would be taught, discussing why the course would be taught that way, discussing why the course material was important to learn, and indicating how to study for the course. Time spent on course policies was assessed with a single item: "Reviewing course rules and policies (for example, penalties for late work and academic honesty)." The last measure was a single item asking about time spent on "teaching course content."

Students' interest in taking the course was assessed with a three-item measure that demonstrated adequate internal reliability (Cronbach's alpha = .73). Participants were asked to rate the extent to which "interest in the topic" and "interest in taking a class from this instructor" influenced their decision to take the course on a scale from 1 (not at all) to 7 (strongly influenced). Participants were also asked to indicate how motivated they were to learn in this class on a scale from 1 (not at all motivated) to 7 (extremely motivated).

Students indicated their satisfaction with the first day of class by indicating the extent to which they agreed with each of nine items on a scale from 1 (strongly disagree) to 9 (strongly agree). These evaluative items included statements such as the following: "Overall I am satisfied with my experience during the first day of this class," "I have a good feeling about this instructor," and "The instructor offered rich and substantial course content on the first day." The internal reliability of this measure was strong (Cronbach's alpha = .95).

RESULTS

Students selected a wide variety of different courses to describe and evaluate. The courses were fairly evenly spread across first year (38.4 percent), sophomore (34.1 percent), and upper level (27.4 percent). When asked whether they had taken the course to fill one or more requirements, 43.4 percent indicated they took the course to fill a general education requirement, 19.4 percent indicated they took it for a minor, and 56.1 percent reported that they took it for a major (these numbers sum to more than 100 because a course could fill both a general education requirement and the requirement for a major or minor). Students' reports of approximate class size indicated that 27.6 percent of the courses were small (five to fifteen people), 53.4 percent were medium (twenty to thirty people), and 19 percent were large (thirty-five or more people). Consistent with the gender balance of the faculty as a whole, more students selected a course taught by a man (59.8 percent) than a woman (40.2 percent).

The more interested that students were in taking a course, the more satisfied they were with how the first day of that course went. In fact, as can be seen in Table 11.1, student interest was the variable most strongly correlated with student satisfaction.

Instructors' use of time was also related to students' satisfaction with the first day of the course. Greater student satisfaction was associated with the instructor's spending more time on the hows and whys of the course, course content, and introductions. Time spent reviewing rules and policies was not related to student satisfaction. Contrary to the claim that having class meet for the entire time is a mistake (Wilson & Wilson, 2007), the proportion of the possible class time that the course met on the first day was also not related to student satisfaction. Having class

Table 11.1 Study 1: Intercorrelations for Student Satisfaction with the First Day of Class, Student Interest in the Course, and How the Instructor Used Time on the First Day

	SI	THW	TI	TC	TRP	PCM
Student satisfaction with the first day of class	.62***	.47***	.18*	.25**	.10	.04
Predictor variable						
Student Interest (SI)	—	.21**	.05	.16*	−.02	.09
Time on Hows and Whys (THW)		—	.42***	.17*	.47***	−.004
Time on Introductions (TI)			—	.04	.30***	.08
Time Teaching Content (TC)				—	.05	.29***
Time on Rules and Policies (TRP)					—	.07
Proportion of Possible Time Class Met (PCM)						

Note: ***$p < .001$; **$p < .01$; *$p < .05$.

meet for most or all of the class period on the first day appears to be the norm at this small liberal arts college: on average, courses met for 81 percent of the possible class time, and half of the courses met for at least 91 percent of the possible time.

Given that four variables were related to student satisfaction, we used regressions to determine which of these variables are related to student satisfaction when controlling for the others. We conducted a stepwise regression using student satisfaction as the dependent variable, and as predictor variables, we used the four ways instructors spent time on the first day and the proportion of time that classes met. Student interest in the course and the amount of time the instructor spent on the hows and whys of the course contributed to the prediction of student satisfaction even when controlling for the other variables. Together student interest in the course and time spent on hows and whys account for 50.1 percent of the variance in student satisfaction with the first day of class: $F(2, 161) = 80.87, p < .001$.

DISCUSSION
The more time the instructor spent discussing the hows and whys of the course, the greater was the students' satisfaction with the first day. This result complements Bain's (2004) finding that the best college teachers

plan their courses by first focusing on the big questions—the overall purpose of the course. Of the thirteen sets of questions that Bain identifies to guide instructors through the process of planning a course, all but one include the word *how*.

Student interest in the course is also a significant predictor of increased student satisfaction with the first day of class. This finding is consistent with the argument that students' prior interest in the course has important consequences for their evaluations of the first day of class; however, it is also consistent with the argument that a strong first day of class increases student interest in the course.

Study 2

Because all the data in study 1 were collected simultaneously, we have no way of knowing whether students' interest in the course reflected their prior interest or whether their interest was influenced by the activities on that first day. We therefore conducted a longitudinal study in which students reported their interest in the course before the first day of class and then completed a survey similar to that in study 1 just after the first day of class.

METHOD

One week prior to the start of the semester, students at two small midwestern colleges were invited to participate in a survey of their interest in each of the classes for which they were registered. After the first day of class, these same students were invited to complete a survey about the first day of class in one of their courses as was done in study 1. Forty-one students (eight men and thirty-three women) completed both surveys.

Students were asked to rate their courses on the following three items on a scale from 1 (strongly disagree) to 7 (strongly agree): (1) "I am interested in the topic of this course," (2) "I want to learn the content taught in this course," and (3) "I am looking forward to taking this course." The items were highly correlated with each other and thus were combined into two overall interest scores: one completed before the first day of class and one completed after the first day of class. The measure showed strong internal reliability at both times (alpha = .92 before the first day of class, alpha = .90 after the first day of class).

Students indicated their satisfaction with the first day of class on the same scale used in study 1. They noted how time was spent on the first day using the same measures as those in study 1 except for the measure used to assess time spent on introductions. The two items from study 1 that asked about time spent having students provide information about themselves were combined, and an additional item asking about time spent on icebreakers was added.

RESULTS AND DISCUSSION

Consistent with study 1, we found that the more interested students were in taking a course, the more satisfied they were with the first day of the course. As can be seen in Table 11.2, this is true both when student interest is measured before the first day of class and after the first day. The strength of the correlation between interest and satisfaction is stronger when interest is measured after the first day than when interest is measured before the first day ($t(38) = 2.25$, $p < .05$). A stronger correlation between interest and satisfaction after the first day of class than before it indicates that interest levels after the first day are better predictors of satisfaction; however, it does not mean that interest in the course was greater after the first day than before it. In fact, the average level of student interest

Table 11.2 Study 2: Intercorrelations for Student Satisfaction with the First Day of Class, Student Interest in the Course, and How the Instructor Used Time on the First Day

	SI-1	SI-2	THW	TI	TC	TRP	PCM
Student satisfaction with the first day	.56***	.77***	.39**	.23	.36*	.18	−.10
Student interest prior to the first day (SI-1)		.60***	.23	.07	.09	.13	−.21
Predictor variable							
Student Interest After First Day (SI-2)			.26+	.041	.19	.10	−.18
Time on Hows and Whys (THW)				.35*	.30°	.66***	−.21
Time on Introductions (TI)					−.23	.13	.02
Time Teaching Content (TC)						.10	.25
Time on Rules and Policies (TRP)							−.22
Proportion of Possible Time Class Met (PCM)							

Note: ***$p < .001$; **$p < .01$; *$p < .05$; + $p = .052$.

was the same before the first day ($M = 5.83$, $SD = 1.33$) compared to after the first day ($M = 5.71$, $SD = 1.27$), $t(40)=.67$, *ns*.

These results suggest that student interest is more likely a cause of student satisfaction on the first day than an effect of it. Even when student interest is measured before the first day of class, this interest predicts student satisfaction with that day. This relationship between student interest and student satisfaction can thus not be a function of instructor behaviors' increasing student interest. This should not be interpreted to mean that nothing the instructor does can change student interest; it simply means that student interest, independent of anything the faculty member does, is a good predictor of student satisfaction on the first day of class.

Instructors' use of time predicted students' satisfaction with the first day of the course (Table 11.2). Consistent with the findings of study 1, greater student satisfaction was associated with the instructor spending more time on the hows and whys of the course and more time on course content. Also consistent with study 1, time spent reviewing the rules and policies of the course was not related to student satisfaction.

As in study 1, we conducted a stepwise regression using student satisfaction as the dependent variable and student interest, the four ways instructors spent time on the first day, and the proportion of time that classes met as possible predictor variables. In this analysis, we used the measurement of student interest done prior to the first day of class so that we could be sure that none of the other variables had a causal influence on student interest. Whereas in study 1 we found that student interest and time spent on hows and whys contributed to the prediction of student satisfaction, in study 2 we found that student interest, time spent teaching course content, and time spent on introductions significantly predicted student satisfaction over and above the other variables in the equation. Together these three variables (interest, content, and introductions) accounted for 48.5 percent of the variance in student satisfaction with the first day of class: $F(3, 37) = 11.61$, $p < .001$.

The discrepancy between the predictors that entered the regression equations in study 1 versus study 2 may be a result of minor differences in the correlation coefficients calculated in the two studies. The more important finding is that instructor behaviors predict student satisfaction over and above student interest. All three instructor behaviors are correlated to student satisfaction at about the same level (in the low 0.3 range). Furthermore, the amounts of time spent on those behaviors tend to be correlated with each other at about the same level; thus, instructors who spend time on hows and whys also tend to spend time teaching content and doing introductions.

Study 3

Another way to examine which instructor behaviors are associated with a good first day of class is to ask instructors themselves. As we did with the students, rather than asking instructors to indicate which things they think are particularly effective, we asked them to describe what they did on the first day of a specific class and then to report how well they thought that particular class went.

METHOD

On the second day of the semester, instructors at two small midwestern colleges were invited to complete a survey about the first day of class in one of their courses. To increase the variability of the quality of the courses, instructors were randomly assigned to consider the best first day of class that semester or the worst first day. The survey was completed by eighty-four instructors (forty-four men and forty women) who varied in terms of faculty rank: 15.5 percent were instructors, 39.3 percent were assistant professors, 14.3 percent were associate professors, and 31.0 percent were full professors. The courses they taught were roughly the same size as those described by students in the previous studies: 34.5 percent had around five to fifteen students, 40.4 percent had twenty to thirty students, and 25.0 percent had thirty-five or more students. Most of the courses were taught as a requirement for a major or minor (78.6 percent), but almost half filled a general education requirement (46.4 percent).

Instructors were asked to indicate their excitement about teaching the course on a scale from 1 (not at all excited) to 7 (extremely excited). They were also asked to rate the extent to which they agreed with the statement, "I feel confident in my students' ability to do well in this class," on a scale from 1 (strongly disagree) to 7 (strongly agree).

Instructors rated their satisfaction with the first day of class on a nine-item scale similar to that completed by students in studies 1 and 2 (Cronbach's alpha = .86). Instructors rated how much time they spent on introductions, course policies, explaining how and why the course would be taught the way it would, and course content using the same measures as described in study 2.

RESULTS AND DISCUSSION

Instructors' satisfaction with the first day of class was strongly related to their excitement about teaching the class and confidence in their students' abilities (Table 11.3). The more excited instructors were about teaching

Table 11.3 Study 3: Intercorrelations for Instructor Satisfaction with the First Day of Class, Instructor Excitement in the Course, Instructor Confidence in Students, and How the Instructor Used Time on the First Day

	IEC	ICS	THW	TI	TC	TRP	PCM
Instructor satisfaction with the first day	.63***	.67***	.28*	.34**	.25*	.03	.37***
Predictor variable							
Instructor Excitement About the Course (IEC)		.54***	.20	.13	.18	−.05	.31**
Instructor Confidence in Students (ICS)			.22*	.21	.30**	−.01	.17
Time on Hows and Whys (THW)				.33**	.10	.45***	.10
Time on Introductions (TI)					−.14	.23*	−.10
Time Teaching Content (TC)						−.11	.45***
Time on Rules and Policies (TRP)							−.23*
Proportion of Possible Time Class Met (PCM)							

Note: ***$p < .001$; **$p < .01$; *$p < .05$.

the class, the better they thought the first day went. Similarly, the more confidence they had in their students' ability to do well in the course, the greater was their first day satisfaction. Faculty excitement about the course is thus related to faculty satisfaction with the first day the same way that student interest is related to student satisfaction.

The same instructor uses of class time that were related to student satisfaction in studies 1 and 2 were also related to instructor satisfaction in this study. The more time the instructor spent discussing the hows and whys of the course, on introductions, and on teaching course content, the more satisfied they were with the first day of class. Although we have no way of testing whether instructor satisfaction is related to student satisfaction, the fact that the same instructor behaviors are associated with both student and instructor satisfaction suggests that instructors and students share similar perceptions of the first day of class. Future research should test whether student and instructor satisfaction are related.

To examine how well the instructors' use of time predicted instructors' satisfaction with the first day of class, we conducted a stepwise regression using satisfaction as the dependent variable and instructor excitement, the ways instructors used class time, and the proportion of class time used as the predictor variables. Instructor satisfaction with the first day of class was best predicted by a combination of three variables: excitement about teaching the course, time spent on introductions, and time spent teaching course content. Together these three variables predicted 52 percent of the variance in instructor satisfaction: $F(3, 75) = 29.73, p < .001$.

Discussion

What instructors do on the first day of class is related to both students' and instructors' satisfaction with that day. Students in previous studies have identified pet peeves that include teaching course content on the first day of class, using icebreakers and introductions, and having the class meet the entire class period (Perlman & McCann, 1999). In contrast, the studies we present here consistently showed that teaching content and doing introductions are associated with greater student and instructor satisfaction with the first day of class. Furthermore, the length of time the class meets is unrelated to students' satisfaction and positively related to instructors' satisfaction with the first day.

Why does this discrepancy between previous research and our findings exist? One possibility is that the previously published studies (Henslee et al., 2006; Perlman & McCann, 1999) asked students to report about the first day of class in general rather than to evaluate the first day of a specific class. Students may in fact dislike learning course content on the first day of class, but they may still find that the first day of class goes better when content is taught. Alternatively, students may have in mind one or two particularly poor first days of class in which the instructor spent the entire class period doing icebreakers or lecturing on course content.

Another possible explanation for the discrepancy is that the previous studies were conducted at large public universities, whereas our studies were conducted at two private colleges, each with fewer than fifteen hundred undergraduates. Perhaps previous research findings are more appropriately generalized to larger institutions, and our findings are more appropriately generalized to smaller institutions. Future research should compare how students at large versus small institutions respond to various approaches to the first day of class.

Whereas the findings of these three studies are largely inconsistent with previous research on student preferences regarding the first day of class, our findings are consistent with previously published advice from faculty developers. Numerous authors recommend that instructors spend time on the first day of class doing introductions or using icebreakers (Eifler, 2008; Lang, 2008; McGlynn, 2001; McKeachie & Svinicki, 2006; Nilson, 2003). Consistent with this advice, we found that the more time instructors evoted to introductions, the greater was the students' and instructors' satisfaction with the first day of class. Similarly, many authors recommend teaching course content on the first day of class (Lang, 2008; McKeachie & Svinicki, 2006; Nilson, 2003). We found that the more time instructors spent teaching course content, the greater was students' and instructors' satisfaction with the first day of class.

Our findings are also consistent with previous studies of specific first-day-of-class activities. Consider, for example, the reciprocal interview activity (Case et al., 2008; Hermann & Foster, 2008; Hermann, Foster, & Hardin, 2010) in which the instructor and students take turns interviewing each other about course-related topics. The instructor asks students to form groups to discuss the syllabus and determine answers to a handful of broad questions provided by the instructor. These questions focus the students on course objectives and the way in which the course will be taught, thus directs their attention to the hows and whys of the course. The time spent in small groups also provides students with an opportunity to introduce themselves to some of their classmates. The instructor then calls on one member of each group to give the group's response to the interview questions. Groups select a different representative to ask interview questions of the instructor on behalf of the group. This provides the instructor with the chance to introduce himself or herself to the students in response to the students' questions.

Conclusion

The results we report here have practical implications for how instructors can ensure that the first day of class goes well. Faculty developers are encouraged to share these findings with the instructors they serve. This could be done during new-faculty orientation sessions, with all faculty members in a faculty newsletter or a workshop, or during individual consultations when instructors discuss poor student course evaluations. Rather than doing what students say they want instructors to do (for example, avoid teaching content and letting class out early), instructors should be encouraged to follow the advice of instructors and faculty developers: make sure students get to know the instructor and one another, focus on the hows and whys of the course, and teach course content.

REFERENCES

Bain, K. (2004). *What the best college teachers do.* Cambridge, MA: Harvard University Press.

Case, K., Bartsch, R., McEnery, L., Hall, S., Hermann, A., & Foster, D. (2008). Establishing a comfortable classroom from day one: Student perceptions of the reciprocal interview. *College Teaching, 56,* 210–214.

Clement, M. C. (2007). Ten things to make the first day (and the rest) of the semester successful. *Teaching Professor, 21*(7), 1–3.

Davis, B. G. (2009). *Tools for teaching* (2nd ed.). San Francisco: Jossey-Bass.

Eifler, K. (2008). Academic speed dating. *Teaching Professor, 22*(6), 8.

Henslee, A. M., Burgess, D. R., & Buskist, W. (2006). Student preferences for first day of class activities. *Teaching of Psychology, 33,* 189–207.

Hermann, A. D., & Foster, D. A. (2008). Fostering approachability and classroom participation during the first day of class: Evidence for a reciprocal interview activity. *Active Learning in Higher Education, 9*(2), 139–151.

Hermann, A. D., Foster, D. A., & Hardin, E. E. (2010). Does the first week of class matter? A quasi-experimental investigation of student satisfaction. *Teaching of Psychology, 37,* 79–84.

Lang, J. M. (2008). *On course: A week-by-week guide to your first semester of college teaching.* Cambridge, MA: Harvard University Press.

McGlynn, A. P. (2001). *Successful beginnings for college teaching: Engaging your students from the first day.* Madison, WI: Atwood.

McKeachie, W. J., & Svinicki, M. (2006). *Teaching tips: Strategies, research, and theory for college and university teachers.* Boston: Houghton Mifflin.

Nilson, L. B. (2003). *Teaching at its best: A research-based resource for college instructors* (2nd ed.). San Francisco: Jossey-Bass/Anker.

Nisbett, R. E., & Bellows, N. (1977). Verbal reports about causal influences on social judgments: Private access versus public theories. *Journal of Personality and Social Psychology, 35,* 613–624.

Perlman, B., & McCann, L. I. (1999). Student perspectives on the first day of class. *Teaching of Psychology, 26,* 277–279.

Wilson, J. H., & Wilson, S. B. (2007). The first day of class affects student motivation: An experimental study. *Teaching of Psychology, 34,* 226–230.

STUDENT AND FACULTY PERCEPTIONS OF EFFECTS OF MIDCOURSE EVALUATION

Whitney Ransom McGowan, Russell T. Osguthorpe,
Brigham Young University

We report on faculty and student perceptions of the effects of midcourse evaluations on teaching improvement and student learning. We provided faculty with a midcourse evaluation tool, surveyed faculty and students, interviewed faculty, observed debriefing sessions, and compared midcourse with end-of-semester ratings. Of 510 mean ratings on individual learning items, 342 (67 percent) mean scores showed improvement from midcourse to the end of the semester. Faculty who read their midcourse feedback, discussed it with their students, and made pedagogical changes saw the most improvement in their ratings.

No instructor wants to be a bad teacher. Some teachers may take great joy in being considered "hard or demanding, but never bad" (Phillips, 2001, p. iv). Rather, individuals who become teachers generally want their students to have "significant learning experiences, grow, and progress" (Fink, 2003, p. 6). Nevertheless, many faculty struggle with their teaching performance. Some give up on themselves, concluding they are not effective teachers.

Faculty improvement is essential for a variety of reasons. First, faculty who improve their teaching tend to experience increased teaching satisfaction. Second, faculty who do not strive to improve in their teaching are less likely to succeed in motivating their students to achieve additional improvement (Trigwell & Prosser, 2004). Good teaching demands that faculty continue to learn and improve.

Most universities offer a variety of services to help faculty improve their teaching, but many of these services are labor intensive and reach only a small minority of those who could benefit most from the intervention.

Teaching improvement seminars and individual faculty consulting efforts require significant time from faculty development specialists and often do not reach faculty in most need of help. The online midcourse evaluation tool used in this study requires almost no investment of professional time from faculty development personnel and reaches far greater numbers of faculty. In this chapter, we investigate faculty and student perceptions of the use of an online, midcourse evaluation tool in improving teaching.

Midcourse Evaluations and Their Effect on Teaching Improvement

In many colleges and universities, students have the opportunity at the end of the course to rate the faculty's teaching. However, the feedback comes too late to benefit the current students directly. It can be used only to benefit the next class of students (Diamond, 2004). Brown (2008) suggested that evaluation reports of faculty should be obtained sooner in the course so that changes can be made before the end of the course.

Cohen (1980) reviewed seventeen studies comparing the impact on perceived quality of instruction of providing midcourse feedback with providing no feedback. He discovered a relatively small impact on teaching effectiveness (effect size = .20). Menges and Brinko (1986) updated Cohen's study six years later and reported a larger effect size when midcourse student ratings were combined with consultation (effect size = 1.10). Prince and Goldman (1981) found that midcourse evaluations led to higher student ratings at the end of a course. Brown (2008) found that 89 percent of students felt faculty should conduct midcourse evaluations because they believed the evaluations would improve instruction as well as their own (student) performance.

Although researchers have studied a variety of issues related to midcourse evaluations, no one has completed a systematic analysis of faculty and student perceptions of the effects of such evaluations on teaching and learning (see Bullock, 2003; Henderson, 2002; Bothell & Henderson, 2003; Johnson, 2003). This study aims to address the gap.

Design of the Research Study

This study used a mixed-methods design to determine faculty and student perceptions of the effects of midcourse evaluations on improving teaching and learning. We received Institutional Review Board approval for this study.

Approximately thirty-four thousand students attend Brigham Young University (BYU), and there are approximately sixteen hundred full-time faculty. BYU values teaching, research, and citizenship equally. End-of-semester online student rating scores are included in summative evaluation of teaching performance for promotion and tenure purposes.

Faculty from all twelve colleges and fifty-two departments were represented in the study. Faculty participants were male and female, included different professorial ranks and tenure status, and showed evidence of their desire to improve their teaching by volunteering to be in the study. Most or all of the faculty in several departments (organizational leadership and strategy, mathematics, the college of nursing, and the counseling and career center) decided to participate, often because their department chairs encouraged them.

Data Collection Procedures

We used a variety of methods, including scores from the midcourse evaluation and end-of-semester online ratings, faculty surveys, faculty interviews, and observations of debriefing sessions.

MIDCOURSE EVALUATION TOOL

Center for Teaching and Learning (CTL) staff created an online evaluation tool containing two survey options to help faculty conduct midcourse evaluations. The first option was a two-question open-ended survey where students indicated in narrative form what was going well in class and what could be improved. The second option consisted of four Likert-scale questions: (1) "I am learning a great deal in this course," (2) "Course materials and learning activities are effective in helping me learn," (3) "This course is helping me develop intellectual skills," and (4) "The instructor shows genuine interest in students and their learning." Response options ranged from strongly disagree (1) to strongly agree (8).

All BYU faculty received an e-mail from the CTL director in September 2008, introducing them to the midcourse evaluation tool and providing a link for them to administer the evaluation. In this e-mail, faculty were encouraged to participate in a study on midcourse evaluations and to use the four-question Likert scale as their midcourse evaluation rather than the two-question evaluation.

Once the faculty member selected the question panel, a survey link was e-mailed to all students in that course. After the survey closed, the faculty member received an e-mail with an attached spreadsheet containing the students' feedback. The midcourse evaluation tool was available from the first week of the semester until the end-of-semester evaluations became available.

FACULTY SURVEY

A total of 105 faculty agreed to participate in the study, administered the four-question midcourse evaluation, and filled out the faculty survey (Exhibit 12.1).

Exhibit 12.1 Faculty Survey

1. What is your name?
2. What is your department?
3. Did you read the responses of your students from your midcourse evaluation? a. Yes. b. No.
4. Did you discuss the feedback you received from the midcourse evaluation with your students? a. Yes. b. No.
5. How valuable was your experience using the midcourse evaluation tool?
6. Do you think conducting this midcourse evaluation will have an impact on student learning in your course? a. Yes. b. No. c. I'm not sure.
7. Did you make any changes in your teaching because of student feedback from the midcourse evaluation, and if so, what?
8. Would you be willing to participate in a 20-minute interview about your experience using the midcourse evaluation tool? a. Yes. b. No.

DEBRIEFING SESSIONS

From the 105 participants, we randomly selected 30 faculty to be interviewed, and we attended eight debriefing sessions conducted in class by some of those 30 faculty. We observed how the faculty approached the debriefing session, documented student feedback, and recorded how the faculty planned to implement changes as a result of student feedback.

STUDENT SURVEY

At each debriefing session, we administered a survey to students about their experience with the midcourse evaluation.

FACULTY INTERVIEWS

The thirty faculty we had selected participated in interviews lasting twenty to thirty minutes each (Exhibit 12.2). Most of these interviews took place after they had received and debriefed with their students their midcourse evaluation results but before they received their end-of-semester evaluation results. The interviews were recorded and coded in NVivo. We then looked for themes and categorized the responses.

Exhibit 12.2 Faculty Interview Questions

1. Describe your experience using the midcourse evaluation tool. Was it easy to use? How long did it take to administer?
2. How did your students respond to the midcourse evaluation(s)?
3. Did you talk with your students about their feedback from the midcourse evaluation?
4. Did you make any changes in your teaching as a result of feedback from students from the midcourse evaluation?
5. Were there any suggestions from students that you did not take? If so, why not?
6. How did you decide which changes to make in your teaching?
7. Did you use the midcourse evaluation tool twice this semester?
8. Will you conduct a midcourse evaluation next semester?
9. Regardless of your student evaluations, do you feel like your teaching improved because you conducted a midcourse evaluation? What evidence do you have to support this assumption?

END-OF-SEMESTER ONLINE RATINGS

The online student ratings system allows students to confidentially rate their BYU learning experience at the end of each semester. Students can provide feedback about their courses and instructors approximately two weeks before the semester ends. The same four questions that are used to measure perceptions of student learning for the midcourse evaluations are used at the end of the semester. Once grades are submitted, faculty can view the results.

Data Analysis

Before we explain the process of data analysis, we provide definitions for the terms we use in this chapter:

- An *individual item rating* is one response (a number from 1 to 8) to one of the four questions pertaining to student learning. For example, when a student responded "strongly agree" to the eight-point Likert-scale question, "I have learned a great deal in this course," that response was converted to the number 8. Each student provided four individual item ratings (one for each of the four learning items).

- An *item mean score* is an average of the individual item ratings for each of the four learning items. For example, if one faculty member taught a course with thirty students, we took the thirty individual item ratings from those students for each of the four learning items (120 individual item ratings). We then averaged the ratings for each of the four items to obtain four item mean scores (one item mean score for each of the four items pertaining to perceptions of student learning in each section).

- A *section mean score* is the average of the four item mean scores for a given course.

- A *composite mean score* is the average of the section mean scores for all courses evaluated in the study.

The composite mean score for the midcourse evaluation was compared to the composite mean score for the end-of-semester ratings to determine the effects of the intervention on students' perceptions of their learning.

We conducted a factor analysis using the extraction method of maximum likelihood and varimax rotation to demonstrate that the mean scores from the four learning items could be combined into a section mean score. Cronbach's alpha for the four items was 0.92. Based on the cumulative percentage from the extraction sums of squared loadings, the total variance that can be explained by these four factors was 81 percent. The factor loadings ranged from 0.84 to 0.92. These results show internal consistency for each of the four learning items and are good indications of students' perceptions of their own learning.

Establishing Trustworthiness

The standards used to establish trustworthiness for the qualitative aspects of this study were credibility, transferability, dependability, and confirmability (Lincoln & Guba, 1985). To establish credibility, we used a variety of data-gathering methods, such as a comparison between the midcourse and end-of-semester scores, faculty and student surveys, faculty interviews, and debriefing sessions. To enable transferability, we provided the CTL with a description of the context of the study, the faculty and their circumstances, and rich details from the interviews, including direct quotes. To establish dependability, we sent the faculty copies of their interview and debriefing session transcripts. We also discussed reflections from the interviews, coding structures, insights that arose while coding the data, and the decisions that were made as part of the study with the director of the CTL, faculty in the instructional psychology and technology department, and administrators. To establish confirmability, we provided copies of the recorded interviews and transcripts and made our notes available on request.

Results

Overall, 305 BYU faculty conducted 646 midcourse evaluations (some sent surveys to more than one course or section). Of these, 249 evaluations (124 faculty) used the four-question survey, to which 3,550 students responded. Of these 124 faculty, 65 said they were willing to allow us to observe a debriefing session and to participate in an interview.

Midcourse and End-of-Semester Quantitative Comparison

Overall, the composite mean midcourse score was 6.37, and the composite mean end-of-semester score was 6.71. We conducted a two-tailed, paired t-test comparing the midcourse with the end-of-semester composite mean scores and did the same for the mean scores for each of the four items. The mean scores for each of the four items, as well as the composite mean score, increased, showing that on average, students' end-of-semester ratings of the four learning items were significantly higher than their ratings of those same items on the midcourse evaluation (see Table 12.1).

We used Cohen's d to further validate the results. The effect size measure represents the standardized difference between the composite means of the midcourse and end-of-semester evaluations. Cohen (1988) defined effect sizes of 0.2 as small, 0.5 as medium, and 0.8 as large, with anything less than 0.2 considered no effect. Out of the 510 item mean scores, Cohen's d was 0.46, representing a medium-effect size. Of the faculty who participated in the midcourse evaluation, there was an overall medium, positive effect. Further details are shown in Table 12.2.

Table 12.1 Midcourse and End-of-Semester Student Ratings of
Four Learning Items

Areas of Learning	Composite Midcourse Mean (SD)	Composite End-of-Semester Mean (SD)	Paired t-Test (p-Value)
Four areas of learning combined ($n = 510$)	6.37 (.77)	6.71 (.72)	.001
Interest in student learning ($n = 128$)	6.84 (.69)	7.08 (.81)	.011
Materials and activities ($n = 127$)	6.12 (.73)	6.44 (.73)	.001
Amount learned	6.33 (.73)	6.61 (.75)	.002
Intellectual skills ($n = 126$)	6.16 (.70)	6.64 (.66)	.001

Table 12.2 Effect Size of Midcourse to End-of-Semester
Ratings Changes

	n	Midcourse Mean	End-of-Semester Mean	Large	Medium	Small	No Effect
Scores that increased	352	6.20	6.86	157 (45%)	75 (21%)	65 (18%)	55 (16%)
Scores that decreased	158	6.74	6.37	37 (23%)	23 (15%)	0 (0%)	98 (62%)

Faculty and Student Surveys

Faculty participants were asked if they read the responses of their students from their midcourse evaluation. Of 103 faculty who responded, 99 (96 percent) said yes and 4 (4 percent) said no. Faculty were asked if they discussed the feedback with their students. Of 105 faculty, 78 said yes (74 percent) and 27 said no (26 percent). Thirty-two faculty members (51 percent) said this was their first time performing a midcourse evaluation, and 31 faculty members (49 percent) said they had completed one before.

Faculty were asked in the survey, "Why did you do a midcourse evaluation?" The 104 faculty who responded to the question provided 118 different reasons. The most common reason was that they wanted to hear the students' opinions (20 responses, 17 percent), followed by feeling that feedback was helpful (17 responses, 14 percent). The third most common reason faculty said they conducted a midcourse evaluation was that they were new faculty or were teaching the course for the first time (15 faculty, 13 percent). The fourth most common reason faculty cited was to improve their teaching (and 28 of the 30 faculty interviewed felt that midcourse evaluations did improve their teaching). The fifth most common reason was to improve student learning.

Of the 126 students from six sections who filled out the survey, 78 (62 percent) had completed a midcourse evaluation before using the online mid-course evaluation tool and 48 (38 percent) had not. Of the 125 students who answered the question, "Did you fill out the midcourse evaluation? If yes, why? If no, why not?" 94 (75 percent) said yes and 31 (25 percent) said no. The most common reason students mentioned for completing the midcourse evaluation was to provide feedback to the instructor (37 students, 30 percent). The second and third reasons were that they received extra credit (25 students, 20 percent) and it was required (20 students, 16 percent). The most common reason students did not fill out the mid-course evaluation was that they forgot about it (14 students), did not receive an e-mail (9 students), were too busy (4 students), and erased it or did it late (1 person in each category). Ninety-seven (78 percent) of the students felt midcourse evaluations were somewhat important or important.

PERCEPTIONS OF STUDENT LEARNING
Of the 30 faculty who were interviewed, 27 (90 percent) felt midcourse evaluations improved student learning. Of the 105 faculty who completed the faculty survey, 62 (59 percent) felt midcourse evaluations improved student learning, and only 12 (11 percent) did not. The rest of the faculty were uncertain and wanted to see their end-of-semester ratings before deciding. From the student surveys, 88 students (71 percent) felt their learning might or would increase because their faculty conducted an evaluation.

ACTIONS TO IMPROVE STUDENT LEARNING
At the end of the midcourse in-class survey, we asked students, "What could be improved? and "How could this course be more effective in helping you learn?" During interviews, faculty were asked, "What changes are you making or planning to make?" (At the time of the interviews, all participating faculty had had the opportunity to review feedback from their students. Some had already started implementing

Table 12.3 Top Student Changes Compared to Faculty Changes

Changes to Improve Teaching	Student Responses ($n = 153$)	Faculty Responses ($n = 76$)
Clearer expectations	60 (39%)	30 (39%)
Active learning	43 (28%)	25 (33%)
Reduce busywork	28 (18%)	6 (8%)
More review	0 (0%)	12 (16%)
No changes	22 (14%)	3 (4%)

changes based on student feedback, and others mentioned changes they planned to make.)

Because we wanted to determine how student suggestions affected teaching performance, we include only the responses from the students of the 22 faculty whose ratings improved by at least 1 point from midcourse to end-of-semester evaluations. We grouped all of the student responses (169) into 29 subthemes, and then seven overarching themes. Top suggestions for improvement from students and actions reported by faculty are in Table 12.3. Three of the four changes were the same for both faculty and students. The first two changes (clearer expectations and active learning) were the top two changes for both groups.

RELATIONSHIP BETWEEN FACULTY ACTIONS AND END-OF-SEMESTER STUDENT FEEDBACK

Of the students surveyed, 56 (45 percent) said they would rate their professor more highly at the end of the semester because he or she had conducted a midcourse evaluation. Student ratings showed improvement in proportion to the extent to which the faculty member engaged with the midcourse evaluation. Faculty who read the student feedback and did not discuss it with their students saw a 2 percent improvement in their online student rating scores. Faculty who read the feedback, discussed it with students, and did not make changes saw a 5 percent improvement. Finally, faculty who conducted the midcourse evaluation, read the feedback, discussed it with their students, and made changes saw a 9 percent improvement.

FACULTY INTERVIEWS

In general, as expressed in interviews conducted after faculty responded to the online survey, faculty thought that doing midcourse evaluations improved student learning. All of the faculty interviewed said they were going to conduct another midcourse evaluation next semester.

Discussion

The results of this study show that faculty and students who participate in midcourse evaluations perceive improvements in student learning and faculty teaching. Although the time between the midcourse evaluation and the end-of-semester student ratings is relatively short (six to eight weeks), quantitative results demonstrate that students' perceptions of their own learning increase significantly when faculty invite their suggestions and then take action to make pedagogical improvements. In brief, small changes in teaching may lead to large improvements in student perceptions of their learning.

These findings are important for those engaged in faculty development. Most centers devoted to the improvement of learning and teaching are eager to find ways to help faculty who struggle in the classroom. Although the data in this study are preliminary and more research needs to be done, the results suggest that the midcourse evaluation tool—because it is completely voluntary and confidential, and because it is easy to administer and act on—is one attractive means of assisting faculty in this area. Using this approach to teaching improvement, the faculty member does not need to be singled out by an administrator to receive help from faculty developers. Rather, the faculty member chooses to take advantage of an unobtrusive intervention that demands only a small amount of time and effort. That being said, research shows that midcourse evaluations can have even greater value when used in a supportive context (Penny & Coe, 2004).

Study Limitations and Additional Questions

Although this study showed that midcourse evaluations can have positive effects on student perceptions of their learning, it does have some limitations and raises a number of additional questions. For example, one limitation is that we did not have a comparison group of courses in which the midcourse evaluation was not administered. Also, students may have based their rating on whether they liked the course content or the instructor rather than the actual instruction.

There are several additional questions to consider for future such studies. For example, to what extent do measures of actual student performance validate student and faculty perceptions of improvements in student learning? How do students respond to pedagogical changes that faculty make as a result of using the midcourse evaluation tool? Do they recognize the changes? Do students act on those changes by making concomitant changes in their learning strategies?

If the midcourse evaluation tool is an effective intervention for assisting faculty who are struggling in the classroom, how can they be encouraged to use the tool and benefit from it? An implicit finding from this study is that personal choice plays an important role in the improvement process. Faculty were not coerced into using the midcourse evaluation tool. Neither were they forced to read or act on the results once the students had offered their suggestions. Thus, how should faculty developers encourage administrators or peers to extend the invitation to struggling faculty to use the tool in ways that will maximize the effectiveness of the intervention?

From the results of this study, it appears that students are generally eager to give feedback to faculty on the quality of their learning experience. However, if midcourse evaluations become ubiquitous and students are required to complete such surveys for every course each semester, will they come to see the evaluation as an additional burden? This concern suggests that midcourse evaluations be kept as brief as possible, requiring only a few minutes for students to complete.

Perhaps the most compelling question that remains to be answered relates to the possible effect of the midcourse tool on the faculty member's ability to read students' reactions to the course. Great teachers are constantly "gathering data" from their students about how well their students are learning (Bain, 2004; Barr & Tagg, 1995). To what extent can the midcourse evaluation tool be used as a learning tool for the faculty member? How can the tool be used to help faculty perceive more clearly how students are learning without administering the midcourse evaluation? This question should be of great interest to any institution interested in establishing an atmosphere of continuous improvement of learning and teaching.

REFERENCES

Bain, K. (2004). *What the best college teachers do*. Cambridge, MA: Harvard University Press.

Barr, R. B., & Tagg, J. (1995). From teaching to learning—A new paradigm for undergraduate education. *Change, 27*(6), 12–25.

Bothell, T. W., & Henderson, T. (2003). Do online ratings of instruction make sense? In T. D. Johnson & D. L. Sorenson (Eds.), *New directions for teaching and learning: No. 96. Online student ratings of instruction* (pp. 69–79). San Francisco: Jossey-Bass.

Brown, M. (2008). Student perceptions of teaching evaluations. *Journal of Instructional Psychology, 35*(2), 177–181.

Bullock, C. D. (2003). Online collection of midterm student feedback. In
    T. D. Johnson & D. L. Sorenson (Eds.), *New directions for teaching and
    learning: No. 96. Online student ratings of instruction* (pp. 95–102).
    San Francisco: Jossey-Bass.

Cohen, J. (1988). *Statistical power analysis for the behavioral sciences* (2nd ed.).
    Mahwah, NJ: Erlbaum.

Cohen, P. A. (1980). Effectiveness of student-rating feedback for improving col-
    lege teaching: A meta-analysis of findings. *Research in Higher Education,*
    13, 321–341.

Diamond, M. R. (2004). The usefulness of structured mid-term feedback as a
    catalyst for change in higher education classes. *Active Learning in Educa-*
    tion, 5(3), 217–231.

Fink, L. D. (2003). *Creating significant learning experiences: An integrated*
    approach to designing college courses. San Francisco: Jossey-Bass.

Henderson, T. (2002). Classroom assessment techniques in asynchronous learn-
    ing networks. *Teaching and Learning in Higher Education, 33,* 2–4.

Johnson, T. D. (2003). Online student ratings: Will students respond? In
    T. D. Johnson & D. L. Sorenson (Eds.), *New directions for teaching and*
    learning: No. 96. Online student ratings of instruction (pp. 49–59).
    San Francisco: Jossey-Bass.

Lincoln, Y. S., & Guba, E. G. (1985). *Naturalistic inquiry.* Thousand Oaks,
    CA: Sage.

Menges, R. J., & Brinko, K. T. (1986). *Effects of student evaluation feedback:*
    A meta-analysis of higher education research. Paper presented at the
    annual meeting of the American Educational Research Association,
    San Francisco.

Penny, A. R., & Coe, R. (2004). Effectiveness of consultation on student ratings
    feedback: A meta-analysis. *Review of Educational Research, 74*(2),
    215–253.

Phillips, R. R. (2001). Editorial: On teaching. *Journal of Chiropractic Education,*
    15(2), iv–vi.

Prince, A. R., & Goldman, M. (1981). Improving part-time faculty instruction.
    Teaching of Psychology, 8(3), 60–62.

Trigwell, K., & Prosser, M. (2004). Development and use of the approaches to
    teaching inventory. *Educational Psychology Review, 16*(4), 409–424.

13

EVOLUTION OF A PEER REVIEW AND EVALUATION PROGRAM FOR ONLINE COURSE DEVELOPMENT

Cynthia L. Adams, Dianna Z. Rust, Thomas M. Brinthaupt, Middle Tennessee State University

The faculty peer assistants (FPAs) program combines a mentoring and peer review process for initial online faculty course development and subsequent course revision. An FPA mentors colleagues during course design and conducts peer reviews when the courses are complete. The program incorporates a peer review and evaluation form that outlines course standards and guides the faculty course developer, the peer reviewer, and the department chair. Feedback about the program from department chairs, faculty course developers, and FPAs was uniformly positive.

With the rapid growth of online courses, higher education institutions are seeking methods to ensure quality and meet accreditation standards. Standards for online courses and peer review are two common tools for quality assurance. In fall 2005, Middle Tennessee State University (MTSU), a large public institution with over twenty-five thousand students, implemented a continuous course development and quality improvement process for online courses that combines mentoring and peer review.

Mentoring and Peer Review Programs

Marek's (2009) survey of library information science faculty in accredited master's programs showed that faculty who develop online courses rely for support most frequently on their peers and then on the institution's information technology workshops. Thus, Marek suggests that an effective model for online course development should include structured peer mentoring.

Several programs exist for mentoring distance learning faculty. One example is Park University's online instructor evaluation system (Mandernack, Donnelli, Dailey, & Schultz, 2005). Online instructors are paired with a faculty evaluator who, during an eight-week term, reviews the instructor's facilitation and delivery of the online course five times. In addition to these formative reviews, which are accompanied by peer mentoring, the academic department completes a summative review at the end of the course.

Another example of mentoring for online course development paired technically savvy graduate students with English faculty in developing online courses for the first time (Alvarez, Blair, Monske, & Wolf, 2005). The authors mention issues with the power relationships between students and faculty as a barrier, but found the program to be valuable for graduate student professional development as well as increasing the number of online course offerings.

In an in-house faculty peer review program for online courses at the School of Nursing at Indiana University (Cobb, Billings, Mays, & Canty-Mitchell, 2001), reviewers include a nursing faculty member and an instructional technology expert. Using a course checklist, the reviewers provide the instructor with a written report that outlines recommendations for improvement and hold a follow-up meeting to answer questions. The primary use of the peer review is for course improvement, since the course is evaluated after it has been taught for one year.

One of the most widely known peer review programs for online courses, Quality Matters (2006), uses a Quality Matters (QM) peer course review rubric with forty standards for online course design. The program uses an interinstitutional and disciplinary peer review team process to evaluate course design, though not delivery. A course that scores high enough on the rubric receives a QM designation.

The MTSU faculty peer assistants (FPA) program draws on other mentoring and review efforts but provides a different approach that addresses what we see as some of the weaknesses and limitations of other efforts. The program also has unique strengths that make it a potential model for other colleges and universities:

- It is conducted in-house and across disciplines.
- The mentoring and review are initiated during course development rather than during or after teaching.
- The program involves the department chairs in the development and approval process.

- The program uses a continuous improvement process that takes place at initial course development and occurs again at the revision of the course every three years.

History of the FPA Program

In 2001, MTSU established a committee and charged it with reviewing new online courses. The committee consisted of several experienced faculty course designers (FCDs) who used an abbreviated rubric and met regularly to review courses. Because of faculty schedules, the committee could not meet as often as necessary, and courses were assigned to individual committee members.

In 2003, the Distance Learning Faculty Services Office sponsored a group of twelve faculty to earn the certified online instructor (COI) designation through the Learning Resources Network (LERN). At a 2004 reorganization meeting, the review committee suggested recruiting COIs to serve as peer reviewers. Most of the initial twelve COIs agreed to serve as peer mentors and selected the name Faculty Peer Assistants Program. One of the original committee members offered a review form based on a rubric developed at the California State University at Chico (2009). The rubric was adopted by the new FPA program members and continues to be used and updated. In summer 2005, the program was piloted, and several courses were successfully reviewed.

Since the program began, forty-four MTSU faculty members have earned the COI, and approximately twenty-five serve as FPAs at any given time. Completion of COI training is a requirement for serving as an FPA, and faculty development opportunities in the areas of peer mentoring, online pedagogy, and course development are continually provided by the College of Education and Distance Learning (CEDL). MTSU faculty peer assistants receive a stipend of $125 per course assignment, which may include several reviews of the same course. At this writing, FPAs have conducted over 150 reviews.

Course Development, Review, and Approval Process

When a potential FCD expresses interest in developing a new online course, the distance learning faculty services office e-mails a course proposal, a standard syllabus template, the peer review and evaluation form (PR form), and abbreviated instructions. Links to more detailed information and training, contained in the websites of distance learning faculty services and the faculty instructional technology center, are also included.

When faculty services receives the course proposal (approved by the department chair) and syllabus, the FCD receives another e-mail that contains the name of the assigned FPA and an online course development agreement. Unlike other mentoring programs (for example, Cobb et al., 2001), assignment of the FPA is made at the beginning of course development. This is especially important for inexperienced FCDs, and it allows mentors to focus on pedagogy at the earliest stages of course development.

Consistent with the recommendation of Lottero-Perdue and Fifield (2010), the mentoring relationship between the FPA and the online faculty course developer is one-on-one. In our program, FPAs are assigned not by rank but by pedagogical experience. This results in some junior faculty mentoring senior faculty, which creates an interesting dynamic. As in the California State University teacher observation/peer support program (Webb & McEnerney, 1995), FPAs are paired with FCDs outside their department for course review. In a cross-department model, faculty can focus on pedagogy instead of being distracted by content, and the reduced likelihood of close colleague mentoring fosters greater objectivity.

When course development is complete, the FCD conducts a self-evaluation using the PR form. This self-evaluation is sent to the FPA, who reviews it and conducts his or her peer review using the same form, and then sends it back to the FCD to address recommended revisions. Depending on the nature and extent of revisions, the FPA may review those changes. When the FCD and FPA are satisfied, the PR form is forwarded to distance learning faculty services. The PR form and course approval form are then e-mailed to the department chair, who is responsible for reviewing the course and approving it for delivery. When the course approval form is signed and returned to faculty services, the scheduling center is notified that the course may be added to the semester schedule.

Although control of the FPA program rests with the faculty services office, FPAs played a major role in developing the program and its guidelines. The FPAs meet annually to review the program and recommend changes, giving them a voice in and control over the program's continuing evolution.

Peer Review and Evaluation Form

The PR form is a rubric that guides the development and review process for new online courses, as well as those being revised on a three-year cycle. It addresses six general review areas and has been revised on an ongoing basis by FPAs. A modified version of a tool developed at California State

University at Chico (2009), the rubric is based on national research regarding online learning. Reviewers rate each area using a three-point scale (LTS = less than satisfactory, S = satisfactory, and X = exemplary), can write in specific comments, and must provide an explanation for any section receiving the LTS rating. (Readers can see the rubric at www.mtsu .edu/learn/faculty/pdf/online_peer_evaluation.pdf.)

The first review area is learner support and resources. This includes such items as instructor contact information, virtual office hours, instructor response time, and emergency contact information. Resource information includes links to a variety of course-specific materials, including media resources such as tutorials and podcasts.

The second review category is course design and organization. In this section, FPAs assess whether the course is logically constructed, the syllabus is complete, requirements are clearly defined, and information is presented clearly. In addition, reviewers rate whether pages are consistently presented to assist students with navigation, whether there is a statement about accommodations available under the Americans with Disabilities Act (ADA), and whether the course is ADA compliant (through such means as alt tags to describe in text the content of images and transcribed text for audio).

The third review topic is instructional design and delivery. In this section, FPAs rate the extent to which interaction, communication, and collaboration are incorporated into the course through opportunities for interactions among students, between students and teacher, and between students and content. They also assess whether learning objectives are identified, whether and how class activities are used, and if multiple learning styles (such as visual and tactile) are considered in the design.

Assessment and evaluation of student learning is the fourth review area. In this section, reviewers examine whether student readiness strategies for online learning are incorporated into the course (for example, a registration permit or assessment tool used at the beginning of the class). In addition, assessments are made of the extent to which course objectives, instructional strategies, and assessment techniques are aligned, as well as whether multiple and ongoing assessment strategies are used.

The next rubric topic is appropriate and effective use of technology. In this area, reviewers determine whether students are given adequate information to access their course materials, if a variety of tools are used (for example, discussion, Web pages, chat, quizzes, and blogs), and if a variety of multimedia and learning objects are used to enhance the course.

The final review topic is opportunities for and use of student feedback. Here, reviewers assess whether students are given opportunities to provide feedback about course design and navigability, feedback is integrated into course design and instruction, and opportunities are available for student self-assessment as well as peer feedback.

Once the reviewers have assessed the six major sections, they provide a summary evaluation of whether the course is ready for delivery. There are three options: (1) yes; (2) yes, with minor modification (additional review not required); and (3) no, with major modification recommended (requires additional review prior to delivery). Reviewers also confirm whether all course materials are located within the course management system and, if not, how and why the course uses other materials.

Challenges and Solutions

Several challenges have been encountered with implementing the FPA program. One area that required early improvement was the responsibility for course final approval. Since department chairs are ultimately responsible for their faculty and department, the CEDL determined that chairs should approve delivery of new online courses developed by their FCDs. Requiring chairs to review the new courses permitted them to review course content and helped build trust between them and the program.

Day-to-day challenges with the FPA program include how to make peer reviewer assignments in an equitable manner. When the program began, e-mails were sent requesting volunteers from the FPA pool. However, some people were assigned multiple courses because they responded first to requests. In addition, colleagues were offering to review their friends' courses. As a result, some FPAs were becoming overloaded and were not providing good mentoring service. To address these issues, a course review tracking system was developed that now allows us to make assignments based on FPA availability and the number of course reviews already assigned to them.

When a course is not recommended for delivery by the FPA or the chair, an opportunity is created for faculty development and course improvement. When the peer review results are less than satisfactory, the FPA sends an informal e-mail to the FCD addressing the concerns and providing an opportunity to make changes before the formal peer review is conducted. On the rare occasion that a course is still not acceptable, the distance learning faculty service office serves as the liaison between the FCD and the FPA to resolve the concerns. Some courses have been reviewed several times (and revisions made) before receiving FPA approval. It is important to note that although the FPAs are charged with providing honest, constructive feedback, FCDs are not required to make the recommended revisions, although most do and are grateful for the guidance. Ultimately the department chair is responsible for reviewing and approving the course for delivery. If a department chair does not approve a course, the distance learning faculty services office serves as liaison and contacts the FCD to request recommended changes. When the changes are made, the chair again reviews the course and approves addition to the semester schedule.

Another challenge occurs when the course review process is not completed in a timely manner. If an FCD has a course that is ready for review but receives no response from the assigned FPA, the faculty services office contacts the FPA. If there are problems or conflicts with conducting the review, as in one instance when an FPA had a family emergency and was unexpectedly out of state for an extended time, reassignment of the course to a different FPA is offered.

The variation in the extent to which FPAs engage in mentoring the FCD is another program challenge. When the FPA program started, it offered just peer review of the quality of online courses. As it evolved, duties extended to mentoring new FCDs. Some FPAs still perceive their duties as simply conducting peer review at the conclusion of course development. Since so many faculty members are new online course designers, FPAs are reminded, through information and training, that mentoring is an important part of the program. The mentoring component includes providing assistance during course design, answering questions and facilitating revisions during the approval process, and providing continued assistance and consultation during the first semester of course delivery.

A broader challenge was gaining buy-in from constituents. There were issues with convincing potential FCDs of the need for a formal review process. Department chairs and potential FCDs also needed to be convinced of the need for the additional levels of bureaucracy that were created. The most important program improvements (chair approval and scheduling controls) were implemented in summer 2007 and were the result of a year of meetings with administrative and faculty groups to obtain that buy-in and support. ·

Because the FPAs are faculty members, they are more likely to be constrained by competing job demands than if information technology staff were serving in this capacity. As Brinthaupt, Clayton, and Draude (2009) noted, faculty interested in integrating instructional technologies experience a number of technology-related barriers (the wide range of options, the pace of changes and innovations) and academic-related barriers (time and effort, tenure and promotion concerns). Many of the challenges we experienced with implementing the FPA program are directly or indirectly related to these kinds of barriers. For example, because the FCDs may want to incorporate technologies that the FPAs are not familiar with, peer mentoring can sometimes be limited in effectiveness. Or FCDs may try to incorporate too many tools into their courses, leading to neglect of pedagogical issues or a slowdown in the development process. FPAs have to find the time to conduct their reviews and must frequently work around the schedules and deadlines of the FCDs while receiving limited compensation, recognition, or credit from their departments or university. Similarly, some FCDs may not see the value of putting in large amounts of time and effort in developing their courses, resulting in less attention to best-practice principles. Thus, there has been an evolving balance among the criteria that the FPA program sets for new online courses, the amount of work the FPAs can devote to peer mentoring and review, and the expectations and preferences of the FCDs.

Our campus has developed mentor guidelines for the FPAs and offers continuous opportunities for professional development in peer mentoring. A customized workshop on peer mentoring was developed for our FPAs by LERN. In addition, new FCDs may review the program and mentors through a Meet Your Mentor site, located within the university's course management system, detailing the FPAs' experiences with distance learning and including personal and professional interests and information. We also include best practice resources for online course development on the site.

An important attribute of the FPA program that sets it apart from other programs is that it supports the Best Practices for Electronically Offered Degree and Certificate Programs advocated by the Commission on Colleges (2000). Some of these best practices include providing training and support to participants, ensuring that electronically offered programs and courses meet institution-wide standards (to provide consistency for students who may enroll in both electronically offered and traditional on-campus courses), maintaining appropriate academic oversight, and having academically qualified persons participate fully in the decisions concerning program curriculum and program operation.

Formal and Informal Evaluation of the FPA Program

To assess the effectiveness of the FPA program, brief surveys were sent to chairs of departments with online offerings, FCDs who had gone through the program, and the FPAs who had worked with the program. The surveys were completed online using a commercial survey program. Respondents rated a variety of statements pertaining to the operation of the program, using five-point Likert scales (1 = strongly disagree to 5 = strongly agree).

Table 13.1 presents the descriptive statistics for the department chairs' evaluation of the FPA program. Chairs reported improved quality of online courses and increased comfort with online offerings. In addition, they reported being satisfied with their degree of involvement in the program, indicated a preference for their faculty to develop more online courses, and felt that the course development process did not need improving. These results suggest that, from the perspective of department chairs, the FPA program has been a success.

The FCDs reported having taught an average of 2.52 (SD = 3.12) online courses and having taught online for an average of 4.90 years (SD = 3.73). Descriptive statistics from the FCDs' ratings of the FPA program are presented in Table 13.2. FCDs were uniformly favorable regarding the FPA program. In particular, they reported that the program improved the quality of their online courses and how they were taught. They were satisfied with the levels of assistance and interactivity provided by their FPA as well as with the PR form. They were more likely to develop

Table 13.1 Department Chairs' Evaluation of the FPA Program

Variable	Mean	SD
The CEDL online course development process has improved the quality of the courses my faculty have created.	4.23	.599
The CEDL online course development process has made me more comfortable about my department offering additional online courses.	4.08	.900
As a chair, I am satisfied with my degree of involvement in the CEDL online course development process.	4.15	.555
In my department, the oversight for online course development is more extensive than the oversight for face-to-face course development.	2.85	1.463
I would like more of my faculty to develop and offer online courses.	3.77	1.166
The quality of the course development process needs to be improved.	2.31	.751

Note: N = 13; response rate = 50 percent.

Table 13.2 FCDs' Evaluation of the FPA Program

Variable	Mean	SD
The CEDL faculty peer review process has improved the quality of the online course(s) I developed.	4.08	1.06
The CEDL faculty peer review process has improved how I teach the online course(s) I developed.	3.68	1.10
I am satisfied with the level of assistance provided by my FPA.	4.06	1.07
The level of interactivity with my FPA was adequate.	3.90	1.05
My experience with the peer review process makes it more likely I will develop additional online courses.	3.75	1.20
The CEDL peer review evaluation form was helpful in the development of my online course.	3.86	1.21
The quality of the faculty peer review process needs to be improved.	2.43	1.14

Note: $N = 52$; response rate = 37 percent.

additional online courses as a result of the program, and they disagreed that the peer review process needs to be improved.

The FPAs reported having conducted an average of 8.67 (SD = 6.69) course reviews to date and having been teaching online for an average of 8.50 (SD = 3.03) years. Table 13.3 presents the evaluative data from the FPAs. Similar to Gibson's (2004) finding of a reciprocal relationship in mentoring, FPAs reported several benefits from participating in the program. Informal comments from the FPAs and the FPA survey results suggest that both the mentor and the mentee receive benefits. In particular, mentors noted that mentoring provided them with ideas to improve their own online teaching, think more critically about their own online courses, and focus on course development best practices. They also reported that working with faculty from other disciplines was beneficial and that the PR Form was helpful.

In summary, department chairs, FCDs, and FPAs rated the program as effective and successful. There were no strong feelings from any of the target groups that the program needed to be improved. Both the FCDs and FPAs reported that participating in the program has improved their own online teaching and course development.

In addition to the survey data, we have information about the program's benefits through informal feedback from department chairs, FCDs, and

Table 13.3 FPAs' Evaluation of the FPA Program

Variable	Mean	SD
Mentoring has provided me with ideas that I have used to improve my online teaching.	4.00	.94
Mentoring has helped me deal more productively with the challenges of teaching online.	3.90	.99
Mentoring has helped me think more critically about my own online courses.	4.10	.99
Mentoring has helped me focus on best practices in course development.	4.10	.99
My own teaching has benefited from working with faculty from other disciplines.	4.20	.63
The stipend I am paid for conducting a course review is sufficient, given the time and effort I typically expend.	3.10	.74
The CEDL peer review evaluation form is helpful in the mentoring process.	4.67	.50
The quality of the faculty peer review process needs to be improved.	2.80	1.14

Note: $N = 10$; response rate = 44 percent.

FPAs. Comments from department chairs indicated that they value the fact that they are involved from the beginning of the course development process to the end (by approving the course development agreement and by approving final development and delivery). Comments from FCDs indicate that they appreciate learning more about the pedagogy behind online instruction, viewing other perspectives on the use of technology, seeing how others have solved issues related to the challenges of teaching online content, and having the opportunity to work with seasoned online instructors throughout the development process. Comments from FPAs indicate that they appreciate the emphasis on best practices and being able to see things from the student perspective.

The systematic review of online courses has larger benefits that could be considered for expansion to the design of traditional courses. Using a standard syllabus template provides students with consistent information about library services for distance learners, services for disabled students, technical support information, online tutoring services, and the distance learning testing center. Improved course quality is an additional benefit to the students. FPAs have made suggestions for improved course navigation, organization, and delivery. Department chair reviews have also improved course quality. For example, one course did not include the approved departmental learning outcomes. The chair recommended this change, and the course was revised accordingly. Although our campus has yet to consider this possibility, the development and implementation of peer review and evaluation programs for traditional courses, modeled after the one discussed in this chapter, might be an innovative and effective next step.

Although the institution has implemented many strategies to improve student outcomes in online courses, we believe that the FPA program has been one of the most significant. In a recent study of 328 students surveyed by the distance learning office, the majority of students indicated satisfaction with online courses (84 percent stating they were satisfied or very satisfied with their course), with 91 percent of respondents stating they would take another online course. Compared to traditional (face-to-face) MTSU courses, 60 percent said they learned the same amount, 25 percent said they learned more, and 15 percent said they learned less.

The strength of the FPA program is that it benefits the institution, mentee, and mentor. The institution benefits by socializing faculty into the distance learning community, meeting accreditation standards, and providing students with improved courses. Mentees and mentors benefit by learning effective online teaching strategies from each other. Most departments at MTSU have only a few faculty members who develop and teach online courses. Similar to the goal of the TOPS program at California State University (Webb & McEnerney, 1995), the FPA program strives to reduce the isolation of teaching. Teaching and learning centers can also reduce the isolation of teaching; however, these centers typically focus on broad teaching issues and the use of technology in teaching in the classroom. MTSU's learning, teaching, and innovative technologies center (LT&ITC) offers workshops that bring together faculty for one-time discussions of using technology in teaching; however, the participants may or may not be teaching online courses. Bringing together isolated faculty who share a common interest in online teaching is a benefit of the FPA program that is not addressed consistently by our LT&ITC. However, both programs are important in recruiting and developing online faculty course developers on campus.

Institutions that would like to implement a similar program should have academic affairs support both in resources and enforcing guidelines for online course development. Faculty buy-in is essential. Although we feel that the FPA program works well, other institutions might consider some alternative approaches. The survey results suggested that the FPAs were rather ambivalent about the compensation for their work, so reducing that amount would probably not be a good idea for this program. Instead of providing FPAs an external certification, an internal program could be developed by the teaching and learning center or information technology department on the campus. In lieu of providing FPAs with a stipend, the institution could allow their service to count as their committee work. Alternatives to paying faculty a development fee for online course development are assigning graduate students to assist faculty or providing faculty release time. At some institutions, a course fee assessed to online courses could offset the cost of online course development.

Our experience with the development and evolution of the FPA program suggests that it has provided many benefits. Students receive a more consistent course experience, which we believe has improved satisfaction and retention. Faculty connect to others in the distance learning field, develop and offer improved online courses, and provide better service to students and the university. Department chairs participate in the program from beginning to end and feel they have some control over what their faculty and department are offering. Giving department chairs a rubric based on best practices with which to evaluate the course has served to educate administrators about effective pedagogy, online and otherwise. Having FPAs residing in the departments provides their colleagues with a readily available source of information about online learning and the processes of online course development.

In summary, the FPA program innovatively and creatively uses limited institutional resources to improve the development and quality of online course offerings. By tapping into the knowledge and experiences of faculty mentors, the program guides course designers, reviewers, and administrators toward the incorporation of best practices.

REFERENCES

Alvarez, D. M., Blair, K., Monske, E., & Wolf, A. (2005). Team models in online course development: A unit-specific approach. *Educational Technology and Society, 8*(3), 176–186.

Brinthaupt, T. M., Clayton, M. A., & Draude, B. J. (2009). Barriers to and strategies for faculty integration of IT. In P. Rogers, G. Berg, J. Boettcher, C. Howard, L. Justice, & K. Schenk (Eds.), *Encyclopedia of distance learning* (2nd ed., Vol. 1, pp. 138–145). Hershey, PA: IGI Global.

California State University at Chico. (2009). *Rubric for online instruction.* Retrieved from www.csuchico.edu/tlp/resources/rubric/rubric.pdf

Cobb, K. L., Billings, D. M., Mays, R. M., & Canty-Mitchell, J. (2001). Peer review of teaching in web-based courses in nursing. *Nurse Educator, 26*(6), 274–279.

Commission on Colleges, Southern Association of Colleges and Schools. (2000). *Best practices for electronically offered degree and certificate programs.* Retrieved from www.sacscoc.org/pdf/081705/commadap.pdf

Gibson, S. K. (2004). Being mentored: The experience of women faculty. *Journal of Career Development, 30*(2), 173–188.

Lottero-Perdue, P. S., & Fifield, S. (2010). A conceptual framework for higher education faculty mentoring. In L. B. Nilson & J. E. Miller (Eds.), *To improve the academy: Vol. 28. Resources for faculty, instructional, and organizational development* (pp. 37–62). San Francisco: Jossey-Bass.

Mandernack, B. J., Donnelli, E., Dailey, A., & Schultz, M. (2005). A faculty evaluation model for online instructors: Mentoring and evaluation in the online classroom. *Online Journal of Distance Learning Administration, 8*(3), 1–30.

Marek, K. (2009). Learning to teach online: Creating a culture of support for faculty. *Journal of Education for Library and Information Science, 50*(4), 275–292.

Quality Matters. (2006). *Quality matters: Inter-institutional quality assurance in online learning: A grant project of MarylandOnline: Summary.* Retrieved from www.qualitymatters.org/documents/final%20FIPSE%20Report.pdf

Webb, J., & McEnerney, K. (1995). The view from the back of the classroom: A faculty-based peer observation program. *Journal on Excellence in Teaching, 6*(3), 145–160.

14

COMPLETING THE FACULTY DEVELOPMENT CYCLE

USING DATA FROM SYLLABI REVIEW TO INFORM ACTION

Phyllis Blumberg, University of the Sciences in Philadelphia

Consistent with the mission of the University of the Sciences in Philadelphia, the Teaching and Learning Center has emphasized implementation of learner-centered practices for eight years. To assess the impact of these development efforts, I reviewed syllabi and course approval forms of seventy-two recently approved courses. The documents revealed a disappointing lack of evidence of learner-centered course design features. Voluntary faculty development programming cannot force faculty to change their course designs. However, the results prompted discussions with administrators and faculty and yielded calls to action for greater implementation of learner-centered practices.

Assessing the impact of one's work is a core principle of effective practice. Once informed by the results of these assessments, we can decide if we need to make changes in what we do (Suskie, 2004). As faculty developers, we work individually with faculty, offer workshops, and coordinate learning communities. Researchers have looked at the effectiveness of the process and format of development efforts (Cox, 2004; Sorcinelli, 1997). The most common measures ask participants immediately after programs or consultations how effective the event was. While individual workshops may not have much impact, a sustained effort focusing on a consistent message, with many follow-ups with faculty individually, usually has a greater impact (Cox, 2004; Eison & Stevens, 1995).

I adapted Suskie's (2004) teaching-learning-assessment cycle to investigate the long-term effects on course design of eight years of sustained faculty development efforts. Suskie's cycle begins with faculty development goals, which lead to learning opportunities whose impact is measured by assessment and whose results inform the redefinition of goals and a plan for action. I employed a variety of learning opportunities to assist faculty in implementing the institution's goal of learner-centered teaching (Weimer, 2002). I evaluated the impact of these efforts by determining the learner-centered status of course design features in a sample of courses. I used the results of this assessment to define new goals, further learning opportunities, and action steps for myself, decision makers, and the faculty.

University of the Sciences in Philadelphia is a private institution of about three thousand students and 175 full-time faculty members. More than 85 percent of the operating budget comes from tuition dollars, and effective teaching is valued and evaluated. Part of the university's mission statement is, "The University will provide a student centered learning and living environment." Faculty members define *student-centered learning* as learner-centered teaching. To be consistent with the university's mission and because a great deal of research supports the idea that learner-centered approaches lead to improved learning (Fink, 2003; Weimer, 2002), I focused on helping faculty members implement this approach to teaching.

Faculty Development Goals

During the 2001–2002 academic year, a strategic planning process identified six strategic imperatives (University of the Sciences in Philadelphia, 2002), of which one was the development of a culture of student-centered learning and living. The tactical planning group on student-centered learning and living, of which I was a member, defined objectives, developed future action steps, and outlined outcome indicators. The faculty members of the task force raised concerns about the phrase *student-centered learning* because it seems to focus on customer satisfaction (Weimer, 2002). The faculty members of the task force and I successfully argued for a change in nomenclature to *learner-centered teaching*, which keeps the emphasis on the students as learners while giving faculty an important role in this learning. While this change may seem like wordsmithing, it was important in promoting acceptance of the planned change in culture.

The tactical planning group identified (among others) the following key outcome indicators of the learner-centered strategic imperative: faculty, staff, and administrators will know what learner-centered teaching entails and how to achieve it; and the curriculum will be consistent with learner-centered teaching in terms of development, content, and delivery (University of the Sciences in Philadelphia, 2002). This study focuses on assessing the achievement of the second indicator.

Learning Opportunities

The Teaching and Learning Center was charged with directing the education needed to achieve the key outcome indicators of learner-centered teaching. Throughout 2002–2003, the center hosted activities focusing on learner-centered teaching, including four day-long workshops given by experts in learner-centered teaching and sixteen discussions. With the combined recruiting efforts of administrators and chairs and my heavy promotion of these workshops, about 70 percent of the faculty attended at least one of these workshops, and the majority of these faculty attended at least two.

At the end of 2003, the center hosted a conference, attended by one-third of the faculty, to define learner-centered teaching and suggest how faculty could achieve it. Participants agreed that the essential aspect of learner-centered teaching was students' taking responsibility for their own learning, and they agreed that faculty needed to facilitate students' progress toward this desired end. The faculty agreed that implementing learner-centered teaching required them to redesign their learning goals, outcomes, teaching and learning activities, and assessments. There could be multiple ways to achieve learner-centered teaching, but they all involved actively engaging the students in their learning (Blumberg & Everett, 2005). From the conference, I developed a consensus statement of the faculty's views of learner-centered teaching, which I used in planning for future educational efforts.

In 2003–2004 I coordinated a learning community for ten faculty members from across the university to explore in depth how to implement learner-centered teaching and design learner-centered courses. These faculty were expected to serve as trainers for others in their departments, sharing with their peers how they changed their teaching and working with individuals who wanted to implement learner-centered teaching.

In the following years, from 2004 to 2009, I continued educating faculty about learner-centered teaching and highlighting local examples of its implementation. Annually since 2003, all new faculty members have participated in a hands-on workshop on teaching, lasting a day and a half, using learner-centered approaches to course design. I offered at least twelve short hands-on workshops each year that focused on aspects of learner-centered teaching such as how to get students to take responsibility for their learning and the varied uses of assessment to guide improvement. All of these workshops allowed time for faculty to alter an aspect of their existing courses. About half of the faculty attended at least one of these workshops each year, and several people attended many of them.

The feedback from these workshops was that they were helpful in fostering implementation of learner-centered teaching. During this five-year
period, the center hosted well-attended poster sessions that featured
examples of faculty using learner-centered approaches (Blumberg,
2004).

   In feedback on these events, faculty said that they developed a sense of
community as teachers (Millis, 1997). It appeared that interest in using
learner-centered teaching was growing (Blumberg, 2004). There seemed
to be good reason for optimism that faculty members were implementing
learner-centered practices.

Assessment Methodology

To complete Suskie's (2004) cycle, I assessed the impact of these faculty
development efforts on course design by assessing the learner-centered
status of a sample of courses at the point of course (re)approval.

Course Selection Criteria and Sample Size

The faculty approved a new general education curriculum in 2007.
In addition to disciplinary knowledge, the courses in the new curriculum
were required to teach skills that transcend the disciplines, including
critical reasoning and problem solving, information literacy, oral and
written communication, and technology. All courses in the new curriculum had to be (re)approved by a curriculum committee. I selected these
courses for review because the approval process could be expected to
give faculty an opportunity to revise the course to meet the new general
education requirements and incorporate learner-centered approaches.
All general education courses were considered with the following additional selection criteria: the second course of a year-long sequence was
selected for review, all one-semester courses were reviewed, and the syllabus of one section of a multisection course was randomly chosen to be
reviewed. Seventy-two small and large enrollment courses met these criteria and were reviewed.

Course Review and Analysis Process

Shulman (2004) suggests using course syllabi as a means to understand
how courses work since they represent a form of scholarship about an individual's teaching and course design. A preliminary review of a few syllabi
indicated that they addressed the course design elements of learner-centered

teaching. With approval from the university's Institutional Review Board, during 2009 I requested syllabi for the selected courses from course instructors and department chairs. I reviewed the course approval form and the most recent version of the syllabus to determine the learner-centered status of each course. The course approval form requires the instructor to list which of the five general education skills the course would address, objectives for these skills, teaching and learning methods to help students master these skills, and how these skills would be assessed. Assessing syllabi and course approval forms for learner-centered elements is not the same as assessing the course, but taken together, the two documents provide a relatively complete picture of the relevant elements of course design.

Assessing Learner-Centered Approaches to Course Design

Weimer (2002) described five practices that need to change to achieve learner-centered teaching: content, instructor's role, responsibility for learning, purposes and processes of assessment, and the balance of power. Blumberg (2009) further defined Weimer's (2002) five practices with specific instructor behaviors that altogether result in a set of twenty-five descriptive components of learner-centered teaching behaviors (Exhibit 14.1). Blumberg (2009) developed a rubric for each of the five practices by listing their components separately in rows. Each rubric identifies four levels of practice for each component: instructor-centered teaching, learner-centered teaching, and two intermediate levels (called lower and higher level of transition) between the two poles. The rubrics were used to rate the degree to which a course was learner-centered. Exhibit 14.2 gives a sample rubric for two components (complete rubrics can be found in Blumberg, 2009).

Exhibit 14.1 Learner-Centered Components Grouped According to Weimer's Practices

THE FUNCTION OF CONTENT

1. Varied uses of content: In addition to building a knowledge base, instructor uses content to help students know why they need to learn content, acquire discipline-specific learning methodologies, use inquiry or ways of thinking in the discipline, and learn to solve real world problems

2. Level to which students are engaged in content

3. Use of organizing schemes

4. Use of content to facilitate future learning

THE ROLE OF THE INSTRUCTOR

1. Creation of a environment for learning through organization and use of material that accommodates different learning styles
2. Alignment of the course components—objectives, teaching or learning methods, and assessment methods—for consistency
3. Teaching or learning methods appropriate for student learning goals
4. Activities involving interactions of student, instructor, and content
5. Motivation of students to learn (intrinsic drive to learn versus extrinsic reasons)

THE RESPONSIBILITY FOR LEARNING

1. Responsibility for learning—a philosophical overview
2. Learning to learn skills for the present and the future, for example, time management, goal setting, and how to do independent reading and research
3. Self-directed, lifelong learning skills, for example, determining a personal need to know more, knowing who to ask or where to seek information, determining when the need is met, and developing an awareness of a student's learning abilities
4. Students' self-assessment of their learning
5. Students' self-assessment of their strengths and weaknesses
6. Information literacy skills (Association of College and Research Libraries, 2004)

PROCESSES AND PURPOSES OF ASSESSMENT

1. Assessment within the learning process
2. Formative assessment
3. Peer and self assessment
4. Demonstration of mastery and ability to learn from mistakes
5. Authentic assessment

THE BALANCE OF POWER (CONTROL ISSUES)

1. Determination of course content
2. Determination of how students earn grades
3. Use of open-ended assignments
4. Flexibility of course policies, assessment methods, learning methods, and deadlines
5. Opportunities to learn

Note: From Blumberg (2009). Reprinted with permission of John Wiley & Sons, Inc.

Exhibit 14.2 Sample Rubrics and Scoring Index for Two Components for the Responsibility for Learning Practice

Likert Scale Scoring Index	Employs Instructor-Centered Approaches 1	Transitioning to Learner-Centered Approaches		Employs Learner-Centered Approaches 4
		Lower Level of Transitioning 2	Higher Level of Transitioning 3	
Component 4: Students' self-assessment of their learning	Instructor believes that instructors alone assess student learning	Instructor does not direct students to assess their own learning	Instructor sometimes provides direction to help students assess their own learning	Instructor motivates students to routinely and appropriately assess their own learning
Component 6: Information literacy skills as defined by the Association of College and Research Libraries (2004)	Instructor does not help students acquire any information literacy skills	Instructor helps students acquire a few information literacy skills	Instructor helps students acquire some information literacy skills	Instructor facilitates students to become proficient in all five information literacy skills

Source: From Blumberg (2009). Reprinted with permission of John Wiley & Sons, Inc.

Using Blumberg's (2009) rubrics, I rated each course on its learner-centered approaches for all twenty-five components. For example, I used various types of evidence to support my rating on the last component of the responsibility for learning practice, which is information literacy. To rate a course on this component, I looked for evidence in the course approval form or the syllabus that the instructor was helping students acquire information literacy skills. If there were no assignments for which the students had to gather information on their own and there were no writing assignments, I rated the course at the instructor-centered level (1). If the course schedule included a class devoted to searching appropriate databases, I knew that at least a few information literacy skills were taught. If there were writing assignments, I looked for statements about plagiarism in the syllabus or a practice exercise on paraphrasing as evidence that the instructor was helping the students gain the information literacy skill of using information ethically and legally.

Data Analysis

Rubrics can be seen as a series of Likert scales and numbers can be assigned to the levels (Exhibit 14.2). I assigned the following numbers to the levels on the rubrics: 1 = instructor centered, 2 = lower level of transition, 3 = higher level of transition, and 4 = learner centered. If I could not determine the level of the component from the syllabus and course approval forms, I assigned it a 1. I was unable to determine the level on fewer than 4 percent of the components across all courses. I recorded on spreadsheets the ratings for each component of each course.

I created a learner-centered index for each course (summative scale) by taking the sum of the scores assigned to each of the components divided by twenty-five (the total number of components considered). The range of the index is from 1 to 4, with the higher number indicating a more learner-centered course. I also created learner-centered indexes for each of the five practices.

Courses were classified according to how often their instructors used the services of the center. Instructors who attended more than 50 percent of the long workshops hosted by the center or met with the director on a regular basis to discuss their teaching were considered high users. Those who attended 25 to 50 percent of the major events hosted by the center or met with the director a few times a year to discuss their teaching were considered medium users. Low users were those who came to fewer than 24 percent of these events and rarely or never consulted with the director about their teaching or course design.

Assessment Results

The learner-centered indexes of the seventy-two courses reviewed clustered in the lower (instructor-centered or lower level of transition) range of the scale (Figure 14.1). Only one course had a high index (above 3.0), thirty-five had indexes between 2.0 and 3.0, and the remaining thirty-six courses (50 percent) had indexes between 1 and 2. Thus, most of the courses hover around the lower level of transition with respect to learner-centered course design. It should be noted that although a course might be rated in the lower level of transition overall, there were variations in the ratings for each component within each course. Some components, such as level of student engagement, tended to be rated more learner

Figure 14.1 Learner-Centered Index for Seventy-Two Courses

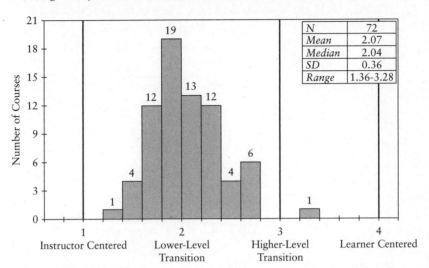

centered, and some components, such as teaching the skills necessary for students to take responsibility for their own learning, were generally rated more instructor centered. The mean index for the responsibility for learning components was 1.98, also around the lower level of transition, and fifty-four of seventy-two (75 percent) courses had a responsibility for a learning index between 1 and 2.

Based on a one-way ANOVA test I concluded that the average learner-centered index does not differ significantly among the departments in which I reviewed more than five courses. I used two separate two-sample t-tests to test for a difference in average learner-centered index between full-time and adjunct faculty and for a difference in average learner-centered index for faculty teaching less than five years and those teaching five or more years. Based on these tests, I concluded that the average learner-centered index for full-time faculty does not significantly differ from the one for adjunct faculty, and there were no significant differences among faculty depending on their years of experience.

Figure 14.2 compares the learner-centered status of courses taught by high ($N = 11$), medium ($N = 7$), and low ($N = 54$) users of the center's services. The mean learner-centered index for high users is higher than the one for nonusers. A significant difference between at least two categories of center users was confirmed by a one-way ANOVA test ($p = 0.0013$). Based on a post hoc analysis conducted using Bonferroni adjustment, there is a significant difference between high and low users ($p < 0.05$).

Figure 14.2 Comparison of Learner-Centered Indexes for Courses
Taught by High, Medium, and Low Users of the Teaching and
Learning Center

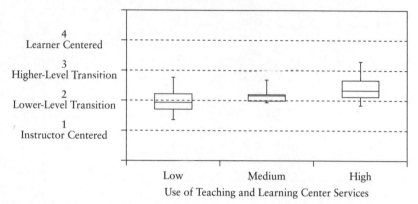

Note: The bottom of the whisker is the lowest value, the lowest line of the box
is the lower quartile (twenty-fifth percentile), the middle line in the box is the
median, the top line of the box is the upper quartile (seventy-fifth percentile),
and the top of the whisker is the highest value.

Limitations of This Study

There is no baseline study of the learner-centered status of courses prior
to the learner-centered strategic initiative. Therefore, this study cannot
infer that any changes were made; it can only determine the status of
course designs at the time of this review. Only one person rated each
of the courses on the components listed on the rubrics. The ratings were
not checked with the instructors of the courses. There was no validation
that the contents of the syllabus and the course approval form reflected
what the instructor actually did in the course. A majority of the courses
are introductory courses taught to first- and second-year students; a study
of upper-division courses might well yield different results.

Although the study found that courses taught by frequent center users
employed more learner-centered approaches than others, it does not
establish a cause-and-effect relationship. The unanswered question is,
"Were these frequent users predisposed to this philosophy of teaching
and course design prior to learning specific techniques, or did these workshops persuade them to change their approach?"

Using the Results: Action Steps

Individually and in groups, I discussed the study, its results, and implications of the results with the provost, deans, appropriate department
chairs, and faculty committees. Each presentation began with the relevant

part of the university's mission statement to remind them that we were supposed to be using learner-centered approaches. I pointed out that the eight years of focused efforts by the center with many faculty attending workshops did not result in many courses using predominantly learner-centered course design elements. The fact that the high users of the center implemented significantly more learner-centered course design elements showed that faculty could implement learner-centered course design at the university even in general education courses. These discussions always led faculty to consider specific ways they could improve their syllabi.

My reports emphasized possible next steps that this university could take to become more learner centered. I described concrete steps that individual faculty members could take, such as teaching students how to use or requiring them to do more self-assessments of their learning and their strengths. My reports contained specific, inexpensive policy recommendations, such as the following: "Faculty need to be evaluated on how learner-centered their teaching actually is. This is not part of the current annual faculty evaluation or promotion and tenure process. Until it is, many faculty members will have little reason to change their teaching."

Further Goals and Actions

The dean of the College of Arts and Sciences (where most of these courses are housed) was interested in the results of this study. She felt that courses in her college should incorporate more aspects of learner-centered teaching and course design because it is consistent with her vision of a liberal arts education. My study prompted the college's strategic planning committee to discuss how learner-centered teaching and course design fit with their vision. As a result, learner-centered teaching is now explicitly mentioned in that college's strategic plan. The plan mentions a few broad-stroke methods, but most of the actual steps will be defined by the tactical planning task force. Since the dean asked me to serve on that task force, I am confident that I will be able to incorporate appropriate specific steps. These steps might identify which components need to be emphasized in a general education curriculum and which might be more appropriate to advanced courses.

At the beginning of 2010, I offered several workshops on how to implement specific aspects of learner-centered teaching, and the dean strongly encouraged her faculty to attend. Next, with her encouragement, I plan to work with individual departments at their meetings. The dean and I are planning a collegewide event to help faculty implement learner-centered course design. Through these steps, more faculty members could design their courses using specific learner-centered strategies, and perhaps even more critical, they will realize why they need to use learner-centered approaches.

My next step is to interview some faculty whose syllabi and course approval forms I reviewed. These interviews will serve two purposes. First, I can determine whether my ratings for their courses are accurate. Second, and more important, is to begin to discuss steps toward specific changes to their teaching and course design.

Discussion

At this university, learner-centered teaching and course design are explicitly mentioned in the mission statement, a strategic imperative adopted by the university, and detailed action steps identified by a tactical planning group. The Teaching and Learning Center has focused on how to implement learner-centered teaching and course design for almost a decade. Yet the results of the study indicated that faculty members were not implementing learner-centered teaching. The consistently low ratings for all components showed that faculty had not aligned their course designs to be consistent with the university's mission, their own statements formed during the consensus conference, or faculty development efforts.

At first I was quite discouraged with these results. For a short time, I even took them personally as this is a small university and I know every faculty member. Since faculty developers are in the habit of solving problems, I thought about possible changes in my faculty development practices. In the future, I will do more one-on-one follow-up after workshops. I will not assume that faculty both heard the message and know how to implement changes.

I speculate that most faculty members did not implement learner-centered course design for a variety of reasons. While the center offered many educational opportunities for faculty to learn about learner-centered teaching and course design and the administration fully supported learner-centered teaching, no real incentives were provided to implement it. Faculty were not given release time to revise their courses. The student course evaluations continued to ask about traditional instructor behaviors such as the effectiveness of presenting the material. Annual evaluations of faculty or those for promotion and tenure did not mention learner-centered teaching or course design. As the ratings of the courses taught by the high users of center services indicate, faculty can learn to change their teaching practices and course design. However, many probably need to be convinced to do so by either pressure or significant rewards.

Voluntary faculty development efforts such as those offered by teaching and learning centers cannot move the majority of an institution's faculty to implement learner-centered teaching and course design without a parallel effort to change the institution's collective policies, structures, and individual beliefs. To truly achieve implementation of unfamiliar teaching philosophies and practices, we need to have a concrete plan for widespread culture change. For example, many faculty members may need support to spend a significant amount of time revising their course design. Such support might take the form of teaching fellowships with faculty working together with the faculty developers, release time, or summer pay. Most of these changes can occur only through administrative decisions and actions.

Conclusion

Disappointing results can be the stimulus for change if they are used properly. In our assessment and accountability culture, coupling data with concrete and specific recommendations provides the impetus for change. The process I describe in this chapter points to the importance of assessing the impact of our work not only as a scholarly activity for our own publications, but also to inform discussions with key decision makers as part of the faculty development assessment cycle.

REFERENCES

Association of College and Research Libraries. (2004). *Information literacy competency standards for higher education*. Retrieved from www.ala.org /ala/acrl/acrlstandards/informationliteracycompetency.htm

Blumberg, P. (2004). Beginning journey toward a culture of learning centered teaching. *Journal of Student Centered Learning, 2*(1), 68–80.

Blumberg, P. (2009). *Developing learner-centered teaching: A practical guide for faculty*. San Francisco: Jossey-Bass.

Blumberg, P., & Everett, J. (2005). Achieving a campus consensus on learning-centered teaching. In S. Chadwick-Blossey & D. R. Robertson (Eds.), *To improve the academy: Vol. 23. Resources for faculty, instructional, and organizational development* (pp. 191–210). San Francisco: Jossey-Bass/Anker.

Cox, M. D. (2004). Introduction to faculty learning communities. In M. D. Cox & L. Richlin (Eds.), *Building faculty learning communities* (pp. 5–23). San Francisco: Jossey-Bass.

Eison, J., & Stevens, E. (1995). Faculty development workshops and institutes. In W. A. Wright (Ed.), *Teaching improvement practices: Successful strategies for higher education* (pp. 206–236). San Francisco: Jossey-Bass/Anker.

Fink, L. D. (2003). *Creating significant learning experiences: An integrated approach to designing college courses*. San Francisco: Jossey-Bass.

Millis, B. (1997). Evaluating a consultation program for parttime adjunct faculty. In K. T. Brinko & R. J. Menges (Eds.), *Practically speaking: A sourcebook for instructional consultants in higher education* (pp. 245–259). Stillwater, OK: New Forums Press.

Shulman, L. S. (2004). *Teaching as community practice*. San Francisco: Jossey-Bass.

Sorcinelli, M. D. (1997). The teaching improvement process. In K. T. Brinko & R. J. Menges (Eds.), *Practically speaking: A sourcebook for instructional consultants in higher education* (pp. 157–158). Stillwater, OK: New Forums Press.

Suskie, L. (2004). *Assessing student learning: A common sense guide*. San Francisco: Jossey-Bass/Anker.

University of the Sciences in Philadelphia. (2002). *Strategic planning document*. Unpublished document.

Weimer, M. (2002). *Learner-centered teaching*. San Francisco: Jossey-Bass.

15

SOCIAL CAPITAL AND THE CAMPUS COMMUNITY

Andrew N. Carpenter, Ellis University
Linda Coughlin, St. Mary's College of Maryland
Susanne Morgan, Ithaca College
Christopher Price, The College at Brockport,
State University of New York

Investigating colleges' and universities' social capital through its five dimensions—civic engagement, norms and trust, collective action, bonding capital, and bridging capital—provides a powerful way of thinking about organizational and faculty development. Four very different institutions of higher learning have promoted their organizational development through efforts that build social capital. We seek to inspire additional application of and research into this topic by demonstrating that confronting the complexities of social capital within diverse campus communities can help faculty developers understand those communities with greater nuance and in ways that improve their ability to design and implement development initiatives.

The study of social capital is most developed in political science, economics, sociology, and community organizing. We submit that the concepts underpinning social capital and its effects on community have value for institutions of higher learning as they develop their organizations and, especially, their faculty. Thus, the question that inspires this chapter is: Might a thorough understanding of the dynamics of social capital allow us to understand our organizations' development potential and give us tools for building stronger communities on our campuses?

The Fundamentals of Social Capital

The metaphor of capital has been used in a variety of contexts. Financial capital is money available for investment; physical capital is real estate, equipment, and infrastructure; human capital is in training that increases productivity on the job; and cultural capital involves in-depth cultural knowledge that can be turned to the owner's socioeconomic advantage (Light, 2004).

A social capital economy can be understood as a system similar to that of a financial economy. A financial economy is based on the exchange of money, and financial capital is the accumulation of financial resources. A social capital economy is based on exchanges between and among people who form social relationships. In the social capital system, the currency is the trust and shared norms of the relationships, and the wealth is social networks.

Theories of social capital investigate how relationships of trust embedded in social networks (Light, 2004) support individuals' and groups' productivity and capacity to plan future action and achieve collective aims. In Farr's (2004) useful characterization, "Social capital is . . . conceptualized as the network of associations, activities, or relations that bind people together as a community via certain norms and psychological capacities, notably trust, which are essential for civil society and productive of future collective action or goods" (p. 9). A key assumption of this chapter is that faculty developers have much to gain by understanding the network of associations operative in their own institutions and by conducting faculty development activities that contribute to social capital. The results can be improved faculty productivity, increased student learning, and a greater institutional capacity to learn and improve.

Before discussing these themes with respect to our diverse institutions, we pause to reflect that the contemporary concept of social capital has a long intellectual history and pedigree that includes work on political economy by philosophers Jeremy Bentham and Henry Sidgwick, work on social structures by Max Weber and Emile Durkheim, and work on democracy and education by John Dewey (Farr, 2004). Farr identified the first use of the term *social capital* by Karl Marx in 1867, but the intellectual history of the concept has much deeper philosophical roots. Marx's use of the term drew heavily on Aristotle's conception of humans flourishing within a social context. Aristotle used the concepts of friendship (*philia*) and political community (*zoon politicon*) to understand the structures of society and political economy and their relationship to individuals' ability to develop their capacities through action in social and political contexts (Gilbert, 1981; McCarthy, 1990).

Most recently, the concept of social capital has gained visibility in the United States through the well-known book *Bowling Alone: The Collapse and Revival of American Community* (Putnam, 2000), which applied Putnam's prior definition of *social capital* as "social organization such as networks, norms, and social trust that facilitate coordination and cooperation for mutual benefit" (Putnam, 1995, p. 67). Rohe (2004) articulated the dynamics of the social capital system by suggesting that a person who engages in civic life builds social networks from which relationships of interpersonal trust develop. Environments rich in networks of reciprocal relations are likely to be able to engage in effective collective action, and that action increases benefits for both the individual and the social organization. Completing the cycle, increased individual and social benefits are likely to prompt increased civic engagement. Other theorists have distinguished two forms of social capital: bonding capital, which brings together people who already know each other, and bridging capital, which connects people who previously did not interact (Vidal, 2004).

It is with these concepts that we analyze efforts to build and exploit social capital at our own institutions. We start by noting that increasing individuals' engagement in the community, for example, by joining or forming social networks, can build interpersonal trust. Putnam (2000) and others suggest that the reciprocal nature of the relationships within social networks increases interpersonal trust. An organization in which social networks exist is better able to engage in collective action to achieve common objectives, in part because of shared norms and thus common goals. Effective collective action can bring benefits to both individuals and the organization. Thus, both individual and organization become wealthier in social capital when there is a higher level of social engagement, and individuals and organizations are likely to increase their social capital further through shared goals and actions. This characteristic of social capital, that new capital can be created, differentiates it from the financial capital system (Light, 2004). That said, there are significant relationships among the various types of capital; for example, the absence of ready financial capital during a time of economic troubles may spur institutions to focus on developing their social capital. Institutions may find that using social capital to fuel collective action may help them cope with difficult financial situations.

Social Capital and the Campus Community

Building community is important in higher education, and concern with community is evident in discussions of student life (Kuh, Kinzie, Bridges, & Hayek, 2007), institutional well-being (Keeling, 2004), and teaching and learning (Fink, 2003). Community is also central in efforts to enhance faculty experience through faculty learning communities (FLCs) (Cox & Richlin, 2004) and through wider intellectual exchange as promoted by the Carnegie Foundation for the Advancement of Teaching and Learning in their Learning Commons project (Hutchings & Huber, 2005).

Our analysis and application of social capital to institutions of higher learning is informed by the contributors to a symposium on social capital in the *Journal of the American Planning Association* (Hutchinson et al., 2004). We submit that the work of community planners is similar to the work of faculty developers, both of whom engage in organizational development from a basis in theoretical and applied research. We also note that our purpose here is akin to that of the planners' symposium, which sought "not to consider social capital as a societal phenomenon, but to explore whether this concept could provide valuable insights, approaches, and tools for planners" (Hutchinson, 2004, p. 144).

In higher education, the concept of social capital has been used directly and indirectly. Cox (2004) reported findings from Putnam's book when he emphasized the importance of community and the value of faculty learning communities (FLCs). Participants in successful FLCs build social capital as they form bonds with each other, establish shared norms, and engage collectively in common scholarly activity. FLCs benefit both the individual faculty member and the institutional culture. We suggest that analyzing these communities in terms of the specific dimensions of social capital could be helpful in maximizing their potential.

Writers such as Boice (2000) urge new faculty to become engaged in their campus communities, and although they seldom mention social capital directly, they imply that civic engagement will help faculty learn norms and build relationships of trust. Boice's research on successful new faculty members has demonstrated that "quick starters" build social capital more effectively than their peers do. A systematic examination of these findings in terms of the dimensions of social capital would be an intriguing way to guide faculty development efforts.

The strong networks formed intentionally by the Professional and Organizational Development Network in Higher Education (POD) serve to increase bridging capital when leading scholars engage with newcomers at conferences and online. Similarly, the Carnegie Foundation for the Advancement of Teaching's advocacy of a teaching and learning commons can be seen as an effort to build bonding capital among faculty worldwide.

Building Social Capital at Four Institutions of Higher Learning

The concept of social capital has been valuable in understanding faculty and organizational development efforts on the campus of each chapter author. Our case studies examine with a new lens—that of building social capital—recent development initiatives at our own institutions. In this chapter, therefore, we are applying the principles of social capital in retrospect by teaching ourselves new insights about what has already occurred. We hope that these insights will inspire readers both to design initiatives that involve social capital building activities and engage in scholarship that applies and extends the principles of social capital development to academic communities.

Ithaca College

Ithaca College is a midsized private comprehensive college with six thousand undergraduates in five schools and a few hundred students in professional graduate programs. There is no collegewide curricular requirement for students, and the 450 full-time faculty members have been quite isolated in their schools. Institutional faculty development efforts have been decentralized, and despite a large budget for individual faculty grants, a faculty member assigned half-time provides the only regular support for individual and organizational development. Into this environment came a new president, provost, and deans of influential schools.

Assessing the well-being of the faculty, these new administrators identified several challenges that relate to social capital. Isolation is typical of much of faculty work; in most disciplines, both teaching and research are individualized, and there is little incentive to work collaboratively. As elsewhere in higher education, the rapid growth of the college in the 1970s created a particular shared faculty identity. The incoming faculty generation does not share the old identity and does not experience an all-college faculty culture.

Anxiety about tenure is high among newer faculty, who sense shifting norms but do not have clear information. The school and college administrations are clear that effective teaching employs methods other than lecture and discussion, that interdisciplinary or integrative learning is critically important, and that continued scholarship is expected of new faculty. However, the middle level, those who review faculty in the departments and schools, are often overly cautious about such contemporary views of faculty work.

Faculty governance is uneven across the college, and there is no clear faculty voice about curriculum and policy. Particularly in the liberal arts school, the largest, faculty are typically far removed from important decisions. Very few faculty members engage in all-college governance activities and when they do, it may be with a sense of futility.

Each of these challenges—a culture of faculty isolation, anxiety about reviews and tenure, and weak faculty governance—points to a pervasive problem of weak social capital. Recent efforts by the faculty development coordinator, the deans, and the president are addressing social capital concerns.

For several years, groups of faculty have built trusting relationships through the all-college mentoring program and tenure seminar. In each of these programs, small faculty groups increase shared norms and reduce isolation and anxiety. The mentoring program consists of small, diverse groups of faculty whose explicit objective is immersion in the campus culture. Approximately one-fourth of the faculty has participated at least once, and they report that the reciprocal nature of the relationships is the major benefit. Faculty at all levels gain insights into other disciplines, new approaches to teaching, and understanding of the college culture. At least five collaborative teaching or research projects have emerged from mentoring groups.

The goal of the tenure seminars, more content oriented than the mentoring groups, is to demystify the tenure process and help faculty create more nuanced analyses of their work. In part, the tenure seminar program has been a "subversive" effort to improve the reviews conducted by committees and department chairs. As junior faculty expand the issues they include in their self-evaluation, they lead their reviewers to address those issues. This collective action by newer faculty is gradually shifting the college's norms and increasing the capacity for effective reviews.

Administrators also support effective collective action from the top; the new president and the dean of the largest school are actively revitalizing faculty governance. The resulting shared social networks affirm the emerging institutional norms and strengthen the social capital of both individuals and administrative units.

An intentional focus on increasing social capital produced the Ithaca Faculty Commons, a new faculty development model designed to maximize resources in a period of budgetary constraint. At the request of the new provost, faculty developed a plan to coordinate the many existing faculty development efforts within a blended online and face-to-face environment. Web 2.0 tools are central to the Faculty Commons, which builds engagement by directing faculty into a sophisticated suite of social networking and other Web-based tools. Individual faculty and staff post the faculty development activities or resources of their committees, offices, or projects. Faculty conduct or archive discussions and presentations through the evolving campus online social networking environment. Faculty engagement drives the success of this model, and the relationships that develop will be an additional benefit.

Bonding and bridging capital also guide faculty and organizational development. With the generational transition, bonding capital is very important. A culture of mistrust of administration and of factions within departments is diminishing as newer faculty members perceive themselves as institutional citizens in addition to disciplinary teacher-scholars. Intentional and increased use of the Web environment increases bridging capital by linking people across status and divisions. For instance, the president is a regular participant in the online social community.

Ithaca College expects that intentionally increasing social networks to build reciprocal trusting relationships will bring benefits for individuals and the institution by increasing faculty retention and effectiveness and increase faculty engagement in the life of the institution.

St. Mary's College of Maryland

St. Mary's College of Maryland is a small, public, liberal arts honors college with two thousand undergraduates and a single graduate program (master of arts in teaching). In a series of faculty discussions of the mission of the college held in 2003, weak organizational communication emerged as a primary issue, and academic excellence was affirmed as the main priority. Online postings of the groups' ideas led to wider discussions and promoted trust in a common goal. Over the next five years, faculty vigorously discussed proposals in small groups and large forums that produced changes in faculty governance and in tenure and promotion processes, and a new core curriculum. The governance changes streamlined multiple campus committees into standing faculty senate committees that now have student and administrative staff membership. These structures allow thorough and speedy review and critique of policies and processes, providing bridges between groups that had seldom discussed these issues before.

As a result of the governance changes, responsibility for faculty development shifted from four division heads to sixteen department chairs. The chairs now meet regularly with the provost and associate provost for academic affairs to debate a wide range of cross-campus issues in a forum that builds bridging capital. Most departments have launched strategic plans, analyzed community standards, developed mentoring standards for both pretenure and tenured faculty, and created assessment plans for their curricula.

Intentional efforts to enhance social capital began in 2006 with week-long teaching excellence workshops open to the entire faculty. The associate provost encouraged the education studies department to develop workshops in collaboration with other interested faculty; their engagement sparked more faculty to become leaders of discussions and active learning sessions focused on liberal arts pedagogy, classroom management, assessment, and international education. After a modest beginning, the workshops now host over 50 percent of the faculty each August. At these workshops, faculty discuss college norms for teaching, groups explore new teaching ideas, and trust builds among group members who normally do not interact to discuss ideas and devise strategies for teaching.

A senior faculty member working with two pretenure faculty developed a new faculty seminar that allows faculty to share their first-year teaching experiences with peers. The organizing group asked the provost for stable funding to ensure its continuation. New faculty meet monthly, visit classrooms of peers and more experienced colleagues, develop group norms and bond in the seminar setting, and become fully engaged in the campus community much earlier than previous cohorts did. The cohorts go on to work together to complete their tenure and promotion portfolios.

The new core curriculum led faculty to collectively study ways to teach four liberal arts skills effectively throughout the curriculum. At the genesis of the new core curriculum, faculty called for more faculty development to build teaching and assessment skills in the newly instituted first-year seminars. The yearly cohort of first-year seminar teachers now brings their experience from the first-year seminars back to their departments to strengthen student skill building in the majors. Such collective action has resulted in an online handbook that outlines best practices and useful examples of pedagogy for critical thinking, oral and written communication, and information literacy across the curriculum.

Collective action led to a major revision of the faculty handbook that now contains previously missing descriptions of academic responsibilities and the processes linked to them, as well as a section of community standards that outlines in one place our former unwritten norms. All committees, both administrative and faculty, post minutes, agendas, and background materials on a campus portal. The administration often asks for written feedback on proposed initiatives and publishes anonymous surveys of opinions and preferences. All handbooks for the faculty, students, board of trustees, and department chairs are available for everyone to read in our online portal.

Each of these major changes occurred by building bridging capital. Small groups of faculty, students, and staff were organized into discussion groups by the faculty senate working with the provost's office. Faculty from disparate departments were intentionally placed together in the groups. The discussions that ensued were richer because they bridged the concerns of multiple campus groups. The linking of campus groups to each other and to authority has engaged the community in the decision-making process, increased communication, transparency, and trust and has made community norms explicit.

Ellis University

In 2009, the first full year of this private, nonprofit, and exclusively online university's operation, Ellis University undertook a series of organizational development initiatives focused on improving the institution's decision-making processes. First, it implemented an institutional model to make its decision making more transparent. Second, it created processes and tools to ensure that its new strategic plan, which was developed by the institution's administration, faculty, and staff, made strong and transparent connections to other policy, decision making, and budgeting systems. Third, the university created a shared governance agreement, and fourth, it created a new faculty senate constitution, both of which its trustees adopted. Taken together, the initiatives helped the institution to make decisions that are data driven, collaboratively achieved with input from essential personnel across the institution, and responsive to the needs of students and other stakeholders. This is why many within the institution considered these initiatives significant milestones in Ellis University's early development; in particular, many faculty and administrators viewed their successful completion as a vital indicator of the new institution's ability to direct its own development, foster innovation, and enhance institutional assessment.

Each of these initiatives also served to build social capital. With respect to norms and trust, the initiatives were intentionally built on the core values that inspired the founding of the institution: educational quality, academic rigor, and institutional integrity. Successful work on the four initiatives increased trust among participants, because their successes reaffirmed key norms and core values and the initiatives involved inclusive and democratic collective action.

The inclusive nature of the initiatives also created a significant opportunity to develop bridging capital. For example, planning and drafting a comprehensive shared governance agreement required substantive discussions among many adjunct and full-time faculty, and between members of those groups and the institution's entire academic administrative leadership. Successfully negotiating this agreement required many collegial discussions and created strong relationships among elected faculty leaders, the institution's president, and the chair of the university's board of trustees. The high level of engagement by faculty, senior administrative leaders, and trustees has served to significantly enhance social capital. For example, nearly all the faculty members involved in the negotiation of the shared governance agreement report that they now trust and respect the institution's president and trustees, and they also report that they feel trusted and respected by those institutional leaders. Likewise, adjunct faculty members involved in these initiatives report they have never felt more valued by, or more strongly connected to, an institution of higher learning to which they had no full-time connection.

In short, by developing and exploiting social capital, Ellis University has achieved a level of collegial interaction and decision making that is unusual among traditional institutions, and even rarer among online institutions. We note, however, that this institution's ambitions are tempered by the difficulty of developing social capital in an exclusively online environment. Two significant problems are that faculty are geographically dispersed, making formal and informal communication difficult, and that the faculty include many adjuncts, a group often marginalized in academic governance. The use of bonding capital provides a significant resource for working on those challenges. Its faculty interacts using a sophisticated virtual campus learning platform that includes multiple social networking functions and widespread use of Web 2.0 communication technologies like wikis and blogs. These tools allow academic stakeholders to begin to address its challenges and to draw on and build social capital as it continues to learn how to overcome them.

The College at Brockport, State University of New York

The College at Brockport is one of thirteen regional comprehensive colleges in the State University of New York system. Since 1997, the college has sought to change its identity to compete for students who traditionally would not have considered enrolling at Brockport. To help bring about this change, the college reorganized the academic affairs division in 2010, going from three schools to four (with a fifth to come two or three years later), in part to create a more entrepreneurial culture among the faculty and administration. These changes have caused predictable anxiety as some faculty are not certain whether or where they fit within this new plan. From a faculty and organizational development perspective, the concern is that some faculty might choose to focus more on their own career at the expense of initiatives that would increase institutional social capital. The challenge is to figure out how to help the faculty, professional staff, and administration reframe this change as an opportunity to work together to improve both their own professional development and student learning. Two initiatives already under way—faculty learning communities and programs to increase student civic engagement—are likely starting points to begin this development work.

Beginning in 2008, FLCs have been piloted as a possible model for all faculty and staff professional development initiatives. The FLC approach helps increase engagement as the participants explore their professional interests with colleagues in other departments in order to achieve individual and collective goals that have a positive impact on the college community. For example, three FLCs (on diversity, service-learning, and online learning) have given the faculty involved a sense of ownership over areas that are often top-down administration-led initiatives. FLCs have the potential to increase levels of trust among the faculty through the creation of a norm of interdepartmental collaboration. In order to make such collaboration more visible, the recently established annual teaching and learning day gives the FLC faculty an opportunity to inform colleagues outside their departments about what they are doing to improve student learning.

In 2004, Brockport joined the American Democracy Project (ADP), an initiative cosponsored by the American Association of State Colleges and Universities and the *New York Times*, that is focused on helping undergraduate students become better citizens. At that time, the campus undertook a civic engagement audit of both the academic curriculum and the cocurriculum (student clubs, student government activities, and other programs outside the academic departments). The audit showed that although civic engagement activities were widespread, there was little awareness among faculty and staff about what was going on outside their own departments. The effort to increase student civic engagement generated significant bridging capital as faculty worked alongside student affairs staff to strategize how to leverage what the college was currently doing to create new programs to meet the ADP goals. While Brockport was able to establish some initiatives (including a speaker series, a freshman summer reading program, an interdisciplinary ADP course, a student living-learning community, and a standing steering committee), the level of bridging capital generated has not been sufficient to make a significant impact on the student population. In order to achieve deeper and more sustained levels of student civic engagement, the college now has a student leadership program and is investigating the establishment of a service-learning program. These programs will require a significant amount of bonding capital among those dedicated to these projects and bridging capital between faculty and professional staff in student affairs.

Summary of Institutional Social Capital Efforts

The preceding discussion of the ways in which the concept of social capital has played out in development efforts on each author's campus is summarized in Table 15.1.

Conclusions and Recommendations for Future Research

From the examples we have discussed from our own institutions, three conclusions stand out. First, learning how to assess social capital at institutions of higher learning can provide powerful new insights into the strengths and weaknesses of development efforts. Second, learning how to identify opportunities to increase social capital may help campuses plan and prioritize future development efforts. Third, learning how to effectively use existing social capital may help developers to maximize the efficacy of their projects and interventions. However, if developers are to learn to assess and use social capital, additional scholarly work is required. In particular, there is an urgent need to design and validate methods for systematically measuring social capital at institutions of higher learning, and there exist numerous significant opportunities to construct theoretical and practical tools that faculty developers can use to assess, build, and exploit social capital at their own institutions.

Social capital is a complex concept, and one of great utility. Confronting the complexities of social capital within diverse campus communities can help faculty developers better understand those communities and thereby improve their capacity to design and to assess development initiatives.

Table 15.1 Social Capital in Development Efforts

	Ithaca College	St. Mary's College of Maryland	Ellis University	The College at Brockport, State University of New York
Type	Private comprehensive	Public liberal arts (honors)	Private comprehensive (online)	Public comprehensive
Number of students	6,000 undergraduate and 450 graduate	2,000 undergraduate and 45 graduate	1,500 undergraduate and 500 graduate	6,900 undergraduate and 1,400 graduate
Number of faculty	450 full time and 200 part time/adjunct	140 full time and 60 part time/adjunct	11 full time and 275 part time/ adjunct	360 full time and 270 part time/adjunct
Civic engagement	Faculty commons	Teaching excellence workshops and first-year teachers' program	Shared governance agreement	Faculty learning communities
Norms and trust	Mentoring program and tenure seminar	Peer-to-peer dialogue one-on-one and in small groups	Open communication and collaboration	Interdepartmental collaboration
Effective collective action	Tenure review improvements Faculty governance enhancements	Faculty governance changes Tenure and promotion process changes New core curriculum	Six new degree programs Formal decision-making model Navigation of regulatory challenges Successful regional accreditation	Academic affairs reorganization Programs to increase student civic engagement
Bonding capital	Recently hired faculty incorporated as institutional citizens	Collaborative development of courses by new first-year-seminar teachers	Faculty participation in a virtual social network using Web 2.0 tools	Faculty participation in annual Teaching and Learning Day event

(*Continued*)

Table 15.1   (*Continued*)

	Ithaca College	St. Mary's College of Maryland	Ellis University	The College at Brockport, State University of New York
Bridging capital	Development of senior-junior faculty relationships through mentoring program Administration building stronger faculty voice	Administration, faculty, students, and staff membership on committees and small group discussions	Interaction of full-time and adjunct faculty, trustees, and administration using new systems of shared governance	Faculty and professional staff participation in faculty learning communities and student civic engagement programs

REFERENCES

Boice, R. (2000). *Advice for new faculty members: Nihil nimus.* Needham Heights, MA: Allyn & Bacon.

Cox, M. D. (2004). Introduction to faculty learning communities. In M. D. Cox & L. Richlin (Eds.), *New directions for teaching and learning: No. 97. Building faculty learning communities* (pp. 5–23). San Francisco: Jossey-Bass.

Cox, M. D., & Richlin, L. (Eds.). (2004). *New directions for teaching and learning: No. 97. Building faculty learning communities.* San Francisco: Jossey-Bass.

Farr, J. (2004). Social capital: A conceptual history. *Political Theory, 32*(1), 6–33.

Fink, L. D. (2003). *Creating significant learning experiences: An integrated approach to designing college courses.* San Francisco: Jossey-Bass.

Gilbert, A. (1981). Historical theory and the structure of moral argument. *Political Theory, 9*(2), 173–205.

Hutchings, P., & Huber, M. T. (2005). Building the teaching commons. *Carnegie Perspectives.* Retrieved from www.carnegiefoundation.org/ perspectives/building-teaching-commons

Hutchinson, J. (2004). Introduction. In J. Hutchinson, A. C. Vidal, R. Putnam, I. Light, X. de Souza Briggs, W. M. Rohe, et al., Using social capital to help integrate planning theory, research, and practice [Edited symposium]. *Journal of the American Planning Association, 70*(2), 143–144.

Hutchinson, J., Vidal, A. C., Putnam, R., Light, I., de Souza Briggs, X., Rohe, W. M., et al. (2004). Using social capital to help integrate planning theory, research, and practice [Edited symposium]. *Journal of the American Planning Association, 70*(2), 142–192.

Keeling, R. P. (2004). *Learning reconsidered: A campus-wide focus on the student experience.* Washington DC: American College Personnel Association and National Association of Student Personnel Administrators.

Kuh, G. D., Kinzie, J., Bridges, B. K., & Hayek, J. C. (2007). *Piecing together the student success puzzle: Research, propositions, and recommendations.* San Francisco: Jossey-Bass.

Light, I. (2004). Social capital's unique accessibility. *Journal of the American Planning Association, 70*(2), 145–151.

McCarthy, G. E. (1990). *Marx and the ancients: Classical ethics, social justice, and nineteenth-century political economy.* Lanham, MD: Rowman & Littlefield.

Putnam, R. D. (1995). Bowling alone: America's declining social capital. *Journal of Democracy, 6*(1), 64–78.

Putnam, R. D. (2000). *Bowling alone: The collapse and revival of American community.* New York: Simon & Schuster.

Rohe, W. M. (2004). Building social capital through community development. In J. Hutchinson, A. C. Vidal, R. Putnam, I. Light, X. de Souza Briggs, W. M. Rohe, et al., Using social capital to help integrate planning theory, research, and practice [Edited symposium]. *Journal of the American Planning Association, 70*(2), 158–164.

Vidal, A. C. (2004). Building social capital to promote community equity. In J. Hutchinson, A. C. Vidal, R. Putnam, I. Light, X. de Souza Briggs, W. M. Rohe, et al., Using social capital to help integrate planning theory, research, and practice [Edited symposium]. *Journal of the American Planning Association, 70*(2), 164–168.

ENRICHING OUR CRAFT

16

TEACHING AND LEARNING TOGETHER

COLLEGE FACULTY AND UNDERGRADUATES

COCREATE A PROFESSIONAL

DEVELOPMENT MODEL

Alison Cook-Sather, Bryn Mawr College

Most models of professional development assume that faculty learning is the purview of faculty colleagues or teaching and learning center staff. A program at Bryn Mawr College challenges that assumption by inviting undergraduate students to serve as pedagogical consultants to faculty members. Feedback from participants suggests that this approach affords faculty and students an unusual opportunity to coconstruct a more informed model of faculty development, deepens the learning experiences of both faculty and students, and recasts the responsibility for those learning experiences as one that faculty and students share.

The vast majority of professional development models assume that either faculty colleagues or the staff of professional teaching and learning centers should be responsible for faculty learning. Reflective and collaborative approaches (Cowan & Westwood, 2006; Huston & Weaver, 2008), faculty learning communities (Cox, 2003; Richlin & Cox, 2004), and peer observation models (Peel, 2005) put faculty into constructive dialogue with one another about what is and what could be happening in their classrooms. With few exceptions (Cox, 2000; Cox & Sorenson, 2000; Sorenson, 2001;

Many thanks to Jody Cohen, James Groccia, Alice Lesnick, Judith Miller, Elliott Shore, and several anonymous reviewers for helpful comments on the manuscript for this chapter.

Werder & Otis, 2010), students are not among the interlocutors or collaborators in faculty learning. Indeed, as Cox and Sorenson (2000) have argued, student involvement "has not only been just a small component of faculty development practices—it has been virtually invisible" (p. 99)

In the Students as Learners and Teachers (SaLT) program at Bryn Mawr College, student involvement is not only visible; it is central to faculty development. College undergraduates assume the role of student consultant and work as partners with college faculty members to cocreate a new model of faculty learning. Part of Bryn Mawr's Teaching and Learning Initiative (www.brynmawr.edu/tli), this program is modeled on a project that positions high school students as consultants to prospective secondary teachers (Cook-Sather, 2002, 2006a, 2009b). Applying to the college context principles of student voice work developed largely within K–12 schools (Thiessen & Cook-Sather, 2007), SaLT complements a new strand of the scholarship of teaching and learning (SoTL) focused on student voice (Mihans, Long, & Felten, 2008; Werder & Otis, 2010).

SaLT: An Overview

SaLT aims to foster dialogue and collaboration across community members who occupy traditionally distinct and delineated institutional roles (Lesnick & Cook-Sather, 2010). Specifically, SaLT aims to support generative dialogue about teaching and learning that rarely unfolds between faculty members and students and, through that dialogue, to affirm and improve teaching and learning in the college's classrooms. Funded by a grant from the Andrew W. Mellon Foundation, SaLT has run every semester since its pilot in spring 2007. It is neither formally evaluative nor intended to be remedial, and faculty involved choose to participate for a variety of pedagogical reasons. Students too participate for various reasons, but all of them desire to be part of a reflective dialogue about what is happening and what could be happening in college classrooms.

Each year all faculty members at Bryn Mawr and Haverford Colleges are invited to apply to participate in a semester-long seminar that includes weekly two-hour meetings, weekly posts to a closed blog, work with a student consultant, mid- and end-of-semester feedback, and development of a final portfolio or a stand-alone partnership with a student consultant that can last anywhere from several weeks to a full semester. One of the seminars is devoted to supporting incoming tenure-track faculty members, who are given a course release by Bryn Mawr and Haverford provosts for their participation. Three other seminars, each with five spaces, are open to all full-time, continuing faculty members, who earn stipends for their participation that are supported by the Mellon grant. Faculty applicants go through a lottery process; those who are selected are assigned student consultants largely according to participants' schedules and, where possible, taking into consideration style and personality. Between 2007 and 2010, SaLT supported eighty-nine faculty members and thirty-nine student consultants in 115 partnerships. Faculty span ranks and divisions range from new to the colleges to those with forty years of teaching experience.

Sophomore through senior students enrolled as undergraduates at Bryn Mawr and Haverford are invited to apply for the role of student consultant. Applicants include students who major in different fields, claim different identities, and bring varying degrees of formal preparation in educational studies (from those with no course work in education to those pursuing state certification to teach at the secondary level). The application process includes writing a statement regarding their qualifications and securing two letters of recommendation—one from a faculty or staff member and one from a student. Student consultants attend an orientation and are supported in their work through weekly reflective meetings.

Students are not enrolled in the courses for which they serve as consultants. Each student consultant has the following responsibilities: meet with the faculty member to establish why each is involved and what hopes both have for the collaboration and to plan the semester's focus and meetings; visit one class session each week; take detailed observation notes on the pedagogical challenges the faculty member has identified; survey or interview students in the class (if the faculty member wishes) for midcourse feedback or at another point in the semester; meet weekly with the faculty member to discuss observation notes and other feedback and implications; participate in weekly meetings with one another and with me in my role as the coordinator of SaLT; and visit one or more faculty seminars five times over the course of the semester. For full-semester partnerships, student consultants work approximately seven hours per week and receive nine hundred dollars. For shorter partnerships, student consultants are paid by the hour.

Both student consultants and faculty members receive handbooks that I revise each semester with input from experienced student consultants and faculty participants. The handbooks outline the key commitments of the SaLT program and, rather than strict prescriptions for practice, offer guidelines for building partnerships.

In addition to the formative assessment conducted throughout the partnerships, at the conclusion of each partnership, all participants answer a series of questions such as, "What are the most important insights, lessons, affirmations, new understandings, and clarifications you take forward with you from this experience?" These questions provide participants an opportunity to revisit issues they explored together during their partnerships and provide essential feedback to me as program coordinator.

Challenging the Norms of Professional Development

Norms within professional development include neither the premise that students have unique perspectives on learning and teaching and should be afforded opportunities to actively shape their education (Cook-Sather, 2006b) nor the premise that we have "an ethical obligation to involve our students more actively [in faculty development]" (Zahorski, quoted in Cox & Sorenson, 2000, p. 98). Therefore, both faculty and student participants must wrestle with the doubts and vulnerabilities prompted by these premises. Faculty must rethink their customary position of authority on pedagogical practice. In one faculty member's words, "There's a need to overcome something that I would have thought had I not heard [their] thoughtful comments: What do students know?" (All quotations included are representative of a perspective shared by at least three participants.) Students must overcome their usual posture of deference to faculty authority. One student explained: "I was hesitant about my ability to do a good job given my lack of background in education, and given that I am just a student."

Regardless of their ascribed authority or lack thereof, both faculty members and students feel vulnerable as they enter into this new partnership. One student consultant explained, "At first I was kind of skeptical because you are a student and these profs have been doing this for quite some time; they have advanced degrees—you're a kid with some college. And you are trying to come in and say, 'Do this better, do that.' You could easily be dismissed." Faculty members also express apprehensions. About the experience of having a student of color serve as a consultant focused on creating a more culturally responsive classroom, one faculty member said, "On the one hand, I felt that she had a certain legitimacy as an informant, but it also made me feel more exposed—that she would be able to see all the things that were problems."

Working together, faculty and students not only overcome their uncertainties but also enthusiastically embrace the notion of students as colleagues in analyzing classroom practice. Explained one faculty member, "I wondered if our students can do the same things as a professional teaching and learning center, but I'm a convert." Another faculty member asserted, "It's more effective to have a student come in rather than a colleague. We look for something different than a student looks for." And a third went further to assert that "by listening to our students, especially in institutions that claim students as colleagues, we can start to fulfill the claims that we make as educational institutions."

By challenging the norms of professional development through inviting students into dialogue with faculty members about classroom practices, SaLT works toward "radical collegiality" in which students are "agents in the process of transformative learning" (Fielding, 1999, p. 22). Faculty and students engage in "a significant reciprocity" through which teachers learn "with and from young people . . . through processes of co-constructed, collaborative work" (Fielding, 2006, p. 311). By affording faculty the opportunity to engage in a richer, more variously informed version of reflective practice (Cook-Sather, 2008), SaLT reconceptualizes faculty learning as part of an ongoing and unending process of dialogue and revision with those usually on the receiving end of pedagogical practice: students.

Cocreating a New Model of Professional Development

SaLT requires deliberate and intentional coconstruction of the faculty-student partnership. This work includes affirming reciprocal interest and respect, identifying pedagogical goals, and finding a language and a mode through which faculty and student consultants interact with one another in order to build confidence and support revisions of practice. Faculty members must assure student consultants that they are open to and interested in what the consultants have to say. Likewise, student consultants must assure faculty members that they are supportive and affirming as well as constructively critical.

Because the goal of this work is faculty learning, faculty members must work to identify and articulate what they want the focus of the work to be and find a good balance between maintaining their existing pedagogical commitments and developing as teachers. One faculty member appreciated "the opportunity to first articulate to myself [and then to my student consultant] what I want to happen in the classroom." Through such dialogue, according to another faculty member, it is possible to clarify and better pursue one's pedagogical commitments. This faculty member explained: "[My student consultant] alerted me to the students' confusion resulting from my style of questioning. . . . Her presence in the classroom made me more aware of how I presented myself in the class and how I 'read' the students and my patterns of interaction with them. Her suggestions enabled me to broaden and diversify patterns of interaction."

While faculty members need to clarify and articulate their pedagogical commitments to both themselves and student consultants, the challenges student consultants face include balancing diffidence with authority, building their confidence, and developing a language with which to offer feedback. Both the premises and structure of the SaLT program "really enhanced my confidence," one student consultant explained, "in the fact that I can do this job and that I have competence in this area." Another student consultant reflected: "It was so nice to think I had a perspective [the professor I was working with] hadn't thought about. And then she would say things I hadn't thought about. So it challenged both of us." Building on the confidence they develop, student consultants learn how to offer feedback in constructive ways. They consistently use phrases such as, "In my own experience as a student" or "If I were a student in this class, I would feel . . ." Such formulations allow professors to hear and receive what student consultants have to say.

If faculty members are not as deliberate, intentional, and careful as they might be in inviting students into this partnership, students can have a hard time developing the confidence they need to support faculty learning. One consultant contrasts experiences with two different faculty members— one in which she felt her efforts to engage in productive dialogue were thwarted and one in which they were embraced: "This time around, because of the way he was reacting to my feedback, I really felt like my role was indeed changing and I wasn't just a student—that I came with a perspective and expertise of a student but that was just as valid as the things he was bringing to the table (as opposed to last time I felt like I was still the little student and he was the big teacher)." This dynamic works both ways: if students are not as deliberate, intentional, and careful as they might be in establishing a partnership with their faculty partners, faculty members can feel too vulnerable to benefit from the partnership.

When both faculty and students achieve a productive balance between affirmation and challenge and navigate their relationship respectfully and responsibly, they develop a "generative and creative" partnership, as one faculty member explained, that allows them "to move in and out of the roles" that they generally occupy. They experience, as one student consultant put it, "teaching and learning as collaboration between all parties involved."

Both the perennial pedagogical challenges that all faculty members face and the process through which they might explore those challenges appear less daunting when faculty members engage with students in constructive dialogue about teaching and learning. As one faculty member explained: "In this project there's some recognition on the part of everyone that nobody's the expert, so you just say what you think. I may choose to believe you or not believe you, but there's not a right answer that you are charged with coming up, no magical solution. You're providing your perspective . . . it's just a conversation, part of a process."

Student consultants also emphasize the dialogical nature of the relationship and the fact that the partners are engaged in an ongoing problem-solving rather than a solution-finding process: "[My faculty partner is] being really receptive to my ideas and we're having a lot of dialogue about ways to generate new, not solutions, but things to try out in the classroom and see how they work." Such a model of faculty learning supports the development of teachers who can communicate, learn, and change, and it supports pedagogy that is always evolving in practice and as a focus of analysis.

Deepening Faculty Learning

Among the wide variety of lessons learned from their work with student consultants, faculty most often identify the importance of the following two: gaining a student perspective on one's practice and expanding strategies for engaging students.

Faculty members highlight the literal fact that a student consultant "has a line of sight into the space of the classroom which I do not have from where I stand." One faculty member offered a vivid illustration of what this new angle of vision affords:

> There are some quiet students in my class—this was really powerful for me—one student was putting up her hand very slightly. I was literally blind to her. [The student consultant] pointed it out. Then [the student] did it next class, and I saw her, and she talked three times. When [the student consultant] told me, I was stunned—I had just missed her. And when she did talk, she said very thoughtful things.

A student consultant's angle of vision opens up space that faculty members cannot see on their own. Through the dialogue in which the faculty-student partners engage, the student's angle of vision also informs faculty thinking about what can happen in that space. One faculty member described her dialogue with her student consultant as "an ongoing intercambio [exchange] in which I was able to get a sense of how others experience the class." She explained that because of this dialogue, "rather than always privilege what worked for me as a student, I work to draw out how different pedagogical practices [and] learning styles can illuminate the space of a classroom for all those around the table."

The perspective and insights faculty members gain through working with student consultants not only enhance their teaching while they are in the partnerships but also shape their subsequent thinking and practice. One faculty member said:

> I like that her presence—her comments, but her presence itself too—not only gives me the benefit of her lighthouse-like observations, but makes me observe from the same kind of remove, even as I am engaged in the everyday work of teaching the class. This split experience of my class as an immediate act and experience, but also a larger narrative that I'm looking down upon, is something I hope to carry into all my teaching.

Using a different metaphor, another faculty member explained: "The student consultant voice remains in my head during lectures [and] discussions and I am trying to rethink my presentations or view them from a student perspective while talking."

In part because they come to value the student perspective and think more deeply about the student experience, faculty members explore several ways to engage students, including making expectations clear and explicit, supporting the development of students' metacognitive awareness, and creating opportunities for students to be more active in and more responsible for their learning. Supporting her claim that her teaching "improved a lot" through her participation in SaLT, one faculty member captured succinctly the importance of making expectations clear and explicit: "I've become more comfortable balancing elements of my teaching style with what students need; for me, this means being rigorous in my expectations for students, but making those expectations extremely clear."

Being explicit about expectations is closely related to another strategy faculty members identify: supporting the development of students' metacognitive awareness—their awareness of their learning and their approaches such that they can make informed and intentional decisions about those. In part because they develop their own metacognitive awareness through the various forums for reflection and dialogue provided by SaLT, and in part because their student consultants emphasize its importance, faculty members deliberately construct activities to support the development in students of metacognitive awareness. As one faculty member put it:

> For most students, metacognition does not just happen—in fact, students are probably unaware of what it is! There is little chance of

developing metacognitive habits if they do not know that they need to do so! Thus, the purpose of [the metacognitive exercises I developed] is not only to help their immediate understanding and my immediate awareness of their understanding, but also (if I tell them so!) to model the metacognitive habits that I hope they cultivate.

Related to the development of metacognitive awareness is the importance of creating opportunities for students to be more active in and more responsible for their learning. Building on the practice of gathering midsemester feedback supported by SaLT (Cook-Sather, 2009a), one faculty member explained: "I've started using midsemester course feedback in order to get a sense of what is engaging for students, what might be standing in the way of full engagement." Another faculty participant stated: "I'm constantly trying to think of ways I can put the pedagogical goals I have for my students in their hands."

Deepening Student Learning

Students who take on the role of student consultant consistently report two ways in which their learning is deepened and expanded. They repeatedly describe becoming better learners and assuming more agency in and taking more responsibility for their education.

Bain and Zimmerman (2009) point out that the most successful students are deep learners, meaning those who are concerned with understanding how to apply their ideas to consequential problems, implications, and ideas and concepts. Such learners are likely to "theorize and make connections with other ideas and problems . . . [and] . . . to become adaptive experts who both recognize and even relish the opportunity and necessity for breaking with traditional approaches and inventing new ones" (p. 10). Student consultants suggest that they develop these capacities in their role. One claimed: "I think that this project has helped me a lot in thinking about myself as a student, what works best for me, and how to work within a structure that a professor has set up to get the most learning out of the experience." Another stated: "I am a much more conscientious student in general now; I ask myself what I could do differently to improve my own classroom experience, rather than complaining about the professor or the course in general."

These increased capacities contribute to the second change that student consultants describe: the ways in which they take more responsibility for their own and others' education (Cook-Sather, in press) and feel they have greater agency in that education. One student consultant wrote: "As a learner, I will be a student who goes after what I want in terms of learning. I won't be afraid to talk to profs if I have issues 'cause I know from this experience that they are open to suggestions, they try to help students get as much as they can out of the course." Another said: "In past discussions I've always been talking about what the profs do to us and it's been a one-way street. And now I am able to look at it as a relationship in the classroom; if we're complaining about something that is going on, it's also the students' role to step up and say something about that."

Sharing the Responsibility for Learning in College Classrooms

By working together to cocreate this form of professional development and deepening their respective learning experiences as a result, both faculty and students begin to see the responsibility for exploring and improving teaching and learning as shared. One faculty member explained: "I work with students more as colleagues, more as people engaged in similar struggles to learn and grow. I have become even more convinced that students are experts in learning and essential partners in the task of creating and developing new courses and refining existing ones." Another faculty member put it this way: "It doesn't mean that you are giving over control of the course. But there are elements of the classroom that we are coresponsible for, that we are traveling through together."

Student consultants made similar statements regarding the shared responsibility that can emerge from this work: "Students are working with faculty to build courses, to build their learning experience" (Cook-Sather, 2009a, p. 237). Another student clearly stated the shared responsibility she feels for teaching and learning: "This experience has made me increasingly alive to both the professor's perspective and to my own responsibilities as a student in creating and maintaining a positive and effective learning environment for all members of the class." And a third named education as the whole college community's responsibility: "It is up to the entire community to make learning spaces function, so that means students have just as much responsibility as professors."

Recommendations for Faculty Developers

Our three years of experience with the SaLT program have suggested some recommended guidelines for those who are considering starting a similar program.

Consider Your Context, and Invite Participant Input

Take into consideration the size and type of your institution as well as the nature and commitments of faculty members and students. With these in mind, design forums and guidelines that will speak to potential participants. In both the creation and the evolution of the program, invite participant input, and, as Cox (2000) has emphasized as well, monitor participant experiences and adjust accordingly.

Create Liminal and Confidential Spaces

Create spaces for faculty learning that are not part of the administration or any particular department (Cook-Sather & McCormack, 2010). Liminal spaces open up possibilities that likely remain closed off when community participants stay in their accustomed locations (Cook-Sather & Alter, 2010). Finally, do not link faculty work within the program to review for reappointment or promotion, and, as Sorenson (2001) has indicated, make sure that participants preserve confidentiality.

Make Participation Voluntary and Faculty Driven

Beyond inviting participant input into the design and evolution of the program, it is essential that both faculty participants and student consultants choose to participate. Furthermore, faculty members, at least initially, should identify the focus of their work with student consultants. This work requires risk, but as one faculty member put it, "This project is making a safer place to be vulnerable and thus learn and grow and be out of your shell." When faculty members feel safe enough to risk learning, they are much more likely to invite both student consultants and students in their classes into dialogue about and collaborative revision of teaching and learning.

Bring Differently Positioned Participants into Structured Dialogue

The forums, guidelines, and facilitation that comprise the SaLT program—handbooks, weekly meetings, reflective assessment questions, active and engaged support by the program facilitator—both affirm and challenge participants to think critically, take risks, and develop new ways of talking with one another about teaching and learning. With such structured support, participants can build enough trust to talk honestly across differences of role and status about the work of education that they share.

Faculty and students open themselves to perspectives and insights they cannot achieve from their own angles of vision and are inspired to act on what they see.

Recognize This Work as Ongoing

Freire (1998) argued that it is our unfinishedness that makes us educable. Affording faculty members opportunities to engage in well-supported, ongoing learning opportunities both accelerates their learning (Cook-Sather & McCormack, 2010) and reminds faculty that learning is a life-long process. Including students among those responsible for teaching and learning in college classrooms extends Shulman's (2004) call to make teaching "community property" and thus affords both faculty members and students an opportunity to deepen their own learning in their respective roles and build a stronger, richer educational community for which both groups share responsibility.

REFERENCES

Bain, K., & Zimmerman, J. (2009). Understanding great teaching. *Peer Review, 11*(2), 9–12.

Cook-Sather, A. (2002). Authorizing students' perspectives: Toward trust, dialogue, and change in education. *Educational Researcher, 31*(4), 3–14.

Cook-Sather, A. (2006a). *Education is translation: A metaphor for change in learning and teaching.* Philadelphia: University of Pennsylvania Press.

Cook-Sather, A. (2006b). Sound, presence, and power: Exploring "student voice" in educational research and reform. *Curriculum Inquiry, 36*(4), 359–390.

Cook-Sather, A. (2008). "What you get is looking in a mirror, only better": Inviting students to reflect (on) college teaching. *Reflective Practice, 9*(4), 473–483.

Cook-Sather, A. (2009a). From traditional accountability to shared responsibility: The benefits and challenges of student consultants gathering midcourse feedback in college classrooms. *Assessment and Evaluation in Higher Education, 34*(2), 231–241.

Cook-Sather, A. (2009b). *Learning from the student's perspective: A sourcebook for effective teaching.* Boulder, CO: Paradigm.

Cook-Sather, A. (in press). Students as learners and teachers: Taking responsibility, transforming education, and redefining accountability. *Curriculum Inquiry.*

Cook-Sather, A., & Alter, Z. (2010). *What is and what can be: How a liminal role changes college students' educational experiences and expectations.* Manuscript submitted for publication.

Cook-Sather, A., & McCormack, E. (2010). *Recurrence and repositioning: Keys to supporting teaching excellence in the liberal arts college.* Manuscript submitted for publication.

Cowan, J., & Westwood, J. (2006). Collaborative and reflective professional development: A pilot. *Active Learning in Higher Education: The Journal of the Institute for Learning and Teaching, 7*(1), 63–71.

Cox, M. D. (2000). Student-faculty partnerships to develop teaching and enhance learning. In J. E. Miller, J. E. Groccia, & M. S. Miller (Eds.), *Student-assisted teaching: A guide to faculty-student teamwork* (pp. 168–171). San Francisco: Jossey-Bass/Anker.

Cox, M. D. (2003). Proven faculty development tools that foster the scholarship of teaching in faculty learning communities. In C. M. Wehlburg & S. Chadwick-Blossey (Eds.), *To improve the academy: Vol. 21. Resources for faculty, instructional, and organizational development* (pp. 109–142). San Francisco: Jossey-Bass/Anker.

Cox, M. D., & Sorenson, D. L. (2000). Student collaboration in faculty development. In M. Kaplan (Ed.), *To improve the academy: Vol. 18. Resources for faculty, instructional, and organizational development* (pp. 97–106). Stillwater, OK: New Forums Press.

Fielding, M. (1999). Target-setting, policy, pathology and student perspectives: Learning to labour in new times. *Cambridge Journal of Education, 29,* 277–287.

Fielding, M. (2006). Leadership, radical student engagement and the necessity of person-centred education. *International Journal of Leadership in Education, 9*(4), 299–314.

Freire, P. (1998). *Pedagogy of freedom: Ethics, democracy, and civil courage* (P. Clarke, Trans.). Lanham, MD: Rowan & Littlefield.

Huston, T., & Weaver, C. L. (2008). Peer coaching: Professional development for experienced faculty. *Innovative Higher Education, 33*(1), 5–20.

Lesnick, A., & Cook-Sather, A. (2010). Building civic capacity and responsibility through a radically inclusive teaching and learning initiative. *Innovative Higher Education, 35*(1), 3–17.

Mihans, R., Long, D., & Felten, P. (2008). Student-faculty collaboration in course design and the scholarship of teaching and learning. *International Journal for the Scholarship of Teaching and Learning, 2*(2). Retrieved from http://academics.georgiasouthern.edu/ijsotl/v2n2.html

Peel, D. (2005). Peer observation as a transformatory tool? *Teaching in Higher Education, 10*(4), 489–504.

Richlin, L., & Cox, M. D. (2004). Developing scholarly teaching and the scholarship of teaching and learning through faculty learning communi- ties. In M. Cox & L. Richlin (Eds.), *New directions for teaching and learning: Vol. 97. Building faculty learning communities* (pp. 127–135). San Francisco: Jossey-Bass.

Shulman, L. S. (2004). Teaching as community property: Putting an end to pedagogical solitude. In L. S. Shulman, *Teaching as community property: Essays on higher education* (pp. 140–144). San Francisco: Jossey-Bass.

Sorenson, L. (2001). College teachers and student consultants: Collaborating about teaching and learning. In J. E. Miller, J. E. Groccia, & M. S. Miller (Eds.), *Student-assisted teaching: A guide to faculty-student teamwork* (pp. 179–183). San Francisco: Jossey-Bass/Anker.

Thiessen, D., & Cook-Sather, A. (Eds.). (2007). *International handbook of student experience in elementary and secondary school.* Dordrecht, Netherlands: Springer.

Werder, C., & Otis, M. M. (Eds.). (2010). *Engaging student voices in the study of teaching and learning.* Sterling, VA: Stylus.

17

USING STUDENTS TO SUPPORT FACULTY DEVELOPMENT

Teresa M. Redd, Carl E. Brown Jr., Howard University

Howard University's Center for Excellence in Teaching, Learning, and Assessment (CETLA) provides faculty development for more than fifteen hundred faculty. Yet it is CETLA's students who make the difference. They are both the motivation for improving teaching and the means to that end. Students have contributed to everything from the design of CETLA's infrastructure, to the implementation of instructional technologies, to the assessment of student learning. Meanwhile, supporting faculty development has contributed to the students' own development. A cost-benefit analysis as well as survey data confirms that working with students at CETLA is a win-win opportunity for the university, faculty, students, and CETLA.

The faces of dozens of students adorn the southern wall of the Center for Excellence in Teaching, Learning, and Assessment (CETLA) at historically black Howard University. These are the faces of CETLA's student assistants. Although CETLA is a faculty development center, students play an indispensable role by motivating and facilitating faculty development. In fact, without its student employees and collaborators, CETLA could not address the pedagogical needs of Howard's faculty in its twelve schools and colleges, and the students, faculty, and university would not reap the unique benefits of CETLA's student partnership.

According to its mission statement, CETLA is "dedicated to developing a cadre of faculty who will produce distinguished and compassionate leaders to serve the nation and the global community. Through faculty training, instructional technology, interdisciplinary collaboration, classroom assessment, and educational research, CETLA strives to ensure that students gain an educational experience of exceptional quality" (Center for Excellence in Teaching, Learning, and Assessment, 2007). Consequently CETLA offers a wide range of workshops, seminars, online tutorials, video-streamed lectures, distance learning courses, and Web-based resources to improve the faculty's teaching with and without technology. To fulfill its mission, CETLA requires a large, skilled staff. Currently it has a permanent staff of five, two instructors, the director, and the assistant director. CETLA has been recruiting, training, and collaborating with students since it opened in October 2003.

Engaging students in faculty development is not new. Since 1996, the national GenerationYES! program has been training K–12 students to help teachers, preservice teachers, and education faculty integrate technology into the curriculum (Generation Yes Youth and Educators Succeeding, 2007). Nevertheless, we found relatively few publications about student assistant programs at faculty development centers on college and university campuses. Our literature review, Web search, and survey of Howard's peer and neighboring institutions (Table 17.1) confirmed that a number of centers hire students to assist with faculty development, but primarily as clerical and research assistants.

Table 17.1 Telephone Survey of Selected Faculty Development Centers

Institution	Student Assistants?	Primary Duties
George Mason University	Yes	Assist with accreditation
Georgetown University	Yes	Assist with training and research
George Washington University	Yes	Perform clerical work
Marymount University	Yes	Perform clerical work, video recording, and develop Web pages
Morehouse College	Yes	Assist with administrative work
North Carolina A&T University	No	
University of Maryland	Yes	Assist with training
University of Virginia	Yes	Perform clerical work
Xavier University	Yes	Perform clerical work

Note: The survey included only centers at Howard University's peer and neighboring institutions.

Centers at Georgetown University and the University of Maryland, College Park reported that they engage students in some teaching-learning activities, namely training faculty to use instructional technology. In addition, we identified several centers that recruit students to assist faculty with other types of teaching-learning activities:

- *Course design*: Michigan State University assigns graduate students to help faculty design distance learning sites. As a result, the students and faculty have not only learned new technologies but gained valuable insights: faculty have considered the design of their courses from a student perspective, while the students have discovered why faculty design courses as they do (Mishra, Koehler, Hershey, & Peruski, 2002).

- *Role playing*: The University of Illinois, Chicago enlists students to improve clinical teaching skills by portraying students in challenging classroom scenarios (Gelula & Yudkowsky, 2003). Like standardized patients in medical schools, these students are trained to act, speak, and respond in a consistent manner as they interact with faculty.

- *Student observer programs*: Several institutions hire and train students to attend a faculty member's classes and discuss their observations with the faculty member in order to improve teaching and learning in the course. Some examples are found at Brigham Young University (Brigham Young University, 1997), Carleton College (Carleton College: Learning and Teaching Center, 2008), Dickinson College (Laws, 1977), and the University of Toledo (University of Toledo Center for Teaching and Learning, 2009).

However, our findings suggest that the role of students at CETLA is noteworthy. At CETLA, we have integrated students into a wide range of activities as a cost-effective means of meeting our faculty's professional development needs. At the same time, through mentoring and peer teaching, we have succeeded in meeting many of our students' needs. Thus, our center has become a teaching and learning center for our students as well as our faculty.

Hiring

While students contribute to CETLA through collaboration, employment is the primary means. Each year we employ approximately ten students who work ten to twenty hours a week. In the summer, half of the students work on projects off-campus, for a total of forty hours for the entire summer.

To recruit students, we e-mail advertisements to the chairs of departments in the Schools of Engineering, Education, Business, and Communications and the College of Arts and Sciences. We also submit ads to the office of financial aid. However, the most successful recruiters are our current student assistants, who gladly refer their classmates and friends. Applicants e-mail their résumés to CETLA, come to CETLA for interviews, and for video, Web, and research positions, they submit samples of their work.

After vetting the candidates, we offer one of four types of compensation: wages, tuition, federal work-study funds, or internship credit. Most of our student employees receive wages or tuition from the student aid pool of CETLA's budget. Over the years, we have transferred an increasing amount of funds from our equipment pool to the student aid pool, so that student aid now represents more than 15 percent of our annual budget. However, sometimes we do not have to pay at all. For example, if a qualified work-study student applies, the federal government covers the cost. And if the student can earn academic credit for a CETLA internship, the student may work free of charge.

Positions and Responsibilities

Once hired, students assume critical roles in CETLA's infrastructure, as the following job descriptions reveal:

- *Webmaster*: Designs, posts, and updates content on CETLA's website; takes photographs as needed.

- *Video editor*: Videotapes guest lectures, guest workshops, keynote speeches, classroom teaching, and special events; edits and publishes videos for streaming.

- *Programmer* (replaced by a full-time staff member in 2007): Builds databases, writes database queries, generates database reports, and troubleshoots to resolve database errors.

- *Instructional technology assistant*: Helps faculty keep up with their colleagues during technology workshops; provides one-on-one, hands-on assistance during open labs; visits faculty offices to teach a five-minute "Blackboard Basics" tutorial; shows faculty how to digitize course materials using CETLA's equipment; assists CETLA's staff with technology projects.

- *Lab assistant*: Sets up computers, peripherals, and networking; fixes computers; loads software.

- *Course redesign assistant*: Creates digital media (for example, animation, video, or Web page) for faculty who have completed CETLA's Course Redesign Seminar.

- *Research assistant*: Conducts bibliographical and Web searches; collects, analyzes, and summarizes data for CETLA's assessment, annual reports, presentations, and publications.

- *Clerical assistant*: Files documents, updates CETLA's sign-in database, delivers mail, and performs other office duties as assigned.

Regardless of their position, student employees are eligible to participate in CETLA's Faculty Resource Network Database (FRieND) Program, which permits faculty mentors to redeem their mentoring hours for time-saving student services through a system called time-banking (TimeBanks, n.d.) For example, in exchange for one hour of mentoring, a mentor can earn an hour of clerical, research, or technology services from CETLA's student employees, such as scanning documents, posting materials online, searching the Web for multimedia resources, or compiling a bibliography from scholarly databases.

Occasionally we assign students tasks that extend beyond their job descriptions so that they can use what they have learned in their major field of study. Consequently we have asked a broadcast major to do a voice-over for a tutorial, a journalism major to interview and write about the featured teacher of the month, and a biology major to introduce an online lab report program to biology teaching assistants. We also have assigned tasks to advance students' learning in their major. For example, we showed a psychology major how to use SPSS to analyze CETLA's "real-world" data; as a result, the student reported that she had gained greater confidence in her introductory SPSS class. Indeed, one survey respondent urged us, "Keep doing what you are presently doing. Challenge your present student employees—give them a chance to do something out of their comfort zone."

Whenever possible, we also assign students to workshops or projects for their own departments. Such assignments allow them to use their knowledge of the discipline to assist their professors and reap the benefits of what their professors learn at CETLA. For instance, we assigned an electrical engineering major to help her professors during a departmental Blackboard workshop. Another time we asked a pharmacy student for assignments and feedback to help us design a workshop for the pharmacy faculty. On another occasion, we asked a psychology major to find writing guides that her professors could share with their psychology classes.

Finally, we encourage all of our student employees to reflect on what they are doing at CETLA, what is happening in their classrooms, and what CETLA can do to improve teaching and learning. As one survey respondent observed, "A student employee brings a fresh perspective to all activities of the center." After all, our student employees are students first, with a keen understanding of what their peers like and understand. Who is better qualified to think of questions for our Blackboard FAQs for Students page, recommend raffle prizes for a student survey, or determine how helpful a chemistry simulation is? Therefore, although we do not sponsor a student observer program, we seek student opinions about the technologies and strategies that we introduce to the faculty. If student assistants find an innovation confusing, hard to use, or boring, we want to know. As another survey respondent observed, a "student's perspective . . . can be invaluable in separating what works from what does not."

Training

Before they can start working in their new positions, students must attend an orientation conducted by Howard's human resource department. Afterward they complete our online orientation to CETLA's policies and procedures. The online orientation is a self-scoring Blackboard mastery quiz, designed by CETLA students as well as staff to be both humorous and informative. To achieve mastery of the policies and procedures, students must repeat the quiz until they have earned at least 80 percent.

While some students bring valuable skills to CETLA, others bring mainly an aptitude for learning. Therefore, we require students to attend our faculty workshops whenever their schedules permit and to watch our online video tutorials. We also ask current CETLA student assistants to train new students, for instance, teach them how to use the self-service digitization station or how to update our sign-in database. What has pleasantly surprised us is how much peer teaching has occurred extemporaneously. For instance, on their own, the video editor has taught the webmaster to edit videos, and the webmaster has taught the video editor to develop Web pages; the programmer has taught the webmaster to embed code, and the webmaster has taught the programmer to design a better user interface. Without being asked, instructional technology assistants have helped one another master the art of constructing Blackboard tests, PBworks wikis, and SurveyMonkey surveys. Even our full-time staff members have learned from students. For example, from watching and working with students, our full-time programmer has become a backup webmaster and cameraman.

Student Collaboration

While CETLA has employed students, it has also sought to collaborate with students outside the center on special projects, especially projects involving art, assessment, and awards. These projects demonstrate how a teaching and learning center can support teaching and reward learning in diverse ways.

Shortly after CETLA opened in 2003, it collaborated with an electronic studio class in the department of art to design the center's logo. During one class period, CETLA's director presented CETLA's mission, goals, and objectives. Later she visited the class to view students' drafts and answer questions. Finally, after reviewing the designs with CETLA's staff, she returned to the classroom to present awards for first, second, and third place. In 2009, CETLA turned once again to students in the department of art to submit their digital artwork for a perpetual slideshow in CETLA's computer classroom. CETLA hoped that the artwork would not only decorate the sterile-looking room but also give the art students' work exposure in CETLA's digital art gallery.

For one of its most successful ventures, CETLA enlisted a graduate class to assess the impact of CETLA's faculty training. Beginning in spring 2008, CETLA began collaborating with the professor and graduate students in a course entitled Effective Use of Technology in Teaching and Learning. Through its partnership with the class, CETLA provided graduate assistants (who were students in the course) for five faculty members to conduct classroom assessment research, which supplied the data for the graduate students' term projects. At the beginning of the term, CETLA introduced the graduate students to resources on teaching with technology, taught a hands-on workshop on survey construction, created a survey item bank based on Chickering and Gamson's (1987) "Seven Principles of Good Practice in Undergraduate Education," and then matched the students with CETLA-trained faculty who were implementing new strategies or technologies. CETLA also assigned one of its own graduate student employees to assist the instructor and students in the course. With the graduate students' support, faculty pursued the following projects: a biology professor assessed the effectiveness of Blackboard in his molecular biology class; a physics professor assessed the effectiveness of cumulative quizzes compared with collaborative learning in a calculus-based physics course; another biology professor assessed students' perceptions of the benefits of multimedia as a tool for learning biology; a chemistry professor assessed students' learning through weekly online surveys so that he would know whether he needed to review any concepts the next week; and a medical professor assessed student satisfaction with her current use of Blackboard and solicited the students' recommendations for other uses. Without student collaboration, CETLA would not have been able to conduct so many studies. Although there were methodological weaknesses in some of the studies, three of the five studies were robust enough to cite in CETLA's annual assessment report.

CETLA has also recruited students to participate in deliberations about its teaching awards. Believing that student evaluations of teaching are essential, CETLA has invited student members of the teaching, learning, and technology committee to serve alongside faculty as judges who review applications for CETLA's annual Teaching with Technology Award. CETLA has also asked its student employees to rate syllabi submitted for CETLA's annual Exemplary Syllabus Award.

Limitations

Despite the benefits, student employment and collaboration have their limits. First, with the ebb and flow of matriculation and graduation, student turnover is high. Whenever we can, we hire sophomores and juniors so that they can work two or three years at CETLA, developing greater expertise and enjoying greater financial security. Since we need an experienced video editor, we have established an apprenticeship to address the turnover problem: each year we hire a junior and a senior video editor. The junior video editor must make a two-year commitment to train as an apprentice under the senior video editor during the first year so that he or she can take over when the senior video editor graduates.

Second, since our students' academic progress takes priority, we have to schedule workshops, videotaping, and open labs around our students' schedules, making sure that the students have enough time to go to class and to study. In fact, the university will not allow full-time students to work more than twenty hours a week or to hold more than one on-campus job. To facilitate scheduling, we teach instructional technology assistants how to use as many applications as possible so that they can substitute for one another if needed. Full-time staff members are also prepared to substitute.

Third, despite their talents and skills, we cannot allow students to perform certain tasks because of security concerns. For instance, even the most trustworthy clerical assistant is not permitted to log into PeopleSoft to submit requisitions, complete the department's timesheet, or create job openings. Sometimes our programmer can assign students to roles that limit their access within a database. However, certain students require unrestricted access. Thus we eventually decided to hire a full-time staff member as a programmer.

Fourth, like security, privacy is also a concern. We restrict students' access to data such as course evaluations, interview transcripts, and grades unless permission has been granted. Indeed, depending on the project, we have required some of our research assistants to earn certification from the Institutional Review Board by completing a series of online modules.

Fifth, many of our students create digital works of art, such as videos, animations, and graphics. Whenever appropriate, we list students' names in the credits. Nevertheless, we require students (as well as faculty collaborators) to sign copyright and performance releases. These releases give CETLA the right to disseminate the media but permit students to include the digital media in their portfolios for subsequent employment or graduate admission.

Assessment

CETLA anonymously surveyed its thirty-nine current and former student employees, and twenty-five responded (Exhibit 17.1 shows the survey).

Exhibit 17.1 Survey of Former and Current Student Assistants

1. In what year did you begin working for CETLA?
2. If you no longer work at CETLA, in what year did you stop?
3. What is your gender?
4. Which program were you in while working at CETLA?
5. How many hours do or did you work at CETLA?
6. What is or was your position at CETLA?
7. The money I earned at CETLA helped me stay at Howard University.
8. While working at CETLA, I developed professional work habits.
9. While working at CETLA, I learned skills that helped me academically at Howard University.
10. I developed skills at CETLA that can help me prepare for a job or graduate/professional school.
11. While working at CETLA, I developed a sense of pride in helping others (faculty or CETLA staff).

12. While working at CETLA, I developed a sense of satisfaction in improving teaching at Howard University.

13. I would recommend working at CETLA to other students.

14. Please list the skills you have developed while working at CETLA.

15. Please list any skills or projects (including internships) you have developed at CETLA for academic credit.

16. Explain your attitude toward the faculty you have encountered at CETLA.

17. What insights as a student employee do you contribute to faculty development?

Of the survey respondents, 88 percent confirmed that supporting faculty development at CETLA had contributed to their own academic and professional development. According to the survey, students acquired technical skills such as shooting videos, adjusting lighting, video editing, photographing, developing Web pages, creating animations, building wikis, generating statistical analyses using SPSS, and constructing Blackboard course sites. Students also cited gaining project management, research, communication, presentation, time management, organizational, teaching, and interpersonal skills. In addition, they credited CETLA with enhancing their problem-solving and analytical thinking and helping them develop a "good work ethic." Some students considered the CETLA staff role models. As one survey respondent stated, they were "great leaders of the Center, very professional and driven by the goals of achieving excellence." On a personal note, another student wrote, "Thank you so very much for your guidance. You have allowed me to watch a very powerful, influential, and still very gentle black woman for the first time in my life!" Yet another student delivered a card saying, "It has been inspiring to see you perform in something to which your passion . . . is so innately tied. I hope I can one day say I am doing the same."

Of the twenty-five survey respondents, 88 percent reported that they had learned skills at CETLA that helped them academically at the university. Several of our video editors earned internship credit from the department of radio, TV, and film for taping and editing our guest lectures. A student programmer presented a database he created for CETLA as his term project in his information systems class. Not only did such skills prove helpful at Howard, but 92 percent of respondents felt that the skills they had acquired at CETLA prepared them for a job or graduate or professional school. It is also worth noting that numerous students have received production credits and developed artifacts for their portfolios. Even more have earned letters of recommendation from CETLA's staff confirming their productivity and professionalism. No wonder all of CETLA's student employees reported that they would recommend employment at CETLA to other students.

In addition to these benefits, 88 percent of the survey respondents agreed that working at CETLA had given them "a sense of satisfaction in improving teaching at Howard University," and 92 percent agreed that they had "developed a sense of pride in helping others" at CETLA. One student wrote, "I believe that I was empowered as a student employee to serve the faculty and vice versa." Two students reported that they had gained greater respect for Howard faculty because of the faculty's "desire to improve" or "drive" to teach. Only one student said that some faculty assumed that the student assistants were "inadequate," and even that student conceded that many other faculty did not hold such assumptions. Other students said they appreciated the opportunity to help fellow students by helping professors. "I was able to understand their point of view and combine it with the wants and needs of my peers," one recalled. Another remarked on the experience of sharing "what faculty need to know to better communicate with their students." Yet another explained, "You help the faculty understand the student perspective. . . . For example, its [sic] good for us at CETLA to encourage the usage of multimedia and graphics on a Blackboard site in order to more fully engage those students." In addition, two students noted that they had improved their own teaching skills, for instance, the "ability to explain things to others."

As this feedback reveals, the students credited CETLA staff and peers with modeling positive behaviors, helping them academically, preparing them for careers, and developing their life skills in a friendly and caring atmosphere. In short, CETLA provides most of the benefits of mentoring identified in Jacobi's (1991) review of the literature. These are not typical supervisor-employee, teacher-student, coworker, or classmate relationships. CETLA staff and students seek to help students improve their lives, not simply finish an assignment. For example, when training students to assist with a faculty workshop on wikis, one staff member showed students how they could use a wiki to apply for a job or graduate school or to coordinate teamwork. Likewise, a staff member training a student for a blog workshop helped her set up a blog to publish her creative writing. As Jacobi explains, "Whereas a traditional supervisor or teacher helps the employee or student to perform specific tasks correctly . . . the mentor typically helps the protégé achieve longer term, broader goals" (p. 513). Perhaps that is why so many of CETLA's student employees maintain contact with CETLA staff and students for years after they graduate.

In addition to the benefits derived by CETLA's student assistants and collaborators, annual workshop and customer service evaluations confirm that faculty benefit from the one-on-one assistance and expertise of CETLA's student assistants. On these anonymous surveys, faculty members report that the students are helpful, efficient, polite, and knowledgeable. But is such student participation cost-effective?

Clearly student employment is cost-effective for CETLA. A comparison with 2009 wages in the Washington, D.C., area (CBsalary.com, n.d) reveals that CETLA saves more than seventy thousand dollars per fiscal year by hiring students as opposed to nonstudent wage employees. The greatest savings stem from hiring students as webmasters and video editors. Moreover, survey results suggest that student employment is also cost-effective for the university as a whole. Nearly two-thirds (64 percent) of the twenty-five respondents agreed that the money they earned at CETLA helped them stay in school. CETLA rarely pays full tuition (or the equivalent in wages), and most CETLA students rely on a scholarship or pay the balance of their tuition out of their own pockets. Thus, without funding from CETLA, many students might drop out of school, depriving the university of revenue.

Conclusion

Our study suggests that CETLA's partnership with students has produced a win-win situation. It is a cost-effective model that benefits Howard University, CETLA, faculty, and students, and it could benefit other institutions. While CETLA enjoys access to students in specialized fields, such as engineering and film, we believe our model is feasible even for centers at small liberal arts colleges that do not offer such majors. Over the years, we have discovered that students often bring unexpected skills and aptitudes from other majors. For instance, an English graduate student became our first webmaster, a health sciences major became our Blackboard expert, and a psychology major became our statistician. If money is an obstacle, we believe that our model can meet that challenge as well. Most centers without budgets or grants to cover student employment can still recruit federal work-study students and student interns. Also, collaborating with classes, as we did for our assessment studies, can provide student support for a center's technology and research projects. We strongly recommend that teaching and learning centers, especially those that are struggling with staff shortages and lean budgets, consider students not only as the reason but as a resource for faculty development.

REFERENCES

Brigham Young University. (1997). *Brigham Young University Faculty Center*. Retrieved from http://lamar.colostate.edu/~ckfgill/publ/progd/brigham.html

Carleton College Learning and Teaching Center. (2008). *Student observer program*. Retrieved from http://apps.carleton.edu/campus/ltc/services/observers/

CBsalary.com. (n.d.). *Salary calculator*. Retrieved from www.cbsalary.com/salary-calculator.aspx

Center for Excellence in Teaching, Learning, and Assessment. (2007). *Mission*. Retrieved from www.cetla.howard.edu/about/mission.html

Chickering, A. W., & Gamson, Z. (1987). Seven principles of good practice in undergraduate education. *AAHE Bulletin, 39*, 3–7.

Gelula, M. H., & Yudkowsky, R. (2003). Using standardized students in faculty development workshops to improve clinical teaching skills. *Medical Education, 37*(7), 621–629.

Generation Yes Youth and Educators Succeeding. (2007). *Summary of GenYES Research*. Retrieved from http://genyes.com/programs/genyes/research

Jacobi, M. (1991). Mentoring and undergraduate academic success: A literature review. *Review of Educational Research, 61*(4), 505–532.

Laws, K. (1977). A classroom observer program. *Liberal Education, 63*(1), 37–43.

Mishra, P., Koehler, M. J., Hershey, K., & Peruski, L. (2002). *With a little help from your students: A new model for faculty development and online course design*. Retrieved from www.punyamishra.com/publications/proceedings/PM_MK_KH_LP_SITE.pdf

TimeBanks. (n.d.). *History and structure*. Retrieved from www.timebanks.org/history-structure.htm

University of Toledo Center for Teaching and Learning. (2009). *Student observer program*. Retrieved from www.utoledo.edu/centers/ctl/observer/index.html

18

THE TA CONSULTANT PROGRAM

IMPROVING UNDERGRADUATE INSTRUCTION AND GRADUATE STUDENT PROFESSIONAL DEVELOPMENT

Mikaela Huntzinger, University of Californa, Davis
Paul McPherron, Southern Illinois University, Carbondale
Madhumitha Rajagopal, Stanford University

Graduate students, particularly at research-oriented universities, are well prepared for future research careers, but they often lack knowledge or training in other aspects of academic life. A teaching assistant consultant program was created to improve the professional development opportunities for campus teaching assistants and provide a community of practice in which graduate students pursue teaching interests, cross-disciplinary collaboration, and service. We offer recommendations for creating similar programs and conclude by recommending the development of communities of practice to create opportunities for graduate students to improve their teaching skills.

Many students enter graduate school with a focus on research and little thought to teaching or service as part of their graduate experience. While these students complete programs in their intended fields and have opportunities to continue on research paths within their disciplines, some decide to pursue careers in which teaching plays a central role. At the University of California, Davis (UC Davis), the teaching assistant consultant (TAC) program has served as a catalyst and key experience in the process of teaching skills development.

The original intention of the TAC program was not to transform its participants; rather, the goal was more concrete to provide cost-effective professional development opportunities for graduate teaching assistants (TAs) campuswide by providing extensive services, from workshops to individual consultations. However, in our experience and that of many TAC fellows, the program also provides a space in which fellows can explore their developing teaching identities. With these twin functions, the TAC program is both an efficient means of providing teaching development opportunities for campus graduate students and a dynamic community of practice (COP) (Wenger, 1998) for its fellows.

Graduate Student Development Programs and Communities of Practice

In recent years, numerous reports, surveys, and research have documented the inadequacy of graduate programs in preparing graduate students for future careers (Association of American Universities, 1998; Austin, 2002; Bellows & Weissinger, 2005; Berberet, 2008; Fleet et al., 2006; Golde & Dore, 2001; Lovitts, 2001). Austin and Barnes (2005) note that graduate education programs send mixed messages about work and expectations in academic life by focusing on research training despite the reality that many graduate students will pursue and thrive in careers that involve large amounts of teaching and service work both inside and outside academe.

There are many potential ways to respond to this discrepancy between graduate training and work expectations following graduate study, including creating more opportunities for graduate students to participate in community service and learn about ways in which they can serve the public good (Austin & Barnes, 2005; Golde & Dore, 2001). UC Davis has responded to the dilemma by enlisting advanced graduate students to meet the campus's extensive demand for teaching development opportunities for graduate TAs in a way that has been as profitable for the participants as it has been for the campus as a whole. In general, group collaboration, which promotes the development of professional identities as members of academic communities, appears to be an effective and transformative tool that can profitably serve as the central element of graduate student professional development programs (Richlin & Essington, 2004; Viskovic, 2006). More specifically, we view the TAC program as a COP in which participants are shaped through their collaboration and in turn shape the practices of the group or community, as described in Wenger (1998):

> Being alive as human beings means that we are constantly engaged in the pursuit of enterprises of all kinds. . . . As we define these enterprises and engage in their pursuit together, we interact with each other and with the world and we tune our relations with each other and

with the world accordingly. In other words, we learn. Over time, this collective learning results in practices that reflect both the pursuit of our personal enterprises and collective social relations. These practices are thus the property of a kind of community created over time by the sustained pursuit of a shared enterprise. It makes sense, therefore to call these kinds of communities *communities of practice*. (original emphasis, p. 45)

Two key aspects of COPs are relevant to the TAC program. First, participants and leaders must seek a continual balance between personal enterprises and social relations, both of which influence and shape the knowledge and practices of the group. A COP is not a collection of passive individuals merely providing a service; a COP must emphasize action and shared knowledge formation (Ramanathan, 2002; Wenger, McDermott, & Snyder, 2002). Second, the shared knowledge produced in COPs varies from "hard" knowledge, such as policy and institutional structures, to more qualitative "soft" knowledge that takes the form of best practices or common sense and is shared through stories and personal experience. The TAC program model is an effective way to offer graduate students from across campus better access to professional development, as implied in the findings of Golde and Dore (2001), Austin and Barnes (2005), and Bellows and Weissinger (2005), and it simultaneously creates a COP for the fellows in the program.

The UC Davis TAC Program

UC Davis, a large research-oriented university, has approximately twenty-five thousand undergraduate students and over seven thousand graduate and professional students. The TAC program is housed in the teaching resources center (TRC), which administers all campuswide faculty and graduate student teaching programs and provides grants for undergraduate course development. Although the center's budget has dropped in recent years and both programs and positions have been cut, the TRC has chosen to continue to fund the TAC program, based on its cost-effectiveness and impact.

The TAC program was established in 1996 to motivate and prepare incoming TAs and to develop resources for TAs' ongoing skill development. Eight to ten graduate students with significant teaching experience participate in the program yearly. One experienced TAC serves as the program coordinator, and an administrator from the TRC serves as the program mentor and "institutional memory." The graduate students in the program work together throughout the academic year, and their time is spent facilitating the annual campuswide TA orientation, offering one-on-one peer consultations with TAs, developing workshops and other resources for TAs, and meeting weekly in their group. Appendix 18A provides an overview of the annual cycle of meeting agendas.

TA Orientation

The first event a new cohort of TACs prepares is the fall TA orientation for the approximately six hundred incoming TAs from about seventy-five departments on campus. The TACs work in teams to develop interactive three-hour workshops for approximately fifty incoming TAs at a time. Over the course of six meetings, the group develops a skeleton master lesson plan for their cohort, which is personalized by each team, and discusses which professional attitudes they want to convey to the incoming TAs, such as emphasizing student-centered learning and keeping reflective records of teaching experiences over time (see Appendix 18B). The TAC coordinator and the mentor lead this training period.

The fact that TA orientation is conducted largely by peer instructors (the TACs) is popular with both the incoming teaching assistants and the TACs. The evaluations received by the TAC presenters during orientation are consistently higher than those received by other presenters (unpublished data).

Consultations

After TA orientation, the TACs develop their skills as consultants during the first several weeks of fall quarter (Appendix 18A). TACs learn the format of and the skills necessary to complete three main types of consultations: midquarter interviews, also known as small group instructional diagnoses (Creed, 1997); videotaping; and classroom observations. TACs examine mock midquarter interview data to practice interpreting them, review teaching videos to consider how to respond to different teaching styles, discuss how to set TAs at ease during consultations, use skits to practice listening for subtext in interpersonal interactions, and play games to explore ways in which they can offer more useful feedback. TACs have conducted 1,524 individualized consultations in the thirteen years since the program was established (Table 18.1).

Consultations provide TAs with an opportunity to gain another view of their classroom and share their opinions and concerns about teaching with a peer consultant (Ballantyne, Hughes, & Mylonas, 2002), and TACs with the opportunity to develop their mentoring and communication skills.

Table 18.1 One-on-One Consultations Performed by the TACs for UC Davis Graduate Student Instructors

	Videotaping	Midquarter Interviews	Classroom Observations
Academic years TACs have provided this service	1996–1997 to 2008–2009	1996–1997 to 2008–2009	2002–2003 to 2008–2009
Total number provided	844	655	25
Mean per year (1 SE)	64.9 ± 4.3	50.4 ±7.2	3.6 ± 1.7

Workshops

After TACs have learned to perform consultations, much of the rest of the year is spent developing workshops (Table 18.2). During the winter quarter of the fellowship, TACs offer three to five workshops on either independent or interdependent teaching topics, and in the spring quarter, TACs offer a certificate-bearing series of six to nine workshops with a single theme. Workshops are highly interactive and rely heavily on small group activities. Participants who attend most or all of the workshops and submit the required assignment (usually a draft statement of teaching philosophy) earn a certificate of completion to put on their curriculum vitae.

The goals of the winter quarter workshops are to allow the TACs to "get their feet wet" with professional development workshops and to offer TAs the chance to learn something about a few specialized topics. To prepare these workshops, TACs split into teams, and each team develops a single workshop. The goals of the spring quarter workshop series are to give TACs the opportunity to teach an entire course for their peers and allow TA participants to explore a single topic in significant depth. Because TACs must work together to create the structure and content of the workshops, this part of the program fosters the type of group collaboration and exploration of identity implied in the notion of a COP. It also requires TACs to work on more practical aspects of group collaboration, such as prioritizing tasks and problem solving.

Table 18.2 Workshops Offered from 1996–1997 to 2008–2009 Academic Years

	Workshops Offered	Individual Attendances
Total number	242	3140
Mean per year (± SE)	18.6 ± 2.2	241.5 ± 24.7

Weekly Meetings

In academia, where research, teaching duties, and other responsibilities weigh heavily on graduate students, it would not be surprising to hear that the fellows allowed the year to slip by without producing significant amounts of work. Yet the TAC program reliably produces many opportunities for individual teaching consultations and participation in teaching workshops for TAs. Research on COPs suggests that this productivity stems from the space the TAC program provides for the fellows to develop their commitment to each other and to their domain of improved teaching (Wenger, 1998; Wenger et al., 2002).

The space, the heart of this COP, is a mandatory two-hour meeting that occurs weekly throughout the academic year. This component inevitably raises eyebrows from many academics unfamiliar with COPs. Busy academics often suggest that they do not want to attend administrative meetings, much less such long and frequently scheduled ones. However, the nearly unanimous view of the individual TACs is that this program could not provide the benefits it does without the weekly meetings. In fact, at the suggestion of an outside reviewer of the group, the TACs recently debated meeting every other week or once a month in order to release their time for other TAC-related activities (they are required to invest an average of six hours per week). However, the TACs decided that despite their busy schedules, they needed the weekly meetings to develop priorities and to get and give feedback. They said that investing two hours per week doing work together was what gave them the motivation and direction to work on their own during the rest of the week. A recent TAC summarizes the value that weekly meetings hold for the TACs:

> The experiences that most stand out for me from my time as a TAC are all related to the sense of community our cohort had. I remember one person saying that he liked coming to the TAC meetings because it was like a 12-step program—we were in a group where we didn't have to be ashamed that we cared about teaching. We all laughed. . . . Maybe my sharpest memory though was developing the first workshop in a small group (three TACs). I remember being surprised and delighted that all three of us actually showed up at the meeting place, ready to work and full of ideas. Until then, grad school had seemed like a place where everyone worked alone and in a funk. But the three of us were excited and happy to be working on this project that wasn't even required by our dissertation committees! Graduate school was very isolating for me, but my cohort of TACs offered me a place to connect. (TAC, 2004–2006)

Although each weekly meeting is different, the components generally remain the same: development of upcoming events and materials, a professional development discussion, and logistics. As a rule, nearly half the time is spent working in small groups to develop upcoming events and materials, nearly half having a professional development discussion, and only a few moments covering logistics. The mood established by the leaders is, ideally, professional but lighthearted, well organized but flexible to respond to group interests.

TACs report feeling a sense of community in the weekly meetings that they often do not feel in their home departments or laboratories. For example, a former TAC describes this "safe" place when narrating her memories of the first TAC meeting:

> In the first meeting, we were talking about something (I can't remember what anymore), and [a TAC] said, "I disagree with that." Everyone faced [the TAC]. There was a small beat of silence. [The group leader] voiced the natural—yet for me powerful—question, "What makes you disagree?" As I glanced around the table, it seemed that everyone's expressions mirrored how I felt at that moment: we were genuinely interested in why [the TAC] disagreed, that there should always be space at this table to acknowledge and incorporate dissent, that we are here to build a collective body of wisdom, experience, and knowledge that arises from understanding everyone's perspective to our utmost ability. I've carried this philosophy with me to every team that I've worked with since this moment. It was in these moments that I came to believe—in a visceral rather than purely intellectual way—that collective attainment (of knowledge, of a practice, . . .) requires everyone to perceive that their ideas are legitimate. In terms of how a team forms a plan for the work ahead of them, "legitimate" doesn't necessarily mean ultimately correct; I mean that all ideas will be given a fair shake on the way to our individual conclusions at the end of the day, and on the way to the collective plan. (TAC, 2006–2008)

In our view, the weekly TAC meeting not only provides TACs with direction, but it also provides an opportunity for TACs to transform their understanding of teaching and learning. The group discussions that follow the reading of pedagogical articles encourage them to grapple with ideas and think creatively about incorporating different approaches into their own teaching. Ultimately the members of each group discuss their ideas in such depth that they tend to discover that group members share an understanding of teaching and learning that they have not read in any one document; that is, they cocreate knowledge.

Requirements and Recommendations for Program Success

Creating and maintaining a successful TAC Program requires resources that include space, funding, and people. Space requirements include a consultation room and a meeting room. Funding requirements include fellowship stipends, salaries, and equipment funds. Each TAC receives a yearly fellowship of three thousand dollars, increments of which are distributed monthly during the academic year. The TAC coordinator receives a 50 percent graduate student researcher salary and does not receive the fellowship. In addition, one full-time staff member dedicates approximately a third of her time to serving as the mentor to the TAC program. Despite these costs, the TAC program is still more cost-effective than hiring one and a half to two full-time-equivalent staff members, the number we estimate would be required to provide services currently offered by the TACs (running the TA orientation, developing two workshop series, and doing over a hundred individual consultations each year).

While space and funding are difficult to acquire, we find that the human resources required of a high-functioning COP such as the TAC program may be the most difficult to develop. This program, which seeks not only to serve as a community for its members but also to produce products for other instructors on campus, requires many different individuals to sustain effort several hours a week throughout the academic year. We have found that a lapse in attention or commitment to the program by almost any member may be accompanied by a lapse in energy and output on the part of the entire group, and because graduate students have their attention pulled in many directions, we find this to be a significant threat.

Wenger and others (2002) note that COPs should "combine familiarity and excitement" and "open a dialogue between inside and outside perspectives" (p. 51). We add four additional suggestions for helping a TAC program to succeed: focus on buy-in from the first group meeting, maintain a safe space for open-ended discussion and play, maintain group knowledge (both hard and soft) while encouraging revision and cocreation of new practices and knowledge, and respond to varying needs of individual TACs, who represent different personality types, have different professional interests, and thrive with different types of mentoring.

Similar to other research on COPs, these suggestions emphasize the importance of authentic group collaboration and participation in the cocreation of knowledge and practice by creating safe spaces such as the weekly meetings (Richlin & Essington, 2004; Viskovic, 2006). This balance between a familiar structure (including the established structures of the TA orientation and the topics of weekly meeting in the first quarter) and the excitement of embarking on creative projects and discussion (often leading to new workshops and interdepartmental collaboration) brings up the inherent tension in COPs between continuity and creativity. In establishing a lesson plan for the TA orientation and mapping out the process of training new fellows, the TAC program can ensure a certain degree of similarity in services from year to year. However, this uniformity has the potential to silence or dominate group discussion, particularly in the fall quarter. The TAC coordinator and mentor must be careful not to allow past practices or the interests, backgrounds, or personality types of individual fellows to dictate group practices. In other words, the TAC program is not static. The description and analysis in this chapter give a generalized view of the program, but we have found that it evolves constantly, which keeps it stimulating for the mentor and TACs who return for a second year.

The interplay of creativity and continuity highlights the role of power and power dynamics within the TAC model. Recent critiques of Wenger (1998) have noted that little attention is placed on how power is negotiated within a COP and how authority is used to achieve goals (Fox, 2000; Roberts, 2006). In our roles as TAC coordinators and mentors, we have seen certain power and control issues threaten to overwhelm the group, including the composition of project teams; the division of work among TACs; debates over lecturing, multiple-choice exams, and project learning; and the perceived dominance of TACs with previous knowledge and research in teaching and education. These issues and others are not insurmountable, but they do require constant attention and dialogue among fellows, and at times they require the creation of new TAC policy and the attention of TRC and university administrators.

Concluding and Looking Forward

The TAC program fosters the creation of collaborative COPs and may be transferable to a range of groups and interactions on a variety of university campuses. For example, a former TAC suggests the versatility of the COP model in emphasizing the process over the content area of the program:

> No single project or experience stands out for me. This is because the power of the program rested in the people participating in it with me. Being in the company of fellow TAs and teachers that were passionate about teaching was inspiring. Not only was that passion contagious, but each member brought their own background, orientation, and strengths to the table. I most remember feeling "opened up" by others' viewpoints while we were engaged in some project. This opening was, for me, one of the most valuable effects of the program. I didn't

> leave the program with a grab bag of tips and tricks. I left with a new
> orientation to teaching and learning. (TAC, 2005–2007)

The TAC program is not unique in its idea of TAs helping TAs; similar programs can be found at many other universities around the United States. Universities structure their programs in unique ways to fit institutional needs, and further investigation of TAC-like programs across the country could explore the efficacy of TAC models and compare the personal stories of TACs. Questions to guide this comparison could include: Are all TAC programs focused, as at UC Davis, on creating a student-run COP, or do other effective models exist? In those identified as COPs, how are power dynamics managed? From a survey of different TAC programs, it appears that almost all programs are located at large research institutions that have well-funded teaching centers. Smaller public universities have generally not invested in TAC-like programs, and a further area of research could be to explore the reasons for this and explore alternative models of TAC programs that do not require significant financial investment.

In an era of ever-tightening budgets and with pressure to prove the worth of programs through assessment and quantitative increases in services, we hope that the TAC model at UC Davis can continue to provide needed services (demonstrating its institutional worth) as well as the freedom and space for professional development (demonstrating its personal worth to participants). We therefore join others (Richlin & Essington, 2004; Viskovic, 2006) in advocating developing and maintaining TAC-like programs. We find that the TAC program is a relatively inexpensive way to create many opportunities for graduate students to improve their teaching skills, either as TACs themselves or as participants in the many programs offered by the TACs.

Appendix 18A: Annual Cycle of TAC Program Meeting Agendas Orientation

Late Summer

Day	Topics
1	Overview of TAC program Professional development (PD): What is good teaching? PD: What do we know about new TAs?
2	PD: Brief overview of five topics of the TA orientation (getting started as a TA, promoting student participation, presenting information clearly, grading efficiently and effectively, ethics) Group review of past TA orientation master lesson plan

3	PD: Getting started as a TA
	TA Orientation practice
4	PD: Promoting student participation
	PD: Presenting information clearly
	TA orientation practice
5	PD: Grading efficiently and effectively
	TA orientation practice
6	PD: Dealing ethically with students, colleagues, and professors
	Dress rehearsal for TA orientation

Note: Each meeting lasts three hours.

Fall Quarter

Week	Topics
1	TA orientation review of evaluations and debriefing
	TAC goals for year
	PD: What is consulting?
2	Big picture of TAC year
	PD: What is good teaching?
	PD: What is improved teaching?
3	How to do a midquarter interview
	Practice interpreting MQI results
	PD: Principles for good practice in higher education
4	Role play: Midquarter interview consultation
	How to do a videotaping
	PD: Watching yourself on videotape
5	Watch video playback consultation
	Role play: video playback
	How to do classroom observations
6	Consultation skills wrap-up
	Brainstorm for winter quarter workshop series
7	Winter quarter workshop series—products this week and next:
	Titles and advertising blurbs
	General goals for each workshop
	Dates and times
	Team members for each workshop
	PD: Promoting teaching through experiential workshops
8	Unfinished workshop tasks from last week
	PD: Learning in workshop settings
9	Small group work on winter quarter workshops
	Fall quarter wrap-up

Note: Each meeting lasts two hours.

Winter Quarter

Week	Topics
1	Practice workshop 1—do a complete dry run
2	Practice workshop 1 again if necessary until team is confident, or begin planning for spring workshop series
3	Practice workshop 2
4	Practice workshop 2 again if necessary
5	Practice workshop 3
6	Practice workshop 3 if necessary or Workshop 4 if it exists
7	Spring workshop series planning—products this week and next: Titles and advertising blurbs General goals for each workshop Dates and times Team members for each workshop
8	Unfinished workshop tasks from last week
9	Practice workshop 1 of spring workshop series

Note: Each meeting lasts two hours. All professional development for winter quarter is decided by the TACs themselves. Each person takes one day and chooses his or her own teaching article to discuss with the group.

Spring Quarter

Each meeting lasts two hours. All professional development for spring quarter is decided by the TACs themselves. Each week the TACs practice the upcoming week's workshop, troubleshooting and revising where necessary. The final week is spent as a cross-over meeting where the incoming cohort is invited to meet and talk with the outgoing cohort.

Appendix 18B: TA Orientation Master Lesson Plan

Following is one version of the skeleton master lesson plan for one three-hour TA orientation workshop. This master was developed from previous cohorts' master lesson plans. The incoming TAC group also suggests interactive activities for each topic in the lesson plan. For example, we have accumulated five scenarios for the "Dealing Ethically" section.

TA ORIENTATION SESSION OUTLINE

- Introduction
- The First Day
  - Setting the atmosphere

- The Rest of the Quarter
  - Doing clear presentations
  - Generating discussion and student involvement
  [Break]
  - Grading student work
- Dealing Ethically with Students, Colleagues, and Professors
  - Open question period
  - Preparing for the future
  - Summary and conclusion
  - Evaluations

REFERENCES

Association of American Universities. (1998). *Committee on graduate education report and recommendations* [Press release]. Retrieved from www.aau .edu/publications/reports.aspx?id=6900

Austin, A. (2002). Preparing the next generation of faculty: Graduate school as socialization to the academic career. *Journal of Higher Education, Special Issue: The Faculty in the New Millennium, 73*(1), 94–122.

Austin, A., & Barnes, B. J. (2005). Preparing doctoral students for faculty careers that contribute to the public good. In A. J. Kezar, T. C. Chambers, & J. C. Burkhardt (Eds.), *Higher education for the public good: Emerging voices from a national movement* (pp. 272–292). San Francisco: Jossey-Bass.

Ballantyne, R., Hughes, K., & Mylonas, A. (2002). Developing procedures for implementing peer assessment in large classes using an action research process. *Assessment and Evaluation in Higher Education, 27*(5), 427–441.

Bellows, L., & Weissinger, E. (2005). Assessing the academic and professional needs of graduate students. In S. Chadwick-Blossey & D. R. Robertson (Eds.), *To improve the academy: Vol. 23. Resources for faculty, instructional, and organizational development* (pp. 267–281). San Francisco: Jossey-Bass/Anker.

Berberet, J. (2008). Perceptions of early career faculty: Managing the transition from graduate school to the professorial career. *TIAA-CREF Institute: Research Dialogue 92.* Retrieved from www.tiaa-crefinstitute.org/ articles/92.html

Creed, T. (1997). Small group instructional diagnosis (SGID) [supplementary materials]. *National Teaching and Learning Forum, 6*(4). Retrieved from www.ntlf.com/html/pi/9705/sgid.htm

Fleet, C. M., Rosser, M.F.N., Zufall, R. A., Pratt, M. C., Feldman, T. S., & Lemons, P. (2006). Hiring criteria in biology departments of academic institutions. *Bioscience, 56*(5), 430–436.

Fox, S. (2000). Communities of practice: Foucault and actor-network theory. *Journal of Management Studies, 37*(6), 853–867.

Golde, C. M., & Dore, T. M. (2001). *At cross purposes: What the experiences of doctoral students reveal about doctoral education.* Retrieved from www.phd-survey.org/

Lovitts, B. E. (2001). *Leaving the ivory tower: The causes and consequences of departure from doctoral study.* Lanham, MD: Rowan & Littlefield.

Ramanathan, V. (2002). *The politics of TESOL education: Writing, knowledge, critical pedagogy.* New York: RoutledgeFalmer.

Richlin, L., & Essington, A. (2004). Faculty learning communities for preparing future faculty. In M. D. Cox & L. Richlin (Eds.), *New directions for teaching and learning: No. 97. Building faculty learning communities* (pp. 149–157). San Francisco: Jossey-Bass.

Roberts, J. (2006). Limits to communities of practice. *Journal of Management Studies, 43*(3), 623–639.

Viskovic, A. (2006). Becoming a tertiary teacher: Learning in communities of practice. *Higher Education Research and Development, 25*(4), 323–339.

Wenger, E. (1998). *Communities of practice: Learning, meaning, and identity.* New York: Cambridge University Press.

Wenger, E., McDermott, R., & Snyder, W. M. (2002). *Cultivating communities of practice: A guide to managing knowledge.* Boston: Harvard Business School Press.

19

READY OR NOT?

AN INTERNATIONAL STUDY OF THE
PREPARATION OF EDUCATIONAL DEVELOPERS

Nancy Van Note Chism, Indiana University School of Education,
Indiana University–Purdue University Indianapolis

This report of an international survey of educational developers describes their entry-level background knowledge and skills for the work of educational development, how they obtained them, and their recommendations on helping prepare new entrants to the profession. Respondents reported that their experiences rendered them moderately prepared for some tasks and less prepared for others, notably consultation. The results can inform increased professionalization of educational development through more systematic preparation of future educational developers.

Educational developers in higher education settings frequently observe that most faculty members are not prepared to teach in any formal or extensive way. What they fail to add is that the same is true for their own profession. The findings reported here document the preparation experiences of entrants to educational development, their assessment of its quality, and their recommendations for the preparation of future entrants.

Conceptual Framework

Literature on the professions consistently names the existence of formal career preparation and an established body of knowledge as requisite characteristics of professions. In addressing the need for formal preparation

My appreciation is expressed to Mellisa Benites Cotera, and to Josh Smith and staff members Jake Stuckey and Eileen Turpin of the IUPUI Center for Urban and Multicultural Education for their help.

of educational developers, Baume (2004) cites the work of many scholars of professionalism, the most well known of whom is Wilensky (1964), whose classic list of characteristics of a profession explicitly identifies emphasis on formal training as a key attribute of a profession. The "systematic preparation and training of practitioners" is also on Knapper's (1998, p. 93) list of hallmarks of a profession.

The association of professions with established bodies of knowledge is also supported by the literature on professionalism, summarized by the observation of Eraut (1994): "The power and status of professional workers depend to a significant extent on their claims to unique forms of expertise, which are not shared with other occupational groups, and the value placed on that expertise" (p. 14). In his conception, Eraut indicates that at certain points in their identity, groups of people performing an activity make conscious efforts to portray themselves as professionals.

The literature on professions also portrays a pattern of advancement from craft knowledge transmitted largely through the interactions of practitioners and their apprentices to more abstract, organized knowledge bases learned through more formal methods, such as classroom instruction, most often coupled with internships or other forms of experiential learning, overseen by a mentor. Examples include medicine, law, social work, and precollegiate teaching. Becher and Trowler Becher (2001) describe this process in academia. Transitions between stages of development within a profession are often characterized by intense debate between those who seek to formalize the preparation of new professionals and those who favor the existing informal system.

It is within this framework of professional knowledge that this study is situated. The study sought to understand the status of the professionalization of the field of educational development and practitioners' views on the nature of the knowledge base they need and how it is acquired.

Literature Review

Educational developers are part of a relatively new group of practitioners who are still struggling with defining the boundaries of their work. Identity literature is common and portrays differences between and across institutions and countries as to what educational developers do. Clement and McAlpine (2008) call educational development an "emerging" field, without a common body of knowledge, "let alone a shared set of convictions or research methods" (p. 1). Carew, Lefoe, Bell, and Armour (2008) speculate that the work is best described as an "elastic practice," whose practitioners rely on "the tailoring of an approach for a specific context, drawing on the toolkit of techniques, experiences, ideas, and theoretical stances that a particular academic developer has collected" (p. 60). The positive side of identity struggles, Grant (2007) points out, is that ambiguous status avoids issues of exclusion, boundary patrolling, and adoption of codified rules of practice.

At the same time, there is concern with preparing new educational developers, particularly as the first generation of developers ages. Over time, practitioners have discussed extensively the knowledge and skills that developers should have (Baume & Kahn, 2004; Bergquist & Phillips, 1995; Brinko & Menges, 1997; Gillespie, Hilsen, & Wadsworth, 2002; Isaacs, 1997; Kahn, 2004; Kahn & Baume, 2003; Knapper & Piccinin, 1999; Lewis, 1988; Outram, 2006; Paulsen & Feldman, 1995). There is also a small literature on how educational developers say they have learned their profession (Fraser, 1999; Graf & Wheeler, 1996; Sorcinelli, Austin, Eddy, & Beach, 2006).

Rowland (2003), comparing teaching and educational development, asks whether educational development is atheoretical (requiring simply a practical feel for what is involved) or theory based (working from an articulated base of ideas about relationships between phenomena). He concludes that both the practical and theoretical are helpful, yet acknowledges the tensions of this middle space. Others such as Kahn (2004) point out that the knowledge bases of teaching and educational development overlap, but "work that involves enhancing a specialist practice will also draw on skills that will not necessarily be developed by simply engaging in the practice itself" (p . 214).

Although such distinctions are drawn between learning to teach and learning the practice of educational development, insights about the nature of experiential learning (Kolb, 1984) and reflective practice (Moon, 1999; Schön, 1983) in learning to teach generally continue to be applied to the development of professional knowledge (Sharp, 2004). The focus is on individual cycles of growth rooted in inquiry into practice and situated within a community of practice.

This study rests on the assumption that although identity issues remain, the existence of the term *educational developer* (or *professional developer, faculty developer*, or *academic developer*) and the expansion of centers for development and professional associations for educational developers worldwide indicate that a core conceptualization of this work has formed, even though its nature is dependent on context, and that consensus on boundary issues is still elusive. This chapter provides a descriptive portrait of what preparation a sample of current educational developers had on entry to their roles, how they evaluated the quality of that preparation, and the types of preparation they would recommend for new developers.

Study Design

The support of a grant from the Professional and Organizational Development Network in Higher Education (POD) enabled this project to be conducted on an international level, affording the opportunity to gather data across national boundaries. Although the context of educational development varies across and within nations, the focus of the study was on ascertaining commonalities while not denying differences. A "maximum variation" sample (Patton, 2002) was thus favored. Methods are described in greater detail in the study report (Chism, 2008) and included a presurvey to ground the categories for the final survey, circulation of drafts of the survey to the heads of major educational development associations for review and subsequent revision, and administration of the survey through the distribution channels of these associations. The final draft of the survey contained items about informed consent and appropriateness of the survey for the respondents, as well as items about their backgrounds, work experiences, and recommendations for the preparation of future developers. A five-point scale was used for the items. An electronic survey format was used, and the survey instrument was available in both English and French. Survey instruments are appended to the formal report (Chism, 2008).

The 565 usable responses came from respondents in over twenty countries and were diverse in demographic makeup and career experience. The majority were female (70 percent) and worked in English-speaking countries—the United States (57 percent), Canada (11 percent), the United Kingdom (13 percent), and Australia/New Zealand (6 percent)—which constituted all but 13 percent of the sample. Most of the participating organizations were unable to provide population characteristics of their lists, a limitation that precluded calculation of a response rate and other demographic indicators. Thus, the emphasis here is on broad patterns and text comments.

Prior Work Experiences

A majority of the developers (67 percent) held faculty positions before entry to the profession. Some worked in central academic support units as directors (5 percent) or staff (15 percent), and others came from central administrative officer positions (6 percent). It is interesting to note that 10 percent had no previous higher education experience. Text comments indicate that these members of the profession came from secondary school positions, corporate training, or other venues.

A little more than half (57 percent) of respondents indicated that they entered the profession as a staff member of an educational development unit, and another 21 percent said that they had informal responsibilities for development. Over a quarter of respondents (26 percent) came into the profession as director of an educational development unit without having had any prior experience as a staff member. This was particularly so for American and Canadian developers, for whom the percentage of respondents indicating entry position as director (36 percent and 25 percent, respectively) was significantly higher than Australian (6 percent) and U.K. (9 percent) developers. One reason might be that it is relatively common in the United States to have development units staffed by only one professional or to use committees or appointments within other units to deliver educational development services. Sorcinelli et al. (2006) report that only 54 percent of the U.S. campuses in their survey have centralized units with dedicated staff.

Most of the respondents held advanced degrees, with 60 percent reporting doctorates and 35 percent master's degrees. No differences in gender representation across degree categories were found, but a significant country difference was found in the higher percentage of doctorates reported by U.S. developers than those from other countries. About 74 percent of U.S. respondents reported having doctorates, compared with 52 percent from Australia and New Zealand, 41 percent from the United Kingdom, 39 percent from Europe, and 36 percent from Canada.

Education was named as the major area of study for respondents' most advanced degree (48 percent). Australian respondents reported the highest percentage of education degrees (70 percent), followed by Canada (64 percent). The percentage in the United Kingdom and the United States was virtually the same, at 44 percent, while Europeans reported 39 percent.

Content Knowledge

With respect to content knowledge, respondents reported having gained their entry-level knowledge through various activities. The most frequently cited activity was reading, followed by conferences and workshops on teaching and learning. Conferences and workshops on educational development and formal course work were rated lowest of the choices provided on the survey item. Those who answered "other" for this item indicated that teaching in secondary school, working as a graduate teaching assistant, or having had a mentor or having worked in corporate training gave them content knowledge for educational development work.

When they were asked to evaluate the effectiveness of their content knowledge experiences for their subsequent work as a developer, respondents generally claimed moderate effectiveness for formal course work and conferences and reading books and articles, and less effectiveness for participation in listservs and online communities.

Respondents rated their entry-level content knowledge as a result of these experiences by indicating that they were somewhat prepared, with average ratings between "some knowledge" and "moderate knowledge" (3 and 4 on a five-point scale) for items about student assessment, instructional design, use of information technology, and evaluation of teaching. They assigned their lowest average rating to knowledge of theories of organizational change (3.13) and faculty development (3.05) and multicultural teaching (3.13) and their highest to knowledge of learning theory (3.90) and active learning strategies (3.99).

Skills Background

With respect to activities that provided skills that educational developers needed, the respondents reported that they engaged in apprenticeships and formal course work, as well as participating in administrative or faculty experiences before working in educational development. They listed additional activities as well: experiences as secondary teachers or graduate teaching assistants, experiences as staff developers in primary or secondary settings, work as instructional technology consultants, and experiences outside education, such as corporate training or project management. Some respondents felt that skills learned through specific experiences were transferable to the work of educational development, such as the one who listed "childbirth education and assertiveness training" and another who listed army service as preparation experiences.

When respondents were asked to evaluate the potential effectiveness of these experiences for providing educational developers with the skills they need, they rated educational apprenticeships and formal course work most highly, with background work experiences as faculty members, directors of other units, and advisory board members next in potential effectiveness.

Based on these prior experiences, respondents rated their entry-level skills on such tasks as supervising staff, preparing conference proposals or publications, event planning, and conflict management from "very little skill" to "some skill" (3 to 4 on a five-point scale), except for the category of presenting work at workshops or conferences, for which they rated themselves as having moderate skill (4.07). The lowest-rated areas were in the categories of performing research or organizational consultations (2.57 and 2.52, respectively), writing grant proposals (2.73), performing teaching consultations (3.08), managing a budget (3.05), and performing program assessments (3.09).

A strong theme in the comments throughout the survey, and especially in the skills section, was concern with the question of whether faculty experience is necessary for the preparation of educational developers. For the most part, those who promote faculty experience or status couch their arguments around issues of respect and credibility rather than the actual skills one acquires as a faculty member. One U.S. respondent stated, "It is critical for educational developers to have experience as a faculty member before attempting to influence faculty members as an educational developer." A respondent from the United Kingdom stated, "It seems to me that the most vital thing is that educational development isn't seen as an alternative career route (or career death) and that educational development professionals continue to be academics (or faculty as you say in the U.S.) with the same expectations for scholarship and teaching, otherwise it becomes increasingly hard to relate to academic colleagues." A U.S. respondent, rather than focusing on credibility, spoke to the depth of skills built during a faculty career: "New faculty developers should come from the faculty. Teaching course design, active learning techniques, etc. can be done by nonfaculty, but it reduces teaching to a 'bag of tricks' rather than a philosophy, values, and vocation."

In contrast, several U.S. respondents argued that faculty experience alone is not sufficient preparation for educational development careers—for example:

> I believe professional development for faculty is a field that must be more clearly understood in higher education. It is a field that requires special training, scholarship, and experience. Too often it seems to be regarded as something that "anyone can do," especially faculty since they teach. I strongly disagree with that philosophy. This field demands its own expertise and scholarship in many areas such as organizational development, teaching and learning, assessment, learning theory, and communication.

Another respondent said, "Educational development needs to be seen as its own discipline. Being a good teacher and a successful faculty member are helpful but not the skill set needed for someone who is more of a coach than a player."

Some respondents isolated teaching experience, rather than having had a faculty appointment, as important preparation for educational developers. While some focused on the credibility argument, others focused more on the understanding and compassion that an experienced teacher can bring to the work. A U.S. respondent stated, "I believe teaching experience in higher education is an important prerequisite for an educational developer. This is because it is important to be able to empathize with faculty when they express their varied concerns about teaching in higher education. In addition to empathy, it is important to provide options for faculty as they deal with the myriad duties, responsibilities, concerns."

A U.K. respondent added, "It is vital that educational developers have had experience and have the credentials as having been—or continuing to be—highly effective teachers in higher education. Without this any other qualification or training is not going to help win over faculty."

Recommendations for Preparation of Future Developers

The final section of the survey asked respondents to go beyond their own personal experiences and provide their recommendation on the potential efficacy of several methods for preparing future educational development professionals, as well as their ratings of the importance of content knowledge topics and skills that future professionals should possess. Respondents favored apprenticeships as the most effective way to prepare future professionals, yet they also expressed strong support for formal course work as part of a degree or specialist program and conference workshops or short courses on educational development. They expressed somewhat less support for Web-based tutorials but still saw some potential in them.

Survey responses documented respondents' opinions on the importance of the specific knowledge and skill areas listed on the survey instrument for the preparation of professionals. Respondents' ratings on the relative value of content knowledge topics recommended for inclusion in preparation experiences for new educational developers were ranked between "moderately important" and "very important" (4 to 5 on a five-point scale). Having knowledge of multicultural teaching received the highest mean (4.72), with evaluation of teaching (4.68), student assessment approaches (4.67), and instructional design (4.65) following closely. Ratings of various skills that respondents thought educational developers should acquire were ranked from somewhat to very important (3 to 5 on a five-point scale), with highest mean ratings going to oral presentation

skills (4.63), followed by consultation techniques (4.48), program administration (4.01), and conflict resolution skills (4.03).

Discussion

The results of this study support and add specificity to anecdotal reports
that portray a rather unplanned entry to careers in educational development. They echo the findings of Fraser (1999), McDonald and Stockley
(2008), and Kahn (2004) about entry to the profession. While most of
the developers surveyed came from other positions within higher education settings, few listed any specific formal preparation for the work of
development. Through their experience, most were familiar with the context of colleges and universities and with the work of faculty members. A
moderate number of new entrants had been exposed to teaching and
learning issues through having served as faculty members or through
reading and workshop attendance, yet fewer than half had attended conferences, workshops, or courses on educational development. Fewer than
a third reported having special preparation in the consultation skills that
educational developers use. As a result, the majority indicated that they
lacked specific educational development content knowledge and skills
upon entry. Clearly there is a steep learning curve for new developers, one
that takes place on the job. In recommending experiences for new developers, the respondents expressed strong support for apprenticeships and
formal course work in educational development, as well as reading on
educational development and conference or workshop attendance.

Based on the framework for this study, the results indicate that if formal preparation experiences are a hallmark of professions, the field of
educational development is still in a formative period. They also indicate
that although more and more developers (such as Eggins & MacDonald,
2003; Felten, Kalish, Pingree, & Plank, 2007; Wilcox, 2009) are pointing
to a scholarship of educational development, it is not being systematically
accessed by those preparing to enter the field. (See Chapter Twenty-One,
this volume, for a discussion of the state of the scholarship of educational
development.) Brew and Pesata (2008) concur: "So it is not uncommon
for senior managers to believe that any university teacher who has taught
students in a faculty is capable of turning into an effective academic
developer overnight without any kind of mentorship, training or understanding of the body of literature that informs academic development
scholarship and practice" (p. 85).

Kahn (2004) points out that it is not uncommon for developers to
work concurrently in fields that require three knowledge bases: initial

discipline, teaching of that discipline, and educational development. Because its practitioners often come to educational development as a second profession after having served in another position, most have not undertaken specialized academic course work or apprenticeships in the field. It is unlikely that they will return to graduate school to prepare for this new career, yet there may be alternatives that are more systematic and perhaps more efficient than the trial-and-error learning that now occurs. For both those who are entering educational development as a first career and those coming from other career paths, much might be gained through studying the theoretical frameworks and research literature informing educational development through entry-level programs, delivered online or at institutes. Skills used in educational development might be honed through apprenticeships at nearby institutions or through an overlap period with their predecessors, overseen by experienced developers who can serve as mentors. These opportunities can be added to the informal methods now available, such as reading and conference attendance, resulting in a more intentional preparation experience for new developers. Cowan (2004) cautions that experience alone is not a sufficient base for learning the practice of educational development: he recommends that reflective inquiry on practice, guided by an experienced developer, must be a hallmark of such approaches.

Professional associations should be called on to take the lead in organizing preparation experiences. This effort will enable the benefits that more effective practitioners can produce at their home institutions and lead to greater professionalization of the field. When practice moves from idiosyncratic to theory based, from personally invented to informed by past study, the field as a whole advances. This argument does not preclude individual creativity or indicate absolute formulas for good practice, but it does underscore that there is now foundational knowledge that educational developers should have. Several associations have already developed initiatives for the preparation of new entrants to the field. Increased formal activity within educational developers' professional associations, such as the certificate programs offered by the Staff and Educational Development Association in the United Kingdom and the POD-sponsored International Institute for New Faculty Developers, may be seen as evidence of growing activity in providing these preparation experiences. More of these initiatives are needed. It is no longer acceptable for centers to appoint directors without substantial knowledge of the field or expect that those with only teaching experience or a faculty title can automatically move into development positions without further preparation.

Interest in establishing and codifying an established knowledge base is supported, as noted above, by current discussion of the scholarship of educational development. Gosling (2007) speaks of the "academicisation" of educational development, arising in response to charges that existing approaches lack a theory base. He indicates that in the United Kingdom, 72.5 percent of educational development units now see contributing to scholarship as an essential part of their mission and that 67.5 percent believe that they must sponsor others' work in the scholarship of teaching and learning. Stefani (2004) optimistically observes that the foundations of the profession are being established: "Formal organization and structure is becoming more evident, with an increasing range of recognized networks involved in promoting and disseminating current scholarship, and research relating to different aspects of academic practice and development" (p. 21).

In addition to welcoming and using scholarship on educational development, additional studies of the efficacy of methods for preparing new developers are needed. Increasing understanding of the skills and knowledge bases needed for the various tasks of the educational developer and how these are best acquired is crucial to the continued maturation of the profession. Without intentional cultivation of the scholarly and practical foundations for practice, the field is doomed to amateur status and uneven efficacy.

As colleges and universities around the world undertake reforms aimed at modernizing and responding to new global imperatives, they need the guidance of educational developers more than ever before. Already those in the field are indicating that filling positions in educational development with prepared individuals has become increasingly challenging (McDonald & Stockley, 2008).

Is the field now mature enough to invest in more formal preparation of educational developers? Are developers ready to state that theirs is a profession that relies on specialized knowledge that new entrants must have? The answer may lie in future new significant and thoughtful preparation vehicles.

REFERENCES

Baume, D. (2004, June). *Professional development, professional recognition and professional standards for higher education teachers and developers.* Paper presented at the annual meeting of the International Consortium on Educational Development, Ottawa.

Baume, D., & Kahn, P. (Eds.). (2004). *Enhancing staff and educational development.* London: RoutledgeFalmer.

Becher, T., & Trowler Becher, P. (2001). *Academic tribes and territories: Intellectual enquiry and the cultures of disciplines* (2nd ed.). Buckingham, UK: Society for Research into Higher Education and Open University Press.

Bergquist, W., & Phillips, S. (1995). *Developing human and organizational resources: A comprehensive manual.* Point Arena, CA: Peter Magnusson Press.

Brew, A., & Pesata, T. (2008). The precarious existence of the academic development unit. *International Journal for Academic Development, 13*(2), 83–85.

Brinko, K. T., & Menges, R. J. (Eds.). (1997). *Practically speaking: A sourcebook for instructional consultants in higher education.* Stillwater, OK: New Forums Press.

Carew, A., Lefoe, G., Bell, M., & Armour, L. (2008). Elastic practice in academic developers. *International Journal for Academic Development, 13*(1), 51–66.

Chism, N.V.N. (2008). *A professional priority: Preparing educational developers.* Indianapolis: Indiana University School of Education, IUPUI. Retrieved from http://ctl.iupui.edu/common/uploads/library/CTL/CTL605522.doc

Clement, M., & McAlpine, L. (2008). In search of a paradigm: The sequel. *International Journal for Academic Development, 13*(1), 1–3.

Cowan, J. (2004). Learning from experience. In D. Baume & P. Kahn (Eds.), *Enhancing staff and educational development* (pp. 192–211). London: RoutledgeFalmer.

Eggins, H., & MacDonald, R. (2003). *The scholarship of academic development.* Buckingham, UK: Open University Press.

Eraut, M. (1994). *Developing professional knowledge and competence.* London: Routledge.

Felten, P., Kalish, A., Pingree, A., & Plank, K. M. (2007). Toward a scholarship of teaching and learning in educational development. In D. R. Robertson & L. B. Nilson (Eds.), *To improve the academy, Vol. 25. Resources for faculty, instructional, and organizational development* (pp. 93–108). San Francisco: Jossey-Bass.

Fraser, K. (1999). Australasian academic developers: Entry into the profession and our own professional development. *International Journal for Academic Development, 4,* 89–101.

Gillespie, K. H., Hilsen, L. R., & Wadsworth, E. C. (Eds.). (2002). *A guide to faculty development: Practical advice, examples, and resources.* San Francisco: Jossey-Bass/Anker.

Gosling, D. (2007). *Educational development in the United Kingdom: Report to the Heads of Educational Development Group.* London: Heads of Development Group.

Graf, D. L., & Wheeler, D. (1996). *Defining the field: The POD membership survey*. Ames, IA: Professional and Organizational Development Network in Higher Education.

Grant, B. M. (2007). The mourning after: Academic development in a time of doubt. *International Journal for Academic Development, 12*(1), 35–43.

Isaacs, G. (1997). Developing the developers: Some ethical dilemmas in changing times. *International Journal for Academic Development, 2*(2), 6–12.

Kahn, P. (2004). Developing professional expertise in staff and educational development. In D. Baume & P. Kahn (Eds.), *Enhancing staff and educational development* (pp. 212–226). London: RoutledgeFalmer.

Kahn, P., & Baume, D. (Eds.). (2003). *A guide to staff and educational development*. London: Kogan Page.

Knapper, C. (1998). Is academic development a profession? *International Journal for Academic Development, 3*(2), 93–96.

Knapper, C., & Piccinin, S. (Eds.). (1999). *New directions for teaching and learning: No. 79. Using consultants to improve teaching*. San Francisco: Jossey-Bass.

Kolb, D. (1984). *Experiential learning: Experience as a source of learning and development*. Upper Saddle River, NJ: Prentice Hall.

Lewis, K. G. (1988). *Face to face: A sourcebook of individual consultation techniques for faculty/instructional developers*. Stillwater, OK: New Forums Press.

McDonald, J., & Stockley, D. (2008). Pathways to the profession of educational development: An international perspective. *International Journal for Academic Development, 13*(3), 213–218.

Moon, J. (1999). *Reflection in learning and professional development: Theory and practice*. London: Kogan Page.

Outram, S. (2006). *Developing the developer: A Higher Education Academy/ SEDA pilot project*. York, UK: Higher Education Academy.

Patton, M. Q. (2002). *Qualitative evaluation and research methods* (3rd ed.). Thousand Oaks, CA: Sage.

Paulsen, M. B., & Feldman, K. A. (1995). *Taking teaching seriously* (ASHE-ERIC Higher Education Report, Vol. 95:2). Washington, DC: George Washington University, Graduate School of Education and Human Development.

Rowland, S. (2003). Academic development: A practical or theoretical business. In H. Eggins & R. Macdonald (Eds.), *The scholarship of academic development* (pp. 13–22). Buckingham, UK: Society for Research into Higher Education and Open University Press.

Schön, D. (1983). *The reflective practitioner: How professionals think in action*. New York: Basic Books.

Sharp, R. (2004). How do professionals learn and develop? Implications for staff and educational developers. In D. Baume & P. Kahn (Eds.), *Enhancing staff and educational development* (pp. 132–153). London: RoutledgeFalmer.

Sorcinelli, M. D., Austin, A. E., Eddy, P. L., & Beach, A. L. (2006). *Creating the future of faculty development: Learning from the past, understanding the present*. San Francisco: Jossey-Bass/Anker.

Stefani, L. (2004). What is staff and educational development? In D. Baume & P. Kahn (Eds.), *Enhancing staff and educational development* (pp. 9–23). London: RoutledgeFalmer.

Wilcox, S. (2009). Transformative educational development scholarship: Beginning with ourselves. *International Journal for Academic Development, 14*(2), 123–132.

Wilensky, H. L. (1964). The professionalization of everyone? *American Journal of Sociology, 70*(2), 137–158.

20

DISTRIBUTION AND PENETRATION OF TEACHING-LEARNING DEVELOPMENT UNITS IN HIGHER EDUCATION

IMPLICATIONS FOR STRATEGIC PLANNING AND RESEARCH

Sally Kuhlenschmidt, Western Kentucky University

This chapter presents descriptive information about 1,267 U.S. teaching-learning development units (TLDUs). It provides strategic planning and research tools previously unavailable. Results indicate that TLDUs occur in at least 21.2 percent of U.S. higher education institutions, and their presence is correlated at a higher level with student enrollment than with number of faculty. The study provides normative data on the nature of higher education in the United States and on TLDUs by Carnegie classification, location, and type of institution. Additional information is provided about the presence of centers at special-focus institutions such as Hispanic-serving institutions.

I thank the Professional and Organizational Development Network in Higher Education and the North American Council for Staff, Program, and Organizational Development for the information they provided on membership and the Hofstra University Center for Teaching and Scholarly Excellence, the University of Kansas, Center for Teaching Excellence, and the University of Victoria, Center for Teaching and Scholarly Excellence for maintaining websites with lists of centers. Finally, I thank Jennifer West and Jaime Trotter for their work in entering and correcting information in the data set.

Difficult budget times often result in administrative requests for data to support the importance of a teaching development center. Administrators may ask for normative data about what types of schools have centers or how common centers are. These data can assist in structuring the argument for the creation or continuation of a teaching-learning development unit (TLDU). The field of teaching development has been hindered because the population of TLDUs has been unknown and because research has had to rely on samples of convenience. Those interested in investigating factors influencing success in the field have had to rely primarily on experiential information and do without the additional dimensions of understanding that accompany systematic research.

Two major efforts to identify the maximum number of faculty development units have been made. Centra's (1976) survey of 756 institutions was the first large-scale investigation and found that 333 respondents (44 percent) had a faculty development unit or coordinator. Erickson (1986) investigated the state of the field by mailing surveys to 1,588 four-year or more institutions. From this sample of 750, 47 percent were identified as having faculty development centers, but 24 percent of the sample were nonrespondents. Both studies relied on self-report. In addition, "faculty development" could include a wide variety of units, from grant offices to funding committees within the discipline, not necessarily a teaching development unit.

Another methodology relies on a sample of convenience. Hellyer and Boschmann (1993) examined faculty development programs at ninety-four institutions in a sample based on the Professional and Organizational Development Network in Higher Education (POD Network) membership, conference attendees, and individuals they knew. Unfortunately, we do not know if the sample was representative or if they simply located centers with directors who were responsive or part of the professional network. This approach may miss centers that are understaffed, underfunded, and overwhelmed, without time to complete surveys or money to attend meetings. Thus, the generalizability of results to the population of TLDUs is unclear.

More recent efforts have looked at subgroups of institutional types. Wright (2000) targeted a population of 125 research universities. At that time she identified 55 centers (44 percent) based on responses to a letter to schools; 33 (26 percent) participated in the survey. Unfortunately we do not know the status of development at the 56 percent of schools (70) that did not respond to the letter.

Frantz, Beebe, Horvath, Canales, and Swee (2005) sent surveys to the 206 centers on the University of Kansas website list and the POD Network listserv, as well as to the small college developer listserv. They received 109 responses but apparently did not investigate duplication of institutions. Their sample, which included only two baccalaureate schools and only one specialized college, showed centers at 59 percent of research/doctoral, 25 percent of master's, 8 percent of baccalaureate/liberal arts, 6 percent of community colleges, and 1 percent of specialized institutions. Interpretation of the data is difficult because we do not know how well this sample reflects the population of teaching development units or if multiple surveys came from the same institution. Wesley (2005) surveyed the seventy-eight Texas two-year colleges on the status of faculty development, with fifty-seven responding in the affirmative, an impressive response rate although the sample was restricted in type of school. Again, faculty development is not necessarily teaching development.

The largest recent collection of center data was by Sorcinelli, Austin, Eddy, and Beach (2006), who identified three hundred institutions as having POD Network members. For the U.S. portion of their sample, 48 percent were at research/doctoral, 25 percent at comprehensive, 12 percent at liberal arts, 10 percent at community colleges (likely underrepresented), and 5 percent at other types of institutions. Because this data analysis is by respondent, it is unclear if the sample proportionately represents institutions. There could have been two individuals from the same institution, thus overrepresenting that school and favoring schools with large staffs or multiple units. This survey informed us about POD Network membership but not about what is typical for centers for teaching.

The flaw in all of these approaches is that the status of teaching development at the nonrespondent schools is unknown. Large numbers of centers could be unnoticed and unmeasured and critical movements or ideas lost. In this study, I have identified centers by using specialized search tools to ensure that every institution is examined for evidence of a center.

Method

Data are available on 4,390 U.S. institutions from the Carnegie Foundation for the Advancement of Teaching (June 19, 2009), which includes the institutional Carnegie classification and information from the Integrated Postsecondary Education Data System (National Center for Education Statistics, 2009). Among the 1,267 TLDUs in the United States identified in this study, there are 933 unique institutions with Carnegie data available.

The data set was assembled by evaluating units identified through multiple sources. It includes appropriate units from the 2006 membership directory of the Professional and Organizational Development Network in Higher Education (2006), interim membership updates through fall 2009 (H. Holmgren, personal communications, March 30, 2007, through October 22, 2009), and various postings to the POD Network listserv (Professional and Organizational Development Network in Higher Education, 2009). It includes the 2009 membership list (by institution) of the North American Council for Staff, Program, and Organizational Development (NCSPOD) (P. Honzay, personal communication, September 22, 2009). In addition, information was incorporated from lists maintained by the University of Kansas (2008), Hofstra University (2008), and the University of Victoria (2007). Specific Google searches were made for TLDUs at Hispanic-serving institutions (HSIs; Santiago, 2006), historically black colleges and universities (HBCUs), tribal colleges (U.S. Department of Education, 2007), and women's institutions. If a unit possessed a distinct graduate teaching assistant program, the program is listed separately in the database. Finally, the remaining three thousand plus institutions were searched using a Google custom search engine that included institutions in which there was no known TLDU. Search phrases included "Center Teaching Learning," "Professional Development," and, for the associate schools, "Human Resources" and "Staff Development." In addition, a random sample of 5 percent of identified TLDUs ($N = 10$ to 23) was taken for each Carnegie classification being searched. The text from the home pages was copied, entered into a frequency word counter, and the ten most frequently used words were searched. The associate schools were the most challenging to research because of a greater variety of administrative location and structures of TLDU responsibilities. Many of their public websites are geared exclusively to student needs. The data set underrepresents these units.

The criteria used to select units for inclusion in the data set included three elements based on my perceptions of the most central characteristics of a TLDU as discussed in the literature and based on the most typical units belonging to the POD Network. First, the unit serves postsecondary instructors, whether faculty, graduate student, or adjunct. The unit may also serve students, staff, or another population. Second, the institution has assigned to the unit teaching development responsibility for those instructors. In addition to centers, qualifying units could include committees, part-time load reassignment, virtual units, system offices, or human resource offices. Finally, the mission includes some actively delivered "pure" pedagogy, not only teaching involved in using technology. Seminars (face-to-face or online) on active learning, teacher learning communities, and consultation on instructional design are examples of activities that met this criterion. A Web page simply listing resources did not meet the criteria for inclusion.

Although the term *center for teaching and learning* is most commonly used, it was found to be problematic. It can include student support units and those that provide primarily technology support or library support and excludes units that are not physical centers (for example, a part-time faculty assignment) or in some other way vary from the "center" ideal yet still do teaching development work among faculty. As a consequence the term *teaching-learning development unit (TLDU)* was selected as a more appropriate generic term following discussion among attendees at the 2009 POD Network Conference who attended a presentation on pilot data.

The data set is a continuously updated document, and results reflect its status at a particular point in time. Data are reported for the data set as it existed on February 9, 2010. The data set is weighted toward those with a Web presence, but lack of a website was not reason to exclude a TLDU if its characteristics were known through another source. In the sample, 128 (10.1 percent) units do not have a home URL that can be accessed. TLDUs without a website may have been mentioned in strategic plans, otherwise notated by other campus units, or been a member of either POD or NCS-POD. Institutions in which faculty resources are located behind a firewall (more common in associate and private, for-profit institutions) are likely under-sampled.

Results

Three types of data are reported for each variable: normative data about the field of higher education in the United States; a description of the sample of TLDUs by that variable;, and penetration, defined as what percentage of the national sample in that variable has TLDUs. .

National Representation of TLDUs

According to the Carnegie data set, there are 4,390 postsecondary education institutions in the United States. There are 1,267 TLDUs in the current data set at 933 unique institutions. Thus, at least 21.2 percent of higher education institutions have a TLDU. This is a lower-bound estimate as the sample likely under-represents some types of institutions.

Enrollment and Number of Faculty

The point biserial correlation between number of full-time-equivalent degree-seeking students and the presence of a TLDU for faculty is $r = .51$ ($p < .0001$; $N = 4,389$), which explains 25 percent of the variance of having a TLDU. The correlation between number of full-time-equivalent faculty and the presence of a TLDU is $r = .39$ ($p < .0001$; $N = 262$), which accounts for only 15 percent of the variance, but there were fewer schools with data on the number of faculty. Thus, the presence of TLDUs is more highly correlated with student enrollment than with number of faculty.

Carnegie Classifications for Institutions with TLDUs

Table 20.1 provides data by Carnegie classification. Associate and master's institutions represent the largest percentages of the TLDU data set but doctoral/research institutions are most likely to have a TLDU—over triple the national rate of 21.2 percent.

Public and Private Institutions

In the United States, 39.6 percent ($N = 1,737$) of institutions are public, 39.7 percent ($N = 1,744$) are private nonprofit, and 20.7 percent ($N = 909$) are private for-profit. In the sample of TLDUs, 69.6 percent ($N = 649$) are at public institutions, 29.4 percent ($N = 274$) are at private nonprofit institutions, and 1.1 percent ($N = 10$) are at private for-profit institutions. The last category is likely under-represented as many of the private for-profit

---

Table 20.1 Carnegie Classifications and Penetration of TLDUs

Classification	Percentage of Higher Education in the United States ($N = 4,364$)	Percentage of TLDU Data Set ($N = 933$)	Penetration
Doctoral/research	6.5% (283)	21.9% (204)	72.1%
Master's	15.2% (663)	28.2% (263)	39.7%
Baccalaureate	17.6% (766)	11.8% (110)	14.4%
Associate	41.6% (1,814)	33.5% (313)	17.3%
Special focus/tribal	19.2% (838)	4.6% (43)	5.1%

Note: Number of institutions is in parentheses.

institutions use firewalls and cannot be searched. Thus, 37.4 percent of public institutions, 15.7 percent of private nonprofit institutions, and at least 1.1 percent of private for-profits have a TLDU.

Geographical and Accreditation Location

Of the TLDU data set, most are in the Southeast, with the next largest group in the mid-Atlantic, closely followed by the Far West (Table 20.2). New England and the Far West have the largest penetration of TLDUs.

Table 20.2 Geographical Location and Penetration of TLDUs

Regions	Percentage of Higher Education in the United States (N = 4,389)	Percentage of TLDU Data Set (N = 933)	Penetration
U.S. service schools	0.2% (8)	0.3% (3)	37.5%
New England	6.1% (269)	8.0% (75)	27.9%
Mid-Atlantic	16.5% (726)	17.3% (161)	22.2%
Great Lakes	14.8% (650)	14.9% (139)	21.4%
Plains	10.1% (444)	8.6% (80)	18.0%
Southeast	24.2% (1060)	22.6% (211)	19.9%
Southwest	8.9% (389)	8.7% (81)	20.8%
Rocky Mountains	3.4% (150)	2.7% (25)	16.7%
Far West	13.6% (599)	16.9% (158)	26.4%
Outlying areas	2.1% (94)	0.0% (0)	0.0%

Note: Number of institutions is in parentheses. New England: Connecticut, Maine, Massachusetts, New Hampshire, Rhode Island, and Vermont. Mid-Atlantic: Delaware, Washington, D.C., Maryland, New Jersey, New York, and Pennsylvania. Great Lakes: Illinois, Indiana, Michigan, Ohio, Wisconsin. Plains: Iowa, Kansas, Minnesota, Missouri, Nebraska, North Dakota, South Dakota. Southeast: Alabama, Arkansas, Florida, Georgia, Kentucky, Louisiana, Mississippi, North Carolina, South Carolina, Tennessee, Virginia, West Virginia. Southwest: Arizona, New Mexico, Oklahoma, Texas. Rocky Mountains: Colorado, Idaho, Montana, Utah, Wyoming. Far West: Alaska, California, Hawaii, Nevada, Oregon, Washington. Outlying areas: American Samoa, Federated States of Micronesia, Guam, Marshall Islands, Northern Mariana Islands, Puerto Rico, Palau, and U.S. Virgin Islands.

Table 20.3 Accreditation Location and Penetration of TLDUs

Regions	Percentage of Higher Education in the United States (N = 4,212)	Percentage of TLDU Data Set (N = 925)	Penetration
National/Specialized	25.4% (1070)	2.8% (26)	2.4%
State	0.3% (12)	0.0% (0)	0.0%
Middle States	12.0% (505)	17.0% (157)	31.1%
New England	5.7% (242)	8.0% (74)	30.6%
North Central	27.0% (1136)	28.2% (261)	23.0%
Northwest	3.8% (159)	8.0% (74)	46.5%
Southern	18.7% (788)	26.2% (242)	30.7%
Western	7.1% (300)	9.8% (91)	30.3%

Note: Number of institutions is in parentheses.

The U.S. service schools appear to have an excellent penetration rate, but the small numbers should be cautiously interpreted.

The North Central and Southern accreditation regions have the largest number of TLDUs. The Northwest has the greatest penetration, double the national rate (Table 20.3), and North Central has the lowest penetration rate of the accreditation regions.

Types of Programs

The 123 land grant institutions represent 2.8 percent of higher education institutions in the United States. There are 21 (0.5 percent) Council of Public Liberal Arts (COPLAC) colleges and 162 institutions identified as medical schools (3.8 percent) in the United States. In the TLDU sample, 6.6 percent (N = 62) were at land grant institutions, 1.5 percent (N = 14) at COPLAC colleges, and 11.6 percent (N = 108) at medical schools. All three of these types of institutions are "friendly" to TLDUs: 50.4 percent of land grant institutions have a TLDU, 66.7 percent of COPLAC colleges, and 66.7 percent of medical schools.

For nonassociate schools, the proportion of undergraduate degrees awarded in the arts and sciences versus professional areas with regard to TLDUs is in Table 20.4. Most TLDUs are found at institutions with both arts and sciences and professional degrees in approximately equal numbers. At institutions whose programs are skewed, TLDUs are somewhat

Table 20.4 Undergraduate Program Classification: Arts and
Sciences Versus Professional

Undergraduate Program Classification	Percentage of Higher Education in the United States (N = 1,571)	Percentage of TLDU Data Set (N = 567)	Penetration
Arts and sciences represent 80% of undergraduate degrees	10.3% (162)	9.5% (54)	33.3%
Arts and sciences represent 60–79% of undergraduate degrees	13.5% (212)	17.6% (100)	47.2%
Balanced degree programs, 41–59% of undergraduate degrees	32.3% (507)	40.6% (230)	45.4%
Professional degrees represent 60–79% of undergraduate degrees	32.0% (502)	28.7% (163)	32.5%
Professional degrees represent 80% of undergraduate degrees	12.0% (188)	3.5% (20)	10.6%

Note: Number of institutions is in parentheses.

more likely to be found at schools with more arts and sciences degrees being awarded.

Table 20.5 addresses the level at which an institution awards graduate degrees in the same areas as undergraduate degrees. Relatively few TLDUs are at institutions that are exclusively undergraduate or exclusively graduate. Most are found at institutions with some but fewer than half of the degrees overlapping. The greatest penetration of TLDUs, however, is in schools in which half or more of the graduate degrees correspond to majors offered to undergraduates.

Diversity

Table 20.6 displays data by institutions that serve minorities and women, including HBCUs, tribal institutions, HSIs, and MSIs (minority-serving institutions). MSIs enroll minority populations, including Pacific Islanders, Native Americans, African Americans, and Hispanics, at a level that exceeds 50% of total enrollment.

Table 20.5 Graduate Degrees' Overlap with Undergraduate Programs

Types of Programs	Percentage of Higher Education in the United States (N = 1,571)	Percentage of TLDU Data Set (N = 567)	Penetration
No coexistence (all graduate or all undergraduate programs)	31.3% (N = 491)	13.1% (N = 74)	15.1%
Some overlap in programs	52.9% (N = 831)	(54.5%, N = 309)	37.2%
High overlap in programs	15.8% (N = 249)	32.5% (N = 184)	73.9%

Note: Number of institutions is in parentheses.

Of all HBCUs, 23 percent have a TLDU, comparable to the national rate of 21.2 percent. For all other diversity categories, TLDUs have below national levels of penetration, with the lowest level (none) at tribal institutions and next lowest at women's institutions, but the total numbers are very small for those two groups.

Table 20.6 TLDUs in Diverse Institutions

Type of Institution	Percentage of Higher Education in the United States	Percentage of TLDU Data Set (N = 933)	Penetration
HBCUs	2.3% (100)	2.5% (23)	23%
Tribal colleges	0.7% (32)	0.0% (0)	0.0%
HSIs	8.8% (385)	7.1% (66)	17.1%
MSIs	18.0% (787)	11.7% (109)	13.9%
Women's institutions	1.2% (53)	0.8% (7)	13.2%

Note: Number of institutions is in parentheses. Rows represent separate analyses as the categories are not mutually exclusive.

Graduate Teaching Assistant Programs

Eighty-five units identified out of the 1,267 (6.7 percent) are either specifically for graduate teaching assistants or offer a program for them. The number of graduate teaching assistant programs is likely an underestimate as identification of these programs relied on existing lists of units, thus suggesting a starting point for further developing the data set.

Discussion

These results serve as a baseline for developing further understanding of the field of faculty development. The lower-bound estimate of 21.2 percent of U.S. institutions having a TLDU reveals room for growth and can serve as a possible argument for uniqueness in tough budget times. In the sample of TLDUs, more are located at master's and associate-level institutions, with the greatest single percentage located in the Southeast and having North Central or Southern accreditation. TLDUs are located most often at institutions with a balance of arts and sciences versus professional degrees and some overlap between graduate and undergraduate programs.

A description of the sample, while interesting for knowing the state of the field, is not as useful as examining where TLDUs have most deeply penetrated a type of institution. TLDUs have been most fully adopted by doctoral/research institutions, with three-quarters having a TLDU. Contrary to expectations, based on this data set, doctoral/research institutions are more likely to have a center than institutions in Carnegie classifications with the reputation of being more devoted to the instructional mission. This difference may be due to greater resource availability from larger enrollments at doctoral institutions, greater need, or some as yet unknown factor. The data on GTA programs are sparse and also need further development.

Institutions with Northwest accreditation are far more likely to have TLDUs (double the national rate). This may be due to a specific requirement that institutions are to provide for the development of faculty on an ongoing basis (Northwest Commission on Colleges and Universities, 2001). In contrast, the requirement of the North Central region, the region with the lowest penetration rate, is less specific: "The organization values and supports effective teaching" (North Central Association of Colleges and Schools, Higher Learning Commission, 2007, p. 6). TLDUs have been most successful at institutions in which more arts and sciences degrees are awarded than professional programs or in which the two are balanced. They are also more successful where graduate programs and undergraduate programs significantly overlap.

Some of these data may be explained by the correlation with enrollment. A larger institution in terms of enrollment is apparently better able to support TLDUs or see the need for such a unit, or perhaps TLDUs encourage greater enrollment. This suggests that if the only consideration were continued existence, TLDUs would be wise to encourage practices that sustain and improve enrollment.

Other favorable environments for TLDUs are land grant, medical schools, and COPLAC schools. TLDUs are underrepresented at institutions that award greater than 80 percent professional degrees. Because they are doing well at medical schools, one inference is that more work is needed at penetrating law, faith, and business schools. Research on why these differences occur could be useful in uncovering values and techniques for TLDU management.

The penetration of TLDUs into historically black colleges and universities (23 percent) is similar to the national rate of 21.2 percent. Penetration of TLDUs fall short of the national rate in all the other categories of diversity (minority serving, Hispanic serving, tribal, and women's institutions). Some of the discrepancy may be due to enrollment size. The largest tribal institution enrolls 1,935 students, and the largest women's institution enrolls 10,750 students. However, HBCUs reflect the national rate, but their largest institution enrolls only 13,067. And the largest HSI enrolls 57,026 yet has a lower than national rate of TLDUs.

For the first time in many years, it is possible to say what is typical or not in terms of institutions supporting the presence of TLDUs. The normative data contained in this report may be useful for many strategic planning tasks of development units. Perhaps more significant for the field is the opportunity to use benchmarking with samples from this data set and even to develop a taxonomy of TLDUs. From this core list of units, it will be possible to identify best practice for various types of units and devise TLDU accreditation standards that can aid in determining time and money allocations. This data set and the opportunity to take random samples will enable researchers to draw stronger inferences. The possibility of investigating and contrasting specific subtypes of TLDUs will allow the field to investigate richer hypotheses and provide more targeted services to their clientele. Sustaining the data set will require cooperation of the research community through sharing newly gleaned information and corrections. The field, and ultimately teaching and learning, is empowered for deeper, richer change.

REFERENCES

Carnegie Foundation for the Advancement of Teaching. (2009). *Carnegie classi-fications data file*. Retrieved from http://classifications.carnegiefoundation .org/resources/

Centra, J. (1976). *Faculty development practices in U.S. colleges and universi-ties*. Princeton, NJ: Educational Testing Service.

Erickson, G. (1986). A survey of faculty development practices. In M. Svinicki, J. Kurfiss, & J. Stone (Eds.), *To improve the academy: Vol. 5. Resources for student, faculty, and institutional development* (pp. 182–196). Stillwater, OK: New Forums Press.

Frantz, A., Beebe, S., Horvath, V., Canales, J., & Swee, D. (2005). The roles of teaching and learning centers. In S. Chadwick-Blossey & D. Robertson (Eds.), *To improve the academy: Vol. 23. Resources for faculty, instruc-tional, and organizational development* (pp. 72–90). San Francisco: Jossey-Bass/Anker.

Hellyer, S., & Boschmann, E. (1993). Faculty development programs: A per-spective. In D. Wright & J. P. Lunde (Eds.), *To improve the academy: Vol. 12. Resources for faculty, instructional, and organizational development* (pp. 217–224). Stillwater, OK: New Forum Press.

Hofstra University, Center for Teaching and Scholarly Excellence. (2008). *Teaching and learning centers in the United States*. Retrieved from www .hofstra.edu/faculty/ctse/cte_links.cfm

National Center for Education Statistics. (2009). *Integrated Postsecondary Edu-cation Data System*. Retrieved from http://nces.ed.gov/IPEDS/

North Central Association of Colleges and Schools, Higher Learning Commis-sion. (2007). *Institutional accreditation: An overview*. Retrieved from www.ncahigherlearningcommission.org/download/Overview07.pdf

Northwest Commission on Colleges and Universities. (2001). Standard 4.1 faculty evaluation. From *Accreditation standards and related policies*. Retrieved from www.nwccu.org/Standards%20and%20Policies/ Standard%204/Standard%20Four.htm

Professional and Organizational Development Network in Higher Education. (2006). *Membership directory and networking guide*. Nederland, CO: Author.

Professional and Organizational Development Network in Higher Education. (2009). *POD listserv*. Retrieved from www.podnetwork.org/listserve.htm

Santiago, D. (2006). Inventing Hispanic serving institutions (HSIs): The basics. *Excelencia in Education!* Retrieved from www.govst.edu/uploadedFiles/ LatinoCenter/InventingHSI.pdf

Sorcinelli, M. D., Austin, A. E., Eddy, P. L., & Beach, A. L. (2006). *Creating the future of faculty development: Learning from the past, understanding the present.* San Francisco: Jossey-Bass/Anker.

University of Kansas, Center for Teaching Excellence. (2008). *Other teaching centers.* Retrieved from www.cte.ku.edu/cteInfo/resources/websites.shtml

University of Victoria, Learning and Teaching Centre. (2007). *Welcome to the Learning and Teaching Centre.* Retrieved from http://web.uvic.ca/terc/resources/idc.htm

U.S. Department of Education. (2007). *White House initiative on tribal colleges and universities.* Retrieved from www.ed.gov/about/inits/list/whtc/edlite-tclist.html

Wesley, J. (2005). *Current characteristics of faculty development in public two-year colleges in Texas* (Unpublished doctoral dissertation). Texas A&M University. Retrieved from http://txspace.tamu.edu/bitstream/handle/1969.1/2572/etd-tamu-2005B-EHRD-Wesley.pdf?sequence=1

Wright, D. L. (2000). Faculty development centers in research universities: A study of resources and programs. In M. Kaplan & D. Lieberman (Eds.), *To improve the academy: Vol. 18. Resources for faculty, instructional, and organizational development* (pp. 291–301). San Francisco: Jossey-Bass/Anker.

21

TOWARD A SCHOLARSHIP OF FACULTY DEVELOPMENT

Mark Potter, Metropolitan State College of Denver

This chapter critically examines the scholarship of faculty development. Using a typology adapted from one developed to understand the scholarship of teaching and learning, I reflect on the primary currents identifiable in the literature. Much of what is published in the field of faculty development consists of descriptions of the development and assessment of particular programs. One approach that is largely missing is the metastudy or review of prior studies that can serve to preserve the findings of scholar-practitioners.

As advice to new faculty developers, Neal and Peed-Neal (2009) wrote in a recent volume of *To Improve the Academy (TIA)* that "faculty development is a craft that must be mastered largely experientially, through imitation, observation, and trial and error, like bartending or dogwalking" (p. 15). I would add that just as with teaching, reading and reflection are essential components of the process of grounding oneself in the field. As a new faculty developer who has entered the field from the ranks of faculty, I have taken the time over the past year and a half to immerse myself in both the scholarship of teaching and learning (SoTL) and the scholarship of faculty development. The comments that follow reflect my ongoing personal grounding and the perspective I have developed toward the scholarship of faculty development.

By several measures, SoTL has matured as a field since the early 1990s. Leaders in the field continue to write of the challenges that remain, particularly in ensuring that SoTL is valued as a form of scholarship on a par with disciplinary research and discovery. Still, when contrasted with the considerably more "adolescent" scholarship of faculty development, SoTL appears as a relatively mature field. The much less formed and smaller body of scholarship of faculty development does not, for example, benefit from the impressive number of journals that publish SoTL work; it does not generate the numerous national and international conferences that SoTL does, and, perhaps most interesting as an indicator, scholars have not yet analyzed this body of literature with the same critical eye they have brought to the SoTL.

Since Boyer's (1990) call for the inclusion of a scholarship of teaching as one of four types of scholarship, subsequent refinement of his argument, along with ongoing critical review of the field, have elevated SoTL to a recognized form of scholarship. Some critical reviews have included attempts to establish typologies through which to view the literature (Nelson, 2003; Weimer, 2006). Weimer lists several benefits that accrue from establishing a typology of pedagogical research (her term for SoTL), including development of a better understanding of the literature in question, the elaboration of an operational definition of the field, the establishment of points of comparison to other types of scholarship that open the way for evaluation, and the elaboration of the range of options accessible to scholars interested in the genre. Although hers is only one of several typologies of the scholarship of teaching and learning, Weimer provides one of the clearest explanations of why to approach the body of scholarship with categories and types in mind.

The critical perspective that Weimer (2006) and others have brought to SoTL can be applied with similar objectives to the scholarship of faculty development. In the process, and specifically by proposing a typology of works that comprise the field, I hope that we can gain a better sense of the parameters and direction of the field along with its strengths and weaknesses. Thus, I begin this undertaking by distinguishing some broad similarities and differences between SoTL and the scholarship of faculty development.

Comparison of Literatures

Certain parallels between the two bodies of scholarship are readily apparent. Both build on entry points for inquiry that cause discomfort among faculty. The following oft-quoted passage from Randy Bass (1999) describing the challenges of SoTL applies equally well to the scholarship of faculty development:

> One telling measure of how differently teaching is regarded from traditional scholarship or research within the academy is what a difference it makes to have a "problem" in one versus the other. In scholarship and research, having a "problem" is at the heart of the investigative process; it is the compound of the generative questions around which all creative and productive activity revolves. But in one's teaching, a

> "problem" is something you don't want to have, and if you have one,
> you probably want to fix it. Asking a colleague about a *problem* in his
> or her research is an invitation; asking about a problem in one's teach-
> ing would probably seem like an accusation. Changing the status of the
> *problem* in teaching from terminal remediation to ongoing investiga-
> tion is precisely what the movement for a scholarship of teaching is all
> about. (p. 1)

Similarly, in faculty development, it may well be perceived that problems are things to steer around, manage through, or fix. Yet they can also
be, as Bass points out with regard to teaching, the entry points of scholarly inquiry.

Like SoTL, characterized by Weimer (2006) as a scholarship of practitioners, the articles and books that comprise faculty development scholarship
are produced by practitioners (faculty developers) studying aspects of
higher education relevant to their day-to-day work. Thus, both scholarships
are distinct from educational research, which is driven by discipline-based
questions and said to be further removed from practice (Weimer, 2006).
Consequently both SoTL and faculty development scholarship are heavily
instrumental in nature. Shulman (2000) credits SoTL for engaging in three
areas: professionalism, pragmatism, and policy. Kreber (2005), however,
criticizes SoTL for what she sees as an imbalance toward instrumentalism:
"Within the discourse on the scholarship of teaching, we read, hear, and
certainly learn much about how to teach certain concepts better, but relatively little about the kinds of learning experiences we hope students will
have during their college and university years and why we believe certain
experiences are more valuable than others" (p. 391). She would like to see
a greater emphasis instead on "critical engagement with the purposes and
goals of higher education and, by extension, the undergraduate curriculum" (p. 391). The study presented in this chapter explores, among other
questions, where the balance between instrumentalism and critical engagement lies in the scholarship of faculty development.

One significant difference between the two bodies of literature stems
from the organizational realities within the academy. Nearly all faculty are
engaged in teaching within their disciplinary contexts. A much narrower
cadre of professionals is committed to faculty development as practitioners, and while differences of style and sets of strengths may distinguish
practitioners, there is not the variety of disciplinary perspectives from
which teaching faculty and SoTL practitioners approach their craft. So
whereas the body of literature in faculty development does not benefit
from the widely diverse perspectives that characterize SoTL, it does not
suffer from the fracturing that characterizes SoTL, wherein it is common

for teaching faculty to limit the already modest amounts of reading they do in the field to articles appearing in journals specific to their disciplines (Weimer, 2006).

Whereas scholars have approached SoTL with a broadly critical perspective and have succeeded thereby in clarifying its parameters, no such perspective has developed with regard to the scholarship of faculty development. I therefore begin with a brief discussion of the general parameters of this literature before adapting and applying a typology and beginning a more systematic review of its main features.

Parameters of the Scholarship of Faculty Development

Faculty development as a practice differs from institution to institution, depending on local needs and culture, and thus it lacks a standard definition that unifies it across higher education (Davis et al., 2003). Moreover, there is no single statement of qualities, standards, or mission around which the scholarship that stems from the practice has coalesced. Just as a review of individual practices can shape the broad understanding of what faculty development is (King & Lawler, 2003), so too can we draw from a review of the scholarship to identify common topical features that shape the outlines of the literature. Here I draw from frequently cited works to establish these parameters. As expected, the practice and the scholarship are closely aligned. Topical features include:

- An emphasis on instructional development, including course design and pedagogy to advance student learning (for example, Bean, 2001; Fink, 2003; Weimer, 1990).
- A commitment to the values of reflection, change, and improvement, with an understanding that faculty operate along a developmental continuum as scholar-teachers, much as students do as learners (for example, Gelmon & Agre-Kippenhan, 2002; Robertson, 1999; Weimer, 2002; Weston & McAlpine, 2001).
- Inclusion of organizational development as integral to promoting faculty development, satisfaction, and vitality (for example, Bland & Schmitz, 1990; Fink, 2003; Ouellett, 2005; Weimer, 1990).

Methodology

In contrast to Weimer (2006), who spent decades reviewing pedagogical literature prior to writing her analysis of that field, my approach to this study has been to pursue an intentional and systematic literature review within distinct limits and undertaken in a far more compressed time frame within the year and a half that I have been a faculty developer. My original ambition had me setting off to read all faculty development articles from the past ten years published in *TIA* and the *Journal of Faculty Development (JFD)*, arguably the two most prominent journals that have as their mission to publish in the field of faculty development. *TIA* publishes for an audience of "faculty development and organizational development professionals, administrators and consultants" (Call for Manuscripts, 2009, unpublished). The *JFD* publishes manuscripts "related to issues in professional development, higher education pedagogy, curriculum, leadership, program design and implementation, and evaluation and assessment" (Journal of Faculty Development, 2009). From this relatively broader range of topics found in the latter, I deselected works more closely related to SoTL or to discipline-driven education and leadership studies in order to include in this study only works that I considered practitioner scholarship on topics related to faculty development. No such selection was necessary from among the articles published in *TIA*.

Such an undertaking quickly proved too great while I was also building a faculty development program to meet the needs of my institution, and I did not complete the entire decade's worth of reading. For this study, I include in my analysis all 114 articles published in *TIA* from 2000 to 2005 (volumes 18 to 22) and 2009 (volume 27). From the *JFD* I include 40 articles published during overlapping years, 2001 to 2004 (volumes 18 and 19) and 2009 (volume 23). Because I do not seek to trace changes over time, the gap in my reading between the years 2005 and 2008 should not affect my findings. Nonetheless, when it became clear that I would not complete the decade, I included the 2009 articles in my reading to verify that there were not recent changes to the field that I might otherwise overlook. My sample is sufficiently large, I believe, to be broadly representative of the decade as a whole in the field.

I have adapted the five major groups from Nelson's (2003) typology of SoTL works to construct my own parallel typology of the scholarship of faculty development. Table 21.1 captures this adaptation.

Several dimensions characterize faculty development literature, and so along with the five groups defined in Table 21.1, I also read for two additional attributes: the purpose of the article (Is it instrumental in its purpose, or is it a critical/theoretical analysis?) and methodology (Is it descriptive, reflective, synthetic, or [quasi-]experimental?). In many cases, these additional attributes can be inferred by the group in which the article is placed. We can expect, for example, that an article in group 2 follows a reflective methodology. Most reports on particular programs (group 1)

Table 21.1 Typologies of SoTL and the Scholarship
of Faculty Development

Group	Nelson's SoTL Typology	Adapted Typology of Scholarship of Faculty Development
1	Reports on particular classes	Reports on particular programs, collaborations, or projects
2	Reflections on several years of teaching experience, implicitly or explicitly informed by other SoTL	Reflections on faculty development experience, implicitly or explicitly informed by other faculty development scholarship
3	Larger contexts: Comparisons of courses and comparisons of student change across time	Larger contexts: Trends in faculty development and comparisons of programs
4	Learning science	Adult development studies
5	Summaries and analyses of sets of prior studies	Metastudies or reviews and summaries of prior studies

Source: Adapted from Nelson (2003).

are instrumental in purpose and descriptive in method, and some studies of larger contexts (group 3) are instrumental in purpose, while others provide critical or theoretical analyses.

The process of assigning groups and determining attributes hinged on the judgment and reflection that I brought to my reading of the articles. My methodology is not even quasi-experimental, and my placement of works into categories is not intended to render replicable results but rather to invoke thematic conclusions. Using my own typology, I consider this work to belong to group 5 (metastudy or review or summary of prior studies), mostly descriptive in methodology (though with considerable reflection brought to bear), and with a purpose more of providing critical analysis than of offering instrumental "takeaways."

Findings

Table 21.2 presents the aggregate placement of articles into the five groups of the proposed typology. Together, groups 1 and 3 (reports on particular programs and studies of larger contexts) dominate the faculty development literature, amounting to approximately 90 percent of all articles published, with the number of articles in group 1 surpassing those

Table 21.2 Assignment of Reviewed Literature to the Typology
of the Scholarship of Faculty Development

Group	Number	Percentage
1	90	58.4
2	9	5.8
3	48	31.2
4	6	3.9
5	1	0.7
n	154	100.0

in group 3 by nearly a factor of two. Reflections on experience and adult development studies comprise a much more modest proportion of the articles, together amounting to around 10 percent, while metastudies and literature reviews barely register in the sample.

With regard to the two additional attributes for which I read, purpose and methodology, tables 21.3 and 21.4 indicate that four-fifths of the articles are instrumental in purpose, reflecting again the dominance of groups 1 and 3, while the most practiced methods, in descending order, are descriptive, descriptive with assessment, and synthetic.

Method is the one dimension where I observed a notable difference between articles from the two publications. Whereas (quasi-)experimental methods are removed from the central trends of this literature, they are found more often in *JFD* (approximately 25 percent of articles reviewed) than in *TIA* (approximately 5 percent of articles reviewed). The *JFD* has on average published roughly half the number of articles each year as *TIA*.

Table 21.3 Purpose of Faculty Development
Literature, by Group

Group	Instrumental	Critical or Theoretical Analysis
1	89	1
2	2	7
3	35	13
4	0	6
5	0	1
n	126	28

Table 21.4 Methodology of Faculty Development
Literature, by Group

Group	Descriptive	Descriptive with Assessment	Synthesis (with or Without Reflection)	Experimental	Reflective
1	41	38	0	7	4
2	0	0	1	0	8
3	12	1	21	10	4
4	0	0	5	0	1
5	0	0	1	0	0
n	53	39	28	17	17

Had I read in the *JFD* over the same years as I did from *TIA*, I estimate that my sample would have included sixty articles from the journal, rather than the forty that it does, and, by extrapolation, articles that follow an experimental method would have numbered roughly twenty-five, or 16 percent of the sample. Even with such a correction, the experimental method would still remain behind description and description with assessment as the main methods within the scholarship of faculty development.

Discussion

The typology proposed for this study accommodates the range of faculty development literature that I reviewed from the two primary outlets of the field. Given these results, and because this typology parallels so closely Nelson's (2003) typology of SoTL, I proceed through this discussion informed by the similarities between the two fields; where observations, critiques, and defenses have been directed toward SoTL, I consider them with respect to the scholarship of faculty development.

Although an advocate of SoTL, Kreber (2005) has nonetheless critiqued that body of scholarship for its strong inclination toward an instrumental approach. Her premise is that "the academy needs to begin to ask more critical questions if the scholarship of teaching movement is to have a lasting, positive and practical impact on our colleges and universities, as well as on the wider society" (pp. 391–392). One's first impression of the scholarship of faculty development, with fully four-fifths of the articles characterized as instrumental in purpose, might be that this criticism applies to it as well. This is indeed a literature that is highly pragmatic and weighted toward meeting generally agreed-on goals rather than questioning or critiquing those goals. Kreber (2003) herself extends her critique to the work of faculty development and offers her vision of how it can move beyond "instrumental learning" and focus instead on addressing the question "of what kind of learning to promote" (p. 296). My reading, however, leads me to argue that Kreber's standard is not the sole criterion by which a contribution to the field can be critical, rather than instrumental, in its purpose. I have applied a broadened conception of what constitutes a critical study to include those that seek to shift the paradigm of instruction in our colleges and universities from instructor centered to learner centered (Barr & Tagg, 1995), and those that seek to reconsider and reposition the role of faculty development within institutions of higher education. The common feature, even accounting for this broadened conception of the critical and theoretical, is that the objectives of the studies extend beyond aiding practical effectiveness to instead bringing change to educational culture.

Specific examples from the sample of articles reviewed for this study illustrate this broader view of what it means to be critical rather than instrumental. Angelo (2001) proposes guidelines for promoting transformative ideas in higher education, including Barr and Tagg's (1995) "learning paradigm." McKinney (2002), alternatively, uses synthesis and reflection to probe the relationship between instructional development, which she considers one component of more general faculty development, and teaching and learning. Both types of "critical" approaches to faculty development posit faculty development initiatives as if they were, as Lieberman (2005) advocates, laboratories for learning organizations intent on a culture of self-examination, evidence, and improvement.

Furthermore, it would be a mistake to dismiss the overwhelming majority of works that appear in faculty development literature as less serious or significant simply because their authors' interests are pragmatic and instrumental. Within groups 1 and 3, where nearly all of the instrumental approaches to faculty development are found, the very purpose of the programs described is often to effect change. Bonilla and Palmerton (2001), for example, describe a focus group approach to learning whether race and gender were real issues in the classroom for both students and faculty, and among their findings was the identification of several troubling issues along with calls to action. DeZure (2003), writing in the aftermath of the terrorist attacks of September 11, 2001, suggests specific steps that faculty developers can take to promote internationalization while acknowledging the urgent need for undergraduate education to focus its efforts on the development of global competencies. From these examples, it is clear that the overlap between two scholarly foci—faculty development and organizational development in higher education—means that even instrumental approaches to faculty development have the potential to effect systemic change in organizations. Within what is predominantly a practitioner literature, therefore, a critical or theoretical approach is not necessary to bring about systemwide changes or even paradigm shifts.

Kreber (2005) issued her critique of SoTL in the midst of a broader discussion regarding its "scholarly" quality. Following Boyer's (1990) broadened use of *scholarship* to recognize that "knowledge is acquired through research, through synthesis, through practice, and through teaching" (p. 24), Andresen (2000) became concerned that the term "may be degenerating into a ubiquitous buzzword" and asked, "What might scholarly teaching look like?" (pp. 138, 142). Weimer (2006) defends the scholarly qualities of pedagogical literature by referencing what she identifies as a shared understanding of the qualities that make a practitioner scholarship viable. Those qualities, she argues, are dissemination of findings among peers and colleagues, creation or enhancement of knowledge and insight, relevant findings with practical application, and the construction of a body of knowledge through incorporation of other past findings. Wisdom of practice, she adds, opens the door to description, outcomes assessment, and reflection—not the strictly hard scientific or experimental methodologies that are commonly expected from the scholarship of discovery—as appropriate methodologies.

These discussions surrounding SoTL raise a similar question with regard to the scholarship of faculty development: Is it indeed a coherent and viable body of scholarship? When measured against the four criteria Weimer described, my answer is *mostly yes*. The works that I encountered unambiguously satisfy the first three of the criteria. This is a body of scholarship in that it is disseminated, with published, peer-reviewed articles and books as the primary format. The ideas and findings contained within the literature establish and enhance our knowledge, and the especially instrumental orientation of the literature underscores its relevance to practical application.

Less immediately clear is whether this scholarship builds intentionally and consistently on past findings. Throughout my review of the literature, several topical strands and clusters of programs with shared goals surfaced. These include, as examples, programs in support of early career faculty development, programs in support of SoTL, and descriptions of particular approaches to strategic planning or positioning faculty development efforts within an institution. Articles solely on the topic of mentoring new faculty, for example, number 6 within my sample, comprise only a subset of articles on the broader topic of early career faculty development. Within such instrumental and descriptive articles (mostly of type 1), numerous as they are, it is not uncommon to find requisite references to seminal works but little attention paid to explaining how the programs being proposed compare with those previously described in the literature as advancing shared goals.

While it might be unfair to expect the authors of each such successive article to provide a full inventory of previously described programs that share common goals, there is ample room within this literature for more works belonging to group 5 (metastudies or reviews and summaries of prior studies), of which I identified a mere 1 out of 154 articles. Both thematically oriented review articles and metastudies can serve to preserve, and evaluate within a broader context, the findings of practitioners who have written of their programs, innovations, and approaches and whose ideas risk becoming lost within the growing body of publications. Indeed, as I complete this study, I am encouraged to see an example of just such an approach to the scholarship of faculty development by Lottero-Perdue and Fifield (2010) in the most recent issue of *TIA* on the topic, no less, of faculty mentoring.

Conclusion

As should be clear by this point, reviews and critiques of the scholarship of faculty development are less common than they are of SoTL. The one such study that I identified in my reading is McKinney's (2002) review of the recent literature in instructional development in higher education. She writes, as I have found, that "it is not surprising that much of the writing in this area is still descriptive" (p. 231). She does not call for a greater emphasis on critical and theoretical analyses but rather asserts that "more frequent use of well-designed experiments would add to the knowledge base" (p. 232).

While my findings confirm the lesser role of the (quasi-)experimental approach, this review leads me to conclude that the greatest impact from this practitioner scholarship, oriented by its nature to produce descriptive works for instrumental purposes, can come from scholar-practitioners broadly incorporating one another's ideas and findings in a more intentional and consistent manner, building on what is known to be effective in specific contexts, and thereby creating a body of knowledge that is tightly connected to the efforts and accomplishments of the past. By doing so, we will achieve what Andresen (2000) identifies as one of the quintessential scholarly attributes, whereby "scholarly knowing, about anything whatsoever, is never final, but always subject to public scrutiny, discussion, reconsideration, and perhaps change" (p. 141).

REFERENCES

Andresen, L. W. (2000). A useable, trans-disciplinary conception of scholarship. *Higher Education Research and Development, 19*(2), 137–153.

Angelo, T. A. (2001). Doing faculty development as if we value learning most: Transformative guidelines from research to practice. In D. Lieberman & C. Wehlburg (Eds.), *To improve the academy: Vol. 19. Resources for faculty, instructional, and organizational development* (pp. 225–237). San Francisco: Jossey-Bass/Anker.

Barr, R. B., & Tagg, J. (1995). From teaching to learning—A new paradigm for undergraduate education. *Change, 27*(6), 12–25.

Bass, R. (1999). The scholarship of teaching: What's the problem? *Inventio: Creative Thinking About Learning and Teaching, 1*(1), 1–10.

Bean, J. C. (2001). *Engaging ideas: The professor's guide to integrating writing, critical thinking, and active learning in the classroom.* San Francisco: Jossey-Bass.

Bland, C., & Schmitz, C. (1990). An overview of research on faculty and institutional vitality. In J. Schuster, D. Wheeler, & Associates, *Enhancing faculty careers: Strategies for development and renewal* (pp. 41–61). San Francisco: Jossey-Bass.

Bonilla, J. F., & Palmerton, P. R. (2001). A prophet in your own land? Using faculty and student focus groups to address issues of race, ethnicity, and gender in the classroom. In D. Lieberman & C. Wehlburg (Eds.), *To improve the academy: Vol. 19. Resources for faculty, instructional, and organizational development* (pp. 49–68). San Francisco: Jossey-Bass/Anker.

Boyer, E. L. (1990). *Scholarship reconsidered: Priorities of the professoriate.* Princeton, NJ: Carnegie Foundation for the Advancement of Teaching.

Davis, G., Foley, B. J., Horn, E., Neal, E., Redman, R., & Van Riper, M. (2003). Creating a comprehensive faculty development program. *Journal of Faculty Development, 19*(1), 19–28.

DeZure, D. (2003). Internationalizing American higher education: A call to thought and action. In C. Wehlburg & S. Chadwick-Blossey (Eds.), *To improve the academy: Vol. 21. Resources for faculty, instructional, and organizational development* (pp. 40–55). San Francisco: Jossey-Bass/Anker.

Fink, L. D. (2003). *Creating significant learning experiences: An integrated approach to designing college courses.* San Francisco: Jossey-Bass.

Gelmon, S. B., & Agre-Kippenhan, S. (2002). A developmental framework for supporting evolving faculty roles for community engagement. *Journal of Public Affairs, 6*, 161–182.

Journal of Faculty Development. (2009). *Journal of Faculty Development, 23*(3), 3.

King, K. P., & Lawler, P. A. (2003). Best practices in faculty development in North American higher education: Distinctions and dilemmas. *Journal of Faculty Development, 19*(1), 29–36.

Kreber, C. (2003). Embracing a philosophy of lifelong learning: Starting with faculty beliefs about their role as educators. In C. Wehlburg & S. Chadwick-Blossey (Eds.), *To improve the academy: Vol. 21. Resources for faculty, instructional, and organizational development* (pp. 288–301). San Francisco: Jossey-Bass/Anker.

Kreber, C. (2005). Charting a critical course on the scholarship of university teaching movement. *Studies in Higher Education, 30*(4), 389–405.

Lieberman, D. (2005). Beyond faculty development: How centers for teaching and learning can be laboratories for learning. In A. Kezar (Ed.), *New directions in higher education: No. 131. Organizational learning in higher education* (pp. 87–98). San Francisco: Jossey-Bass.

Lottero-Perdue, P. S., & Fifield, S. (2010). A conceptual framework for higher education faculty mentoring. In L. B. Nilson & J. E. Miller (Eds.), *To improve the academy: Vol. 28. Resources for faculty, instructional, and organizational development* (pp. 37–62). San Francisco: Jossey-Bass.

McKinney, K. (2002). Instructional development: Relationships to teaching and learning in higher education. In D. Lieberman & C. Wehlburg (Eds.), *To improve the academy: Vol. 20. Resources for faculty, instructional, and organizational development* (pp. 225–237). San Francisco: Jossey-Bass/Anker.

Neal, E., & Peed-Neal, I. (2009). Experiential lessons in the practice of faculty development. In L. B. Nilson & J. E. Miller (Eds.), *To improve the academy: Vol. 27. Resources for faculty, instructional, and organizational development* (pp. 14–31). San Francisco: Jossey-Bass.

Nelson, C. (2003). Doing it: Examples of several of the different genres of the scholarship of teaching and learning. *Journal on Excellence in College Teaching, 14*(2), 85–94.

Ouellett, M. L. (Ed.). (2005). *Teaching inclusively: Resources for course, department and institutional change in higher education.* Stillwater, OK: New Forums Press.

Robertson, D. L. (1999). Professors' perspectives on their teaching: A new construct and developmental model. *Innovative Higher Education, 23*(4), 271–294.

Shulman, L. (2000). From Minsk to Pinsk: Why a scholarship of teaching and learning? *Journal of Scholarship of Teaching and Learning, 1*(1), 48–53.

Weimer, M. (1990). *Improving college teaching: Strategies for developing instructional effectiveness.* San Francisco: Jossey-Bass.

Weimer, M. (2002). *Learner-centered teaching: Five key changes to practice.* San Francisco: Jossey-Bass.

Weimer, M. (2006). *Enhancing scholarly work on teaching and learning: Professional literature that makes a difference.* San Francisco: Jossey-Bass.

Weston, C., & McAlpine, L. (2001). Making explicit the development toward the scholarship of teaching. In C. Kreber (Ed.), *New directions for teaching and learning: No. 86. Scholarship revisited: Perspectives on the scholarship of teaching* (pp. 89–97). San Francisco: Jossey-Bass.

22

REFLECTIONS ON INTERNATIONAL ENGAGEMENT AS EDUCATIONAL DEVELOPERS IN THE UNITED STATES

Virginia S. Lee, Virginia S. Lee & Associates

An important aspect of the increasing complexity of the higher education landscape is its gradual internationalization. However, neither our colleges and universities nor we as educational developers have unequivocally embraced internationalization. In this chapter, I offer examples of international engagement and a framework for thinking about them. I argue that international engagement in the form of an evolving global scholarship and practice of educational development represents the ultimate extension of our thought and practice as educational developers.

Since the founding of the Professional and Organizational Development Network in Higher Education (POD) in 1976, the higher education landscape has changed greatly. As student enrollments in colleges and universities have increased, higher education has become more democratized, and today's student body includes more first-generation college students, more students of color, and more nontraditional students than ever before. The assessment movement has caught hold, and with it has come a growing demand for accountability from the American public as so-called consumers of higher education. Simultaneously the academic disciplines have evolved, and new fields of study have appeared, including alternative epistemologies arising from feminism, African American studies, critical theory, postmodernism, and multidisciplinary approaches. Instructional technologies have become more pervasive and varied (Lee, 2010). And economic downturns have challenged institutions to do more with less.

An important part of the increasing complexity of the higher education landscape is its gradual internationalization, which mirrors the growing globalization of contemporary American society (for the distinction between globalization and internationalization, see Altbach & Knight, 2007). However, colleges and universities have not unequivocally embraced internationalization. On the one hand, the number of international students rose to 671,616 in 2008–2009, an 8 percent increase over the previous year. The increase in Chinese students was particularly notable: a 21 percent increase overall, with an impressive 60 percent increase at the undergraduate level (Fischer, 2009). Rapid development in China has created a demand for higher education that its own university system is still unable to fulfill. At the same time, the weakness of the dollar relative to other foreign currencies has made American higher education more affordable, and institutions are aggressively marketing their programs to international students. The number of colleges and universities offering degree programs and opening branches abroad has also increased, although the actual number of branches is not well documented. (The American Council of Education, 2009, sent surveys to 88 institutions reportedly operating 197 branch campuses abroad, but received responses from only 20 institutions with information on 40 branch campuses.) Enrollment in study-abroad programs has continued to increase. In 2007–2008, 262,416 American students studied abroad, an 8.5 percent increase over the previous year. And in a recent study, 83 percent of institutions surveyed indicated they wanted to send more students abroad and were taking measures to do so (Institute of International Education, 2009). Finally, in its publication *College Learning for the New Global Century*, the Association of American Colleges and Universities (2007) describes the essential student learning outcomes of its LEAP campaign including the following under Personal and Social Responsibility: "civic knowledge and engagement—local and global" and "intercultural knowledge and competence."

Yet despite the rising foreign demand for U.S. higher education, only 39 percent of institutions in 2006 made specific reference to international or global education in their mission statements. And fewer institutions required a course with an international or global focus as part of the general education curriculum in 2006 (37 percent) than five years earlier in 2001 (41 percent; Green, Luu, & Burris, 2008). Similarly, American students' own interest in acquiring knowledge about other countries and cultures, either through study or actual experience, is tepid. Although 91 percent of American institutions offer study-abroad opportunities, only 1.4 percent of approximately 18 million students study abroad. Furthermore, although enrollments in foreign language courses increased steadily during the 1960–2002 period, total enrollments in U.S. institutions of higher education increased more rapidly. As a result, in 2002 only 8.6 percent of students studied a foreign language compared to 16.1 percent in 1960 (Welles, 2004). Finally, Hayward (cited in DeZure, 2003, pp. 43–44) concludes that postsecondary graduates are poorly informed about other countries, consistently underperforming compared to students from other developed countries on global competency and geographical surveys.

Consequently, at a time when foreign demand for American higher education is rising and the world is flattening, the response of American higher education and its student body to the fact of globalization is ambivalent at best. The ambivalence is one manifestation, I believe, of widespread complacency due to our persistent sense of separation from the rest of the world and of invulnerability as the dominant world power in the past century. But our sense of separation and domination is an illusion. It took events as dramatic as the fall of the World Trade Towers on September 11, 2001, and the global financial crisis to shatter illusions of separation and domination, if only for a moment. The magnitude of our collective shock, bewilderment, and outrage—to foreign attack and our own Trojan horse of easy credit gifted to the rest of the world—was in direct proportion to the magnitude of our complacency. Something unshakable in the American psyche had been severely shaken.

International Engagement as Educational Developers: Representative Examples

Globalization is a fact: whether as citizens or educational developers, we are so embedded in an international context that, like the "American" car, the very distinction between domestic and foreign seems specious. The relevant question clearly is not, "Should we engage internationally?" but "How much?" and "How?"

In my role as POD president and as an independent consultant, I have had several opportunities to engage internationally: a two-week residence as a senior visiting fellow in educational development at the University of Windsor in Canada (September 2007); as program chair of the International Consortium for Educational Development (ICED) 2008 Conference in Salt Lake City, Utah and as POD representative to the ICED Council (June 2008); a week-long consultation at a Canadian college in Doha, Qatar (December 2008); as POD representative to the ICED Council meeting in Dublin, Ireland (June 2009); and as an invited keynote speaker, panelist, and workshop presenter at a national conference on educational development in Beijing, China (July 2009). Through these experiences, as well as my participation in POD leadership and governance, I have observed various modes of engagement in international contexts. These modes of engagement in turn reflect underlying assumptions about the mutual roles and expectations of and between our international counterparts and us. A few examples follow.

Example 1: The Relative Importance of International Engagement in POD's Strategic Plan

In recent executive and core committee meetings, we have had several discussions regarding the importance of international engagement in POD's strategic plan. Often international engagement is represented as a separate sphere of activity from services to members, professional development, and organizational development, with the obvious implication that use of resources for international engagement necessarily means fewer resources for other areas. We have also discussed whether "international" is a form of diversity and, if so, whether it is on equal footing with other forms of diversity, such as race, ethnicity, or sexual orientation. Two practical implications of these discussions are whether POD should be represented on the ICED Council and with what (if any) POD funding; and whether we should designate the Institute for New Faculty Developers, the *International* Institute for New Faculty Developers, what the latter designation signifies, and what (if anything) it promises in the way of special programming.

Example 2: Being an Expert on Educational Development in International Contexts

The growing importance of higher education in Asia, the Middle East, and other parts of the world has created a growing interest in educational and, more broadly, academic development. Not only are universities in these areas increasing the number of faculty members to accommodate a growing student body, they are also seeking ways to develop the professional capabilities of their faculties in teaching, research, and administration. As a result educational developers from the United States, United Kingdom, Canada, Australia, and other developed countries are increasingly called on to share their expertise with colleagues in the developing world.

What mutual expectations and assumptions underlie these consulting relationships? In July 2009, seven POD members joined colleagues from Australia, Hong Kong, and Norway as invited keynote speakers, presenters, and panelists at an educational development conference in Beijing, China. The conference was a staging event for the founding of a faculty development network in China. The structure of the conference—a mostly unilateral sharing of educational development ideas, concepts, and practices developed in Western contexts with a largely passive Chinese audience—embodied a clear set of assumptions about knowledge and technology transfer: the expectation that those who knew more assisted those who knew less, presumably to become more like themselves; the universality and generalizability of concepts such as educational development, leadership, and mentoring; and the related irrelevance of cultural, organizational and linguistic context.

It was hard to know whether attempts to deviate from these assumptions were successful. Wishing to engage participants more, was it acceptable for presenters to change the conference plan when the program had been carefully vetted through unknown authorities during the entire planning process? And the response to periodic opportunities for active engagement, a sacred cow in Western contexts, was mixed. Some conference delegates participated enthusiastically, while others took a break or seemed distracted. Report-outs from small group discussions were somewhat chaotic; for example, group spokespersons seemed reluctant to relinquish the floor once they had it. And we later learned that concepts such as leadership and mentoring did not translate readily into the Chinese context. I left feeling the conference had been important as a symbolic staging event, but wondered how we might do it differently the next time.

Example 3: Exporting a Western Curriculum to a Non-Western Context

When U.S. institutions establish degree programs and branch campuses overseas, American instructors often teach the curriculum to a non-American student body. The question arises, To what extent is a curriculum culturally neutral? To the degree that the curriculum is not neutral, who makes the accommodation—curriculum designer, instructor, student—and what does that imply?

In December 2008 I consulted with a Canadian college in Qatar with Canadian instructors teaching a Canadian curriculum in technical subjects to a Qatari student body. I observed instructors making on-the-ground adjustments to accommodate an array of unforeseen issues, including the communication abilities of students whose native language was not English; challenges in motivation due to the wealth of the students' families and the assurance of employment regardless of academic performance; students' extensive familial obligations; the importance of social interaction; the novelty of gender-integrated classes in a radically segregated society; and the relevance of the curriculum to students' future employment (for example, in the petroleum industry). In addition, the concept of education is still new in a tiny country whose traditional fishing and pearl hunting culture was displaced only in the 1940s by the discovery of vast oil reserves off its coast.

International Engagement as Educational Developers: A Framework

The concept of elasticity of practice provides a useful bridge between the different modes of international engagement noted above. According to Carew, Lefoe, Bell, and Armour (2008), *elastic practice* describes "the process of tailoring a specific approach or instance of Academic Development from the full professional 'toolkit' (techniques, experiences, ideas, values, theories) that academic developers collect during their evolution as practitioners." In the process, "multiple theoretical bases are melded or successively employed to support an adaptive, responsive approach to practice" (p. 1). Elasticity of practice is relevant at any level of professional engagement, from our own academic department to the international arena. For educational developers, the hypothetical decision not to engage internationally would represent extreme inelasticity of practice and a mode of engagement here called *isolationism*. It mirrors the national policy of the United States of a similar name between the two world wars and still exerts a strong pull on the American psyche.

Within POD (see example 1), isolationism as a response to globalization reflects one way of resolving the tension between the traditional values and priorities of POD and the demands of a new higher education context (Lee, 2008a). For some, our historic commitment to the provision of services to our largely domestic membership, as articulated in the POD 2007/2012 Strategic Plan (POD, 2006), presents a conflict for resources with international engagement. However, given the fact of globalization today, support of international engagement is not inconsistent with continued strong support of our membership (goal 1), professional development (goal 2), organizational development (goal 3), or diversity (goal 5). Internationalization is a reality on our campuses, and because we are the largest and one of the most well-established educational development networks in the world, international colleagues attend our conferences and institutes for new faculty developers and regularly seek our counsel regarding educational development initiatives in their own countries. Engaging internationally provides a good example of how we are reinterpreting a traditional value of collegiality and service to our members and making it responsive to the current context.

Leaving the extreme inelasticity of isolationism, I consider two other modes of international engagement: colonialism and postcolonialism (Manathunga, 2006). In an international context, the colonialist mode of engagement is common and more readily visible in our interactions with colleagues in developing countries (see example 2). It is more elastic than isolationism, because there is at least some stretching of practice to acknowledge an international colleague. Within the colonialist perspective, we as American educational developers view the international colleague as an entity to be developed. The desire to develop the international colleague may be superficially benign, a genuine and seemingly disinterested desire to help the international colleague become "better" (often meaning "more like ourselves"). That is, our international colleague is like ourselves, except that she or he is at an earlier stage of development. I call the desire benign and disinterested because there is no explicit intention to develop the international colleague at his or her expense, serve an agenda of imperialist domination, or hold the colleague in a bond of obligation and dependency. There is also a comfortable clarity in the mutual roles and expectations of this perspective.

But the mode of engagement is more insidiously colonial, because it ignores (or only vaguely acknowledges) cultural context and, thereby, the identity of the international colleague as truly other. Manathunga (2006) asserts that the hegemony of educational psychology in educational development and its focus on universal and generalizable principles of learning and development within the individual partly supports the colonialist perspective. She also points to a celebratory and progressive liberal ideology that blithely ignores difference in the spirit of we-are-all-the-same. A practical implication of the colonialist perspective is a still relatively inelastic practice with no accommodation to the otherness of the international colleague because the otherness is still largely unseen. If accommodation occurs, the onus lies with the international colleague. To the extent that both parties are complicit in the mutual expectations of this perspective, however, the international colleague has little permission to accommodate.

Within the postcolonial perspective, as educational developers we engage more critically and with greater awareness with the international other(see example 3). As a result, our practice becomes far more elastic as we adapt our existing toolkit to accommodate the needs and perspectives of the other. To a far greater extent than in the example above, we see instructors at the Canadian college in Qatar taking a colonial mode of engagement (that is, the export of a Canadian curriculum) and adapting it over time as they learn more about the needs and capabilities of their students. In contrast to the clarity of roles and expectations in the colonialist perspective, in our postcolonialist interactions with international colleagues, we move into a "contested, unstable space" where "identities can be explored, interrogated, problematized, blurred and engaged with and cultural change may take place" (Manathunga, 2006, p. 21). In the process, all of our conventions, comfortable truisms, and tidy categories—for example, learner centeredness, student engagement, academic time on task—are open to scrutiny and critique. Likewise, the international other needs to be willing to enter the same space with us. For example, the Qatari students need to give up notions of authority and the expectation of passivity in the colonial mode of engagement in order to engage in the learning process. Together we create a unique adaptation of our practice to the demands of a particular cultural context. In the process, our practice as educators and educational developers becomes increasingly flexible, nuanced, and sophisticated.

International Engagement as Educational Developers: Levels of Engagement

Thinking of the progressive levels of our engagement as educational developers, moving from the academic department through the institution and beyond, international engagement represents the last practical level of activity (Macdonald, 2009). Offering the most novel of experiences, international engagement is also the maximal test of the fundamental premises of our practice (Smith, 2009) and its flexibility, and, arguably, it offers the greatest opportunity for growth, both personally and collectively. Table 22.1 summarizes selected activities at each level of activity—department, institution, nation, globe—as well as possible conflicts that may arise and need to be resolved at each level. The conflicts are the "contested, unstable spaces" (Manathunga, 2006) that also represent opportunities for the growth and development of our practice. Each level necessarily encompasses the activities and conflicts of the previous levels and their resolution.

I believe the most compelling challenge at the global level—the most elastic extension of our practice—is the articulation of a meaningful and practical agenda for international educational development that at once incorporates and transcends the interests of individual nation states. The Bologna Declaration—an effort to strengthen the European higher education area by making academic degree standards and quality

Table 22.1. Representative Activities and Conflicts at Different Levels of Engagement in Educational Development

Level	Representative Activities	Representative Conflicts
Department or school	Course and curriculum design Course and program assessment Work related to disciplinary accrediting bodies Peer review Chair development	Content versus learner orientation Common understanding of the discipline, student learning outcomes Reconciling conflicting demands of disciplinary or regional accrediting body and institutional requirements
Institution	General education and other campuswide program reform efforts Student retention and graduation Addressing rising enrollments with fewer resources Roles and rewards	Negotiating the relationship between general education and the major Balancing conflicting demands of teaching, research, service; allocation of resources, including time Balancing effective teaching practices with higher faculty-to-student ratios
Nation	Articulating educational agenda, including student learning outcomes that address the national agenda Advocacy on behalf of the value of educational development Advancement of own educational development research and practice agenda Increasing visibility of self and institution through conference presentation and publication Service and leadership in national organizations and initiatives	Balancing national commitments and needs of own campus Resolving conflicts of what is in the national interest with respect to higher education Balancing autonomy of institutions and federal standards of accountability Articulation of common values among different institution types in national organizations In external work, accommodating to requirements of different institution types

| Globe | Articulating an international agenda for educational development
Assisting emerging educational development networks
Sharing approaches to educational development across national borders through international organizations, conferences, publication | Resolving problems of communication due to language differences, uses of different terminology, variations in national context, and cultural norms
Reconciling international and national educational development interests
Balancing commitments to one's own institution, national and international networks |

assurance standards more comparable and compatible throughout Europe—represents the most relevant existing experiment in this direction. The primary impetus for the declaration was to ensure mobility and employability throughout Europe and to improve international competition and the attractiveness of European higher education throughout the world (Clement, McAlpine, & Waeytens, 2004). Countries in Europe had to recognize that they had a larger, more critical interest that was better served by acting collectively rather than individually and that higher education was a critical piece of the equation. Analogously, given the fact of globalization and the related inconvenient truths of global warming, financial interdependence and instability, and the fragility of international peace and security, we may realize that as a globe, we ultimately share a set of interests far more critical than our competitive advantage relative to other nations and that here too, education is a critical piece of the equation.

Recommendations and Conclusions

Implicit in a global scholarship and practice of educational development is a tension between our individual efforts as educational developers, bound by local cultural and societal contexts, and the larger landscape of educational development worldwide. On the one hand, a global scholarship and practice of educational development acknowledges local and national variations and promises a productive synthesis among them. It also posits a practice in which educational development is put to the service of a global agenda that transcends local boundaries and national interests (Lee, 2008b). For us as educational developers, a global scholarship and practice of educational development represents the ultimate contested, unstable space and the ultimate extension of our thought and practice.

As we move into the final years of implementation of the 2007–2012 POD strategic plan, I encourage us to become clearer on our international interests and their importance relative to other activities and priorities of the organization. At the very least, we should strengthen our representation on the ICED Council, sending a clear message to our international colleagues that we value that commitment. We should find better ways of sharing the discussions within and activities of ICED with the POD membership. We should encourage publication by international colleagues in member journals such as *To Improve the Academy* and publication by our members in *International Journal for Academic Development*. We should include more POD conference sessions and *To Improve the Academy* articles related to the internationalization of the academy and its implications for educational development.

As representatives of the world's largest educational development network and the dominant world power, we will be called on by our international colleagues to share our expertise. International work places a special burden of thorough advance preparation to ensure that our efforts have real, as opposed to symbolic, impact. It also requires close collaboration between the consultant and her international hosts during the planning of the visit and clear communication as the dynamics of the visit unfold. An orientation to the higher education context, current educational development practices, and cultural traditions, expectations, and norms of the conduct of the host country relevant to anticipated work is essential. Educational development concepts such as faculty governance, mentoring, and leadership, developed in largely Western contexts, are not readily understood in other countries where higher education is far more centralized. Where English is the second language, a glossary of educational development terms is useful. Even in other English-speaking countries, such as the United Kingdom and Australia, terminology is often subtly different from American use, resulting in an illusion of comprehension or a vague haze of incomprehension in conversation, and clarification of terminology is advisable here as well. Excellent translation is essential depending on the level of English proficiency of the international hosts and participants. Sending written transcripts of keynote addresses and papers well in advance of the visit is important for simultaneous translation and for interactive sessions, exceptionally skilled translators are mandatory. Finally, early in-country practitioners of educational development, particularly those with English fluency, provide a bridge between practice in the United States and the host country; engaging them as collaborators during the planning and implementation phases of the visit is another excellent strategy. (Many of these recommendations come from a debriefing document prepared by the members of the international delegation to the 2009 Beijing Conference.)

To quote Ji Xianlin, the master of Chinese culture who died during the Beijing conference in July 2009, "Cultural exchange is the main drive for humankind's progress. Only by learning from each other's strong points to make up for shortcomings can people constantly progress, the ultimate target of which is to achieve a kind of Great Harmony" ("The reluctant master," p. 8).

REFERENCES

Altbach, P., & Knight, J. (2007). The internationalization of higher education: Motivations and realities. *Journal of Studies in International Education, 11*(3–4), 290–305.

American Council of Education. (2009). U.S. branch campuses abroad. *ACE Issue Brief.* Retrieved from www.acenet.edu/AM/Template.cfm?Section=I nfoCenter&TEMPLATE=/CM/ContentDisplay.cfm&CONTENTID =34786

Association of American Colleges and Universities. (2007). *College learning for the new global century.* Washington, DC: Author.

Carew, A. L., Lefoe, G., Bell, M., & Armour, L. (2008). Elastic practice in academic developers. *International Journal for Academic Development, 13*(1), 51–66.

Clement, M., McAlpine, L., & Waeytens, K. (2004). Fascinating Bologna: Impact on the nature and approach of academic development. *International Journal for Academic Development, 19*(2), 127–131.

DeZure, D. (2003). Internationalizing American higher education: A call to thought and action. In C. M. Wehlburg & S. Chadwick-Blossey (Eds.), *To improve the academy: Vol. 21. Resources for faculty, instructional, and organizational development* (pp. 40–55). San Francisco: Jossey-Bass/ Anker.

Fischer, K. (2009, November 16). Number of foreign students in U.S. hit a new high last year. *Chronicle of Higher Education.* Retrieved from http://chronicle.com/article/Number-of-Foreign-Students-in/49142/

Green, M. F., Luu, D., & Burris, B. (2008). *Mapping internationalization on U.S. campuses: 2008 edition.* Washington, DC: American Council on Education.

Institute of International Education. (2009). Expanding study abroad capacity at U.S. colleges and universities. *IIE Study Abroad White Paper Series No. 6.* Retrieved from www.iie.org/Content/NavigationMenu/Research_and_Evaluation/Study_Abroad_White_Papers/StudyAbroad_WhitePaper6.pdf

Lee, V. S. (2008a, October). *Presidential address.* Presented at the POD Network/NCSPOD Conference, Reno, NV.

Lee, V. S. (2008b). Reflections on the 2008 ICED conference. *HERDSA News, 30*(2), 21.

Lee, V. S. (2010). Program types and prototypes. In K. H. Gillespie & D. Robertson (Eds.), *A guide to faculty development* (2nd ed.). San Francisco: Jossey-Bass.

Macdonald, R. (2009). Academic development. In M. Tight, K. H. Mok, J. Huisman, & C. Morphew (Eds.), *The Routledge international handbook of higher education* (pp. 427–439). London: Routledge.

Manathunga, C. (2006). Doing educational development ambivalently: Applying post-colonial metaphors to educational development? *International Journal of Academic Development, 11*(1), 19–29.

Professional and Organizational Development Network in Higher Education. (2006). *2007/2012 strategic plan.* Retrieved from www.podnetwork.org/about/strategic_plan.htm

The reluctant master. (2009, July 12). *China Daily,* p. 8.

Smith, K. (2009). Transnational teaching experiences: An underexplored territory for transformative professional development. *International Journal for Educational Development, 14*(2), 111–122.

Welles, E. (2004). Foreign language enrollments in United States institutions of higher education, fall 2002. *ADFL Bulletin, 35*(2–3), 7–26.